JUDGES BEYOND POLITICS IN DEMOCRACY AND DICTATORSHIP

Why did Chilean judges, trained under and appointed by democratic governments, facilitate and condone the illiberal, antidemocratic, and antilegal policies of the Pinochet regime? Challenging the common assumption that adjudication in nondemocratic settings is fundamentally different and less puzzling than it is in democratic regimes, this book offers a longitudinal analysis of judicial behavior, demonstrating striking continuity in judicial performance across regimes in Chile. The work explores the relevance of judges' personal policy preferences, social class, and legal philosophy but argues that institutional factors best account for the persistent failure of judges to take stands in defense of rights and rule of law principles. Specifically, the institutional structure and ideology of the Chilean judiciary, grounded in the ideal of judicial apoliticism, furnished judges with professional understandings and incentives that left them unequipped and disinclined to take stands in defense of liberal democratic principles before, during, and after the authoritarian interlude.

Lisa Hilbink is a two-time Fulbright grantee to Chile and Spain. From 2000 to 2003, she was Post-Doctoral Fellow in the Princeton University Society of Fellows and Lecturer at the Woodrow Wilson School of Public and International Affairs. Her doctoral thesis, on which this book is based, won the Best Dissertation Award for 1999/2000 from the Western Political Science Association. Dr. Hilbink is a member of the American Political Science Association, the Law and Society Association, and the Latin American Studies Association. She is now Assistant Professor at the University of Minnesota, Twin Cities.

CAMBRIDGE STUDIES IN LAW AND SOCIETY

Cambridge Studies in Law and Society aims to publish the best scholarly work on legal discourse and practice in its social and institutional contexts, combining theoretical insights and empirical research.

The fields that it covers are studies of law in action; the sociology of law; the anthropology of law; cultural studies of law, including the role of legal discourses in social formations; law and economics; law and politics; and studies of governance. The books consider all forms of legal discourse across societies, rather than being limited to lawyers' discourses alone.

The series editors come from a range of disciplines: academic law, socio-legal studies, and sociology and anthropology. All have been actively involved in teaching and writing about law in context.

Series Editors

Chris Arup
Victoria University, Melbourne
Martin Chanock
La Trobe University, Melbourne
Pat O'Malley
University of Sydney, Australia
Sally Engle Merry
Wellesley College, Massachusetts
Susan Silbey
Massachusetts Institute of Technology

Books in the Series

The Politics of Truth and Reconciliation in South Africa
Legitimizing the Post-Apartheid State
Richard A. Wilson

Modernism and the Grounds of Law
Peter Fitzpatrick

Unemployment and Government
Genealogies of the Social
William Walters

Autonomy and Ethnicity
Negotiating Competing Claims in Multi-Ethnic States
Yash Ghai

Constituting Democracy
Law, Globalism and South Africa's Political Reconstruction
Heinz Klug

The New World Trade Organization Agreements
Globalizing Law through Services and Intellectual Property
Christopher Arup

The Ritual of Rights in Japan
Law, Society, and Health Policy
Eric A. Feldman

The Invention of the Passport
Surveillance, Citizenship, and the State
John Torpey

Governing Morals
A Social History of Moral Regulation
Alan Hunt

The Colonies of Law
Colonialism, Zionism, and Law in Early Mandate Palestine
Ronen Shamir

Law and Nature
David Delaney

Social Citizenship and Workfare in the United States and Western Europe
The Paradox of Inclusion
Joel F. Handler

Law, Anthropology, and the Constitution of the Social
Making Persons and Things
Edited by Alain Pottage and Martha Mundy

Judicial Review and Bureaucratic Impact
International and Interdisciplinary Perspectives
Edited by Marc Hertogh and Simon Halliday

Immigrants at the Margins
Law, Race, and Exclusion in Southern Europe
Kitty Calavita

Lawyers and Regulation
The Politics of the Administrative Process
Patrick Schmidt

Law and Globalization from Below
Toward a Cosmopolitan Legality
Edited by Boaventura de Sousa Santos and Cesar A. Rodriguez-Garavito

Public Accountability
Designs, Dilemmas, and Experiences
Edited by Michael W. Dowdle

Law, Violence, and Sovereignty among West Bank Palestinians
Tobias Kelly

Law and Society in Vietnam
The Transition from Socialism in Comparative Perspective
Mark Sidel

Legal Reform and Administrative Detention Powers in China
Sarah Biddulph

The Practice of Human Rights
Tracking Law between the Global and the Local
Edited by Mark Goodale and Sally Engle Merry

JUDGES BEYOND POLITICS IN DEMOCRACY AND DICTATORSHIP

Lessons from Chile

Lisa Hilbink

University of Minnesota, Twin Cities

CAMBRIDGE
UNIVERSITY PRESS

CAMBRIDGE UNIVERSITY PRESS
Cambridge, New York, Melbourne, Madrid, Cape Town, Singapore, São Paulo, Delhi

Cambridge University Press
32 Avenue of the Americas, New York, NY 10013-2473, USA

www.cambridge.org
Information on this title: www.cambridge.org/9780521876643

First published 2007

Printed in the United States of America

A catalog record for this publication is available from the British Library.

Library of Congress Cataloging in Publication Data

Hilbink, Lisa, 1967–
Judges beyond politics in democracy and dictatorship : lessons from Chile / Lisa Hilbink.
    p. cm. – (Cambridge studies in law and society)
Includes bibliographical references and index.
ISBN 978-0-521-87664-3 (hardback)
1. Justice, Administration of – Chile – History.   2. Judges – Chile – History.   3. Judicial
power – Chile – History.   4. Law reform – Chile – History.   5. Democracy – Chile – History.
6. Constitutional law – Chile – History.   I. Title.
KHF2500.H55   2007
347.83'014 – dc22   2007000395

ISBN   978-0-521-87664-3 hardback

To Dad,
   who gave me my sense of justice,
and to Mom,
   who devoted her life to peace.

CONTENTS

ACKNOWLEDGMENTS

They say it is difficult to let go of one's first book, and that is particularly
true in my case. Despite the many sources of moral and material support
I received from the time I began this project, as a dissertation, to the
late phases of the book revisions, it was still difficult to convince myself
that it was, or would ever be, ready for public consumption. Because of
this, I held on to it for too long and racked up an inordinate number of
debts, which I can only modestly acknowledge in these few preliminary
lines.

To begin, I would like to express my sincere gratitude to the various
institutions that provided funding for the research and writing of this
book. The original research in Chile was made possible by a grant from
the J. William Fulbright Foreign Scholarship Board. Follow-up trips
were supported by grants from the University Committee on Research
in the Humanities and Social Sciences, the Woodrow Wilson School,
and the Faculty Research Grant Committee of the Program in Latin
American studies, all of Princeton University. Much of the reading and
thinking that went into the theoretical framework of the book was done
during my years as a Wilson-Cotsen Fellow in the Princeton University
Society of Fellows in the Liberal Arts. I thus owe a tremendous thank
you to both the Woodrow Wilson School and the Society of Fellows for
their financial support during that time. Finally, I thank the College of
Liberal Arts and the Department of Political Science at the University
of Minnesota, which provided the general research funds on which I
drew for write-up support and assistance.

I also extend profound thanks to the many Chilean individuals and
institutions who aided and cooperated in this study. Many judges and
lawyers, whom I promised anonymity, gave me interviews of two or
more hours; others typed out long answers to each of my questions.
I am most honored by and very appreciative of the time and trust
they offered me. I am also grateful to the personnel of many institutions which facilitated my work, including persons at the Biblioteca
de la Corte Suprema, the Biblioteca del Congreso, the Biblioteca

Nacional, the Comisión Chilena de Derechos Humanos, the Fundación Archivo y Documentación de la Vicaría de la Solidaridad, and, above all, the Universidad Diego Portales, Facultad de Ciencias Jurídicas y Sociales.

Chilean scholars Jorge Correa, Hugo Frühling, and Augusto Varas deserve special recognition for their guidance at crucial stages of the study. Rodolfo Aldea, José Luis Cea, Fernando Escobar, and Alex Wilde also provided invaluable insights, advice, and *pitutos*. In addition, I thank faculty members at the Diego Portales Law School from whom I learned so much both in private discussions and public seminars: Mauricio Duce, Gaston Gómez, Felipe González, María Angélica Jiménez, Cecilia Medina, Jorge Mera, Carlos Peña, and Cristian Riego. Finally, for their intellectual support and friendship, I want to thank Mario Bugueño, Javier Couso, Pablo Policzer, and the late Marta Pérez. Long conversations with each of these individuals broadened and deepened my general understanding of and love for Chile and helped make this book much richer.

In the United States, I have personal and intellectual debts on both coasts, as well as in my new – or, better put, rediscovered – home in the heartland. I could not begin to offer sufficient thanks to my adviser, Paul Drake, and to the other members of my dissertation committee at the University of California-San Diego (UC-SD), Ann Craig, Harry Hirsch, Jim Holston, Alan Houston, and Carlos Waisman. Each contributed in essential ways to my intellectual and professional development during my time at UC-SD and has continued to support me in the years since then. I am also grateful to the great UC-SD friends that helped keep me sane during graduate school and beyond, especially Octavio Amorim-Neto, Steve Applebaum, Michele Chang, Maureen Feeley, Chris Fry, Bill Griswold, Kim Harley, Sohie Lee, Minna Mahlab, and Jay Moody.

As a post-doc at Princeton, I had the extraordinary privilege to work with a wide range of brilliant faculty, visiting scholars, and graduate students who stimulated my thinking on law, politics, and justice and gave generously of their time to help me improve my work. These include Jeremy Adelman, Pablo de Grieff, Patrick Deneen, Jim Doig, Kent Eaton, Christopher Eisgruber, David Erdos, Carol Greenhouse, Gabor Halmai, Valerie Hunt, Stan Katz, Steven Macedo, Diane Orentlicher, Kal Raustiala, Bruce Rutherford, Kim Scheppele, Paul Sigmund, Nate Skovronick, Martin Stein, Keith Whittington, Melissa

Williams, Deborah Yashar, Mariah Zeisberg, and the directors and fellows of the Society of Fellows. I am particularly indebted to the members of our first-book writing group, Ana María Bejarano, Erica Cosgrove, and Sarah Pralle, who suffered through the reading of my extremely long and dense dissertation chapters, gave me excellent feedback, and became dear friends.

My good fortune continued when I joined the Department of Political Science at the University of Minnesota, where I have enjoyed the professional support and friendship of extraordinarily gifted, sensitive, and good-humored colleagues. While I am grateful to so many of them for their contributions to my "subjective well-being," I owe particular thanks to Sally Kenney, David Samuels, Bill Scheuerman, and Kathryn Sikkink, each of whom read chapters of the book manuscript and gave me valuable comments, criticisms, and advice.

I also have debts to numerous individuals in my wider intellectual community who read and critiqued pieces of this work along the way, and/or offered general support and encouragement. These include John Brigham, Daniel Brinks, Rebecca Bill Chávez, Jodi Finkel, Bryant Garth, Tom Hilbink, Diana Kapizewski, Brian Loveman, Michael McCann, Jonathan Miller, Tamir Moustafa, Tony Pereira, Miguel Schor, Dru Scribner, Hootan Shambayati, Matthew Taylor, and Joe Thome. For their excellent research and/or editing assistance at different stages of the manuscript drafting, I thank Glen Gutterman, Jennifer Kwong, Matías Larraín, Daniel Levin, and Marcela Villarrazo. Dan, in particular, deserves a huge thank you for his enthusiastic and meticulous work on the draft I sent for review. Last, but not least, for their gentle guidance and incredibly efficient editorial work, I thank John Berger of Cambridge University Press, and the project manager at Aptara, Inc., Barbara Walthall.

The contributions of all the individuals and institutions listed above are important but can only pale next to those of my amazing and wonderful family. The enormous and repeated sacrifices they made in order to support the research and writing of this book humble me. It is not easy to have an academic mother, wife, daughter or sister, particularly one whose research requires that she spend long periods in foreign lands, but my children, husband, parents, and brother have all endured and supported, with unflagging love, humor, and flexibility, the ups and downs of the crazy life I (and, hence, they) lead. My deepest thanks thus go to Ron and Dottie Hilbink, Tom Hilbink, Ed and Merry

Gerber, and Jamie, Noah, and Liliana Gerber for their endless emotional and material support. Sadly, the one who gave the most of all – my mother, Dottie – is no longer here to read these lines. She passed away in July of 2006, but her intellectual influence and gifts of self are reflected in every page of this work. It is thus to her, and to my brilliant and loving father, that this book is dedicated.

INTRODUCTION

On September 11, 1973, General Augusto Pinochet helped to lead the overthrow of one of Latin America's most celebrated democratic regimes. As part of the coup, Chile's military leaders bombed the presidential palace, shut down the Congress, closed or banned political parties, and purged the state bureaucracy. They left the courts, however, completely untouched. In the face of state terror, Chilean human rights defenders thus placed their hopes in the judiciary as the only branch of the democratic state left intact.

To the dismay of justice seekers, Chilean judges cooperated fully with authoritarian regime in the months and years that followed. Not only did the courts grant the military government nearly complete autonomy to pursue its "war" against Marxism, but they also offered repeated legal justification of the regime's expansive police powers. Judges unquestioningly accepted the explanations offered by the government regarding the fate of the disappeared and readily implemented arbitrary decrees, secret laws, and policies that violated the country's legal codes. The Supreme Court, mouthpiece of the judiciary, publicly endorsed General Pinochet's seizure of power and declared that writs of habeas corpus disrupted the Court's ability to deal with the "urgent matters of its jurisdiction." Indeed, of the more than fifty-four hundred habeas corpus petitions filed by human rights lawyers between 1973 and 1983, the courts rejected all but ten (Constable and Valenzuela 1991: 122). Moreover, the Supreme Court unilaterally abdicated both its review power over decisions of military tribunals and its constitutional review power.[1] Throughout, the justices insisted that the military government was restoring the rule of law, even as the generals made a mockery of the Constitution. Even after civilian rule had been restored, judges continued to endorse the legal edifice constructed by the leaders of the authoritarian regime (including the military's self-amnesty), and left largely unchallenged the principles and values embodied therein.[2]

This performance – which extended from passive capitulation to outright collaboration in authoritarian rule – demands explanation at several levels. To begin, such judicial behavior, in any context, shocks the moral conscience. As with antebellum American judges who applied the Fugitive Slave Laws, German judges who implemented Nazi law, or South African judges who imparted legal legitimacy to apartheid (Cover 1975; Müller 1991; Dyzenhaus 1991; Osiel 1995), one is driven to ask how and why professionals charged with administering justice could turn a blind eye to – or worse, offer justification for – state-sponsored (and often arbitrary) degradation, repression, and brutality. Such behavior is at odds both with (Western) society's moral expectations for professionals, in general, and for judges, in particular. As Paul Camenisch has argued, professionals are "bearers of a public trust, bestowed upon them in the form of a professional degree and title, and endowing them with a monopoly in the provision of a service which is crucial to society." They have "significant power which can be used either for great societal benefit or to considerable societal harm," and thus "they can rightly be accused of failure not only when they use their power, influence and expertise for the wrong purposes, purposes which are positively harmful, but also when they fail to use them for the proper purposes, or even fail to do so with sufficient energy and perseverance" (Camenisch 1983: 15 and 17). Like physicians who provided their professional services to the regime's torturers, then, judges who offered legal endorsement of state-sponsored brutality opened themselves up to ethical critique. But of course *judges* are subject to particular scrutiny because, as professionals, they are trained and take oaths to administer *justice*, or at least to uphold the constitution and the laws, which contain principles

---

[1] For the official critique of the conduct of the judiciary under the military regime, see Ministerio Secretaría General 1991: Vol. 1, Ch. 4.

[2] This only began to change in the late 1990s, following institutional reform and the detention of General Pinochet in London. The extent and limits of this change will be discussed in Chapter 5.

of justice. The judges in Pinochet's Chile had been trained and appointed under a democratic regime and had taken an oath to uphold the constitution of that regime, which provided a host of liberal and democratic protections. Why was it that they so easily ignored that oath and supported, sometimes passively, other times actively, the illiberal, antidemocratic, and *anti-legal* agenda of the military government?

This question becomes even weightier when considered in light of Chile's political culture and history. In a continent plagued by political violence and instability, pre-Pinochet Chile had often been touted as "exceptional" (Valenzuela 1989: 160 and 172).[3] Whereas the political histories of other countries in the region often featured "brutal, distorted, manipulated, political institutions and pseudo-liberal democratic regimes" (Diamond and Linz 1989: 20) and "[an absence of] traditions of participation, contestation, and toleration of dissent" (Waisman 1989: 63), Chile stood out for its "high level of party competition and popular participation, open and fair elections, and strong respect for democratic freedoms" (Valenzuela 1989: 160; see also Valenzuela and Valenzuela 1983). In fact, a 1965 index that ranked countries in terms of democratic performance placed Chile in the top 15 percent, above the United States, France, Italy, and West Germany (Bollen 1980).[4] Chile also boasted a "strong historical tradition of respect for the rule of law and a constitutional framework of presidential government" (Valenzuela 1995: 31). In contrast to Brazil or Mexico, where the law is very unevenly applied across the territory, or to Argentina, which is notorious for its systemic corruption, Chile has long distinguished itself by its rule-bound and orderly society. As one prominent Chilean social scientist argued in 1974: "One of the most characteristic political realities of Chile is the importance of legality as a superior standard [*instancia*] to which all behaviors and the resolution of conflicts between people and institutions are referred. . . . Legality is the foundation of the government's legitimacy" (Arriagada 1974: 122).[5] Why

---

[3] See also Blakemore (1993), who notes that, in the nineteenth century, Chile was considered "the England of Latin America"; and Dahl (1971), in which Chile figures as a prominent case of successful democratic development.

[4] For a more critical perspective on Chile's "democratic exceptionalism," see Loveman and Lira (2002).

[5] Similarly, Chilean constitutional lawyer José Luis Cea (1978: 6) notes that at the conclusion of the 1960s, "the Chilean population, by and large, had been educated in respect for the principle of legality, which it had internalized as its own. In accordance

was it that Chilean judges so easily abandoned these alleged national traditions?

The behavior of Chilean judges is particularly remarkable when contrasted to that displayed by judges in countries with ostensibly far less democratic and legalistic traditions, such as Brazil and Argentina.[6] After the 1964 coup in Brazil, the Supreme Court, left intact by the junta, repeatedly called the generals on their affront to the historic Brazilian constitution, *even after* the military attempted to stack it with more sympathetic judges (Karst and Rosenn 1975; Feinrider 1981; Nadorff 1982; Osiel 1995).[7] Lower courts and even military courts also sought to limit what the military government could do in the name of national security, although the former were quickly deprived of their independence (Ballard 1999: 241; Pereira 2005: 77). In Argentina, a thoroughly purged judiciary first capitulated almost completely to the ruling junta, but, toward the end of the regime, began issuing general rulings limiting the military's power (Helmke 2002).

The central question that this book seeks to answer is thus: Why did Chilean judges who had been trained under and appointed by democratic governments facilitate and condone authoritarian policies? Put differently, why in a country with such a long history of democratic practice and respect for legality, a country whose human rights movement was one of the strongest on the continent, did judges make no public and concerted effort to defend liberal democratic principles and practices, not only under Pinochet but well into the 1990s? In answering this question, the book speaks to debates in public law and comparative politics regarding the roots of judicial behavior, the definition and limits of judicial independence, and the way the judicial role should be conceived and constructed to promote the rule of law and rights protection.

> with said principle, the rulers as well as the ruled could act only to the extent that an explicit legal precept, technically generated, had previously ordered, permitted, or prohibited that action."
>
> [6] It is also surprising given that Chile's judiciary was commonly thought to be *much* more independent than its Argentine counterpart (Verner 1984).
>
> [7] In October 1965, the Brazilian junta passed Institutional Act No. 2, which expanded the Supreme Court from eleven to sixteen members and gave exclusive judicial appointment power to the executive. This did not achieve the desired level of compliance from the high court, however, so in late 1968 and early 1969, through Institutional Acts 5 and 6, the junta reduced membership on the court back down to eleven and forced three of the acting justices into early retirement, which led the Supreme Court president to resign in protest (see Ballard 1999: 241).

OVERVIEW OF THE ARGUMENT

The main argument put forth in this book is that the behavior of Chilean judges under Pinochet is attributable largely to institutional factors. Although I also highlight the importance of the personal political views of some judges, particularly on the powerful Supreme Court, that factor alone is not sufficient to explain the courts' paltry defense of liberal democratic principles not just during, but also before and after, the authoritarian interlude. To account fully for the weak response of the judiciary to violations of constitutionalist principles (i.e., liberal and democratic rights and limited power), it is necessary to understand how the institutional setting fostered and amplified illiberal and even antidemocratic attitudes, but constrained the development and expression of liberal democratic perspectives.[8] The institutional structure and institutional ideology of the Chilean judiciary, historically constructed around the concept of apoliticism, provided professional understandings and incentives that rendered even democratic-minded judges unequipped and disinclined to take stands in defense of liberal democratic principles.

Some definitions and clarifications are necessary to make sense of this claim. To begin, by "institutional structure" I mean the organizational rules governing the powers and duties of different offices within the institution, including their relationship to each other and to other government offices. By "institutional ideology" I mean the discrete and relatively coherent set of ideas shared by members of the institution regarding the institution's social function or role, that is, the professional norms that guide behavior within the institution (Smith 1988). These norms were both embodied in and reproduced by the institutional structure. In saying that these institutional features were historically constructed around the concept of "apoliticism," I mean that they were developed in the nineteenth and early twentieth centuries with the goal of keeping judges insulated from and out of the debates and affairs of the elected branches. Beyond simply securing judicial independence from partisan manipulation – a worthy ideal – the judicial structure and ideology in Chile built a high conceptual wall between "law" and "politics." However, far from rendering the judiciary politically neutral, these institutional features worked to foster and enhance a strongly

---

[8] On how institutions "refract and constrain" outcomes, see Thelen and Steinmo (1992: 3).

conservative and generally anticonstitutionalist orientation among judges. Rather than invoke the rights guarantees or liberal-democratic structure of the national constitution to limit abuses of public power and promote equality before the law, then, Chilean judges, some actively but most passively, rendered decisions that bolstered the power of state officials and reinforced the traditional social hierarchy, long before and well beyond the seventeen-year dictatorship.

As I will explain in Chapter 2, the judiciary's institutional ideology has its roots in nineteenth-century legal positivism, which consigned judges to be "slaves of the law" (Jaksic 1997: 266). This view developed into what I identified in my research as a legal essentialist or "antipolitics" conception of the judicial role among judges. Judges understood "law" and "politics" as two entirely distinct and unrelated pursuits, and considered the goals of judges and legislators to be completely separate and divergent. In this fetishized view of the law,[9] the less "political" judges were, the more "legal" they would be.

Such an understanding, I argue, was strengthened and reproduced by the institutional structure that was established in the 1920s, when reformers sought to end executive manipulation of the courts and professionalize the judicial career.[10] It was at this time that the formal judicial hierarchy was established and the Supreme Court was given control over discipline and promotion within the career, even controlling nominations to its own ranks. Although this structure successfully increased judicial independence from executive control, it henceforth provided incentives for judges to look primarily to their superiors – rather than to any other audience or reference group – for cues on how to decide cases. Judges thus learned that to succeed professionally, the best strategy was to eschew independent or innovative interpretation in favor of conservative rulings that would please the high-court justices. In this way, conservatism and conformity were continually reproduced within the inward-looking judicial ranks.

It was for these reasons that after the 1973 military coup even judges personally at odds with the laws and practices of the military regime were professionally unwilling or unable to defend liberal democratic

---

[9] I thank Carol Greenhouse for this phrasing.
[10] By professionalization, I mean a process by which an institution is transformed such that the criteria for selection and promotion within it are made on the basis of specialized knowledge and demonstrated skill or merit, rather than primarily through personal or partisan favors.

principles and practices. Publicly challenging the validity of the regime's laws and policies in the name of liberal-democratic values and principles was viewed as unprofessional "political" behavior, which threatened the integrity of the judiciary and the rule of law. Under the watchful eye of the Supreme Court, any judge who aspired to rise in the ranks of the judiciary learned not to take such stands. Instead, judges conformed to the conservative line set and policed by the Supreme Court.

In making this institutionalist argument, I do not mean to imply that the judiciary functioned in a social and cultural vacuum. Indeed, I make clear that the institutional structure and ideology of the Chilean judiciary embodied and reproduced the interests and ideas of its nineteenth- and early twentieth-century designers. My explanation is, therefore, historically bounded. Yet this study offers more than a particularistic interpretation of judicial performance in Chile. It uses the Chilean case both to test and to generate hypotheses regarding the sources of judicial behavior under both democratic and authoritarian regimes.[11] The hypotheses I explore in this study include explanations of judicial behavior based in personal policy preferences, legal philosophy, class-based interests, and regime-related variables such as fear and manipulation by the executive. My analysis of the Chilean case demonstrates the limits of each of these explanations on its own, and offers instead a more complete institutional argument, whose general elements can in turn be tested in future comparative research.

The main theoretical contribution of this longitudinal case study, then, is its identification of the sources of a clear pattern of judicial behavior that persisted across regimes in Chile. The sources of this behavior are not, however, unique to Chile. In the final chapter of the book, I present evidence from secondary sources on a variety of other cases that suggest broad applicability of my argument, and with these additional cases in mind, I proffer several lessons for scholars and policy makers. The first is that formal judicial independence, even when achieved and respected, is not sufficient to produce a judicial defense of rights and the rule of law. Indeed, institutional variables appear to impact significantly whether or not judges will be willing and able to assert themselves in defense of rights and the rule of law. Second, judicial behavior scholars need to pay more attention not only to the way

[11] For discussions of the value of case study to theory-building in political science, see Lijphart 1971; Eckstein 1992; King, Keohane and Verba 1994; Rueschemeyer 2003; Gerring 2004.

institutions constrain the expression of judges' preexisting attitudes but also to how they constitute judges' professional identities and goals. Judicial role conceptions matter, and we need to understand better how they are formed, maintained, or altered. Finally, apoliticism appears to be the wrong ideal around which to construct a judiciary in service of liberal democracy. Although judicial independence and professionalism are legitimate *desiderata* for any polity committed to the rule of law, it is neither possible nor desirable to construct a judiciary beyond politics. For when judges are prohibited by institutional structure and/or ideology from engaging with the wider polity, they are unlikely to cultivate the professional attributes necessary for them to defend and promote liberal-democratic constitutionalism. An "apolitical" judiciary is thus far better suited to authoritarianism than to democracy.

METHODOLOGY AND DATA REPORTING

This book offers a longitudinal analysis of judicial performance in Chile from 1964 to 2000. It is based primarily on archival research and interviews conducted in Chile during a one-year period in 1996, as well as two shorter visits in 2001. I chose 1964, the beginning of the presidency of Eduardo Frei Montalva, as the start date for my analysis of primary data because it was precisely at this time that Chile was deemed most democratic. Examining judicial behavior (both decisions and other public declarations and acts) during this period, as well as during and after the dictatorship, allowed me to determine if and how behavior changed with regime change. The main sources of this data were judicial decisions in civil and political rights cases, published in the three main jurisprudential journals: *Revista de Derecho y Jurisprudencia*, *Gaceta Jurídica*, and *Fallos del Mes*. To locate these cases, I used the indices of each volume, searching for references to civil and political rights as well as to other terms that signaled government involvement, such as the Law of Internal Security. I then read them all and analyzed them for their legal reasoning and their political content. I also recorded which judges participated in or dissented from each decision, searching for patterns at the individual level. For the authoritarian period, I supplemented the data from the jurisprudential journals with information in the monthly and annual reports of the *Vicaría de la Solidaridad* and the archives of the *Comisión Chilena de Derechos Humanos*, which were the two main institutions from which the struggle for human rights was conducted. Although I discuss some of these latter cases in the text, the quantitative analysis, summarized in the tables in each chapter, is based solely on the published cases.

I should note that Chile's jurisprudential journals do not provide exhaustive records of all decisions rendered by the courts, but are, rather, collections of cases selected by the editors for their juridical or social interest or importance. There simply is no accessible "raw" source of judicial decision data for the period I covered in Chile. The advantage of this is that the number of decisions I worked with was manageable enough that I could read them all and analyze them in detail. The disadvantage is that I cannot say that the decisions I analyzed are an unquestionably representative sample of all the decisions rendered. However, given that the editors of the different sources were of very different political persuasions, and given that I interviewed legal scholars from across the political spectrum for this study, always asking them for further case references, I am confident in the general representativeness of the sample.

Interviews were a second major source for my analysis. On three different research trips (one in 1996 and two in 2001), I conducted a total of 115 interviews with legal scholars and practitioners, former ministers of justice, and, most importantly, judges. In 1996, I interviewed thirty-six acting high-court (AHC) judges (fifteen of seventeen Supreme Court members and twenty-one members of the appellate courts of Santiago and San Miguel)[12] plus ten lower-court and/or former judges. In 2001,

---

[12] The thirty-six represented two-thirds of the total (fifty-four) of acting high court (AHC) judges in the Metropolitan Region (greater Santiago). I selected high court judges because it is they who have jurisdiction in areas of constitutional justice (writs protecting constitutional rights and writs of inapplicability due to unconstitutionality), as well as in cases involving violations of the Law of Internal State Security. (As Chilean human rights lawyer Roberto Garretón notes, first instance judges "had little to do with problems of constitutional justice under the military regime" In addition, all high court judges also have worked in first instance courts earlier in their careers, many under the military regime, and thus could speak to that experience as well. I felt justified limiting the study to Santiago for three interrelated reasons: First, most judges work outside of Santiago early in their careers, so interviewees in Santiago bring perspectives from the provinces; second, the Santiago Appeals Court is often a springboard into the Supreme Court, and thus its members are more likely to be future Supreme Court justices than those from the regions (Navarro Beltrán [1988] calculates that 45 percent of all Santiago Appeals Court judges go on to become Supreme Court justices); and third, the judiciary, like the country, is highly centralized and the views and decisions of the Supreme Court and the Santiago Appeals Court draw the most public attention and define the judiciary in the public mind.

I interviewed fifteen judges, ten of whom I had interviewed in 1996. All interviews were semistructured and lasted anywhere from forty-five minutes to four hours. Through the interviews, I probed the judges' role conception, their political leanings, and their understandings of the institutional and/or political constraints that they were subjected to under different regimes and administrations. I sought to ask questions in the most open-ended way possible, so as not to lead the subjects or to put them on the defensive. Because interview responses cannot necessarily be taken at face value, I sought to triangulate and contextualize the responses through interviews with a variety of actors, and, where possible, through archival material.

Because interviewees were promised anonymity, their names appear only in Appendix B, where they are listed alphabetically, and are not tied personally to their statements cited in the text. Instead, throughout the text I use a coding system that identifies subjects only by category and assigns them each a number that corresponds to the year and the (random) order in which I interviewed them. For example, the appellate court judge that I interviewed first in 2001 is identified as "ACJ01–1;" the seventh Supreme Court justice interviewed in 1996 as "SCJ96–7," and so on. The key to the categories is as follows:

SCJ   Supreme Court Justice
ACJ   Appellate Court Judge
LCJ   Lower Court Judge
FJ   Former Judge
AI   Abogado Integrante
HRL   Human Rights Lawyer
OL   Other Lawyer and/or Law Professor (includes Ministers of Justice)

A third major source of information for the analysis was records of the plenary sessions of the Supreme Court, including the annual evaluations. Through these materials, I was able to see when and how the Supreme Court exercised its disciplinary and promotion power over the judicial hierarchy, and if there was any evidence of their changing or retracting decisions in the face of disagreement from the executive.

Finally, I drew on numerous secondary sources, such as major newspapers and magazines, biographical encyclopedias, law school theses, judicial memoirs, and scholarly journal articles and books. These were particularly useful in providing historical background to the study's focus period, as well as for contextualizing and expanding the data from decisions and interviews.

PLAN OF THE BOOK

This book proceeds as follows. Chapter 1 provides a discussion of the specific theoretical debates to which the analysis seeks to contribute, and elaborates the book's arguments. Specifically, it serves to situate the arguments in comparative politics debates on the role of courts in democracy and democratization, in the (American-dominated) literature on judicial behavior, and in terms of specific works on judicial complicity with illiberal/authoritarian rule. Chapter 2 offers a historical background, explaining the ideas, interests, and events that informed the construction of the judiciary in Chile, as well as an account, based on secondary materials, of judicial performance during the nineteenth and first half of the twentieth centuries.[13] It serves to demonstrate that the roots of judicial behavior in late-twentieth-century Chile lie in institutional norms and structures established long before General Pinochet arrived on the scene.

Chapter 3 turns to an analysis of judicial behavior in the years immediately preceding the Pinochet dictatorship (1964 to 1973), extending and deepening the argument begun in Chapter 2 by delving into primary sources. It elucidates how during the presidencies of Eduardo Frei Montalva and Salvador Allende, when Chile was considered to be one of the most democratic countries in the world, its courts played a role in the system that was quite illiberal and undemocratic. Although the chapter acknowledges the personal conservatism of certain members of the Supreme Court to be a relevant factor in the explanation for this performance, it argues that the behavior of most Chilean judges during this period (and beyond) did not reflect exogenous personal attitudes, social ties, or commitments. Rather, their conservative behavior was a response – sincere, strategic, or both – to institutional dynamics.

Chapter 4 continues the book's primary analysis, contextualizing and dissecting the performance of the Chilean judiciary during the authoritarian regime, and underscoring continuities with the preauthoritarian past. In order to account for the change in the legal context marked by the introduction of a new constitution in 1980, the chapter is divided

---

[13] For a basic description of how the Chilean judicial system functions, including definitions of many legal terms that appear throughout the text, refer to Appendix A.

into three parts. Part I covers the period 1973–1980, when the 1925 Constitution was (nominally) still in place, and Part II discusses the period 1981–1990, after the 1980 Constitution came into force. Part III analyzes judicial behavior throughout the authoritarian era, discussing the evidence for the competing hypotheses presented in Chapter 1, and arguing that it was institutional factors that ensured that all but the most exceptional judges would refrain from asserting themselves in defense of liberal democratic principles and practices during this period.

Chapter 5 examines judicial performance in the first decade of the postauthoritarian era (1990–2000), showing that the overarching pattern of judicial behavior detailed in previous chapters persisted long after the formal transition to democracy. The chapter reveals that it was not until after judicial reforms took effect and Pinochet was detained in London that the judiciary's treatment of authoritarian-era human rights abuses began to change. In rights cases that postdated the return to democracy, however, the more traditional behavior continued. Extending the argument developed throughout the book, the chapter contends that this behavior was institutionally conditioned.

Chapter 6 summarizes the analysis, presents supporting evidence for the argument from a variety of other countries, and develops the theoretical and practical implications that I derive therefrom. It emphasizes that although the institutional features to which the book attributes judicial performance in Chile have specific and demonstrable roots in Chilean history, comparable structures and/or professional ideologies, grounded in the ideal of judicial apoliticism, can be found in many other cases, including, among others, Italy, Spain, Japan, and South Africa. By contrast, in cases in which such structures and ideologies have been absent, such as Argentina and Brazil, more rights-defensive judicial behavior has been possible. The chapter closes by discussing the broader lessons that can be taken from the analysis of Chile and these other cases.

CHAPTER ONE

THE JUDICIARY, THE RULE OF LAW, AND DEMOCRACY: ASPIRATIONS AND IMPEDIMENTS

This book examines how and why Chilean judges trained and appointed under democratic governments lent such robust support to the Pinochet regime. Although the analysis has obvious relevance for Chileans and scholars of Chile, it was motivated by and speaks to much broader theoretical concerns. Comparative politics theorizing on democratization has recently begun emphasizing the need for the rule of law to support and sustain democracy, and the need for judicial reform as a primary means of building the rule of law (Linz and Stepan 1996; Frühling 1998; Hammergren 1998; Domingo 1999; Prillaman 2000; Zakaria 2003). However, there remains relatively little description in the literature, much less empirical analysis, of how the judiciary functions (or has functioned) in most democratizing countries, and especially not in Latin America.[1] Thus, it is still unclear what precisely about judicial institutions requires reform in such countries, or what the limits of institutional reform might be. Meanwhile, in the American public law literature, abundant analysis of judicial functioning, particularly at the Supreme Court level, has produced heated debates regarding if and how institutions affect judicial behavior. However, these debates are greatly limited by an almost exclusive focus on the American case. This book thus brings theoretical concepts and debates from

---

[1] This is slowly changing as a new generation of scholars addresses this lacuna for the Latin American region. See, for example, Arantes 1997; Domingo 2000; Popkin 2000; Chavez 2004; Helmke 2005; Staton 2004; Sieder, Schjolden, and Angell 2005; Finkel forthcoming.

public law to bear on comparative politics theories of democratization, and contributes empirical insights from a comparative (non-U.S.) case to address theoretical debates in public law. In the mode of new institutionalist analysis, it seeks to explain how institutional attributes of the judiciary contributed to judges' antidemocratic performance in Chile. Based on the findings, it then takes a first step toward answering the general question of under what institutional conditions judges might be more likely to question and challenge undemocratic and/or illiberal governmental action, and to promote the liberal principles and practices that, I will argue, make democracy meaningful.

THE JUDICIAL ROLE IN DEMOCRACY AND DEMOCRATIZATION

During the past twenty years, theories of democracy and democratization have come to a growing consensus around the value of the liberal concepts of rights and the rule of law. Whereas in the past, some democratic theorists, particularly those on the Left, tended to reject these concepts as either irrelevant to or in fundamental tension with democracy, today many explicitly acknowledge the rule of law and rights protection as either supportive of or integral to any meaningful democracy (Laclau and Mouffe 1985; Bobbio 1987; Held 1987; Habermas 1996; Shapiro 1996; Touraine 1997). Having observed (or experienced) the outcome of government unfettered by law, previous skeptics have (re)valorized the idea of governance in accordance with key legal principles such as consistency, security, continuity, public accountability, and due process (Hutchinson 1999). Scholars across the political spectrum now agree that a healthy democracy requires that "the acts of agencies and officials of all kinds are subject to the principle of legality, [that] procedures are available to interested persons to test the legality of governmental action [and that there is] an appropriate remedy [applied] when the act in question fails to pass the test" (Merryman 1985: 141). Moreover, most scholars now reject the idea of a harmonious collective will common in some earlier theories of democracy and accept the permanence of conflicts and antagonisms.[2] Recognizing the diversity that (increasingly)

---

[2] Prominent democratic theorists such as Robert Dahl (1971) and Giovanni Sartori (1962) have long argued this view, but they are now joined by others who previously rejected it.

characterizes modern societies, they emphasize the need to limit the power of governing coalitions so as to protect dissent, promote debate, and safeguard the fundamental interests of individuals and groups within the opposition (Mouffe 1993: 104-5; Holmes 1995: Ch. 1; Touraine 1997: 28). In other words, today's democratic theorists argue not only that there must be restraints on the routine conduct of government officials, but also on lawmaking itself (Dyzenhaus 1999; Tamanaha 2002).

At a minimum, democratic theorists argue that to function properly the democratic process requires respect for citizens' basic political rights (Dean 1967; Ely 1980). These include the right to vote for almost all adults, the right to run for office, the right to free expression (including criticism of any and all aspects of government), the right to alternative sources of information, and the right to associate and assemble peacefully (Dahl 1989: 220). As Stephen Holmes (1988: 233) writes, "democracy is government by public discussion, not simply the enforcement of the will of the majority. . . . Consent is meaningless without institutional guarantees of unpunished dissent [and] popular sovereignty is meaningless without rules organizing and protecting public debate." Without the protection of what Carlos Nino (1996: 201) calls "a priori rights" (those that are preconditions for free political participation), the democratic process loses its validity.

Some scholars argue for more than this procedural minimum, holding that with the values of autonomy and human dignity at its core, the modern ideal of democracy necessarily involves guarantees of certain substantive individual rights.[3] Voters may empower leaders to represent and lead them, but, whether their party wins this time around or not, they expect the government to respect their inherent dignity, that is, to show equal concern and respect for those whose lives it can affect (Beatty 1994: 19–23).[4] Although such authors disagree about which rights are fundamental – that is, about what is necessary to preserve individual dignity – they are united in the belief that there are some rights that must be protected from or promoted by the democratic process. In other words, some policies, no matter how much popular democratic support they have, are illegitimate because of the harm they

---

[3] By substantive rights, I mean those not directly related to the democratic process. Note that such rights can be either "negative" or "positive." See Dworkin 1978; Kateb 1992; Touraine 1997.

[4] This is also the general argument of Dworkin (1978).

cause to some, and potentially all, citizens.[5] Liberal theorists generally agree that laws and practices violative of bodily integrity, due process, free religious belief and practice, or private, consensual sexual expression have no place in a democracy.[6] Liberals disagree, however, about what, if any, limits are appropriate for socioeconomic policy: Some (the libertarians) believe restrictions on private property and commerce are illegitimate (e.g., Nozick 1974), whereas others (those sharing socialist concerns) hold that such restrictions are required in order to ensure basic subsistence and equality of opportunity for all citizens (e.g., Rawls 1971; Sen 1999).[7]

This emphasis on substantive rights protection is reflected in contemporary popular understandings and expectations of democracy around the world. In Western Europe, for example, scholars speak of a "second democratic revolution," driven by a new consciousness on the part of citizens of their rights and a growing demand that government enforce respect for these rights. This revolution "from sovereignty to justiciability" entails a move away from a focus on political will and majority power toward an emphasis on (constitutional) law and the protection of minorities (Garapon 1999: 44; Toharia 2001: 29–30). Similarly, in both Latin America and Eastern Europe, the latest wave of democratization was as much about securing fundamental rights as it was about restoring elections and the democratic process. As Elizabeth Jelin and Eric Hershberg (1996: 3) explain, in Latin America in the 1980s, "basic human and civil rights became the center of political activism and intellectual preoccupation. Calling on the state to guarantee and protect individual rights, and insisting that public officials be held accountable for their actions, social actors articulated new demands that were pivotal to the process of rebuilding democratic institutions, or, in some countries, of constructing such institutions for the very first time." Likewise, in Eastern Europe, many citizens understood democracy's promise to be that individual dignity would, at last, be respected and protected by

---

[5] Many liberals would argue that these restrictions must apply to legislation affecting noncitizens as well.

[6] As Judith Shklar (1987: 2) argues, "Government must resort to an excess of violence when it attempts to effectively control religious belief and practice, consensual sex, and expressions of public opinion." See also Kateb 1992; Holmes 1995.

[7] Using slightly different reasoning, Judith Shklar argues that legally guaranteed proprietorship "cannot be unlimited, because it is the creature of the law in the first place, and also because it serves a public purpose – the dispersion of power" (1989: 31).

the government. Kim Lane Scheppele (2001: 32) notes that in Hungary in the 1990s, "it was common . . . for [citizens] to say that something was 'undemocratic' when it violated basic rights." Democracy "was not associated with republicanism or elections" but rather "with a substantive set of rights to be treated decently and with respect."

Both in theory and in the popular imagination, then, the rule of law and respect for rights (however defined) is central to the legitimacy and fairness of a democratic regime (Beatty 1994: 3).[8] And although courts are not the only institutions responsible for defending rights (Tushnet 1999; Whittington 2003), scholars and citizens of new democracies have increasingly turned their attention – and hopes – to the judiciary.

This focus on courts derives in part from an analysis of democratic weakness (past or present) as resulting from the excessive concentration of power in the legislature and/or the executive in many countries.[9] In this view, there have not been enough healthy mechanisms of "horizontal accountability" to keep elected officials within legal and constitutional bounds. Although regular, free, and fair elections and freedom of the media and assembly may be present in many countries, allowing for what Guillermo O'Donnell (1999: 39) calls "vertical accountability," there is often an absence or serious weakness of "state agencies that are authorized and willing to oversee, control, redress, and/or sanction unlawful actions of other state agencies [or actors]." The development of a strong and independent judiciary, as perhaps the most crucial of a network of overseeing agencies, is thus viewed as an important means to advance the rule of law, protect constitutional rights, and thereby strengthen a democratic (or polyarchic) regime.

The emphasis on courts also can be attributed to a positive perception of the role of the judiciary in American democracy, in general, and in the U.S. "rights revolution" (Epp 1998), in particular.[10] As several authors have noted, a global "judicial turn" began in Europe after World

---

[8] As Murphy argues, whereas the strain between (liberal) constitutionalist and democratic theory "is always real and often serious," they are both grounded in a commitment to protecting human dignity and "to an extent, the two theories need each other" (1993: 6).

[9] In presidentialist systems, such as those of Latin America, excessive executive power is the general concern; in parliamentary systems, in which the legislature produces the executive, the concern is often expressed in terms of unchecked parliamentary sovereignty.

[10] The significance of the judicial role in the expansion of rights in the United States has, of course, been challenged. See, for example, Rosenberg 1991.

War II, as a result of, among other things, the emergence of the highly juridical United States as "an ideal to be emulated" (Cappelletti 1971; Vallinder 1994: 97). This has been enhanced by disillusionment in many countries with political parties and legislatures – that is, with politicians, in general. As elected officials are increasingly viewed as narrowly partisan, corrupt, or simply incapable of protecting citizens' rights and interests, people in many societies are turning to judges as an alternative (Garapon 1996; Toharia 2001: 30–31).[11]

Equally if not more important in this judicial turn has been the work of national and cross-national organizations in promoting human rights. As David Beatty (1994: 3) points out, "For ordinary people, invoking the authority of law [has become] one of the most obvious ways of ensuring [that] the power of the [democratic] state would not be abused in the way which made colonial, fascistic, and communist governments so notorious in the past." Indeed, "a human rights revolution, rising from the ashes of 20th century horrors," has put pressure on "courts outside of the United States to create expansive protections for rights" (Scheppele 2000: 2).

Yet just because there is demand or hope for judicial rights protection in many countries today does not mean that citizens of such countries will necessarily find their judges to be responsive to their rights claims. Despite the faith of some authors in judges as the guardians of human rights, and despite diverse examples of judges taking important stands in defense of liberal-democratic principles, it is simply not the case that judges will always "tend to operate on behalf of internationally-recognized norms of human dignity" (Ackerman 1997: 790–791). As the literature on judicial complicity in undemocratic or illiberal rule attests, and many other cases of judicial passivity indicate, judges are not necessarily responsive to citizens' rights claims, and in some cases may work explicitly against them (Cover 1975; Dyzenhaus 1991; Müller 1991).

SO WHY BOTHER WITH JUDGES?

Not all democratically committed theorists agree that an empowered judiciary is necessary to securing rights. Indeed, the recent international embrace of judicial review has emerged after more than a century and a

---

[11] Also, as many analysts have pointed out, it may be convenient for politicians to delegate unpopular or particularly controversial decisions to the courts.

half of suspicion of, in not outright scorn for, the idea in many countries outside the United States.[12] Even in the United States, proponents of judicial review have always had to defend themselves against accusations that they are hostile to popular sovereignty. Because judicial review (at least as practiced at the federal level in the United States) empowers unelected, tenured officials to overrule legislative majorities, it is said to pose a "counter-majoritarian difficulty," which requires justification in a democratic system.[13]

Some deny that such justification is possible. For example, political theorist Jeremy Waldron (1999) argues that it is inconsistent to demand respect for individual moral autonomy (as in rights theory), but to mistrust the exercise of that moral autonomy through the democratic process. Because definitions of and relationships between rights can never be settled definitively, any liberal society will have the difficult task of resolving such matters; but to delegate this task to a small, unelected, tenured set of individuals (high court judges) is an affront to the most basic principle of democracy: political equality. Majoritarian (or "radical") democrats such as Waldron accept that rights protection, even beyond that necessary to the democratic process – is integral to democracy. What they object to is the delegation of the power to define and protect rights to an unelected (and hence unaccountable) elite.[14] Like Jacksonian democrats in the nineteenth-century United States, their view is that if the constitution does not provide clear answers regarding how to define and balance rights, then why should judges, rather than elected representatives, be the ones to exercise that important discretion (Dahl 1957; Rosenberg 1991; Mandel 1994; Kennedy 1997; Tushnet 1999; Hirschl 2004)?

Four main points can be made in defense of a significant role for judges. First, the primary empirical referent for radical democrats is often the U.S. Supreme Court, which has particular institutional

---

[12] Note that I follow C. Neal Tate in defining judicial review broadly, as the judicial practice of reviewing legislation or administrative acts for their adherence to a set of rules or standards, express or implied, in the constitution or other laws. See Tate 1992: 3–13. See also Cappelletti 1985 and Stone 1992.

[13] As Bruce Ackerman notes, Alexander Bickel's "counter-majoritarian difficulty" is "the starting point for contemporary analysis of judicial review" (1984: 1014). See Bickel 1962.

[14] Waldron characterizes the U.S. Supreme Court as "a nine man junta clad in black robes and surrounded by law clerks" (1999: 309). See also Sartori 1962 and Dahl 2001.

characteristics – such as appointment, tenure, standing, and decision rules – that may be particularly inappropriate or problematic from a democratic standpoint. For example, the small size and (related) limited diversity of the U.S. Supreme Court and the fact that decisions can turn on the vote of one individual (in five to four rulings), are especially galling to anyone committed to political equality. However, these characteristics are not universal, and different institutional rules might improve the democratic legitimacy of such a court (see Hilbink 2006).

Second, although Waldron is correct in his view that judges will inevitably come to their office with the same combination of self-interest and principle as do legislators, he, too, quickly dismisses the idea that although they perhaps are no better than legislators at making difficult policy decisions, judges *are* different in important ways. They generally have different training and different institutional constraints and incentives shaping the way they approach their work than do legislators (Rubin 1991; Peretti 1999). In particular, the fact that they are not subject to popular election may (under the right institutional conditions) allow them to make more sincere, principled decisions (Eisgruber 2001). Viewed negatively, the participation of such judges in the policy/lawmaking process provides a check on the will of the majority; but viewed positively, it offers an additional and distinct channel for political voice and deliberation, which might, as the Federalists hoped, encourage moderation and promote more principled and/or more inclusive policy (Bellamy 1996; Hutchinson 1999; Peretti 1999).

This more positive view is not just theoretical. Catalina Smulovitz (1995) writes that in Argentina after 1983, judicialization became an alternative recourse for articulating and institutionalizing political demands, demands that politicians could ignore or postpone indefinitely, but that courts, because of the rules that govern them, could not.[15] Moreover, as Heinz Klug (2000: 160–161) argues in reference to the South African case, a properly structured and enabled constitutional court can provide "a unique institutional mechanism for the management of [what otherwise appear to be] irreconcilable political conflicts." He explains that "[u]nlike the executive and the legislature which are viewed as dominated by particular, even if frequently changing political interests," the South African Constitutional Court serves as a forum in which opposing forces can "imagine the possibility of achieving, at least

---

[15] A similar point is made for European cases in Giles and Lancaster 1989, Shapiro and Stone 1994, and Scheppele 2001 and 2003.

in part, their particular vision within the terms of the Constitution," while also "shap[ing] these imaginings through the creation of external reference points [namely international human rights standards] which delegitimize incompatible alternatives or visions" (Klug 2000: 177).

A third and related argument against the radical democratic view is that allowing courts constitutional jurisdiction helps to encourage a "culture of justification," which is by some accounts the essence of the rule of law. In an effort to transcend the standoff between radical democrats (such as Waldron, or others inspired by Jeremy Bentham) and liberal neutralists (such as Ronald Dworkin), legal theorist David Dyzenhaus has recently argued that the rule of law should be reconceived as *the rule of a culture of justification* (Dyzenhaus 1999), that is, as a system in which "government is subject to the constraints of principles [which are internal to the idea of law itself] such as fairness, reasonableness, and equality of treatment" (Dyzenhaus 1998: 152). Without requiring a commitment to any more specific set of liberal principles, as in Dworkinian theory, one can still admit and find virtue in a system that involves "controls [that] operate in the very determination of what law is" (Dyzenhaus 1999: 7). Stephen Macedo highlights this virtue in the American case:

> Constitutionalism is about the individual's right to challenge governmental acts in independent courts of law . . . requiring officials to justify their acts in publicly reasonable constitutional terms. . . . The power of courts stands for the special form of respect we pay to those on the losing side of electoral struggles and legislative battles, and those who feel victimized by officials executing the law. The courts embody (not alone, but most dramatically) a common determination to accompany the application of power with reasons, a regulative desire to govern ourselves reasonably. (1988: 255)

A final point to be made against the radical democrats is that their case offers little insight into or hope about how to construct and nurture a culture of respect for rights if it is not already well established. They emphasize that without a liberal political culture[16] and a "right" public political understanding, both rights and democracy are in peril (Waldron 1999: 308). As Robert Dahl argues, the preservation of rights and liberties "can depend only on the beliefs and cultures shared by its political, legal, and cultural elites and by the citizens to whom these

---

[16] "Liberal" here meaning grounded in a belief in the moral autonomy and integrity — that is, the equal moral worth — of each individual.

elites are responsive" (2001: 99).[17] Not only will shared "norms, beliefs, and habits... provide support for the institutions in good times and bad," but they will also "inevitably" provide for the expansion of the "sphere of rights, liberties, and opportunities" (Dahl 2001: 138).

Although I agree that without a measure of republican virtue and a spirit of liberty among both rulers and ruled, formal institutions are likely to function perversely and bills of rights to serve as no more than "parchment barriers," I reject the implication that the only way to achieve greater rights protection is by changing an entire national "culture." No culture is monolithic. In most modern societies, liberal beliefs and republican virtue fluctuate, or are shared unevenly by different sectors of the population at different times. Moreover, courts do not merely reflect but also help construct culture, particularly in transitional periods (Teitel 2000: 4 and 23). As H.L.A. Hart famously argued:

> A society is a something in process – in process of becoming. It has always within it... seeds of dissension. And it has also within it forces making for moderation and mutual accommodation. The question – the relevant question – is whether the courts have a significant contribution to make in pushing... society in the direction of moderation – not by themselves; of course they can't save us by themselves; but in combination with other institutions. Once the question is put that way, the answer, it seems to me, has to be yes.[18]

As this quote suggests, courts *alone* cannot prevent tyranny or secure greater respect for rights.[19] Nonetheless, it is possible for judges to contribute positively to the construction of a more liberal regime and,

---

[17] Similarly, Waldron contends that rights are "respected more on account of the prevalence of a spirit of liberty among the people and their representatives – a political culture of mutual respect – than as a result of formal declarations or other institutional arrangements" (1999: 308).

[18] Cited in Karst and Rosenn 1975: 98.

[19] Indeed, Charles Epp has shown that responsive judges are only one of the variables necessary for a "rights revolution" to take place. Along with constitutional promises (bills of rights), responsive judges do present *opportunities* for legal mobilization, but a broad and successful transition to a regime of expanded individual rights protection requires "a support structure of rights-advocacy lawyers, rights-advocacy organizations, and sources of financing." This structure can provide consistent support for "widespread and sustained litigation," as well as for action aimed at securing the governmental and societal cooperation necessary for implementation of judicial decisions (Epp 1998: 8–9, 18).

hence, a more meaningful and sustainable democracy (Epp 1998; Stone Sweet 2000; Teitel 2000; Scheppele 2001). As Allan Hutchinson argues, courts should be understood "as democratic institutions which have a vital and complementary role to play in the continuous process of discussion and reflection about what democracy means and demands" (1999: 218).[20] The question is: under what conditions are judges likely to be willing and able to play this role?

This book addresses this question through the analysis of a negative example, Chile, where judges were, with few exceptions, unwilling or unable to take stands in favor of liberal democratic principles. The idea is that if we can understand the sources of undesirable judicial behavior, we can, by inference, generate hypotheses about the conditions that might allow for more positive outcomes in other times and places (see Osiel 1995: 487–488).

THE ROOTS OF JUDICIAL BEHAVIOR IN GENERAL

Most of the existing literature on judicial behavior, whether normative or empirical in orientation, focuses on the United States, and in particular on the U.S. Supreme Court. A small subfield of comparative judicial studies does exist, but it has, until recently, remained rather isolated from the larger debates in both public law and comparative politics. Most studies have tended to concentrate on the high court of a single nation, and have not followed a common methodology or research agenda (e.g., Kommers 1976; Paterson 1982; Stone 1992; Jacobsohn 1993; Tate and Haynie 1993; Edelman 1994; Volcansek 2000). The past fifteen to twenty years have seen efforts to encourage more systematic and cumulative cross-national research, but progress in this regard has thus far been slow.[21] Indeed, it remains the case that even comparative political scientists "know precious little about the judicial and legal

---

[20] Peretti 1999 makes a similar argument.

[21] John R. Schmidhauser (1987) was one of the first such efforts. Since then, a few edited volumes have begun to examine issues such as judicial review and judicial activism or policy making from a comparative perspective, and some journals have recently devoted issues to judicial politics in different countries (1987). See, for example, Waltman and Holland 1988; Holland 1991; Jackson and Tate 1992; Tate and Vallinder 1995; Kenney, Reisinger, and Reitz 1999; *West European Politics* 15:3 (July 1992); *Comparative Political Studies* 26:4 (January 1994); *International Political Science Review* 15:2 (1994).

systems in countries outside the United States" (Gibson, Caldeira, and Baird 1998: 343).[22]

With most scholars focused narrowly on the U.S. Supreme Court, the debate on judicial behavior[23] was polarized for many years between "legalists," or those who attributed case outcomes to the content of laws and legal norms, and "political jurisprudence" scholars, or those who explain judicial decision making as a function of variables outside of and unrelated to the law. In general, lawyers fell into the former category, and social scientists into the latter.[24]

Until quite recently, the dominant model within the political jurisprudence school, at least within political science, was the attitudinal model (Schubert 1965; Schubert 1974; Rohde and Spaeth 1976; Segal and Spaeth 1993). As the name implies, the attitudinal model argues that the behavior (votes) of U.S. Supreme Court justices directly reflects their individual policy preferences – preferences that precede their arrival on the bench. According to this model, developed most fully by Harold Spaeth and Jeffrey Segal, judges are only concerned with achieving their preferred policy outcomes, not with making good or consistent law. Even strong legal norms such as *stare decisis* have minimal influence on the way justices vote (Spaeth and Segal 1999; Howard and Segal 2002).

The gradual accretion of studies on other courts in the United States (appellate, trial, and state courts), as well as the move into the study of courts by analysts of legislative and executive politics, however, has given rise to a new focus in judicial studies. Challenging the idea that policy preferences get translated directly into judicial decisions, many

---

[22] A study of the articles published in *Comparative Politics, Comparative Political Studies*, and *World Politics* between 1982 and 1997 indicates that, of 727 articles published, only 9 dealt with courts. The author of the study notes that even these articles would have been absent if CPS had not published its 1994 special issue on courts. See Hull 1999: 121, 124.

[23] For a good discussion of the history of judicial behavior studies, on which this account also relies, see Maveety 2003b.

[24] The divide between lawyers and social scientists on this issue is not completely rigid. Political jurisprudence has its roots in legal realism, originated by lawyers such as Oliver Wendell Holmes, Karl Llewllyn, and Jerome Frank in the early twentieth century, and their views regarding the sources of judicial behavior are shared by legal scholars in the contemporary Critical Legal Studies movement. Also, although few social scientists would fall into the purely "legalist" category, many scholars have and continue to argue for the importance of certain legal and judicial norms in judicial decision making.

theorists now argue for the importance of strategic calculation in judicial decision making and of the influence of institutional context on such calculation.[25] The primary advocates of this approach are Lee Epstein and Jack Knight, who tout this development as a veritable revolution in judicial studies (1998). Citing roots in Walter Murphy's *Elements of Judicial Strategy*, they advocate the adoption of a strategic approach to unify the field, an approach based in three basic assumptions: (1) judges make goal-oriented decisions, and act "'intentionally and optimally' toward a specific objective"; (2) in the decision-making process, judges consider the preferences of other actors and their likely actions and reactions; and (3) judges' actions will be structured by the institutional context, both formal (laws) and informal (norms and conventions), in which they function (Epstein and Knight 1998: 9–18). Because of this last assumption, Epstein and Knight can be considered part of the "new institutionalism" movement in political science (which is, in fact, not so new [see Gillman 2004; Melnick 2005]).[26] Identifying themselves as and allying with rational choice theorists in political science and economics, however, they represent only one vein of institutionalist theory in judicial studies (and in political science as a whole).

Another notable group of judicial scholars, the "historical institutionalists," also emphasizes the important influence of institutions in their analyses of judicial functioning, but they do not accept the idea that judges (or other actors) always and everywhere act "intentionally and optimally" to achieve their goals. Moreover, they place more emphasis on the need to identify, through close historical and ethnographic research, what the various goals of potentially strategic actors might be, rather than positing those in advance (e.g., Smith 1988; Gillman 1993; Kahn 1994; Gillman and Clayton 1999). As Cornell Clayton and Howard Gillman emphasize, another difference between rational choice and historical institutionalist judicial scholars is that the latter tend to "resist[] the . . . tendency to reduce courts to individual, quantifiable units of analysis and instead seek[] to emphasize the cognitive structures that attach courts and judges in general to culture and society" (1999: 4).

[25] On this shift, see Baum 1997; Epstein and Knight 2000.
[26] Interestingly, neoinstitutionalism has become so influential that even the standard-bearers of attitudinalism, Spaeth and Segal now emphasize the unique institutional context that permits the sincere expression of policy preferences on the U.S. Supreme Court (1999: 18).

In contrast to the attitudinalists and other theorists of the behavioralist movement, both rational choice institutionalists (or strategic approach scholars) and historical institutionalists agree that judicial norms and legal traditions (i.e., variables that are endogenous to the legal system) can shape judicial behavior. The difference is that historical institutionalists argue that these variables *both* "constitute and constrain judicial attitudes and motivations" (Clayton and Gillman 1999: 4), whereas rational choicers only see them as potential constraints on previously existing goals (Maveety 2003b: 26–27).

This book offers an explanation that bridges these two perspectives. On the one hand, it argues that strategic calculations, shaped heavily by institutional characteristics (both formal and informal), are an important part of the explanation for judicial behavior in Chile. It thus provides (further) evidence that judicial behavior, like all human behavior, has an important strategic element. Furthermore, it generates hypotheses about the way particular institutional characteristics, in any context, are likely to channel judicial behavior. On the other hand, the book also emphasizes the ways that institutional factors shape judicial identity and, thereby, *constitute* the goals that judges have, rather than simply constraining the achievement of preexisting goals. Moreover, to support the argument, the book brings to bear data that are primarily historical and interpretive. The argument is based on an inductive analysis, both quantitative and qualitative, of all the civil and political rights decisions published for this period, of the record of other official judicial acts and speeches, and of semistructured interviews with judges and lawyers. Information on the history of the judiciary and the context of judicial decision making during the focus period provides a broader understanding of the role that the judiciary, as an institution, has played in the Chilean political system over time.[27] Finally, the study fits in the historical institutionalist mold in that it was motivated by and seeks to address explicitly normative concerns about judicial behavior. I chose the topic of this book out of a deep interest in and concern for democratization in Chile and other developing countries,

---

[27] As Rogers Smith argues, historical institutionalists in the field of public law attempt to "recognize [the] historical roots" of inherited legal principles and institutions "and attend carefully to the role – great or small – they have played politically, attempting to judge their characteristic tendencies, strengths, and weaknesses in the crucible of social life" (1988: 105).

where scholars, citizens, and policy makers are still trying to figure out what has gone wrong in the past and what kinds of changes might help promote a better – that is, a more stable and meaningfully democratic – future. This book thus speaks not only and not primarily to American judicial behavior scholars but also to scholars of comparative politics concerned about promoting a supportive role for judges in emerging and established democracies alike.

JUDICIAL BEHAVIOR IN ILLIBERAL CONTEXTS: SPECIFIC HYPOTHESES

Although there exist some well-known and high-quality works analyzing judicial capitulation to or complicity in authoritarian regimes, they are few compared to the number of works on judicial behavior in general. In this section, then, I present possible explanations for the performance of Chilean judges under Pinochet as derived from analyses of judicial behavior in both democratic and nondemocratic cases. These explanations fall into four main categories: regime-related, attitudinalist, class-based, and legal theory. I will discuss each in general and as it applies to the Chilean case, arguing that although each has partial explanatory power, an institutional explanation more accurately and completely accounts for judicial performance under authoritarianism in Chile.

The Regime-Related Explanation

The first and most obvious possible explanation for judicial capitulation to authoritarian rule in any country is that authoritarian leaders manipulated the courts, through either purges, threats, or jurisdictional restrictions. Obviously, when judges are handpicked by regime leaders, or cowed by fear for their personal safety or economic security, one cannot expect significant resistance.[28] However, as in Chile, authoritarian leaders sometimes see benefits to respecting the independence of the courts: If they leave the courts alone, they can deflect charges that they have no respect for the law.[29] Instead, as José Juan Toharia argues

---

[28] Even with purges, however, resistance is still possible. See, for example, Osiel 1995; Solomon 1996; and Helmke 2005.

[29] For an excellent summary of the various motivations authoritarian rulers can have for respecting or granting judicial independence, see Moustafa 2007.

with reference to Spain under Franco, authoritarian leaders are likely to pursue the strategy of allowing judicial independence and impartiality while restricting jurisdiction (1974–1975). C. Neal Tate concurs, noting that the "objective would be to leave the courts with only routine, non-threatening decisions to make, preserving their utility, but reserving the important and threatening litigation for decision by more controllable agencies, e.g., military courts" (1993: 318). He adds, however, that "there is no guarantee that these tactics will be successful. If, in spite of the establishment of parallel courts, regular courts continue to accept cases which fall within the special jurisdiction of the parallel courts, and challenges denying the parallel courts' jurisdiction in cases they have begun to hear, the strategy will fail. Similarly, if the courts entertain challenges to the validity of the crisis decrees and regulations, then the strategy will fail" (Tate 1993: 319; see also Osiel 1995).[30]

In Chile, the Pinochet regime pursued the strategy of restricting civilian jurisdiction, expanding military jurisdiction to levels comparable only to Francoist Spain. However, even before the strategy was formalized into law, human rights lawyers brought challenges to its constitutionality, challenges which the courts repeatedly rejected. Indeed, it was the judges themselves who tended to interpret their own role very narrowly, abdicating the authority they had to reign in the state's police powers or protect constitutional rights. My analysis of judicial decisions revealed that this general pattern was evident long before the 1973 military coup, persisted through even the weakest moments of Pinochet's seventeen-year rule, and continued well after the transition to civilian rule in 1990.[31] Furthermore, both archival sources and interviews with judges, lawyers, and legal academics pointed more to institutional factors than to regime-related factors as explanations for judicial performance across time. It cannot be said, then, that regime-related variables offer a straightforward or complete explanation for judicial behavior in Pinochet's Chile.

---

[30] Tate notes that in the face of judicial resistance, the only option left to a crisis regime is coercion, which the judiciary obviously has no means to resist. However, by resorting to coercive treatment of judges, the regime "vividly illustrates the hollowness of its professed respect for constitutionality" (1993: 319), or as Dyzenhaus puts it, forces the regime into a "rule of law dilemma" (1998: 159).

[31] The continuity of judicial behavior in Chile across regimes calls into question theories that hold that they key to the assertion of judicial authority is diffuse political power or party alternation (e.g., Ginsburg 2003; Ramseyer and Rasmussen 2003).

The Attitudinal Explanation

With regime-related variables thrown into question, many scholars of judicial behavior would immediately suspect that it was the judges' personal policy preferences that explain their support, implicit or explicit, for the Pinochet regime (e.g., Segal and Spaeth 1993). In this view, little resistance from the judiciary reflects little personal opposition to the government (whatever its stripe) on the part of judges. This has certainly been the popular interpretation of judicial behavior among Chileans. Many press articles, both during and after military rule, implied judicial complicity was a function of ideological sympathy and/or a lack of individual moral integrity (e.g., Pozo 1983: 9–10; Luque and Collyer 1986: 23–27).

My research revealed that individual political attitudes are part of the explanation; alone, however, they cannot account for the sustained and highly uniform behavior of judges throughout the institution. To begin, the research showed that not all nor even a clear majority of judges in the hierarchy personally approved of the political values and practices of the Pinochet regime. Crucially, however, at the time of the coup in 1973, a powerful bloc of Supreme Court justices *did* sympathize ideologically with the military leaders. This was important because of the power the Supreme Court exercised over the rest of the judicial hierarchy. The Court controlled discipline and promotions within the judiciary, and thus any judge who aspired to rise in the judicial ranks had to curry favor with – or at least not invite scrutiny by – his or her superiors. A right-wing bias at the top of the judiciary thus meant a likely right-wing bias (even if only strategic) all the way down. In other words, the political bias of the Chilean judiciary cannot be understood as a simple function of individual-level attitudes; rather, institutional dynamics were also at play.

Moreover, the fact that the 1973 Supreme Court sympathized with the Pinochet regime can itself be attributed, in part, to institutional factors. At the time of the coup, a majority of the justices on the Court had been appointed by the progressive presidents Eduardo Frei and Salvador Allende. Without understanding how the appointment process works in Chile, one might assume, then, that these justices would sympathize with and defend the mainly working class and/or left-wing victims of the regime, and certainly not lend continuous support to the military regime. However, and as I will demonstrate in subsequent chapters, because the Supreme Court itself selects the nominees for appointments to its own ranks, the Court actually has more control over its ideological composition than the executive does, and the influence it exerts was and is conservatizing. In addition, having been socialized into the ideology of the institution, even judges who maintained private doubts or concerns about authoritarian policies were not compelled by their professional understandings or role conceptions to take stands against the military regime. Thus, although there were also conjunctural factors at work, and although some members of the Court would have certainly been right-wingers regardless, even the aspect of the explanation that appears most "attitudinal," then, is itself partially institutional.

The Class-Based Explanation

Another possible (and related) explanation for judicial capitulation to authoritarianism, particularly in the Chilean case, in which the military staged a coup against the socialist government of Salvador Allende, is that the judges were defending their class interests. This would be the obvious response from many critical legal theorists, who argue that courts *always* serve the interests of the powerful, whether under democratic or authoritarian regimes. Because, in many countries, judges do tend to come from elite backgrounds, and are thus socialized in similar family, community, and educational institutions, their approach to interpreting law and administering justice may well be a function, conscious or not, of class interests (Kairys 1982; Unger 1986; Kennedy 1997; Hirschl 2004).

The first point against this argument as it applies to Chile is that many lawyers and politicians who proved ardent defenders of human rights, or at least critics of military rule, came from elite social backgrounds. Moreover, some lawyers and politicians who initially supported the coup later became fervent public critics of the military regime, whereas judges' behavior remained quite consistent over time.

Second, my research showed that, by the middle of the twentieth century, the Chilean judicial ranks were no longer filled with elites (as they had been in the nineteenth century). Analysis of the background information I collected in my interviews, such as father's occupation, high school attended, and family landholdings, revealed that almost 80 percent of respondents came from lower-middle to middle-class backgrounds, whereas only a small minority were of upper-middle to upper-class extraction. Because entry-level judicial posts were very low paying and not very prestigious, the judicial career attracted those who desired a stable income and career, rather than those who had the social connections or financial cushion to pursue a (potentially less secure) future in private legal practice (Couso 2002: 177). Thus, most judges serving in the 1970s and 1980s did not come from social backgrounds that would *necessarily* incline them to support a conservative social and political agenda.[32]

The class background of most judges does factor as part of the explanation, but in a way that only makes sense within the judiciary's institutional context. The judicial career in Chile was structured such that it attracted individuals who were not part of the traditional sociopolitical elite, who needed a dependable income, and who could only improve their social standing by rising in the judicial hierarchy. As noted in the previous section, promotion within the judicial hierarchy required pleasing or submitting to one's superiors. The institutional features of the judiciary were thus unlikely to attract individuals with a predisposition to take creative or independent stands in the first place, much less to make nonconformity an attractive option on the job, regardless of the wider political context.

The Legal Theory Explanation

A final possible explanation, and the one that has attracted the most attention from those troubled by judicial complicity in authoritarian regimes, is that the judges' professional understandings of the nature of law and adjudication rendered them unwilling or unable to hold regime leaders legally accountable for repressive acts and policies. The most common culprit is legal positivism,[33] which analysts blame for leading judges to believe that their role is passive and mechanical; that is, that their function is to apply the letter of the law without concern for the outcomes of their decisions or for the preservation of general

---

[32] Moreover, as Rueschemeyer, Stephens, and Stephens emphasize, all class interests are inevitably socially constructed (1992: especially 53–57). See also Scott (1985) at 43.

[33] Legal positivist philosophy asserts that there is no necessary connection between legal validity and moral defensibility. A valid (and hence binding) law is one enacted consistently with the society's rule of recognition, that is, with the settled practice determining the procedures by which norms become laws. Rule application, that is, adjudication, should respect ordinary linguistic practice and legislative history. A particularly strong version of positivism, formalism, refers to the judicial inclination to apply canonical rules in a mechanical fashion, irrespective of the purposes and policies underlying them. It thus denies the possibility of judicial discretion. Textualism, or the judicial practice of referring strictly to the text of a law in the practice of interpretation, is a manifestation of formalism.

principles of the legal system (Fuller 1958; Cover 1975; Dyzenhaus 1991; Dubber 1993; Ott and Buob 1993). Judges who work under legal positivist assumptions, or what David Dyzenhaus calls "the plain fact approach," believe they have a professional duty to execute the will of the legislator(s), regardless of the law's content (1991). This conviction incapacitates them in the face of "wicked law," and thereby renders them easy servants of authoritarianism. Defenders of legal positivism counter that the major alternative, natural law philosophy,[34] offers no more security against tyranny and repression than does positivism, and in fact, may offer less. The "absolute values" shared by judges and used to interpret or even bypass the positive law may not be the ideal values that liberal humanist proponents envision, particularly in authoritarian contexts (Hart 1958; Raz 1979; MacCormick 1993). In other words, judicial reasoning in accordance with "higher law" will not meet liberal standards of justice when the "higher law" itself is not politically liberal (as in Nazi Germany, apartheid South Africa, or Chile under Pinochet's 1980 Constitution).

As I will explain in the next chapter, Chile's legal tradition since independence is strongly legal positivist, and many Chilean analysts have laid the blame for judicial complicity during the Pinochet years at the doorstep of legal positivism (Cea 1978; Cúneo 1980; Squella 1988 and 1994). My research partially confirmed this, revealing a widespread tendency on the part of judges to use a "plain fact approach" – or at least a plain fact justification – in adjudication. In decisions, judges frequently insisted that they had no choice but to defer to the executive or legislature, and in interviews, most judges emphasized that they were duty-bound to remain "apolitical."

However, both case analysis and interviews also revealed that (at least some) judges were willing and able to appeal to principles beyond the letter of law, *so long as the outcome favored or restored the (conservative) status quo*. In other words, although there did seem to be a general tendency among judges to avoid evaluating the legitimacy of government policy, some did deem it appropriate to review and even challenge the actions

---

[34] Natural law philosophy is based on the view that there is an inherent, or conceptual, connection between law and morality. In the strong version of natural law theory, no rule can be legally binding unless it is also morally defensible. In the weaker version, the understanding is that it is socially desirable for judges, in hard cases, to look beyond a rule's wording and the specific intention of its authors, to more general moral principles embedded in the fabric of legal doctrine.

of the sitting government when those actions somehow threatened the traditional social order (i.e., under Presidents Frei and Allende). These judges did not consider such activism "political," but viewed it rather as an appropriate, professional response to administrations that promoted radical social change.[35] In turn, they did not consider judicial support for the Pinochet regime (whether passive or active) "political," as Pinochet himself pledged to rid the country of "politics" and to restore the country's traditional values.

My claim, then, is that there was an "antipolitics" ideology at work in the Chilean judiciary, but one that cannot be understood as a simple function of legal positivism. Unlike "plain fact" positivists, judges could and sometimes did publicly assess the legitimacy of executive and legislative acts. However, they did so only when the resultant rulings favored or restored the *status quo*, and could thus bear a mantle of "apoliticism." To take principled stands in defense of those who *challenged* the traditional order, by contrast, was deemed "political" and unprofessional. This understanding was transmitted and reinforced by the autonomous, bureaucratic institutional structure of the Chilean judiciary, where the Supreme Court both defined what it meant to be "apolitical" and policed the understanding within the judicial ranks. Any judge who desired to be respected by colleagues and to rise in the career had to be careful to avoid appearing "political." The best career strategy – or for some simply the best way to fulfill one's role as a judge – was thus to avoid taking any stands at all, as passivity would never be interpreted as "political" behavior.

THE INSTITUTIONAL ARGUMENT

As is clear from the preceding discussion, each of the conventional explanations for judicial capitulation to authoritarian rule applies partially to the Chilean case, but none provides a completely satisfying account. I thus offer as an alternative an institutional argument, which integrates some of the insights from the competing hypotheses and more accurately explains the phenomenon in Chile. Specifically, I argue that the institutional structure and ideology of the Chilean judiciary together rendered it highly unlikely that judges would be willing and/or able to take stands in defense of liberal and democratic principles.

---

[35] For a similar argument regarding the judiciary in Weimar Germany, see Kahn-Freund 1981.

The argument has two main elements: one structural, one ideological. When I refer to the institutional *structure*, I mean the formal rules that determine the relationship of judges to each other and to the other branches of the state, and thereby offer incentives and disincentives for different kinds of behavior. Particularly important are the rules governing the judicial career, that is, rules regarding appointment, promotion, remuneration, and discipline. When I refer to the institutional *ideology*, I mean the understanding of the social role of the institution into which judges are socialized, the content of which is maintained through formal sanctions and informal norms within the institution.

The institutional structure of the Chilean judiciary can be described as that of a highly autonomous bureaucracy. Although there have been some changes to the structure in recent years, the following describes it accurately from the late 1920s until 1997:[36] Judges entered the career at the bottom rung, wherever there was a vacancy, and sought to work their way up the hierarchy. Salaries for district-level judges were very low, particularly compared to what lawyers could expect to earn in private practice. Yet tenure was generally secure and a judge with a good record could hope to move up in rank (and hence pay) through appointment to a higher court. To do so, however, the judge had to curry favor with his or her superiors, who controlled the disciplinary process within the judiciary and played a dominant role in the appointment and promotion process. Indeed, to enter the judiciary, an individual had first to approach the appellate court with jurisdiction over the district where a post was available. The appellate court composed a list of three candidates from which the Ministry of Justice (MJ) selected the appointee. To advance to the appellate level, the judge had to be nominated by the Supreme Court to appear on a similar list of three nominees from which the MJ made its appointment. Finally, to get to the Supreme Court itself, an appellate judge had to be nominated by the Court. The Court composed a list of five nominees, two of which appeared by right of seniority,[37]

---

[36] Recent changes will be discussed in Chapter 5.

[37] The 1925 Constitution specified that two individuals on the lists of five and one on the lists of three had to be chosen on the basis of seniority. The others were to be chosen on "merit," the meaning of which was left to the discretion of the superior court justices. This system remained in force until 1981. The 1980 Constitution established that only one of the nominees on any list be reserved for the individual with most seniority and added the requirement that said individual have an impeccable evaluations record.

but the other three that the Court chose by plenary vote. The MJ made its appointment from this list.[38]

In choosing the nominees, the higher courts always referenced the judge's disciplinary record and the formal evaluations that the judges had received. The Judicial Code (which dates to 1943) defines internally punishable (i.e., noncriminal) judicial "faults and abuses" to include any expressions of disrespect for hierarchical superiors, or, in the case of appellate judges, any "abuse of the discretionary faculties that the law confers on them." The respective superiors have the duty to respond to all such "faults and abuses" and to choose the appropriate disciplinary measures, ranging from a private reprimand to suspension for months at half-pay.[39] The Supreme Court has the ultimate responsibility to over-see the conduct of all the judges in the nation. To this end, the Court conducts regular performance evaluations for all judicial employees. These evaluations were triannual until 1971, when they became annual. The Supreme Court meets in January of each year to discuss the perfor-mance of every employee of the institution, from the most menial worker (e.g., the elevator operator) to the most senior appellate court judge.[40] Before 1971, judges were evaluated every three years on the "efficiency, zeal and morality" of their performance. In 1971, a four-list system was instituted: A List One rating meant good performance, a List Two sig-naled some dissatisfaction above, a List Three rating served as a stark warning (as two consecutive years on List Three meant dismissal), and a List Four rating meant immediate removal.[41] The formal criteria of eval-uation were still the same ("efficiency, zeal, and morality"), but because the justices (as before) did not have to justify the evaluations in any way

---

[38] I reviewed all the minutes of the plenary sessions from 1964 through the late 1990s (I couldn't access those after 1998), and there was never an instance of the MJ rejecting the list of nominees and requesting that another be drafted. Moreover, when I interviewed former ministers of justice, they all grumbled about the fact that they frequently had to choose "the lesser of the evils" from the list; that is, it was clear that they felt constrained by the process. Those who worked in the Allende administration, in particular, felt that the Court had intentionally stacked the list with more conservative judges. Their response was thus to name the individual who appeared on the list by seniority, regardless of his technical qualifications.

[39] See *Código Orgánico de Tribunales*, articles 530–545.

[40] Evaluations of district-level employees are supposed to be based on reports provided by the respective appellate courts, but the Supreme Court still votes on them.

[41] See *Código Orgánico de Tribunales*, articles 270–277.

(indeed, the votes were anonymous), subordinates had to be sure not to anger their superiors or, indeed, give them any reason to scrutinize or question their work.

This autonomous bureaucratic ("apolitical") institutional structure, I argue, gave strong incentives for judges to play, primarily if not exclusively, to the Supreme Court. Professional success was clearly linked to pleasing, or at least never upsetting, the institutional elders. From their earliest days in the career, then, judges had to worry about how their superiors would perceive and assess their work. The likelihood that they would so worry was heightened by the fact that entry-level posts were very poorly compensated. Those who accepted them generally had low levels of financial independence, and thus relied on the security of the job and the promise of upward mobility within the judicial hierarchy. The incentives operating on judges thus encouraged conformity and reproduced conservatism within the institution.

I am not the first to make this observation. Several prominent Chilean scholars have called attention to the corporatist nature of the judiciary and have noted (and lamented) the lack of internal judicial independence (Frühling 1980 and 1984; Correa 1993; Peña 1994). My work confirms and builds on their insights, providing systematic empirical evidence for a thirty-five-year period covering both democratic and authoritarian regimes.

The second part of my argument, regarding the institutional ideology of the judiciary, also owes something to Chilean analysts. As mentioned earlier, many prominent Chilean legal scholars have emphasized the positivist or formalist legal culture that prevails in their country, and in which judges are trained and function (Novoa 1964; Lowenstein 1978; Cúneo 1980; Squella 1988 and 1994; Correa 1990; Correa and Montero 1992). Legal education has traditionally been done in the exegetic method (memorization of codes), such that students learn "the law," but are not encouraged to examine and critique the reasoning behind it, nor even to learn how law functions in practice. Students, including judges, are taught to think of law in purely bookish and technical terms, and, importantly, they are taught that the only legitimate source of law is the legislator; the role of the judge is merely to apply the law in accordance with the rules of interpretation outlined in the Civil Code. Judges are expressly prohibited from engaging in partisan political activities.[42] All of this positivist indoctrination is so strong,

---

[42] See the *Código Orgánico de Tribunales*, article 323.

the argument goes, that judges come to think of their work in almost mechanical, or formalist, terms. They seek to apply the written law "regardless of the consequences or the specific circumstances of the case," and they eschew any analysis based on general principles (Cea 1978). Thus, under the dictatorship they were able to apply authoritarian policies without reserve because it was simply not a part of their role perception to assess the legitimacy of legislation nor to recognize and accept responsibility for the outcomes of their decisions.

My research showed, however, that some Chilean judges were in fact quite able to (and did) think of their work in nonformalist terms, and that they were willing to depart from the letter of statutory law both before and after 1973. As subsequent chapters will demonstrate, when left-wing presidents sought to exercise (longstanding legal) executive prerogatives to advance their reform agendas, the courts proved cognizant and capable of invoking constitutionalist principles to check government excesses. Notwithstanding this, my research also showed that a taboo against "political" behavior was clearly at work within the institution. To understand the significance of this norm, it is necessary to explain how the term "political" was defined within the institution and how that definition was maintained.

As I show in Chapter 2, the definitions of the "political" and the "judicial" were established in the nineteenth century, when Chilean statebuilders sought to achieve political stability through the "rule of law." To this end, they imposed a strict understanding of the separation of powers doctrine: judges handled private law (property and contract), politicians handled public law (public order and morality).[43] Judicial adherence to this division of authority was secured through partisan manipulation of the courts. In the constitutional overhaul of the 1920s, judicial independence was secured by eliminating the power of the executive to discipline and appoint judges, and transferring that power to the Supreme Court. In addition, the Court was given the power of judicial review for the first time. However, there was no purge of the judicial ranks, and legal and judicial training remained the same. Thus, nineteenth-century views regarding the legitimate scope of judicial (and political) authority were, effectively, frozen in to the judiciary, as those at the top of the hierarchy (the Supreme Court justices) were newly empowered to promote to their own ranks those who best emulated their own professional, if not also personal, attitudes and practices. At

---

[43] This interpretation is supported by Barros (2002: 112–114) and Couso (2002: 152).

the same time, they had, through the evaluations system, an effective means of deterring dissent. In the decades that followed, the judiciary thus remained quietist in the face of abuses of public power.

This behavior changed, however, when the progressive governments of Eduardo Frei and Salvador Allende began using executive power to challenge the sanctity of private property (the traditional judicial domain) and the social order that this concept supported. Led by the Supreme Court, judges began invoking rights principles to defend traditional values and interests. Yet they did not understand this activism to be "political." Judicial authorities reserved the term "political" to delegitimize the activities of the few judges who publicly demonstrated sympathy with or defense of the ascendant Left. Likewise, following the military coup, the judicial elite applied the label "political" to the expression of criticism or opposition to Pinochet's self-proclaimed "apolitical" (and clearly pro-private property) regime.[44]

In contrast to many Chilean authors, then, who tend to portray the country's judges as small-minded, bureaucratic automatons, focused only on their corporate interests and seemingly oblivious to the content of the laws they applied,[45] I contend that there was a more substantive ideology at work. The "antipolitics" ideology of the institution embodied and served to perpetuate traditional, nineteenth-century views of sociopolitical legitimacy. Judicial defense of these views, and the interests that stood behind them, was considered "neutral" and professional – that is, purely legal – whereas even a principled defense of other views, or the interests that stood behind them, was considered "political" and hence *un*professional.[46]

My argument is that, in combination, the structural and ideological features of the Chilean judiciary effectively served to mobilize bias (Thelen and Steinmo 1992: 10) – specifically, a conservative bias. These features allowed and supported the expression of traditional, conservative juridicopolitical views by actors in the institution, while discouraging and sanctioning the development and expression of alternative views. Because of the institutional structure, the primary, and in some ways, exclusive "audience" or "reference group" for judges was

---

[44] On the "antipolitics" of the authoritarian regime, see Loveman and Davies 1997 and Munizaga 1988.

[45] See especially Correa (1993) for a focus on the origins and implications of this concept of judicial independence. See also Vaughn 1993.

[46] On a similar phenomenon in the U.S. case, see Sunstein 1987.

the Supreme Court, whose members were not representative of the diversity in the wider polity.[47] They were clearly more conservative than the majority of society, in part because of the way the same institutional features had shaped their views. Given the power they bore over their subordinates' careers, it is clear that the expression of alternative juridicopolitical views was severely constrained. The institutional ideology also helped to preclude the expression of alternative views because it equated professionalism with apoliticism. To behave professionally, so as to merit respect from peers and secure success in the career, meant to remain above "politics," or at least to appear to do so. This meant that passivity was prized, in general, and activism was only deemed acceptable when it was aimed at preserving or restoring the sociopolitical status quo. With this prevailing understanding of professionalism in the institution, and with the conservative Supreme Court monitoring adherence to this understanding, it is no wonder that Chile's judges offered little resistance to the abusive policies of the Pinochet regime.[48]

To summarize, then, the central claim of this book is that the institutional features of the Chilean judiciary promoted a conservative bias among judges, which in turn explains why the judges offered such little

---

[47] I borrow the idea of "audience" from Schattschneider (1960) and the notion of judicial "reference groups" from Guarnieri and Pederzoli (2002). The claim fits nicely within the framework of Baum 2006.

[48] This argument bears some resemblance to that of Müller (1991), which explores how and why judges and lawyers cooperated so fully with the Hitler regime. Müller attributes this behavior to both "intellectual affinity between [traditional German] conservatives and Nazis" and the "loyalty to state leadership" (rather than to the law) or "fixation on government [which characterized] such a large part of the [German] judiciary" (1991: 294 and 297). Moreover, he suggests that these qualities were institutionally cultivated. From 1878 forward, and despite formal independence from the government,

> judges could be dismissed at any time during their [12–20] year training and assistantship [i.e., prior to being granted an official judgeship]. This period offered ample opportunity to observe the candidates, to remove those elements associated with the opposition, and to suppress every liberal tendency. The only candidates who survived this ceaseless scrutiny were those who were loyal and compliant to a particularly high degree – those who, in other words, accepted the social and political order unconditionally. (1991: 6)

The major difference, of course, is that in Germany, it was the Ministry of Justice (i.e., the government) that controlled judges' careers, not the judicial elite itself, as in Chile and other cases discussed in Chapter 6.

resistance to the undemocratic and illiberal regime of General Pinochet. Both the role conception into which judges were socialized and the incentive structure in which they functioned discouraged them from taking principled liberal-democratic stands, before, during, and after the authoritarian period.

CHAPTER TWO

THE INSTITUTIONAL CONSTRUCTION
OF THE JUDICIAL ROLE IN CHILE

The Chilean judiciary,[1] in its basic institutional structure, is the oldest
in Latin America. In 1974, the Supreme Court celebrated "150 years
of uninterrupted institutional life" (*Sesquicentenario de la Corte* 1974),
making it by at least one account "the most stable institution in Chile"
(Bravo Lira 1990: 36). In a region known for its political and institutional instability, this is certainly remarkable. Yet, as this book reveals,
this century and a half of stability did not come without a price. Indeed,
as Chile evolved from a quasi-authoritarian republic (in the 1830s) to
one of the world's most vibrant democracies (in the 1960s), the judiciary
proved to be not merely stable but sclerotic.

This chapter begins to make this point by offering a brief history
of the institutional development and political role of Chile's judiciary
from the dawn of the republic to 1964 (the year my primary analysis
begins). My objective is to show that long before General Pinochet
arrived on the scene, the stage was set for judicial cooperation with his
regime. As I will explain, nineteenth-century Chilean statebuilders and
twentieth-century reformers constructed the judiciary around the ideal
of "apoliticism." This institutional construction, in which judges were,
first, ideologically and, later, structurally, separated from political life,
discouraged independent thinking and innovation, and, instead, reproduced conservatism and conformity. Judges had neither the professional

---

[1] Throughout the book, I use the term "judiciary" as a translation of the Spanish "*poder
judicial*," referring to the court system.

understandings nor incentives to do anything but accept and emulate the traditional perspectives and practices of the institutional elders. Thus, although the judiciary was, by the mid-twentieth century, staffed largely by members of the emergent middle class and boasted high levels of independence and professionalism,[2] judges were largely unwilling or unable to take stands in defense of liberal and democratic principles. Indeed, as I will show in this and subsequent chapters, whether under democratic or authoritarian regimes – that is, despite dramatic changes in the political and legal context in which they functioned – the courts were remarkably consistent in the values and interests they defended or left defenseless. In short, the extremely "stable" institutional setting in which judges learned and practiced their vocation rendered their performance extremely – and tragically – "stable" as well.

LAW AND COURTS IN COLONIAL TIMES AND IN EARLY INDEPENDENCE

Before proceeding with a discussion of the judiciary's institutional and political trajectory in Chile's republican era, it is important to establish what preceded it and what those who constructed the Chilean judiciary were attempting to accomplish. Chile, like all the newly independent states of Spanish America in the early nineteenth century, emerged from a colonial era whose legal system was characterized by privilege, jurisdictional divisions, morally oriented legal interpretation, and the union of administrative and judicial authority. In the medieval Castilian tradition, the administration of justice was considered the highest attribute of sovereignty; the essence of royal authority was the granting of grace and favor. As J. H. Parry notes, "The principal task of government was considered to be that of adjudicating between competing interests, rather than that of deliberately planning and constructing a new society" (1966: 194). Therefore, the principal organ of government was the judicial tribunal (Phelan 1967: 122).

---

[2] The term "judicial independence," as used here and throughout this book, refers to freedom from partisan manipulation of judicial decision making through control of judicial discipline and tenure or interference with the decisional process (see Brinks 2005).

Members of different estates were subject to the jurisdiction of the same courts.[3] However, there was no equality before the law because "the rights, privileges, and obligations of each person came from the functional corporations and the estate to which he belonged ... the social status of a culprit influenced the nature of his punishment" (Phelan 1967: 213).[4] Moreover, conflicts involving the church, military, and commercial entities were resolved according to separate rules and in separate tribunals (*fueros*). Decisions of the ecclesiastic tribunals could be appealed to the *Real Audiencia*, but in general, the perspectives and interests of the Audiencia coincided with those of the church.

The dominant legal philosophy of the period was church-backed natural law. Legal argumentation was fundamentally morally oriented, and gave scant attention to the literal content of legal rules. Indeed, "the empire was governed by several codes of law which often conflicted with one another" (Parry 1966: 193). Thus, legal analyses focused on the purposes to be attained by the rules and on the overarching goals of the legislator (Frühling 1984: 9–10).

After the declaration of Chile's independence in 1810, the leaders of the young republic agreed on the illegitimacy of the principles that had undergirded colonial rule but could reach no consensus on what should replace them. Thus, during the first two decades of Chilean independence, constitutions were written and rewritten as leaders grappled with the grand ideals of the Enlightenment and the realities of state- and

---

[3] As in the rest of colonial Spanish America, subjects could bring conflicts before three to four levels of authorities, the first being the local *alcalde* (mayor) or the *corregidor* (provincial governor) and the last being the *Consejo Real y Supremo de las Indias* in distant Spain, which ruled only on civil cases. The *Consejo* was established in 1524, had ten to fifteen members, and responded directly to the king. The *Real Audiencia*, which was composed of approximately four magistrates, served as the highest court of appeal within the colony, and the court of last resort in criminal cases. The *Real Audiencia* also could send one of its members as a *juez de comisión* to investigate serious or notorious crimes in the outlying provinces. The members of the *Audiencia* were appointed by the king on the basis of aristocratic patronage, academic training, and previous experience. The mission of the *Real Audiencia* was to see that the activity of the government remained within the boundaries of the Law, or more broadly, to link the colonies to the king (Parry 1966: Ch. 10; Karst and Rosenn 1975; Phelan 1967; Frühling 1984: 7–8).

[4] Punishments were generally physical for the poor and financial for the rich. Phelan notes that, in other colonies, banishment to remote and isolated Chile was viewed as one of the worst punishments possible!

43

nation-building. "The new republic drifted from one makeshift political experiment to the next" (Collier 1993: 3) as "armies, rebellions, and bandits [moved in succession] across the country" (Loveman 1988: 119).[5]

The mantle of liberalism was claimed by all of the postindependence contenders for power, but the interpretations given to it varied tremendously (Collier 1967: Ch. 4; Frühling 1984: 14; Jocelyn-Holt 1999). As Brian Loveman and Elizabeth Lira put it, "although it was 'liberty' for which they fought, it wasn't obvious for which liberty they were fighting, nor the liberty of whom or for what. The loyalties were divided and confused" (1999: 62). The elite of the period may have held liberalism to be "the paradigm of modernity, the latest and most worthy of imitation in Western civilization," but they also "demonstrated the necessity of adapting [its] principles to the reality of the country, to the feeling and conscience of a national identity with which they were preoccupied" (Cea 1987: 25).[6]

The aspiration to liberalism was evident in the 1823 Constitution and the 1824 *Reglamento de Administración de Justicia*. These founding documents offered liberal protections against torture and self-incrimination, for the presumption of innocence, and for no punishment without trial, among others.[7] They also gave the Supreme Court "directive, correctional, economic, and moral oversight of all of the courts of the nation,"[8]

---

[5] In the meantime, both a (national) court of appeals and a Supreme Court (the *Supremo Tribunal de Justicia*) were created to replace the *Real Audiencia*, while the *alcaldes* continued to serve as first instance judges. Because the earliest constitutions focused almost exclusively on the executive and legislature and said almost nothing about the judiciary, Spanish laws regarding judicial organization continued to function, as did all the laws from the colonial period "with the exception of those in conflict with the present liberal system of government" (López Dawson 1986: 39). Moreover, from 1814 to 1817, Spanish judicial institutions were reinstated.

[6] As Iván Jaksic puts it, "the efforts to define the nature of republican institutions in accordance with liberal ideology often clashed, during these years, with a strong tendency to continue the Bourbon tradition of centralized administration" (2001: 95).

[7] Indeed, "every Chilean constitution of the [revolutionary] period contained a section, however small, guaranteeing individuals against legal injustices and detailing their legal rights" (Collier 1967: 157). On the founding generation's interest in rights generally, see Kinsbrunner 1973.

[8] These laws also established the judicial hierarchy which more or less remains today, with the Supreme Court at the top, the court(s) of appeals under them, and the departmental and instructing judges (first instance) below them. However, the

as well as the duty to "protect, realize, and stake claims before the other powers for individual and judicial rights (*garantías*)" (*Sesquicentenario de la Corte* 1974).[9] However, as Raúl Tavolari notes, the 1823 Constitution also charged the Senate with protecting and defending these rights, such that it was unclear which body (the Supreme Court or the Senate) should exercise this function in any given case (1995: 51–52). Moreover, the prevailing concern of the period increasingly became order rather than liberty. Ideological struggles and civil turmoil had been the hallmark of the country since independence. Many early statesmen expressed their unease and even "horror" at the disorder that plagued the young nation (Jocelyn-Holt 1997: 79–80). Rather than liberalism, they thus turned increasingly to republicanism as a guiding philosophy. They emphasized that in order to tame the passions that had engendered the violence of these early years, virtue had to be cultivated among the citizenry. And in their view, the path to a virtuous republic rested in law, which, when properly enforced, could transform customs (Jocelyn-Holt 1997: 84; Jaksic 2001: 179). Leaders such as Mariano Egaña and Andrés Bello "were convinced that if certainty in the interpretation of legal rules was ensured, political stability and economic progress would follow" (Frühling 1984: 16).[10] They thus set out to construct a legal regime that would offer generality and predictability, at least for those citizens who "mattered" socially, and thereby promote social and political stability.[11] Influenced by perspectives and models from Europe,[12] they advocated legal codification and the creation of a faithful judicial bureaucracy. It was only after 1833, however, that they were able to realize this project (Jaksic 2001: 158).

alcaldes retained the functions of the last group in departments where there was no legally trained judge.

[9] These have remained the fundamental attributes of the Supreme Court ever since, and thus it celebrated its sesquicentennial in 1974.

[10] See, for example, Andrés Bello's essay, "Observance of the Laws" (Jaksic 1997: 261–269).

[11] Thus, for example, by 1824 the law established that all economically significant civil cases and all criminal cases involving serious penalties had to be adjudicated by legally trained judges outside the political administration (Frühling 1984: 23 and 26).

[12] Bello, for example, spent nineteen years (1810–1829) in London, where he was exposed to the work of Jeremy Bentham. Much of Bentham's thought was too radical for Bello's taste, however. Instead, he sympathized with and "absorbed much of the anti-Jacobin tenets of the Holland House reformers who embraced the views of Edmund Burke" (Jaksic 2001: 99).

LAW AND COURTS UNDER THE PORTALIAN REPUBLIC

The 1833 Constitution, which ushered in the era known as the Portalian Republic, after statesman Diego Portales,[13] aimed above all at establishing a strong, effective, and stable government. The express purpose of the Constitution was to bring political disturbances and partisan fluctuations to an end (see Collier 1967: 333; Frühling 1984: 19; Loveman 1988: 124). Like Bello and Egaña, Portales wanted public tranquillity, which would allow business to flourish, and he believed that this could only be achieved via "a strong government, centralizing, whose men are true models of virtue and patriotism, and [that can] set the citizens on the road of order and virtues" (Kinsbrunner 1973: 61). Only in the distant future, when the people had become sufficiently virtuous, could the government be completely liberal and free (Kinsbrunner 1973: 61; Collier 1967: 339).

Thus, although a measure of popular representation was secured via limited suffrage,[14] the idea of equality before the law was ensconced in the Constitution,[15] and a number of liberal rights were formally protected,[16] the real emphasis of the era, both legal and practical, was on limiting challenges to executive authority and maintaining order.[17]

---

[13] Brian Loveman notes that although "Portales played almost no official role in elaborating the Constitution of 1833 . . . the centralized, authoritarian character of the constitution owed as much to Portales as to its principal author, Mariano Egaña" (1988). Jay Kinsbrunner directly challenges this view in his *Diego Portales: Interpretive Essays on the Man and Times* (1967). Simon Collier claims that Andrés Bello "was consulted in private about the draft of the constitution" and "may even have had a hand in the final editing" (1967: 332). Iván Jaksic confirms this, noting, "there can be little doubt of Bello's participation" (Jaksic 2001: 103).

[14] The vote was granted to all literate males over twenty-five (or twenty-one if married) who enjoyed a certain economic status (property, invested capital, income). This limited suffrage was, internationally speaking, quite normal for the period.

[15] The 1833 Constitution, Article 12, Number 1 established that "There are no privileged classes in Chile."

[16] See the 1833 Constitution, Article 12, Numbers 2–7, which protected the right to labor, the right to movement within the national territory, the inviolability of property, the right to petition authorities, and freedom of expression. Note that freedom of religion and freedom of political association were not protected, and freedom from arbitrary arrest was not an absolute guarantee. See also Lastarria 1856: 37.

[17] "The liberal ideology which lay at the heart of the Chilean revolution was rejected in practice by the Portales regime, while Mariano Egaña and others led a conscious retreat from liberal doctrine" (Collier 1967: 358).

In addition to veto power, emergency powers, and extraordinary powers to govern by decree, then, the President of the Republic also was given strong control over the judiciary. Although the president could not appoint judges at will,[18] he was empowered to oversee the prompt and adequate administration of justice, as well as the official behavior of judges.

As a result, the principles of judicial tenure and independence took on quite restricted meanings in practice. Twice in the 1830s, the president used his power to suspend or fire members of the higher courts when their decisions did not reflect the interests of the government (Frühling 1984: 21).[19] And in 1837, in the midst of a war with Bolivia and Peru, President Joaquín Prieto and his Minister of War and the Interior, Diego Portales, decreed that such political crimes as treason, sedition, uprising, and conspiracy would not be judged by the ordinary courts, but by permanent councils of war established in the capital of each province. The councils of war included one member of the judiciary, namely, the local judge of the respective province, and two military officials appointed by the president. They could apply any penalties they deemed appropriate, including death, and their decisions and sentences could not be appealed. Consequently, "those who 'disturbed public order' or were 'disrespectful toward the government' faced banishment or even execution" (Loveman 1988: 127; Loveman and Lira 1999: 57). These special war tribunals functioned until 1839, when they were dissolved by law (Frühling 1984: 21).

It was not only the exaggerated powers of the president that restricted the judicial role in politics during this period. The 1833 Constitution neither recognized the judiciary as a full state power, nor gave it powers of judicial review (Articles 108–114). Instead, it assigned Congress

---

[18] Article 82, No. 7 of the 1833 Constitution established that the President of the Republic was to appoint judges from lists of nominees prepared by the Council of State, a body composed of two cabinet ministers, two members of the Supreme Court, an ecclesiastic, a general of the army or navy, a chief of some office of the treasury, two former cabinet ministers or diplomats, and two former provincial officials. Nominations were to be based on the proposals of the five-member Supreme Court, which submitted biannual reviews of judicial functionaries, although for many years, the Council could add its own names to the list and the President of the Republic could demand one (and only one) alternative list.

[19] Frühling notes that in "the most notorious" of these cases, the president fired members of the Martial Court for their decision *not* to impose the death penalty on a general who had plotted to start a revolution in 1836.

the power of general interpretation of the Constitution, following the French model of parliamentary sovereignty.[20] When Congress was not in session, a "conservative commission," composed of seven senators, elected by their peers, was to "oversee the observance of the constitution and the laws" (Kinsbrunner 1967: 60).[21] Although habeas corpus was to be enforced by the courts, the law left the details of this procedure unspecified and unresolved until the adoption of the Law of Organization and Attributes of the Tribunals in 1875. The Constitution further limited the reach of the courts by granting jurisdiction in contentious administrative cases (conflicts derived from contracts entered into either by the government itself or by its agents) to the Council of State (Article 104).[22] The defenders of this article of the Constitution argued that the judiciary should not interfere with the highest interests of society, which only the government could represent (Frühling 1984: 22).

Moreover, scholarly legal doctrine from this period through 1925 consistently emphasized the duty of the courts to apply the letter of the law and denied them even the power to question laws passed by unconstitutional methods (Bertelsen 1969). Andrés Bello, author of the Chilean Civil Code and founder of the University of Chile, was instrumental in propagating this positivist conception of the judicial role.[23] Between 1830 and 1837, Bello published more than fifty articles on the administration of justice in the official government publication, El Araucano (Bravo Lira 1991: 56). In these articles, he advocated procedural reforms of the judiciary that would tightly control its decision making. He argued:

> Often a law may seem unjust to a judge: he can believe that it is a rash one; he can find his opinion buttressed by doctrines that seem to him to be worthy of respect, and it may be that his idea is not mistaken. Yet he cannot act against that law, nor can he ignore it, for if judges were able to do so, decisions would no longer be ruled by law but by the magistrate's private opinions.

[20] On this model, refer to Cappelletti 1971 and Merryman 1985.
[21] Kinsbrunner emphasizes the check that the legislature placed on the executive from early on, but Lastarria notes that the conservative commission was never convened (1856: 89). Frühling (1984) argues that because of the permanent practices of electoral intervention by the administration, the president managed to get his will echoed in Congress.
[22] On the composition of the Council of State, see note 18.
[23] For a definition of legal positivism, see Chapter 1.

Thus, he stated, "the judge is the slave of the law, . . . he has no power over it."[24] Under Bello's influence, many laws were passed in the 1840s and 1850s detailing the procedure that judges had to follow in deciding cases before them. The Civil Code of 1855, which is still in force today, made clear that judges could not interpret the laws according to their spirit or purpose when their literal content was clear (Article 19). It also declared that usage and custom were not sources of law to be considered by the interpreter, unless otherwise specified by law (Article 2) (Frühling 1984: 29–30).[25]

It should be noted, however, that Bello's legal positivism had a different inspiration than that associated with Enlightenment thinkers and propagated after the Revolution in France. As noted earlier, Bello and his followers were concerned above all with securing order and stability in Chile (see Jaksic 1997: xlvii).[26] Their greatest fear was not that judges would subvert the popular will or inflict arbitrary and inhumane punishment on citizens[27] but, rather, that they would use their individual discretion to favor particular parties in different cases, thereby dividing and eroding the authority of the state and sowing the seeds of anarchy and chaos.[28] In order to support the construction of the new republican state, law needed to serve the authority of the government. Above all, then, it had to be clear, uniform, and predictable. To allow judicial discretion in the application of the law would be to divide sovereignty and

---

[24] From "Observance of the Laws" (Jaksic 1997: 266). As Enrique Navarro Beltrán notes, Bello also frequently sustained that judges are mere delegates of the executive (1988: 85).

[25] This was not unique to Chile, but was the judicial role constructed in all of Latin America, following the Napoleonic model. See, for example, Adelman 1999.

[26] Jaksic emphasizes Bello's anti-Jacobin views and his belief in the importance of continuity with Spanish traditions (2001: Ch. 3 and Ch. 6).

[27] Frühling notes that Mariano Egaña, who studied the French and English legal systems in the 1820s, wrote to his father that democracy was the greatest enemy that America had (1984: 16). He was particularly worried about factionalism, anarchy, and their potential effects on economy. Jaksic writes that as Director of the Colegio de Santiago in the 1830s, Bello included works by Bentham, Locke, and Rousseau in the law curriculum, but "mainly to refute them" (2001: 110).

[28] Bello's arrival in Chile "was punctuated by a civil war resulting from political experimentation along republican lines in the 1820s. Order, it appeared to him and others in Chile, could only be ensured by a political system that provided for strong executive powers, limited the number of elected offices . . . and discouraged popular mobilization" (Jaksic 1997: xlviii).

to introduce conflict into the heart of public authority.[29] This would lead to an erosion of order and the eruption of civil war, which would make freedom and progress impossible.[30]

On this Hobbesian logic, Andrés Bello and his fellow statesmen thus constructed a justice system based on legal codification and strict judicial restraint. Judges were to be slaves *not* to the law as the product of democratic deliberation and the guarantee against government oppression but, rather, to "the law," which, having proven its value over centuries in Rome, Spain, and the New World colonies, would be incorporated into the country's codes drafted by Bello and others, and would, through its qualities of timelessness and neutrality, inspire respect and obedience among the citizenry.[31]

Diego Portales, meanwhile, shared the objectives of order and stability but held that the key to a just and effective rule of law rested in the judges themselves:

> there is no good law if it is not carefully upheld; we contend that good agents (*encargados*) make good laws, since it is with the same laws that both good and bad justice is administered. . . . [T]hey may make excuses for themselves with the confusion and discord of the laws; but they would have to confess that this is purely a pretext . . . (Bravo Lira 1991: 54).[32]

For the most part, the quality of the "agents" was guaranteed by the fact that judges came from the same elite families and legal-political circles that presidents did (see Garth and Dezalay 1997; Gil 1966: 127). However, as noted earlier, Portales and his followers had no qualms about intervening in the judiciary to ensure that judges would be "good

[29] Useful to understanding this logic is Michael P. Zuckert's (1994) account of the Hobbesian rule of law. See also Herzog 1989: Ch. 4.

[30] Mariano Egaña, for example "called for 'inexorable laws' to contain disorder and to set up a supreme and unquestionable executive authority." In 1824, he stated, "I am certain that nothing would discredit us more than constant alterations in our laws" (Collier 1967: 336 and 340). Bello shared this view, which was part of his more general philosophy on the importance of clarity and unity in both language (grammar) and law (Jaksic 2001: 153–154).

[31] Indeed, codification in Chile can be described accurately as the pruning and organization of existing (i.e., Spanish) law, with relatively minor innovations (Jaksic 2001: 161–174). Interestingly, José Luis Cea claims the Spanish influence was so profound that even by 1970, "Chile had not succeeded in building what might properly be called a native legal culture" (1978: 15).

[32] Jocelyn-Holt emphasizes Portales's skepticism about law (1997: 156).

agents" of the sovereign will, as interpreted (above all) by the executive. As one contemporary Chilean constitutional law scholar has put it, "The authority [i.e., the executive] was to operate within the laws, but [only] to the extent that these gave him broad powers to impose order." In essence, this meant that presidential power could not be controlled by juridical means (Cea 1987: 26–27).

In the first half of the nineteenth century, then, a legalism evolved in Chile that combined the legal positivist principles of Andrés Bello with the authoritarian intervention and limitations inspired by Diego Portales. Law thus had far less to do with liberty, equality, and popular sovereignty than with order, clarity, and stability; and judges, as "slaves of the law," were charged with serving and upholding order and stability above all. In the mind of the country's political elite, to question the state's authority (which was concentrated in the executive) was to court anarchy. Judges were accordingly discouraged from articulating any legal interpretations at odds with those of the president. Consequently, "Judicial protection of citizens against government action was virtually unknown in the 19th century, even in cases where citizens were supposedly protected by habeas corpus. . . . Judges depended on the executive for appointments, and faced intimidation when they were not creatures of the president" (Loveman 1993: 393). In addition, it should be noted that although the system did progress toward some level of legal generality, this generality did not extend to citizens of the lower social strata. Landlords continued to administer justice on their estates and, until 1875, minor civil disputes of all sorts were adjudicated by delegates from the government who were not required to follow a specific set of procedural rules. As Hugo Frühling puts it, "the ideology of an harmonious order formed by contract transaction was constantly challenged by a rural and urban reality of authoritarian and hierarchical domination of the masses" (1984: 37; see also Blakemore 1993; Drake 1993). In practice, then, legal formalism coexisted with multiple forms of discretion.

LAW AND COURTS BEFORE AND DURING
THE PARLIAMENTARY REPUBLIC

In the second half of the nineteenth century, the pattern described here continued, although divisions among the elite did bring about some important legal changes. Diego Portales was assassinated in 1837 and soon thereafter, rival members of the elite began to critique and reform the government structure he had created. The authoritarian domination of the executive was gradually replaced with the supremacy of the legislature, and the jurisdiction of ordinary courts was expanded via the abolition of ecclesiastical, military, and commercial *fueros*. Such changes resulted primarily from the struggle of different elite groups seeking to protect their economic or religious interests from state intervention (Frühling 1984: 47; Cea 1987).

Among the constitutional reforms passed between 1871 and 1874 were limitation of the president to one term, congressional approval of the cabinet, and restriction of the president's exceptional powers. In addition, an electoral reform divested the control of elections from municipal governments, which were controlled by the executive, and gave the power of election oversight to juntas of the wealthiest taxpayers in each district. The vote was made secret and new rules nearly tripled the electorate (Frühling 1984: 48–50).[33] All of this greatly enhanced the power of political parties vis-à-vis the president.

In 1875, the Law of Organization and Attributes of the Tribunals (LOAT) clarified and consolidated the jurisdiction of the ordinary courts.[34] It increased the Supreme Court from five to seven justices and specified the Court's duties to include review (*casación*) of legal appeals of appellate court decisions and decision-making power over writs of habeas corpus and extradition requests. In addition, the LOAT established the judicial career, meaning that judges were expected to start as district-level judges and move up the hierarchy to appellate courts, and possibly even the Supreme Court, based on their performance (as evaluated by their superiors and members of government responsible for judicial appointment) (Illanes Benítez 1966: 309–18; López Dawson 1986). Finally, the LOAT dramatically circumscribed the jurisdiction of military tribunals, such that they could only judge infringements of military laws by military men, and reduced the competence of ecclesiastic courts in civil matters to recognizing the validity or nullity of

---

[33] See also the discussion in Loveman and Lira 1999: 199–201. They emphasize the liberal reformist spirit that characterized the 1870s and 1880s, noting the important liberalization of penal law in the form of the 1874 Penal Code, and highlight the fact that the period 1861 to 1891 was the longest period in Chilean history in which no state of constitutional exception was declared.

[34] It should be noted that this law, with minor modifications, governed judicial organization and practice until 1942, when the Organic Code of the Tribunals was written to replace it. The 1942 Code remains in force today.

Catholic marriages.[35] Commercial courts, or *consulados*, had for their part been abolished in 1866.

In 1889, under the presidency of reformer José Manuel Balmaceda, another law established new and stricter requirements of seniority and competence for judicial appointment, and curbed executive power to intervene in the judicial selection process. From this point forward, the president was required to appoint judges from a list of only three names drawn up by the Council of State, which itself had to select nominees from larger lists submitted by the nation's high courts. The law also regulated the president's ability to review sentences and to suspend judges, establishing formal complaint and accusation procedures, and it required that any temporary (substitute) judicial appointments made by the president be reviewed by the Council of State (de Ramón 1989).

Chilean historian Armando de Ramón contends that all of these changes, along with the expansion of judicial personnel in the 1870s and 1880s, infused the country's judiciary with a cadre of highly professional, respectable, and potentially innovative men (de Ramón 1989). According to several Chilean analysts, it was during this period that the principle of the separation of powers became institutionalized and the judiciary gained legitimacy (Frühling 1984: 58).[36] However, as Frühling notes, "lack of access to the judicial system and the fact that minor disputes were adjudicated in a much more informal way" meant that the poorer strata of the population identified very little with the law on the books (1984: 59). It was not until 1901 that a judgeship was established in each department of more than thirty thousand inhabitants, and in less populated places, administrative resolution of conflicts was still the norm (Henríquez 1980).

Moreover, following the civil war of 1891,[37] the victorious oligarchical parties conducted a major purge of the judiciary, replacing 80–86 percent of Balmaceda's potential innovators by 1893 (de Ramón

[35] This ended in 1884 with the Law of Civil Marriage, which granted power of adjudication to ordinary courts. See Frühling 1984: 56–57.

[36] Garth and Dezalay argue that the legitimacy of the law in Chile, both before and long after such reforms, was "itself tied to the families behind the law, meaning in turn that this legitimacy also rested relatively less on specialized professional knowledge" (1997: 20). This would seem to challenge to some extent the idea that the judiciary rose (and fell) in prestige along with the Balmacedist reforms.

[37] For a summary of the various factors that precipitated the civil war, see Loveman 1988: 176–187.

1989: 38). The new members of the judicial corps, both immediately and over the following thirty years, were by all accounts chosen more for their partisan loyalties than for their professional merits.[38] Under the "parliamentary republic" established by the victors of the civil war (namely, leaders of the traditional oligarchical parties), a prebendal system governed appointments in the public administration, the army, and the judiciary (Gil 1966: 128; Cumplido and Frühling 1980: 71–113).[39] Although this system was resisted in some quarters, especially in the army, opposition from within the judiciary was minimal. This was due in part to the positivist ideology that attributed a merely passive and subordinate role to the judges and, no doubt, to the fact that the new appointees shared social ties and ideological sympathies with the party elites (Cumplido and Frühling 1980).[40]

During the parliamentary republic, then, constitutional practices and interpretations produced the hegemony of the Congress, rendering constitutional amendment unnecessary. With a disempowered president, and the judiciary at its service, the oligarchy was thus able to use the state to its particular benefit. As a result, the judiciary, which had been a rather prestigious, albeit quite powerless, institution in the 1870s and 1880s, became by the 1920s the object of disdain, at least among certain sectors of the population.[41] As one journal article put it in 1919, "There is no older, more persistent, or more hypocritical lie than that which praises the judiciary."[42] In 1925, the poet Vicente Huidobro stated the matter more bluntly:

> The Chilean justice system would make one laugh if it didn't make one cry. [It is] a justice system which carries in one tray of the scales the truth and in the other, a cheese, [with] the scales tipping toward the side of the cheese. Our justice system is a putrid abscess which pollutes the air and makes the

---

[38] In addition, the Supreme Court was expanded twice during this period, to ten members in 1902 and to thirteen members in 1918 (Pérez-Barros Ramírez 1984).

[39] It should be noted that the nitrate boom of the late nineteenth century enriched the Chilean state and made the expansion of the bureaucracy possible; however, the posts therein were filled almost exclusively by partisan appointees.

[40] Scholarly doctrine continued to espouse the positivist principles advocated by Bello earlier in the century. On this, see Bertelsen 1969.

[41] Gil goes so far as to say that during this period Chilean tribunals fell rapidly "from a position among the most highly considered courts of Latin America . . . to being the least respected" (1966: 128).

[42] Cited in de Ramón 1989: 34.

atmosphere unbreatheable. Harsh and inflexible for those on the bottom, soft and smiling with those at the top. Our justice system is rotten and must be cleaned out entirely ... [43]

In sum, although the 1870s and 1880s saw the curbing of presidential prerogatives over the courts, the unification of jurisdiction, and some efforts to "professionalize" the judiciary,[44] the era of the parliamentary republic (1891–1924), characterized by prebendal manipulation of state agencies, ensured that none of the previous reforms would lead to any sort of judicial challenge to the legal understandings of the ruling oligarchs. Judges continued to defer almost completely to the authority of the conservative legislators.[45] Thus, as new social sectors began organizing and questioning the legitimacy of the oligarchical regime as a whole, the prostrate judiciary drew increasing scorn. And so the opportunity was ripe for a major change when social upheaval and a series of military interventions brought an end to the parliamentary republic.

THE JUDICIARY IN CONSTITUTIONAL TRANSITION AND DICTATORSHIP

As many analysts have noted, nineteenth- and early-twentieth-century politics in Chile was basically an "aristocratic game" in which the oligarchical parties (the Liberals and the Conservatives) took turns in office, largely ignoring the social changes that were planting the seeds of major challenges to their hegemony (see Cea 1987; Blakemore 1993; Garth and Dezalay 1997).[46] But by 1920, the "social question" had become too big to ignore. The middle and working classes had organized and were demanding new protection and representation from the state.

---

[43] Cited in Mariana Aylwin, et al. 1996: 274.

[44] By "professionalization" I mean the creation of a "merit-based" bureaucracy, in which members move up the ranks of a hierarchy based on some combination of seniority and performance, and are thus (ostensibly) less beholden and/or vulnerable to the whims of governing politicians.

[45] As Gil writes, under the parliamentary republic, the "allegiance of judges was given to the political parties to which they owed their appointments, just as it had formerly been given to the chief executive in the preceding period" (1966: 128).

[46] For details on the numerous pro-labor proposals that were rejected by the Congress between 1890 and 1924, see Remmer 1984.

The social and political agitation came to a head under the presidency of Arturo Alessandri Palma (elected in 1920), leading to a standoff between the Liberal president and the Conservative Congress and to the first of a series of military coups on September 11, 1924. From 1924 to 1932, different factions of the military, periodically in alliance with Alessandri and for a time led by strongman Carlos Ibáñez (1927–1931), revamped the Chilean political system, introducing a new constitution to shift the balance of power from the Congress back to the president and instituting a new role for the state in the economy.[47] They thus launched the era of the "developmental state."

Part of the effort to establish this new activist state entailed the "professionalization" of the civil service and other state agencies.[48] In view of the fragility of the political and social consensus of the period, the reformers, mostly lawyers themselves, had a special sensitivity to the need for ensuring, at least formally, the independence and impartiality of the courts (Frühling 1984: 101). To this end, the new Constitution (of 1925) placed the power of nomination for judicial vacancies completely in the hands of the judiciary; that is, it formally ended government intervention in judicial nominations. From 1925 forward, the Supreme Court itself drew up the five-person lists of nominees for vacancies in its own ranks, as well as the lists of three for openings on any court of appeals. Appellate courts, in turn, became responsible for composing the lists of three nominees for any open first instance judgeship in their district.[49] The President of the Republic was to select appointees from these lists and could not remove them from their posts except by a formal impeachment process. The Supreme Court, by contrast, retained the right, on a two-thirds vote of its membership, to remove any judge for "bad behavior." An internal evaluation system, instituted in 1927, made the threat of removal more serious by giving the Court the power to review and classify (in lists of descending merit) all judicial employees for the efficiency, zeal and morality

---

[47] On the politics of this transitional period, see Stanton 1997.

[48] For my definition of professionalization, see note 44. On the economic and political reasons behind this drive for professionalization, see Sánchez Noguera 1991: 27–38.

[49] The Constitution specified that two individuals on the lists of five and one on the lists of three had to be chosen on the basis of seniority. The others were to be chosen on "merit," the meaning of which was left to the discretion of the superior court justices. This system remained in force until 1981.

of their work every three years. (This was changed to once yearly in 1971.)[50]

The 1925 Constitution also made the judiciary officially a power of the state and gave the Supreme Court the power of judicial review for the first time. Although a ruling on unconstitutionality only applied to the case in question (i.e., only had *inter partes* effects), it was a major innovation (Gil 1966: 125).[51] On appeal from a party in a case before any court in the country (*recurso de inaplicabilidad por inconstitucionalidad*), the Supreme Court could now declare any law inapplicable because of either unconstitutional procedure in the passage of the law or unconstitutional content of the law. In addition, the Constitution gave the judiciary the power to decree the immediate liberty of those detained or imprisoned with infractions of constitutional principles, and, by eliminating the conservative commission of the Senate and the Council of State, it placed the protection of essential rights and constitutional guarantees definitively in the courts.[52] Finally, the Constitution mandated the creation (via supplemental laws) of administrative courts to handle conflicts arising between citizens and state agencies.[53]

[50] One historical note: from 1924 to 1937, Supreme Court membership was reduced to eleven, ostensibly for fiscal reasons. However, it was restored to thirteen members in 1937 and remained at that number until 1984.

[51] Bertelsen notes that in discussions of the commission which drafted the 1925 Constitution, Alessandri argued that judicial review with *erga omnes* effects (i.e., applying to all cases involving the same law) would be "dangerous" (1969). However, he did propose that courts at all levels be given the power to declare unconstitutionality, a proposal which was not accepted by his colleagues, who feared this would threaten legal uniformity and certainty. See also Frühling 1984.

[52] The 1925 Constitution did set some limits on rights guarantees, however, namely by providing for states of exception in the case of both internal commotion and external threat of war (Art. 44, secs. 12, 13 and Art. 72, sec. 17).

[53] Despite the fact that five bills intended to create these tribunals were introduced in Congress between 1927 and 1970, the requisite law was never enacted (Cea 1978: 27). However, later statutes granted the ordinary civil courts the power of revising certain administrative measures (Frühling 1984; Navarro Beltrán 1988). Note that the 1925 Constitution also created the Electoral Qualification Tribunal, which was to determine the facts and render judgments regarding the probity of all congressional and presidential elections. The tribunal was composed of two sitting Supreme Court justices, one appellate justice from Santiago, and two former presidents or vice presidents of the Senate and the House of Deputies. Its membership was to be renewed every four years.

The formal powers of the judiciary, and especially the high courts of the nation, thus increased substantially with the adoption of the 1925 Constitution. At first glance, the granting of such powers seems rather surprising, given the lack of prestige from which the judiciary was suffering at the end of the parliamentary republic. However, such a change makes sense once one recalls the political conditions surrounding the drafting of the new constitution. As Kimberly Stanton explains, Alessandri and the military agreed to have a handpicked comission draft the 1925 Constitution "due to shared fears that an assembly would produce the wrong results." Their fear was at least partly due to the results of an independent (i.e., unofficial) "constituent congress" held previously by professionals and intellectuals which was deemed to have a "communist tint" (Stanton 1997: 7). The members of the appointed commission, particularly those in the critical subcommittee led by Alessandri himself, were products of an elite strongly anchored in the legal sphere. This elite believed fully in the law, although as Bryant Garth and Yves Dezalay point out, this faith derived more from the extended family relationships around the law and legal institutions than from a respect for the autonomy of law.[54] Moreover, this commission – not surprisingly – saw a need for controls on expanded state activity (Frühling 1984: 101).[55] Thus, Alessandri and his associates made the constitution a controlling document for the first time in the history of the republic, granting the Supreme Court the explicit (albeit limited) power of judicial review. At the same time, they attempted to insulate the judiciary from future political intervention and manipulation. In other words, just as the lower classes were beginning to exercise significant influence in the formal political sphere, the traditional elite embraced the ideas of judicial review and judicial independence.[56] Had the new Constitution been drafted by a constituent assembly, rather

---

[54] Garth and Dezalay explain that "the law school, especially at the University of Chile, provided a place where the members of elite families who needed to have a profession could mix with the sons and daughters of economically successful immigrants and then form alliances that could be used in political parties and activities" (1997: 8).

[55] To this end, the *Contraloría General de la República* was also created in 1927 (and then given constitutional status in a 1943 amendment) with the mission of controlling the legality of state acts. The *Contraloría* supervises the use of public funds and reviews the legality and constitutionality of executive decrees.

[56] The strengthening of judicial independence and the introduction of judicial review in Chile at this time support Ran Hirschl's "hegemonic preservation" thesis (2004).

than by a small, self-appointed elite, the structure and powers attributed to the judiciary might well have been quite different.[57]

In addition, to the extent that leaders of the period located any problem in the judiciary, they identified this in specific personnel, whom the new rules of judicial selection, plus a measure of strong-arming, would either reform or eliminate. In this sense, they followed in the footsteps of Diego Portales. In 1927, Colonel Carlos Ibáñez (then Minister of the Interior, but soon to have himself elected president) initiated a purge to rid the judiciary of those judges he viewed as most venal and corrupt.[58] Acting on his orders, the Minister of Justice explained,

> Few services of the state require more attention from the government than our administration of justice. Various are the factors that, aggravated by the passage of time, without the proper response, and counting on the country's patience, have created a heavy atmosphere of lenience and even impurity around the magistrate, [which is] swayed by political interests, but haughty and stubborn in its relations with the other powers of the state. (de Ramón 1989: 53)

At least one Chilean analyst argues that this was the ideal moment to carry out a thorough housecleaning in the judiciary, removing what he believes were (in the vast majority) conservative lackeys of the oligarchy that had appointed them (de Ramón 1989: 53).[59] However, the effort escalated into a full-blown confrontation between the executive and a faction of the Supreme Court, which balked at the brutal and illegal procedure being followed to remove judicial employees.[60] The whole affair ended with the deportation of the president of the Supreme Court

---

[57] Henríquez notes the irony of making all laws subordinate to the control of a document drafted by such a small, self-appointed elite (1988: 130). Also note that in the plebiscite held to ratify the 1925 Constitution, more than half of eligible voters abstained, citing as one of their reasons the fact that the document had not been prepared by a constituent assembly. See Verdugo, Pfeffer, and Nogueira 1994: 22–23.

[58] For an excellent account of this effort, and its aftermath, see Sánchez Noguera 1991. Note that Ibáñez held himself out as the savior that would rescue the entire Chilean public administration from the corruption into which it had sunk.

[59] Few would disagree that the judiciary at this time was filled with political appointees and was widely perceived as corrupted. See Gil 1966, as well as Sánchez Noguera 1991 who cites numerous newspaper articles from that period.

[60] Sánchez Noguera writes that "The governmental initiatives were viewed [by the judges] as an usurpation of [their] exclusive prerogatives and as the imposition of new political ideals on a branch of the state that had nothing to do with them" (1991: 47).

(brother of the President of the Republic), the forced resignation of four of his supporters, and the expulsion of a handful of other judges.[61] Meanwhile, most of their colleagues kept silent and waited out the storm.

The sociopolitical and ideological composition of the judiciary thus remained basically the same as it had been for at least thirty-five years, with those at the top of the hierarchy vested with more power than ever over their subordinates. Moreover, having witnessed the fate of those who had stood up to Ibáñez before he became president, it was unlikely that any ideological innovators in the judicial ranks would assert themselves under his subsequent four-year dictatorship, which was characterized by labor repression, widespread censorship, restricted political party activity, and torture, imprisonment, and exile of the political opposition.[62]

Indeed, the jurisprudential record of the period overwhelmingly reveals judicial passivity and submissiveness to the executive. Francisco Cumplido and Hugo Frühling summarize the jurisprudence of the years 1924–1932 as generally renouncing the power of courts to determine the validity of laws declared by *de facto* powers, thereby granting them official legitimacy. In other words, just as they would after 1973, the courts held the laws of the various *de facto* governments of the period to be of equal validity to those of representative governments. Moreover, judicial leaders asserted that ruptures of the constitutional order need not affect the functioning of the judiciary, thereby delinking the legitimacy of the judiciary from the democratic system (Cumplido and Frühling 1980).

Exemplary is the 1927 Supreme Court ruling in a case challenging the constitutionality of a "decree with the force of law,"[63] which argued

---

[61] Although this was viewed as scandalous by many in the traditional elite, it was, in fact, minor compared to the purges that Ibáñez carried out in other areas of the public administration.

[62] For primary evidence regarding how members of the judiciary perceived and reacted to the attack by the Ibáñez dictatorship, see passages from the sessions of the 1931 investagory commission on the acts of the dictatorship cited in Lira and Loveman 2006.

[63] In Chilean law, a "decree with the force of law" is a decree issued by the executive on matters constitutionally reserved to the parliament. Such decrees require express and previous delegation by *law* of powers by the parliament to the president. Many legal scholars contest the constitutionality of such decrees, but between 1925 and 1967, the mechanism was used 23 times (Cea 1978: 127, note 5).

that although in theory, a law based on the assumption of extraordinary powers by the president contradicts constitutional norms, "it is necessary to recognize that the respect for and carrying out of these norms depends on factors of political or social order which are in any case out of the scope of a strictly juridical pronouncement."[64] In other words, the Court argued that under certain circumstances, the law on the books was irrelevant, and, furthermore, that judges had no business questioning the executive's decision to suspend legal rules for "reasons of state;" to do so was considered "political" and thereby inappropriate to the judicial role.

The idea that the judiciary is somehow separate from the democratic constitutional order was evidenced in a statement made by president of the Supreme Court, Braulio Moreno, in the inaugural speech of the 1925 judicial year. In that speech, he claimed that even if the replacement of one junta by another is a "serious break in the nation's regime, it must be kept in mind that guarantees of respect for the independence of the judiciary were given."[65] In other words, from the perspective of the judiciary, law transcended politics, even the most fundamental of politics: regime change. Basic legal principles, as embodied in Chile's legal codes, remained the same under democratic or authoritarian governments, and so long as the experts on those codes – the judges – were left free to apply them, the rule of law, and the order and stability it engendered, would prevail. An independent judiciary thus had no necessary connection to democracy.

The judiciary's lack of vocational identification with or commitment to any overarching democratic principles is also manifest in the ineffectiveness of habeas corpus during this period. Although the intense social and political agitation of these years led to frequent citizen petitions for the writ, the courts found numerous ways to stall and circumvent their duties in this area. The situation became so serious that three prominent lawyers (Daniel Schweitzer, Jorge Jiles, and Luis Naveillán) issued a formal request to the Supreme Court for an *auto acordado* to regulate the processing of habeas corpus (*recurso de amparo*) cases.[66] They noted that in 1924, 1925, and 1930–1932, judges had found "a thousand subtle

---

[64] Cited in Bertelsen 1969: 157.
[65] Cited in Cumplido and Frühling 1980: 104.
[66] An *auto acordado* is an official statement issued by the plenary of the Supreme Court which clarifies some procedure internal to the judiciary not specified in the Code of the Tribunals or other laws.

maneuvers" to avoid carrying out and applying legal measures related to the writs, constantly feigning ignorance regarding the obligation to decide a case within twenty-four hours (or, in exceptional cases, within six days), and demanding successive reports "as if it were their duty to try those who are denied their liberty rather than to stop the abusive detention of individuals." This had led to unacceptable delays (months and even years) in the processing of the petitions, and the Supreme Court had adopted no resolutions to impede other authorities from dis-obeying, leaving unresolved, or frustrating the resolution of cases of alleged arbitrary arrest and detention (Tavolari 1995: 64–65).[67]

Yet another testimony to the quietism and lack of democratic com-mitment of the judiciary during this period is a 1932 book by an appellate court judge who was expelled from the judiciary by his superiors. The book, entitled *The Dwarves of Liberty*, condemned the judiciary, and especially the Supreme Court, for its submissiveness and lack of inde-pendent spirit. The author claimed that the tight hierarchical structure of the judiciary bred docility and submissiveness, and rewarded flattery over competence. He argued that conservative politicians sought to grant ever more autonomy over appointments to the judiciary because "they continue to believe that the science of legislation is nothing more than a problem of pen, paper, power, and will." In his view, however, giv-ing more such power to the Supreme Court was the worst error possible, as such an arrangement fed "inconfessable and ignoble instincts" among the superiors and exacerbated the "ego-massaging and obsequiousness" of the inferiors. In lieu of the three-year qualifications by the Supreme Court, he argued for public (i.e., citizen) evaluations of judicial perfor-mance and suggested that election of judges would be the best means of attracting dynamic and upright people to the judiciary (Labarca Fuentes 1932: 104 and 101).

To summarize, then, leaders of this transitional period in Chilean political development recognized the need to reform the judiciary.

---

[67] In response, the Court thus issued an *auto acordado* on December 19, 1932, elimi-nating administrative requirements to resolve habeas corpus writs and calling on the appellate courts to adopt the measures authorized by law to sanction public employ-ees not in compliance with judicial orders. Their statement read, "It should not be possible to leave a person's liberty in the hands of a functionary who is remiss or maliciously guilty on his fulfillment of [such] an obligation." This commitment was sadly forgotten again after 1973. See Chapters 5 and 6.

However, they attributed the judiciary's lack of prestige to the corruption of a few key members, and seemed to believe that new rules designed to "professionalize" the institution (the internal qualifications system and high court control of judicial nominations), along with a targeted purge of ideological enemies, would restore the courts' image of independence and impartiality in the eyes of the public.[68] Thus, rather than allowing emergent political groups to participate in any redefinition of law and the judicial role, they reinforced the ideological and institutional tendencies cultivated in and around the judiciary in the mid-nineteenth century.

As a result, even as the new Constitution granted the judiciary, and especially the Supreme Court, important new powers, innovation in the judicial role was rendered highly unlikely by three factors: the overall continuity in judicial personnel from the parliamentary era; the increased control of the Supreme Court over the judicial hierarchy; and the authoritarian context in which the new powers were introduced. All of these factors preserved and strengthened the traditional, conservative hegemony in the judiciary. So far as the populist strongman Ibáñez was concerned, the resultant passivity of the judiciary was surely very welcome. However, what it meant for wider society was that at this critical juncture in Chilean political development, the gulf between the rule of law and democracy expanded.

THE DEVELOPMENT OF CONSERVATIVE JUDICIAL ACTIVISM FROM 1932 TO THE 1960S

From 1932 until 1973, Chile underwent a process of significant social democratization. The electorate shifted leftward, forcing the gradual decline of the nineteenth-century conservative parties. New political parties of the Center and Left, with strong ties to groups in civil society, established themselves as major contenders in the political game,

---

[68] José Luis Cea notes that Alessandri and company put emphasis on "juridico-formal" issues rather than on sociopolitical problems, the latter of which would have been difficult to solve given the lack of agreement on their causes (1987: 30). Note the similarity of this approach to that of Andrés Bello and associates in the nineteenth century: In both periods, the political elite believed that well-crafted laws, imposed from above and faithfully applied by an "apolitical" judiciary, could produce social harmony.

and even the Right produced somewhat reformist candidates.[69] As noted earlier, a new, active role for the state in the economy had been forged by Alessandri and Ibáñez with the aim of promoting and guiding industrialization and advancing socioeconomic justice. As the decades progressed, both the number of state agencies and their mandates expanded dramatically, including administrative bodies and special tribunals established to channel social and political conflicts away from the nineteenth-century-minded ordinary courts (see Frühling 1984; Correa 1993).

Even Alessandri and Ibáñez, in their efforts to address labor conflicts and general unrest, had avoided the judiciary. In late 1924, for example, Alessandri had established special tribunals of conciliation and arbitration presided over by a representative of the executive branch, a representative of the employees, and a representative of the employers, none of whom required legal expertise. These tribunals had jurisdiction over lawsuits brought by workers or employers related to collective or individual labor contracts and to other issues regulated by labor legislation, and they were given "imperium," that is, the power to demand police assistance to enforce their decisions. In 1931, Ibáñez had replaced these (via decree) with formal labor tribunals staffed by legally trained judges. However, the Minister of Social Welfare was in charge of their appointment, and their decisions could be appealed to new appellate labor courts, staffed by one appellate court judge, one representative of the employers, and one representative of the employees. The decisions of these latter could not be appealed to the Supreme Court and any complaints regarding the behavior of the judges were to be directed to the Ministry of Social Welfare. As the 1931 Labor Code stated in Article 573, "there can be no appeal against the sentences of the labor courts" (Frühling 1984: 122 and 126).[70]

---

[69] For more on this period, see Drake 1978; Cea 1987; Drake 1993; Aylwin et al. 1996.

[70] A similar approach was used in the implementation of agricultural reform, which began in 1962 under President Jorge Alessandri Rodríguez (son of Arturo Alesssandri). New autonomous executive organs were created to carry out the reform, the most important of which were the Corporation for the Agrarian Reform (CORA), which was in charge of realizing expropriations and redistribution of land, and the Institute of Farming Development (INDAP), which provided technical and financial assistance. Special agrarian tribunals, composed of one judge, one representative of the property holders, and one representative of the President of the Republic, were conceived to deal with reform-related conflicts in the first instance. Unlike the

The labor tribunals quickly came under attack from lawyers and newspapers generally aligned with the interests of the employers. They claimed that the labor tribunals were biased against the employers and tended to abuse their discretionary faculties. This critique was indirectly supported by the Supreme Court, which asserted that it had been robbed of its rightful jurisdiction in labor matters. Thus, in 1933, the government reassigned "directive, corrrectional, and economic jurisdiction" over the labor courts to the Supreme Court.[71] This modification was not meant to create a "third instance" for labor conflicts. Article 573 of the Labor Code was still in force, prohibiting the use of the *recurso de casación* (an appeal based on the contestation of a lower court's application or interpretation of law) against decisions of the labor courts (see Novoa 1993: 310–312). All that the change signified was that the Supreme Court could review labor cases for possible misconduct by labor judges.

However, the Supreme Court found a covertly activist means of imposing its traditional, conservative perspective on both case outcomes and general legal interpretation (Henríquez 1980: 112–16). On reclaiming disciplinary control over labor courts, the Supreme Court launched a practice of accepting *recursos de queja*, exceptional appeals against a "mistake or abuse by the judge," as if they were simple appeals (*recursos de apelación*).[72] The Court thereby acquired final interpretive power over, first, labor legislation and, later, other areas of the law. Interestingly, while in 1930, *recursos de queja* constituted less than 10 percent of cases seen by the Supreme Court, by 1933, they had become a third, and by the late 1960s, they were nearly half of all the cases on the high court's docket (Henríquez 1980: 112).[73] The Court

labor courts, however, they were from their inception to be subject to the supervision of both the respective appellate courts and the Supreme Court. These courts were actually not convoked until 1965, after the election of Eduardo Frei Montalva, when the pace of the reform was stepped up dramatically. See Henríquez 1980.

[71] Later, in the early 1940s, a law was passed requiring that all labor appeals courts be staffed by full-time members of the judiciary (Frühling 1984: 128 and 131–132). See also Henríquez 1980: 24.

[72] In 1965, the Supreme Court adopted an *auto-acordado* formally making the *recurso de queja* more like a *recurso de apelación*.

[73] This practice was extended into and exacerbated in the 1970s and 1980s. See Valenzuela Somarriva 1990: 137–169.

clearly used the *recurso de queja* as a way of asserting control over legal interpretation and case outcomes rather than as a means of disciplining judges. Rarely did it apply the sanctions associated with the acceptance of a *recurso de queja*.[74] Although lower judges thus did not suffer from immediate sanctions, their authority was significantly circumscribed.

Through such discretionary power, the Chilean judiciary opposed the government's actions toward more social justice and egalitarianism from the 1930s forward.[75] In general, judges took a very traditional stance regarding the protection of private property and freedom of contract, and justified their decisions in formalistic language. As a representative example, Chilean lawyer and political scientist Hugo Frühling cites a 1957 case involving 1954 rent legislation designed to protect tenants from unreasonable rent charges and eviction.[76] In this case, the Santiago Court of Appeals ruled in favor of the landlord, claiming that the tenant did not prove he had fulfilled all his contractual obligations (i.e., that had paid all rent on time), even though he had no outstanding debt with the landlord. The court further argued that because the legislation "gravely affects the right to property and the autonomy of will by interfering with and annulling freedom of contract, the judge has to carefully and clearly take into account the wording of the law so that he does not commit excesses to augment these defects." As Frühling notes in regards to this case, "It is obvious that the Court did not think in terms of interpreting the law in accordance with its [the law's] stated objective, i.e., to protect tenants' right to live in a house as long as they paid the rent and complied with their contractual obligations. Rather, the Court considered limitations on freedom of contract as exceptions or partial departures from principles of law the deviation from which should be viewed with care and even suspicion" (Frühling 1984: 172, 186, and 188). Although the courts "couldn't go against the thrust of the governmental policies which were supported by the electorate," they "seemed determined to preserve a sphere of autonomy free

---

[74] These sanctions consisted of fines and/or suspensions, which affected the offending judge's yearly evaluation and hence his (or her) ability to rise in the hierarchy.

[75] There are obvious parallels here to the Lochner era in the United States (see Gillman 1993), and to the Weimar period in Germany (see Kahn-Freund 1981). Whereas in the United States, however, institutional factors permitted the judiciary to adjust to the new political reality of the New Deal era, in Chile, as in Germany, the "civil service" judiciary remained hostile to "the development of the law through social conflict [and change]" (Kahn-Freund 1981: 178).

[76] The case is *Fuentes viuda de Fuenzalida vs. Cuadra Pinto, Dario* (1957).

from sometimes capricious . . . legislative intervention" (Frühling 1984: 195).[77]

Such determination was not evident in public law cases, however. Although the 1925 Constitution had given the judiciary new and specific powers to check the excesses of the other branches of the state, judges chose only to assert this power, and even then in limited ways, in cases related to property rights. In cases involving alleged violations of civil and political rights, such as habeas corpus, due process, freedom of expression, freedom of association, and freedom of assembly, the courts time and again deferred to, and hence upheld, the absolute authority of the executive.

To begin, the judiciary gave the legislative branches free reign to declare constitutional states of exception *preventively*, that is, to restrict or suspend constitutional liberties as a response to a potential, rather than established, internal threat.[78] The 1925 Constitution allowed for the declaration of a state of siege in cases of either foreign attack or "internal commotion," and permitted the passage of legislation limiting basic civil and political rights "when supreme need for the defense of the state, preservation of the constitutional regime, or internal peace may so demand."[79] A state of siege and laws restricting constitutional rights were only to be declared by Congress, although the president was authorized to declare a state of siege if Congress was not in session, in which case an ending date had to be established.[80] Under a constitutional state of exception, the president was permitted to subject persons to house arrest or detention in places other than jails for common criminals, to censure the press, to impede the circulation of printed matter that tended to alter the public order or subvert the constitutional regime, and to search homes without warrants (Loveman

---

[77] Novoa also offers examples in which the Supreme Court applied rent control laws so rigidly that they dismissed the claims of the renters, even when the amounts charged clearly exceeded legal limits (1993).

[78] Loveman notes that between 1933 and 1958, "sixteen separate laws imposed almost four years of these regimes of exception on the country. This did not include at least a dozen states of siege [declared by decree] during the same years" (1993: 352).

[79] Because both a state of siege and legislation granting the government "extraordinary faculties" usually went hand in hand, some consider them to be a single institution. See, for example, Caffarena de Jiles 1957.

[80] See Article 44, No. 13, and Article 72, No. 17 of the 1925 Constitution. In practice, however, the president found ways to bypass Congress. See Mera, González, and Vargas 1987b.

1993: 352; see also Caffarena de Jiles 1957; Mera, González, and Vargas 1987b). In cases brought before it, the Supreme Court never challenged the interpretation of the government regarding threats to public order, nor sought to establish the meaning of the concept of internal commotion.[81] When a petition for habeas corpus (*recurso de amparo*) was brought against a detention or expulsion during a constitutional state of exception, the Court consistently declared that it lacked the authority to question either the government's motives for a given detention or to evaluate the facts upon which it was ordered. In one case, the Court went so far as to assert that the President had no obligation to specify cause for detention (Frühling 1984: 258).[82] The justices grounded these decisions in a narrow and controversial interpretation of the separation of powers, claiming that actions taken by the administration under a state of siege were "political" matters in which the strictly legal actors of the judiciary were prohibited from interfering (Mera, González, and Vargas 1987b; Verdugo 1989).

In 1936, the Valparaiso Court of Appeals ruled that preventive detentions ordered under a state of siege decreed by the president immediately expired once Congress reconvened, but the Supreme Court reversed the decision. In an extraordinarily formalist move, the Court argued that because the Constitution stated (Article 72, number 17) that a presidential siege decree will become a legislative bill in the subsequent session of Congress, the state of siege can be neither repealed nor amended except via the processing of the bill.[83] A few days later, the Court ruled in another *recurso de amparo* that the Valparaiso Court's decision had been unsound because an automatic expiration

---

[81] This was even true under the (second, and this time elected) administration of Carlos Ibáñez (1952–1958), who made frequent and cynical use of the state of siege. (I thank Brian Loveman for this point.)

[82] Frühling is referring to the *Santiago Wilson* case of 1936. Caffarena de Jiles, writing in 1957, notes that between 1930 and 1957, there were forty-four months, twenty-nine days of constitutional exception, and asks "Has there really been 'internal commotion' every time an estado de sitio was declared? . . . Why do our courts fall in the grave error of sustaining that they don't have the power to review the orders of detention that the president issues during states of exception, thereby misunderstanding their fundamental mission of being the bulwark of constitutional guarantees?" (Caffarena de Jiles 1957: 24 and 26).

[83] *José Donoso y Otros (amparo)*, treated by Frühling 1984: 240. Frühling notes that the appellate court decision had been striking, for it invoked the spirit of the Constitution and the need to better enhance and protect rights.

of the state of siege would cause uncertainty and thus endanger public order.[84]

Similarly, in a 1948 *recurso de inaplicabilidad por inconstitucionalidad* brought against a law passed by Congress that imposed a state of exception, the Supreme Court ruled that "the need or convenience for enacting such a law is to be solely assessed by the legislative branch."[85] Here again the Court argued that there were areas of legislative decision making that, due to their "political" (as opposed to "strictly legal") nature, could not be reviewed by the courts, despite the fact that the legislature was supposed to act in accordance with certain constitutional standards. The Court accordingly gave Congress and the executive free reign to invoke "reasons of state," however vaguely or weakly justified, to impose a state of exception and to restrict individual rights.

Concomitantly, the courts consistently limited their own scope of power to interpret laws of internal security. The most notorious of these was the 1948 "Law for the Permanent Defense of Democracy," passed under the presidency of Gabriel González Videla. The law prohibited "the existence, organization, action and propaganda, oral, written, or via any other medium, of the Communist Party, and, in general, of any association, entity, party, faction or movement, which pursues the implantation in the Republic of a regime opposed to democracy or which threatens the sovereignty of the country."[86] It also simultaneously modified, in an authoritarian direction, a host of other laws related to political expression and organization (see Loveman and Lira 2002: 139–161). As the Chilean legal scholar Felipe González notes, the law was vague and sweeping in its wording and called for harsh, disproportionate penalties, even for the mere act of organizing. Nonetheless, in cases in which aspects of this law were challenged, the courts upheld its application, dismissing constitutional guarantees as a source for the adequate interpretation of the law, refusing to analyze whether or not the act in question was a genuine threat to internal security or public order, and ignoring the issue of intention on the part of the accused to harm the juridical goods protected by the law (González 1989: 20). In a 1949 *recurso de inaplicabilidad por inconstitucionalidad* brought

[84] The second case was *Anibal Jara* (*amparo*). See Frühling 1984: 241–242.
[85] The case was *Juana Mardones* (*inaplicabilidad*), discussed in Frühling 1984: 243.
[86] It should be noted that these types of laws were common throughout Latin America during this period.

against the Law for the Permanent Defense of Democracy, for example, the Supreme Court ruled that the text of the law "complements" and hence does not "contradict" the Constitution.[87] Thus, in a case in which it "had the opportunity to establish a criterion in these matters, and more than this, could have perfectly assumed its role as a state power," the Court "limited itself to considerations of a formal nature, restricting itself in its field of action" (Mera, González, and Vargas 1987a: 10).

In subsequent *recursos de amparo* related to this law, courts (appellate and Supreme) invoked Article 4 of the 1925 Constitution, which stated that no magistrate, person, or group of persons could attribute to himself any authority or rights other than those expressly conferred to him by the laws. As they had in the past, then, they asserted that the principle of the separation of powers prohibited the judiciary from examining alleged executive branch violations of citizens' personal liberties (Mera, González, and Vargas 1987a: 10). In one case, they even went so far as to say that detentions ordered in the exercise of emergency powers were "untouchable orders."[88]

In public law cases, then, the tendency of the Chilean courts was to circumscribe their own authority. Even after 1958, when the Law for the Permanent Defense of Democracy was repealed and a new and substantially less authoritarian Law of Internal State Security (*Ley* 12.927) was adopted, the courts continued with this jurisprudential line. The wording of the legal text was far less important than the (institutionally rooted) attitude of the courts in shaping legal outcomes.[89] Through their unwillingness to review, evaluate, and (when appropriate) challenge the decisions and acts of the executive in such cases, they demonstrated themselves to possess a greater commitment to public order than to individual citizen rights. Because this stance was very different from the more activist stance they took in defending individual property rights, their claims to apoliticism began to ring hollow with much of the public.

---

[87] The case, *Frías contra Zañartu*, is mentioned in González 1989: 20; Bertelsen 1969.

[88] The 1949 case was *Graciela Alvarez (amparo)*, noted in Frühling 1984: 258; Mera, González, and Vargas 1987b: 65; Caffarena de Jiles 1957.

[89] This is the conclusion of González in "Modelos Legislativos" (1989). See also the discussion of the Supreme Court's approach to *recursos de inaplicabilidad por inconstitucionalidad* in Valenzuela Somarriva 1990.

CONCLUSION

By tracing the institutional development of the Chilean judiciary from the end of the colonial period through the mid-twentieth century, this chapter has uncovered the historical roots of judicial performance under the Pinochet regime. Not only has it illuminated the origins and nature of the institutional features to which I attribute outcomes in my focus period (1964–2000), but it has also identified some patterns in judicial behavior that were to recur in later years. The chapter thus provides the foundation for the argument I will build in subsequent chapters: that the performance of the Chilean judiciary under Pinochet was not simply a function of regime-related factors, judges' personal political preferences, class loyalties, or legal philosophy, but was rather the result of long-standing institutional dynamics that gave the courts a conservative bias.

As I have shown, from the birth of the republic in the early nine-teenth century, Chilean leaders were concerned with the need to build a rule of law, upheld by "apolitical" judges. Judges were trained to be dutiful "slaves of the law," but in a context in which law, at least public law, was understood as the will of the executive. Rather than defend legal principles embodied in the constitution, or in the idea of constitutionalism, then, judges were expected to defer to the other ("political") branches of government. To do otherwise would be to tread on forbidden "political" ground and to threaten the rule of law.

Whereas during most of the nineteenth century fidelity to this narrow role was ensured through executive intervention in judicial appointment and discipline, by the end of the 1930s institutional reforms had safely insulated judges from executive and legislative manipulation, and judicial tenure became secure. The judiciary became an autonomous bureaucracy in which judges were both structurally and ideologically separated from the politics of the elected branches. Judges were thus not only expected but allowed and able to base their decisions on their understanding of the law, rather than on ("political") signals from non-judicial actors.[90]

[90] Indeed, to the extent that elected officials anticipated judicial challenges to their policies – namely, in the areas of property and contract regulation – they sought not to manipulate the courts, but to circumvent the judiciary through the creation of special tribunals or administrative agencies under their control.

Yet as my review of the literature on judicial performance in the post-1932 period indicates, the enhanced independence, professionalism, and formal authority of the judiciary did not produce politically neutral judges. Indeed, judges used their newly secured autonomy not to uphold faithfully the positive law but, rather, to defend private property and contract from increasing levels of state regulation, and, in the area of public law, to give elected officials free reign to maintain order. They held quite consistently to a strict separation of powers doctrine, according to which legal oversight of the private sphere constituted the core and exclusive "judicial" function, while questioning of executive or legislative decisions on questions of public law was inappropriate meddling in "political" matters.

The argument that I will make and defend in the chapters that follow is that judicial behavior before, during, and after the Pinochet regime (that is, from the mid-1960s through the 1990s) can be best explained by the institutional variables identified above. My claim is that the structural reforms of the 1920s served to freeze in a nineteenth-century understanding of law, society, and the judicial role. The rigid hierarchy established by these reforms empowered conservatives on the higher courts, and in particular the Supreme Court, to reinforce and reproduce their own views through discipline and promotions within the institution. Thus, even as the country underwent significant social and political democratization, reflected in and advanced by the elected branches of the state, the courts remained grounded in and committed to predemocratic and in many ways illiberal understandings of sociopolitical organization and legal legitimacy. Otherwise put, judges of the 1960s, 1970s, and 1980s did indeed have a conservative bias, but it was a bias that was constructed and maintained by factors endogenous to the institution.

CHAPTER THREE

CONSERVATIVE ACTIVISM IN THE HEYDAY OF DEMOCRACY, 1964–1973

In the previous chapter, I sketched the historical construction of the judicial role in Chile around the ideal of "apoliticism." I described the development of the institutional ideology that forbade judges to interfere in "political" questions, and I explained how the structural reforms of the 1920s, while enhancing judicial independence and professionalism, empowered the conservative judicial elite and, thereby, served to perpetuate nineteenth-century understandings of "law" and "politics" within the institution. In the decades that followed, Chilean judges hence displayed very conservative (that is, predemocratic and politically illiberal) professional attitudes and practices, even as the country as a whole underwent a process of significant democratization.[1]

In this chapter, which covers the years 1964–1973, I defend that claim through an analysis of judicial behavior in civil and political rights cases, archival records, and interview material. My objectives are twofold. First, I seek to demonstrate that the substantive role of the judiciary in Chilean politics did not change radically with the advent of the Pinochet regime. Indeed, during the years leading up to the military

---

[1] Increased literacy rates and the full incorporation of women into the suffrage beginning in 1952, as well as general population growth, had led to a rapid electoral expansion. From a total electorate of some 500,000 persons in 1938, the voting population leapt to 2,500,000 by 1963. A major part of the electorate consisted of rural and urban laborers, who accounted for some 70 percent of the economically active population. See Drake 1978: 17 and 21–22, cite at 21. See also Aylwin et al. 1996: 248–249.

coup, when Chile was considered one of the most democratic countries in the world,[2] its courts played a role in the system that was quite illiberal and undemocratic. As in the past, judges generally deferred to the executive in the area of civil and political rights, leaving individual citizens at the mercy of the state. Although some judges, particularly at the Supreme Court level, began taking stands in defense of citizens' rights, they did so almost exclusively in cases involving conservative interests. The courts thus manifested a weak and inconsistent commitment to rights protection, as well as to the principle of equality before the law central to both liberalism and democracy.

Second, I attempt to show that this judicial performance was significantly shaped and constrained by institutional variables. Although there was a minority of judges who had personal ties and commitments to the political Right, my argument is that the striking bias of the judiciary as a whole can only be satisfactorily explained by institutional factors. The institutional structure of the judiciary, in which the Supreme Court exercised control over judicial discipline and promotion, gave strong incentives for judges to emulate or otherwise curry favor with their superiors. Judges learned that the best way to ascend the judicial hierarchy was to conform to the professional standards modeled by the institutional elders. Although these standards were occasionally enforced by the Supreme Court, my claim is that their normative power alone served to keep many judges "in line." In other words, it was not only the institutional structure but also the institutional ideology of the judiciary that shaped judicial behavior. Above all, this institutional ideology held that the judicial role was and must remain completely apolitical. As shown in Chapter 2, this consigned judges to a largely passive role in public law cases.[3] In the 1964–1973 period, however, the Supreme Court engaged in and endorsed the active defense of traditional (understood to be timeless, natural, and apolitical) interests and values against what it labeled the "political" machinations of the Frei and especially the Allende governments. Any judges who sympathized or cooperated with the Allende government were thus cast as unprofessional "political" actors, whereas those who challenged the government were painted to be dutiful defenders of the "rule of law."

---

[2] Refer to the Introduction to this volume.
[3] Though, as further demonstrated in Chapter 2, it permitted significant activism in private law matters (esp. property and contract).

I should underscore two points before proceeding. The first is that I am not seeking to pin blame on judges as individuals for playing a largely illiberal and undemocratic role in this period. Although one of my objectives in this chapter (as in others) is to illuminate the nature of that role, and although I am ultimately critical thereof, I am not seeking to condemn the judges for not having made alternative choices. Indeed, the larger point of this book is that judges' views were constituted and their choices constrained by institutional factors that were not of their own making. I mean to show that given the institutional setting in which they functioned, their behavior was not outrageous, but rather logical and quite predictable. Second, and relatedly, I am not seeking to paint the judges in this chapter as the villains, and the Frei and Allende administrations as the heroes. Although my focus is on illiberal and undemocratic *judicial* behavior, I am not claiming that the behavior of other political actors as this time was always, or even generally, liberal democratic. Indeed, the long-standing abuse and perversion of professed liberal ideals on the part of the traditional elite had provoked a political reaction, not just in Chile, but in all of Latin America, against liberalism in this period (Borón 1993). Thus, this chapter should in no way be read as a clear-cut story of good, liberal-democratic politicians versus evil, illiberal and antidemocratic judges. The moral of the story is, ultimately, one that points to a need for judicial reform, but not exactly of the sort that the progressives of the late 1960s and early 1970s envisioned.

THE JUDICIAL ROLE IN THE FREI AND ALLENDE YEARS

The election of Christian Democrat Eduardo Frei Montalva in 1964 marked a decisive victory for progressive forces in the Chilean polity.[4] Frei, whose campaign promised a "Revolution in Liberty," emerged with 56 percent of the vote and a clear mandate for socioeconomic reform.[5] As president, Frei instituted a major agrarian reform, increased public housing, and encouraged rural unionization and mass-level political activity (see Loveman 1988; Collier and Slater 1996; Gazmuri 2000).

---

[4] By "progressive," I mean those committed to promoting greater equality between citizens.
[5] Frei owed his triumph to an electoral alliance with the Right, designed to prevent a win by the Socialist-Communist coalition (the FRAP).

While eschewing Marxism, he nonetheless supported a quite radical redistribution of wealth and power in Chile.

Six years later, a majority of the electorate remained committed to social change,[6] but was strongly divided over the form and pace that change should take. Moreover, they faced ever fiercer opposition from the right-wing minority. The 1970 election was hence a tight three-way contest between the candidates of the Left, Center, and Right. Despite threats from the far Right and the now well-documented U.S. covert intervention,[7] the left-wing candidate, Socialist Salvador Allende Gossens, garnered a plurality of the popular vote (36.2 percent). With support from the Christian Democrats, he was subsequently confirmed by Congress as President of the Republic. Allende attempted to pursue a legal path to socialism via the acceleration of agrarian reform and, in the name of the proletariat, state takeover of major industries. Unlike Frei, however, he lacked majority support in Congress for most of his program, and so he sought to implement many of his policies using special powers reserved (by law) to the executive. As time went by, many of his supporters took matters into their own hands. The tactics of both the extreme Left and the extreme Right grew ever more radical (Garcés 1973; Sigmund 1977; Valenzuela 1978).

During these years of rapid change and social conflict, the public paid great attention to how the courts resolved important cases brought before them. Despite significant public critiques of the formal legal system (Novoa 1964), the discourse of law remained a powerful one in Chilean political life, and it was important for most players in the system to be able to claim that the law was on their side (Arriagada 1974; Cea 1978). For the government, such a claim had traditionally been easy to make. First, the political system was heavily presidentialist; that is, it concentrated much decision-making power in the hands of the executive (Silva Cimma 1977; Faundez 1997). Moreover, and as noted in the previous chapter, the courts had historically deferred to and upheld the absolute authority of the executive, on the grounds that judges had no authority to intervene in "politics." Thus,

---

[6] The platform of the Christian Democratic candidate, Radomiro Tomic, was, in many ways, indistinguishable from that of Socialist Salvador Allende.

[7] See Documents of ITT published in *El Mercurio*, April 2 and 3, 1972; United States Senate, Senate Resolution 21, *Hearings by the Select Committee to Study Governmental Operations with Respect to Intelligence Activities, Vol 7: Covert Action* (Dec. 4 and 5, 1975); and Kornbluh 2004.

Table 3.1. Decisions in civil and political rights cases, 1964–1973

| | Pro-Left | | Pro-Right | | |
	Appellate	Supreme	Appellate	Supreme	Total
Pro-State	7	1	7	3	18
Pro-Individual	2	0	5	7	14
Subtotal	9	1	12	10	–
Total	10		22		32

Presidents Frei and Allende both expected the courts to rule in their favor.[8] Instead, during this period Chilean judges demonstrated an increasingly strong willingness to challenge the executive in the name of the civil and political rights of individual citizens. However, they extended such rights protection very unevenly, actively defending conservative values and interests but reverting to positivist and even formalist reasoning in cases involving defendants of the ideological Left. When the Left called attention to this practice, the Supreme Court claimed that such critiques were motivated by narrow "political" passions, which audaciously challenged the sober and objective reasoning of the courts. The judges and their supporters portrayed themselves as servants of transcendent and immutable principles and public values, while they accused their critics of engaging in *politiquería* (petty partisan politics).

My independent analysis of the thirty-two civil and political rights cases published for the period, however, reveals that the critics were right.[9] As Table 3.1 shows, decisions at the appellate and high court levels were more than twice as likely to go in favor of right-wing interests

[8] In a 1972 interview, Eduardo Novoa, Allende's legal advisor, expressed indignance at the fact that the judiciary was now claiming it had power to review administrative acts, claiming that the courts were "intervening in materials that the law itself says cannot be reviewed by them." See Gonzaléz Bermejo and Vaccaro 1972: 32. Silva Cimma supports this view (1977: 170–173).

[9] I coded these cases on two variables: whether the ruling favored left-wing or right-wing parties and interests, and whether the ruling came down on the side of the state or the individual. The polarization of the period made the political coding quite straightforward, as, with good knowledge of the context, it was easy to determine whether the decision involved a victory or a defeat for the Left and the Right, respectively.

as in favor of left-wing interests.[10] Moreover, if one isolates the Supreme Court outcomes, the decisions were ten times as likely to favor the Right.

Perhaps most striking, though, is the difference within the group of decisions that could be categorized as "pro-individual rights." In contrast to the eighteen pro-state decisions, which were almost evenly split in terms of the political side they benefited, the fourteen decisions that upheld individual rights were made almost exclusively in favor of members of the political Right. Specifically, twelve of the pro-individual rights decisions (or 86 percent) were also "pro-Right," whereas only two (or 14 percent) were "pro-Left." This severe imbalance in rights protection belies any professed commitment on the part of judges to democratic rule of law principles.

Before proceeding with my explanation for this behavior, I offer a few examples to illustrate the pattern. I begin with a landmark case of 1967, in which the Supreme Court ruled that a lower court had the authority to review presidential decrees for constitutionality and to apply or refuse to apply the decree based on that review.[11] The ruling, in the case *Juez de Letras de Melipilla con S.E. el Presidente de la República*, was a dramatic break from the judiciary's traditional deference to presidential authority on questions of public law. In the past, this deference had held even in cases (such as this one) involving a "decree of insistence," a legal instrument allowing a decree to go forth, despite legal objections, with the official assent of all cabinet members.[12]

The case arose in November 9, 1966, when the Frei administration seized the estate of a landowner whose employees had illegally struck. Arguing that, by the Law of Internal State Security,[13] it had the right to take over the management of any industry or market essential to

---

[10] I did not include lower courts because, for most of these cases, the first instance was at the appellate level.

[11] This case was widely cited in my interviews with legal scholars as one of the most important and influential of the period.

[12] In Chile, presidential decrees are automatically reviewed for legality and constitutionality by the Comptroller General. However, the "decree of insistence" was a widely accepted and frequently exercised instrument used to overrule the Comptroller in the country's strongly presidential system (Silva Cimma 1977; Cea 1978: 36). For example, President Ibáñez issued 355 such decrees between 1952 and 1958.

[13] The Law of Internal State Security (*Ley de Seguridad Interior del Estado*, no. 12.927), written in 1958, moderated and replaced the harsher Law for the Permanent Defense of Democracy passed under President González-Videla in 1948. See details in note 18.

the national defense, to the supply of basic goods to the population, or to the public utility, the government issued a decree ordering the resumption of work on the estate and appointing an *interventor* to take over temporary administration of the estate.[14] When the Comptroller General ruled the decree unconstitutional, the government responded with a decree of insistence. In response, the owner of the estate filed a suit with the local judge, claiming infringement of his property rights, and the local judge found in his favor on grounds that the government's decree did in fact exceed the limits of constitutionality. Claiming that the judge had no legitimate power to challenge the executive in this way, the government brought the case before the Supreme Court.

In a dramatic assertion of judicial power, the Court ruled that the local judge was fully competent to rule as he had in the case. The Court invoked the duty of the judiciary "to protect the fundamental rights of the human person," even in cases where the constitution seemed to give the last word to the executive.[15] As one justice wrote in a concurring opinion:

> To deny the courts the right to hear property disputes or *recursos de amparo*, which the affected parties bring when their essential rights are threatened by an illegal decree or an abusive act of authority, would be to disregard the primordial obligation that the judiciary has to render justice and to secure respect for the rights of the inhabitants which the law submits to its protection and care.[16]

---

[14] It should be noted that this practice, of ordering workers back to work by decree and assigning a government official to manage the farm until the conflict was settled, was officially legalized as an article of the Agrarian Reform Law, which passed in July 1967 (eight months after this particular conflict). The provision could be used, as it sometimes was, to repress illegal strikes, or "as a pretext to place a governmental representative in the farm and begin organizing the *campesinos* for expropriation of the property." This latter application of the provision was occasional under President Frei and became routine under President Allende (Loveman 1976: 258–259, 271, and 282).

[15] RDJ 64 (1967) 2.1: 109–120. RDJ refers to the *Revista de Derecho, Jurisprudencia y Ciencias Sociales y Gaceta de los Tribunales*.

[16] RDJ 64 (1967) 2.1: 109–120. There was a dissenting group of five justices in the case, including two of the three that had been appointed by President Frei (Juan Pomés and Rafael Retamal). The dissent was grounded in the traditional separation of powers argument, holding that judges had no place reviewing executive decisions involving questions of domestic order and security.

The Court thus endorsed the idea that judges had the authority and the duty to defend constitutional rights. It did so, however, in a case that directly challenged the prerogative of the Frei government, taking a stand in favor of traditional property rights even as the whole concept of property was being rethought and redefined, with majority support, by the country's elected leaders.[17] Moreover, because the decision departed from the deference that the courts had traditionally shown toward the government, the decision appeared to reflect a bias in favor of conservative forces.

This perception was enhanced by the judiciary's inconsistent treatment of two suits brought by the Frei government which were quite similar in their general facts. Both cases involved alleged violations of the Law of Internal State Security, which extended significant powers to the president to preserve societal order, broadly defined.[18] In the first case, the defendants were members of the right-wing National Party who, in the national and international press, had attacked the "weak and vacillating" foreign policy of the Frei government, and whose party platform called for the imposition of a "regime of iron authority" to stem the "period of disorder" that the Frei government had initiated. In the second case, the defendant was Socialist Party senator Carlos Altamirano, who had given a speech at an academic conference in which he at once

[17] Indeed, in January 1967, the Frei administration had succeeded in getting a constitutional amendment passed changing the article guaranteeing the right to property to allow government expropriation in the interest of society with less rigid terms of indemnification. For more information on the legal aspects of the agrarian reform and its treatment by the judiciary, see Thome 1971; Henríquez 1980.

[18] The 1958 Law of Internal State Security established specific penalties for "those who incite or induce subversion of public order or an uprising against, resistance to, or overthrow of the constituted government; those who perform similar acts with respect to the Armed Forces or the *Carabineros*, to incite them to indiscipline or to disobey the orders of the legitimate authorities; those who meet to propose the overthrow of the constituted government or to conspire against its stability; those who form private militias; and military personnel who disobey orders given by the constituted government." It also declared it a crime to spread or foment theories intended to destroy or alter by violent means the social order or the republican and democratic form of government, as well as to engage in acts intended to spread tendentious or false information for the purpose of harming the democratic and republican order, the constitutional order, or the security of the country. Finally, the law also sanctioned public offense to the symbols of the nation or to the constituted authorities and acts that disrupted or destroyed public services (Organization of American States 1985: 177–178).

criticized the Frei government and suggested that Cuba offered a good model for Chile to follow.[19]

In the National Party case, the Frei administration had arrested three PN leaders on grounds that they had "gravely offended the patriotic sentiment," "propagated tendentious and false information designed to perturb the security of the country," "insulted and defamed the President and the Minister of Foreign Relations," and "incited subversion of public order" – all violations of the Law of Internal State Security.[20] The three PN members[21] promptly filed a *recurso de amparo* in the Santiago Appeals Court.[22]

In an unusual "after hours" decision,[23] the appellate judges ruled (3–0) to uphold the writ on the grounds that "the existence of facts which themselves present the characteristics of the specific crimes [imputed]" had not been established. On appeal six days later, the Supreme Court upheld the appeals court ruling, stating that:

> within the freedom to express opinions without prior censorship, which the Constitution guarantees to all the inhabitants of the Republic, political parties have the right to express publicly the judgment which the acts of the Government deserve and to criticize its actions, unless these opinions constitute an incitation to subversion . . . or an insult to His Excellency, the President of the Republic or to his Cabinet Ministers, *which in the present case has not been established from their text.* Nor has there been grave offense to patriotic sentiment, an offense . . . *which must be a matter of fact and not simply of simple declarations.*[24]

---

[19] Because Altamirano enjoyed senatorial immunity, his prosecution had to proceed in two steps: first, the government had to convince the courts to remove his immunity (*desafuero*), and only then could he be tried for the alleged crimes.

[20] Cabinet minister Bernardo Leighton stated, "It is evident that the party is trying to create a climate of alteration of our democratic regime." Quoted in *El Mercurio*, September 3, 1967, p. 43.

[21] The individuals were Victor García Garzena, Sergio Onofre Jarpa, and Alfredo Alcaino Barros.

[22] The case is referred to as *García Garzena, Victor y otros* (*recurso de amparo*), and the appellate and Supreme Court decisions were issued on September 2 and September 8, 1967, respectively.

[23] The court had never before convened on a Saturday afternoon to decide a specific case (personal communication with Chilean law professor Felipe González, May 23, 1996).

[24] From text of the case as presented in *RDJ* 64 (1967) 2.4: 266–272, my italics. The ruling was six to one, with the dissent from Frei appointee, Rafael Retamal.

Thus, the courts clearly saw fit the evaluation of the facts of the case against the claims of the government, and were willing to take a stand in defense of the constitutional right of free expression. The PN members were immediately released from custody.[25]

By contrast, in the Altamirano case, *Carlos Altamirano O.*, the same courts abandoned any commitment to the constitutional protection of free speech and put no challenge to the government's charge that the Socialist senator had violated the Law of Internal State Security by insulting the president and propagating violence. In the first phase of the prosecution, the Santiago Court of Appeals voted (in plenary) to revoke the senator's immunity on the sole grounds of insults to the president.[26] On appeal, the Supreme Court (also in plenary) unanimously upheld that ruling and gave new life to the charge of propagating violence. The high court made reference to the entire document from which the libelous and subversive lines were extracted to show that the senator's intention was to celebrate and encourage the emulation of the Cuban revolutionary model, which clearly and unapologetically involved violence.

Two months later, a Santiago Appeals Court judge, specially appointed by the Supreme Court, convicted Altamirano on the charges for which his immunity had been revoked. The ruling stated that "[t]he constitutional precept that consecrates the freedom of expression without previous censorship has left free the determination of the cases in which people incur responsibility for crimes and abuses committed in the exercise thereof to the law, such that it is *incumbent upon the legislator, and not upon the judge*, who is limited simply to applying it, *to prevent that right from being unjustifiably spoiled.* The legislator makes a political appraisal; the judge, a juridical one."[27] In other words, the judge argued that legal limits to the constitutionally protected freedom of expression were not subject to judicial evaluation. In contrast to that in the

---

[25] Eight months later, the charge itself was ruled upon by the Santiago Appeals Court, which claimed that if the Supreme Court had found no grounds for detention of the accused in the habeas corpus decision, then the case itself had to be definitively closed. See *RDJ* 65 (1968) 2.4: 95–99.

[26] The vote was thirteen to one. The dissenter was Abraham Poblete (an Alessandri appointee). Interestingly, the court did not find sufficient grounds to revoke Altamirano's immunity in the case pressed by the military. However, they were overruled by the Supreme Court, with only one dissent from Eduardo Ortiz (an Alessandri appointee). See *RDJ* 64 (1967) 2.4: 276–281.

[27] *RDJ* 64 (1967) 2.4: 272–276, emphasis added.

National Party case, this ruling placed special emphasis on the textual legal limits to the freedom of speech and on the limited responsibility of the judiciary to defend against these. The courts thus sent the message that aggressive right-wing speech was legitimate dissent, protected by the constitution, but aggressive left-wing speech was not.[28]

In similar political rights cases under President Allende, the courts, led by the Supreme Court, also ruled in favor of the political Right, extending protection to individuals critical of the executive but not to those critical of the opposition in Congress. For example, when the Allende government prosecuted far-right journalist Rafael Otero for public libel and an attack on public order (i.e., violations of the Law of Internal State Security),[29] the Supreme Court ruled that Otero had not demonstrated any libelous intent nor any intent to disrupt public order. Overruling the appellate court, which had sided with the government, the Court argued that it was incumbent upon judges to conduct an evaluation of not simply the words and phrases used by the defendant but also the background and purpose which motivated the use of those words and phrases.[30] In other words, they asserted the power, indeed the duty, of the courts to weigh carefully the subjective aspects of such a case, rather than simply to accept the analysis of the plaintiff (in this case, the executive).[31]

---

[28] The courts also ruled against left-wing journalists in two other cases of the period: *Contra Raul Pizarro Illanes y otro*, which denied *amparo* (habeas corpus) to the director of *El Clarín*, on grounds that he had abused his freedom of expression by publishing articles that contained libelous statements against an appellate judge; and *Contra Jorge Insunza Becker*, in which the appellate court revoked the immunity of Deputy Insunza for libel against the police (*Carabineros*) when he was director of the Communist newspaper, *El Siglo*. See also the contrast in treatment of two cases involving threats to national security from the far Right and the far Left (*RDJ* 66 (1969) 2.4: 302–305; *RDJ* 67 (1970) 2.4: 112–120).

[29] In an official letter sent to President Allende to request authorization for a national radio and television station, Otero had made a statement implying that Allende's decisions were subordinated to instructions from a Cuban diplomat, an implication which, in the view of the government, constituted a public libel and an attack on public order. The case was *Contra Rafael Otero Echeverría*, *RDJ* 68 (1971) 2.4: 77–81.

[30] *RDJ* 68 (1971) 2.4: 77–81. The ruling was six to one, with Eduardo Varas, an Ibáñez appointee, dissenting.

[31] Interestingly, though, the Court would not go so far as to rule the Law of Internal State Security's limits on free speech unconstitutional, even when Otero's lawyers brought such a charge. See *RDJ* 68 (1971) 2.4: 292–296.

By contrast, a few weeks later, the Santiago Appeals Court denied that it had the power to review the subjective aspects of a similar case, brought by four opposition congressmen against the director and owner of *Puro Chile*, a pro-Allende newspaper. Arguing that the text of the Law of Internal State Security bound them to render a conviction, the court confirmed the guilty ruling handed down by a specially appointed judge.[32] In other words, the appellate judges ignored the jurisprudential reasoning articulated by their superiors only a few weeks before, but followed their ideological lead. They found that in implicating the congressmen in question (Francisco Bulnes, Julio Durán, Jorge Lavandero and Raúl Morales) in various unseemly and even criminal acts,[33] as well as using derogatory terms to describe or refer to them, the newspaper had committed repeated acts of "defamation and contumelious insult" against public authorities. The intent to offend was clear, they argued, from the paper's word choice; journalists, as "professionals who are supposed to know what their social function is, and to what legal limits and ethics they are subject" should know better. Thus, it was clear that the paper had deliberately sought, without sufficient proof, to discredit the congressmen, and, in so doing, had committed a crime against public order. "It is the law itself which presumes that such acts in some way alter public order. Thus, it is not appropriate for the judge to contradict the explicit text of the law," read the decision.[34] It thus departed from the more activist perspective proffered by the Supreme Court in the Otero case.

---

[32] The director of the newspaper was sentenced to 541 days of internal relegation and to pay the costs of his trial, and the owner was ordered to pay fines amounting to 8,000 escudos plus related legal fees.

[33] The paper had published copies of documents that it claimed showed the involvement of the congressmen in the "campaign of terror" to prevent Allende from assuming the presidency, including the assassination of constitutionalist General René Schneider in 1970. It should be noted that the articles in question all appeared between July and December of 1970, and that one of the congressman, Raúl Morales, had been under official suspicion of involvement in the assassination until the Supreme Court, in a highly controversial ruling, dismissed charges against him on January 4, 1971. The paper had also targeted one of the men for alleged marital and sexual improprieties.

[34] *RDJ* 68 (1971) 2.4: 46–56 at 50, 52, and 53. In the first instance, the decision (*Contra José Antonio Gómez López*) was rendered by appellate court justice, Rubén Galecio, and then confirmed by Santiago appeals court judges, Marcos Aburto, Antonio Raveau, and (substitute judge) Jorge Barros.

The *Puro Chile* decision also departed from the Chilean judiciary's historical definition of public order as defined by and in relation to the executive.[35] In this case, the newspaper in question was clearly aligned with the Allende government, and so its articles were obviously not written to upset the public order as defined and upheld by the executive. The courts, however, determined that the notion of public order included the authority of other powers of the state, and that it could be disturbed *even when* the executive deemed it under control. In this sense, the ruling did represent a more assertive judicial stance.[36]

Over the course of 1972 and 1973, relations between the Supreme Court and Allende's Popular Unity government grew increasingly acrimonious. In situations in which citizens carried out illegal, and sometimes destructive or violent, seizures of farms or factories,[37] Allende's policy was to prohibit the police from executing judicial commands to use force against the perpetrators (Arriagada 1974: 251).[38] Judges and many lawyers interpreted this as general disrespect for the law, and an attack on judicial independence and power (*Libro Blanco* 1973; Arriagada 1974; Echeverría and Frei 1974; Silva Cimma 1977; Cea 1978; Soto Kloss and Aróstica 1993). In addition, Allende permitted unprecedented acts of protest against the judiciary (Athey 1978),[39] and the language used to critique the judges in the pro-Allende press was often crass and offensive (Echeverría and Frei 1974; Gardner 1980). However, it was equally true that the Supreme Court applied much

---

[35] See Chapter 2 of this volume, as well as Mera, González, and Vargas 1988: 35.

[36] The courts also challenged the government's monopoly on questions of order in the case *Juan Cembrano Perasso y otros (recurso de amparo)*, June 26, 1973, in which they deemed the police raid of a new television station at the University of Chile (in which some weapons were found) to be "arbitrary and illegal." At the appellate level, *amparo* was granted by Marcos Aburto, Osvaldo Erbetta, and Gustavo Chamorro. The decision was confirmed in the Supreme Court by José María Eyzaguirre, Luis Maldonado, Victor M. Rivas, Enrique Correa, and José Arancibia. See *Fallos del Mes* No. 176 (July 1973):107–108.

[37] Although such illegal takeovers were not officially promoted by the Allende government, "factions of the Popular Unity coalition actively encouraged [them], and the Allende government acquiesced in and took advantage of the process to further its own attempts at structural change through the [existing law]" (Gardner 1980: 174).

[38] *RDJ* 70 (1973). The minority within the UP coalition that favored the insurrectional route to socialism thus gained the upper hand via "the tactic of *faits accomplis* and using coercion . . . against the very government" (Cea 1978: xxv).

[39] *RDJ* 70 (1973).

stricter standards to and launched far more criticisms of the Allende government than they had against any previous administration (DeVylder 1974; Athey 1978; Kaufman 1988). Moreover, when Allende supporters pointed this out, the Supreme Court responded by reasserting their objectivity and dismissing the critics as impassioned, self-interested, ignorant, and unethical.[40]

The conflict between the judiciary and the executive came to a head in mid-1973, as "the court . . . moved away from an initial concern with specific legal violations to participation in a broader attempt to use juridical norms to discredit the government publicly" (Gardner 1980: 170). In his speech inaugurating the judicial year 1973, the new Supreme Court president, Enrique Urrutia Manzano, denounced the government's policy of discretionary enforcement of judicial orders as an assault on the Rule of Law:

> We understand the Rule of Law (*Estado de Derecho*) in a very simple way: that condition in which the law doesn't infringe upon the attributes constitutionally granted to the Public Power; in which the rights which the Constitution grants to the citizens are effective and not trampled underfoot, such that administrative officials honestly carry out their functions without altering the ends for which their offices were created and that they make use of their powers without fraud, and that, [any abuse is promptly punished.] Finally, and we emphasize this, giving it the greatest importance, by the Rule of Law, we mean that condition in which judicial rulings are duly carried out.[41]

Two and a half months later, in a now-famous memo sent to Allende on May 26, 1973, the Court stated forthrightly:

> This Supreme Court must bring to your attention, for the umpteenth time, the illegal attitude of the administrative authority in the illicit intromission in judicial affairs, as well as the obstruction of the national police in the carrying out of orders emanating from a criminal court, which according to the law, must be executed by that body without any impediment; all of which signifies an open persistence in rebelling against judicial resolutions, underestimating the alteration that such attitudes or omissions produce in the juridical order; moreover, this signifies not simply a crisis of the Rule of Law . . . but rather an urgent or imminent breakdown of law and order in the country.[42]

[40] *RDJ* 70 (1973):169–170.
[41] *RDJ* 70 (1973): xxiv.
[42] *RDJ* 70 (1973): 212.

An infuriated President Allende responded seventeen days later with a sharp letter inveighing against the Court for misrepresenting the legal conditions of the country and thereby contributing to the generation of a state of public disquiet. He claimed that it was the executive, not the judiciary, that was in charge of controlling public force and maintaining public order, and that, hence, the government had the prerogative to apply discretion in this sphere. He also expressed anger at the fact that in recent months, the Court had brought its criticisms of his government directly to the press, rather than taking up their concerns confidentially with his administration. In closing, he disputed the positivist defense that the Court had repeatedly offered to dismiss charges of class bias:

> such an argument ignores the fact that the laws are interpreted; and it is in the act of interpretation, in the meaning and reach which is given to the terms used in the [legal] texts, that the assessments of the judges are displayed, [and] underlying those is a concept of social relations and of the hierarchy of legal values.

The Court's concept in this regard, was at odds with the reality of the country, Allende claimed, and its inopportune public statements never "favored social peace or the re-establishment of democratic dialogue."[43]

The Court's embittered response to these allegations, dated June 25, 1973, was followed by official condemnations of the Allende administration by the leaders of the two houses of Congress, by the Bar Association, and by resolution of the Camara of Deputies.[44] In this dramatic statement, the Court expressed its outrage at what it saw, in Allende's previous memo, as "an attempt to submit the decision-making power of the judiciary to the political necessities of the government." It also curtly reminded the president that the Supreme Court "deserves respect from the other powers of the state" both out of constitutional duty and "because of its honor, deliberation, humanity and efficiency." Moreover, the Court insisted that it had the power and the duty to "contradict at times the most fervent desires of the executive" and that all administrative functionaries were legally bound to comply with the decisions of the judiciary. Finally, the Court rejected Allende's suggestion that

---

[43] *RDJ* 70 (1973): 225–226.
[44] It should be noted that the National Association of Magistrates, from which the pro-Allende forces had split off or been forced out (depending on the account), also officially registered its disapproval of the "attacks on the judiciary" on June 23, 1973. See Echeverría and Frei 1974: 160–162.

the courts of law should abandon legal formalism to pursue a particular brand of social justice in specific cases, a turn that they believed would be arbitrary and "even criminal."[45]

Indignant about the "disrespectful" tone in which it was written, Allende refused to respond to this memo.[46] However, by this time, so many voices were raised in a clamor against Allende's policies that his response mattered little.[47]

EXPLAINING THE JUDICIAL ROLE UNDER FREI AND ALLENDE

It should be clear from the preceding account that, despite judges' fervent and repeated claims to the contrary, the Chilean courts did not play a "neutral" or "apolitical" role in the nine years leading up to the military coup of September 11, 1973. Even as the majority of the population moved leftward on the political spectrum, the judiciary, under the direction of a powerful Supreme Court, threw its support squarely behind the country's most conservative sectors. In so doing, they antagonized the Left, emboldened the Right, and eroded the possibility that more moderate forces would prevail on either side of the burgeoning political battle.[48] The question is *why* did judges behave in this way?

Scholars of the American attitudinalist school would hypothesize that *personal policy preferences* explain the behavior of Chilean judges. Testing this hypothesis for the Chilean case is more challenging than for the United States for several reasons. First, Chilean judges, who enter the career right out of law school, are prohibited from affiliation with any political organization and from participating in public policy debates. Thus, generally speaking, there is little independent evidence of the political preferences of individual judges. Second, the judicial appointment process in Chile is much more bureaucratic and opaque

---

[45] *RDJ* 70 (1973): 226, 227–228, and 241.

[46] *RDJ* 70 (1973): 241.

[47] Echeverría and Frei note that "the importance of [the June 25 memo to President Allende from the Supreme Court], which has already been widely diffused, is unquestionable. First, because of the depth and seriousness of its contents and, second, because it emanated from an institution like the Supreme Court, head of one of the powers of the State" (1974: 24–25).

[48] As one prominent conservative lawyer declared approvingly, "Without the judiciary, there wouldn't have been a military coup in Chile" (Interview OL96–8, October 7, 1996, 15:30).

Table 3.2. Individual votes of supreme court justices, 1964–1973

	Favoring Left	Favoring Right	Total votes
Pre-Frei Appointees (n = 10)	13 (24%)	41 (76%)	54
Frei/Alende Appointees (n = 8)	10 (33%)	20 (67%)	30

than in the United States. As noted in Chapter 1, the President of the Republic does not nominate judges, as in the United States, but, rather, must choose appointees from nomination lists composed by the Supreme Court (for vacancies on the high court and all appellate courts) and by the appellate courts (for lower-court posts). Furthermore, before 1998, there was no congressional (or any other) involvement in the appointment process. Unlike in the United States, then, one cannot easily identify any given judge with a particular president or political party (and thereby infer his/her policy preferences). Finally, and relatedly, the press has traditionally given scant coverage to judicial appointments. Hence, one cannot even turn to journalistic accounts to code judges' political leanings.

In secondary sources, as well as in the course of my interviews, however, particular justices – namely, Israel Bórquez, Enrique Urrutia, José María Eyzaguirre, and Ricardo Martín – were repeatedly identified as having had clear right-wing ties and sympathies (Velasco 1986: 155, 166; Silva Cimma 2000: 321). Bórquez, in particular, was said to be rabidly right-wing. Not surprisingly, the individual voting records of these justices in the Supreme Court decisions I analyzed for this period reflect this: Bórquez voted for the Right at a ratio of 7:1, Urrutia at 6:1, Eyzaguirre at 6:1, and Martín 3:1. For these individuals, then – all of whom were appointed to the Supreme Court before Frei's election in 1964 – the attitudinalist explanation might suffice. Attitudinalism seems insufficient, however, to explain the behavior of all judges during this period, even all Supreme Court justices.

Table 3.2 offers for comparison the combined voting records of the ten justices appointed to the Supreme Court prior to 1964 (i.e., under more conservative presidents) and of the eight named between 1964 and 1973 (i.e., under the progressive presidents Frei and Allende). It shows that while the (ten) pre-1964 appointees (including the individuals named in the previous paragraph) accounted for almost two-thirds of all the votes cast in this sample during the 1964–1973 period, and although 76 percent of those votes were pro-Right, it would be incorrect to attribute the bias to this group alone. Indeed, the (eight) post-1964 appointees, who might have been expected to be less conservative, voted pro-Right a full 67 percent of the time, not dramatically less than the pre-1964 group. Moreover, if one takes only the votes cast after Allende's election, the two groups supported the Right at the same rate (61 percent).

Interestingly, at the appellate level, where the vast majority of judges had risen to their posts before 1964 (i.e., before the Frei presidency), the overall voting patterns were somewhat less biased in favor of the Right. Appellate court judges cast pro-Left votes 42 percent of the time, as compared to only 27 percent for the Supreme Court. Indeed, more striking than the political bent of the vote pattern at the appellate court level is the bias in favor of the state: Appellate judges voted on the side of the state in 73 percent of all instances, compared to the Supreme Court justices, who did so 54 percent of the time. I will return to this latter point, but suffice it to say here that any clear (exogenous) "attitudinalist" effects appear to be limited to a vocal minority on the Supreme Court.

Seeking to explain why many judges not associated with the political Right came to close ranks with their more conservative brethren, critics on the Chilean Left have attributed the perceived bias in judicial decision making to *class loyalty*. They claim that judges ruled in favor of property owners and right-wing politicians and journalists because of their common place in the traditional social hierarchy – that is, because of their shared social ties and interests with the country's elite (Novoa 1993 [1970]). Although this may have been the case for a small minority of judges, my research revealed that, in fact, by the 1960s, the judiciary was no longer a bastion of the oligarchy, but was, rather, solidly middle class. In the nineteenth century, judges had come mostly from elite families, but with the "professionalization" of the state in the 1920s, the judiciary became much more open to nonelite aspirants.[49]

This was evident not only in secondary sources (de Ramón 1999; Couso 2002: 177; Dezalay and Garth 2002: 226) but also in the social

---

[49] As in much of the public administration in Chile, the Freemasons, who were generally associated with the middle class (Lomnitz and Melnick 2000), had a strong presence in the judiciary. Indeed, according to a number of my interviewees, the unspoken agreement had long been that in judicial promotions, there should always be some parity between Catholics and Masons.

Table 3.3. Social background of high court judges*

Respondent	High school	Father's occupation	Landowning	Lived abroad
1	Upper Middle Class	Farmer	Yes	No
2	Middle Class	Municipal Employee	Yes**	No
3	Middle Class	Attorney	No	No
4	Middle Class	Military	No	No
5	Lower Middle Class	Navy Pharmacist	No	No
6	Lower Middle Class	Public Servant	No	No
7	Lower Middle Class	Judge	No	No
8	Upper Middle Class	Farmer	Yes	Yes
9	Upper Middle Class	Doctor	No	No
10	Middle Class	Merchant	No	No
11	Middle Class	Mechanic	No	No
12	Lower Middle Class	Miner	No	No
13	Middle Class	Accountant	Yes**	No
14	Upper Class	(Not Given)	(Not Given)	Yes
15	Upper Middle Class	Merchant	No	No
16	Upper Class	Diplomat	Yes	Yes
17	Middle Class	Attorney	No	No
18	Lower Middle Class	Farmer	No	No
19	Lower Middle Class	Policeman	Yes**	No
20	Middle Class	Attorney	No	No
21	Middle Class	Merchant	No	No
22	Lower Middle Class	Merchant	Yes**	No
23	Lower Middle Class	Public Employee	No	No
24	Middle Class	Merchant	No	No
25	Middle Class	Accountant	Yes**	No
26	Upper Middle Class	Farmer	Yes	No
27	Upper Middle Class	Dentist	Yes	No
28	Lower Middle Class	Policeman	No	Yes
29	Middle Class	Attorney	Yes	No
30	Middle Class	Merchant	No	No

* Information obtained in written questionnaire, returned by 83 percent of the judges in my sample.
** Respondent indicated that family owned land but, given his/her other responses or specific clarifications, such ownership would not classify him/her as a member of Chile's "landed elite."

background information that I gathered in my interviews with judges (see Table 3.3). This data, which included high school attended, father's occupation, mother's or maternal grandfather's occupation, and prior or present landholdings, showed that a full three-fourths of respondents came from lower-middle- to middle-class backgrounds, whereas only about one-fourth were of upper-middle- to upper-class extraction. Few judges came from landed families, most had fathers who were merchants or public employees, and all but a handful attended lower-middle- to middle-class high schools (many of these public).[50]

Judges offered narratives of their career trajectories that underscored their economically modest backgrounds. Several noted that they chose the judicial profession after working in nonlettered posts in the judiciary to fund their studies. One mentioned that he had been an orphan, and would never have been able to go to university were it not for the free education system (Interview ACJ96-19, May 28, 1996, 13:00). Another explained that on finishing law school, he did not have the money to start an independent legal practice or the contacts to enter into a company as an in-house lawyer, where he would have been paid well. Thus, his options were either to go into a big law firm where he would be exploited for an indefinite number of years, or go into the judiciary, where the pay was low but the job was secure and one could work one's way up by merit (Interview FJ96-1, June 11, 1996, 9:00). Still others described having just scraped by early in their careers, when they earned very little money and had families to support (Interviews ACJ96-14, May 14, 1996, 14:30; ACJ96-10, May 9, 1996, 10:00; ACJ96-19, May 28, 1996, 13:00).[51]

Clearly, then, the bias of the judiciary cannot be attributed to class, at least not understood in objective terms. Some judges may have identified with the traditional elite, but my claim is that this identification was constructed *within* the institution. Seeking to please their superiors and move up in the judicial ranks, middle-class judges learned to "mimic the conduct and aristocratic demeanor of some of the elite judges who were still there when they began their careers" (Dezalay and Garth 2002: 226).[52] Indeed, precisely because they tended to be individuals without significant financial cushions or well-heeled social networks, they came to identify their own interests – in job security and social dignity – with those of the institution and its elite. Because the Allende government made no secret of its mistrust of the courts and sought significant reform of the judiciary, many judges reacted by throwing

[50] I am indebted to Javier Couso and Matías Larraín for helping me interpret the sociological data.

[51] In past decades, judges were some of the lowest-paid state employees. Unless they came from moneyed families, they couldn't expect to live anything but a modest middle-class lifestyle. Partially for this reason, in the 1950s and early 1960s, many judicial posts went unfilled because of the dearth of aspirants. In recent years, reformers have begun to attend to this problem (Vargas and Correa 1995).

[52] For a good (if disturbing) example of this behavior, see Silva Cimma 2000: 321–322.

their support to the Right (Velasco 1986: 153; Interview HRL96-8, October 17, 1996, 16:00).

In so doing, judges demonstrated that they were not necessarily bound by the legal positivist principles of strict fidelity to statutory law and deference to the legislator. As several of the examples discussed earlier illustrate, Chilean judges, particularly at the level of the Supreme Court, proved willing and able to appeal to constitutionalist principles and to use these to evaluate the legitimacy of government claims and policies. This dispels the idea that judicial behavior was driven primarily by *legal philosophy*.

The argument I offer, then, is that the conservative bias of Chilean courts during this period (and beyond) is best explained by the *institutional structure and ideology* of the judiciary. The *institutional structure* of the judiciary, in which the Supreme Court controlled discipline and promotion, gave incentives for judges to follow closely the examples set by their superiors. Given that most judges depended on the security of their posts and the promise of promotion to guarantee their livelihood and perhaps improve their social status, they had every reason to play along with those who controlled their careers, and even to absorb or adopt their perspectives. This structure served to reproduce a very conservative understanding of the judicial role, or what I am calling the *institutional ideology*. The core of this ideology was a belief that adjudication was and should remain strictly apolitical. In general, this meant that judges were to restrict themselves to a passive, subservient role vis-à-vis the executive, as emphasized in Chapter 2. But, under Frei, and particularly Allende, activism of a conservative nature was condoned and rewarded within the institution, since the judicial elite considered this to be a reaction against the (imminent or potential) "politicization" of law and justice and, therefore, not itself "political."[53] Judges who desired to increase their chances of promotion or simply to maintain their professional integrity (the two were not unrelated) thus had to take care to demonstrate their commitment to this particular brand of "apoliticism." At best, then, the institutional setting encouraged judges to avoid taking any stands at all against the government, to be quietist and deferential. At worst, it permitted and amplified the defense of conservative values and interests, while discouraging the expression of alternative perspectives.

---

[53] There are strong parallels here with the ideology of the Weimar-era judiciary in Germany, which produced a very similar pattern of rulings (see Kahn-Freund 1981).

Table 3.4. Individual votes of high court judges in rights cases, 1964–1973

	Appellate courts	Supreme court	Total
Pro-State	67	45	112
Pro-Individual Rights	25	39	64

In support of this claim, I cite first the strong statist tendency evident in the data. Most judges were clearly disinclined to challenge the reasoning of state officials in the name of individual rights. As Table 3.4 shows, at the appellate level, judges deferred to the executive at a rate of three to one. The tendency at the Supreme Court level was less strong but, overall, justices still favored the state slightly more than half the time.[54] Moreover, of the thirty-nine pro-rights votes by Supreme Court justices for the period, 59 percent were made by six individuals (one-third of the eighteen justices).[55] In other words, an activist minority skewed the overall results.[56] Most of the time, judges didn't consider it proper to interrogate the state's reasoning. As in the past, judges often claimed that they simply did not have jurisdiction to review the facts of the case before them and offer an independent evaluation to test the claims of elected officials.

Such a position was generally the safest for judges to take, particularly for those at the district and appellate levels. Many judges that I interviewed noted that if a judge had aspirations to get to the Supreme Court, it was best not to take professional risks. For instance, one retired judge spoke of a personal conversation he had had in the early 1970s

[54] Indeed, it is very interesting that when given the opportunity (in the case *Contra Rafael Otero Echeverría (recurso de inaplicabilidad)*, December 13, 1971), the Supreme Court refused (unanimously!) to rule portions of the Law of Internal State Security unconstitutional, even though the law clearly interfered with the liberty of expression and the individual who challenged the law's constitutionality was of the political Right.

[55] The individuals in question were Justices Bórquez, Eyzaguirre, Urrutia, Varas, Maldonado, and Rivas. The first four were pre-Frei appointees (and three of four noted conservatives), whereas the latter two were appointed under Frei.

[56] This was not at all the case at the appellate court level, where votes were much more evenly spread (and much more statist overall). Indeed, if one takes the votes of the activist Supreme Court judges as a percentage of the total votes at both levels, then 14 percent (one-seventh) of all judges account for 38 percent of all pro-rights votes.

with Supreme Court justice, José María Eyzaguirre, in which Eyzaguirre told him,

> If you want to get to the Supreme Court, the first thing you have to worry about is that your seat is stable, . . . that is, you need to avoid serious problems. When there are complications, don't burn yourself (*no se quema*). [Better to] wait, stall, declare yourself without jurisdiction, go on to another case. That's the basic thing; that's how you get to the Supreme Court. If you look at everyone on the Supreme Court, you see that those who are there don't commit themselves, don't let themselves get burnt (Interview FJ96-4, June 17, 1996, 12:30).

That other judges had absorbed this message was very clear. "In Chile, the obsequious judge is rewarded, not the best trained or the most intelligent. . . . Everyone prefers to take the comfortable position: avoid compromising oneself. And why? Because everyone wants to be promoted!" confessed one (Interview FJ96-2, June 13, 1996, 13:00). "All that a mediocre judicial employee has to do to be favorably evaluated is be very friendly with the Supreme Court and accept any kind of request that the Court makes," stated another; "In contrast, a judge who is very independent of such influence will surely not receive the same [positive] evaluation (Interview ACJ96-10, May 9, 1996, 10:00). "When the Court doesn't know a lower judge, they always give him a good evaluation . . . but those who take stands, those who are known for not being with this gentleman or that other, run risks," maintained a third (Interview FJ96-4, June 17, 1996, 12:30). "Like in the army, there is a certain 'verticality' in the organization of the judiciary," explained a fourth, "First instance judges don't make their voices heard because they think that the appellate court might intervene and critique them and the justices of the appellate courts don't intervene or make their voices heard because that could be the object of criticism by the Supreme Court" (Interview ACJ96-5, May 2, 1996, 18:00).[57]

My research into the judicial role under Frei and Allende indicated that these views were not unfounded, for the Supreme Court did flex its muscle on occasion, reminding wayward subordinates to stay in line. For example, when the newly formed National Association of Magistrates

---

[57] By contrast, several *abogados integrantes* interviewed for this work claimed that they were more independent than career judges because they did not have to worry about the disciplinary control of superiors (Interviews AI96-1, May 20, 1996, 10:30; AI96-2, June 12, 1996, 16:00; and AI96-3, June 19, 1996, 12:00.)

organized a strike in November of 1969,[58] the Supreme Court issued a declaration denouncing the organizers for usurping the Court's role as the unique representative of the judiciary before the government, and warning them that they were violating fundamental institutional norms.[59] The strikers subsequently added to their demands a modification of the judicial evaluation system, "which they considered a weapon used by the Supreme Court to pressure their subordinates" (Matus 1999: 209). This demand was not met, but its articulation is revealing of the perspective of lower court judges vis-à-vis the institutional structure.

Further evidence comes from the Allende period, when the Supreme Court president warned subordinates not to succumb to the political "proselytizing" of the Left, and spoke of "measures" that would be taken to avoid this.[60] The public reprimand and suspension of Judge Oscar Alvarez, who was an open supporter of the Allende administration, served to make this threat credible. The judge, Oscar Alvarez, of the La Serena Appeals Court, had been a member of the judiciary for nineteen years and had been serving on a commission of judges that worked closely with the Ministry of Justice under Allende to help draft bills on judicial reform.[61] The Supreme Court formally accused Alvarez of

---

[58] Frustrated with persistently low wages and weak administrative support, judicial personnel demanded a 60 percent increase in the judicial budget. The Supreme Court did not support the strike. Nonetheless, after six days, the strikers reached an accord with the government, agreeing to a 35 percent budget increase beyond the adjustment for inflation. In addition, the government agreed that the strike leaders should not be punished or suffer deductions in pay for work days lost.

[59] Records of the plenary sessions of the Supreme Court, Volume 15, October 27, 1969.

[60] See *RDJ* 69 (197) 1: xv.

[61] The Allende administration attempted to assert some influence on the judiciary by forming an advisory committee of sympathetic judicial personnel within the Ministry of Justice called the Comité de la Unidad Popular (CUP). These individuals were called upon to collaborate in the improvement of the judicial system, by finding ways to make it more representative of, sympathetic toward, and accessible to the popular classes. In addition to drafting proposals for legal changes, they also served as consultants in the judicial appointment process, informing the government on which judicial nominees might be most inclined to support UP legal interpretations and reforms. Although such an approach on the part of the executive to judicial appointments was certainly nothing new, the open and vocal participation of members of the judiciary in this process, selected so obviously for their ideological sympathies, was deemed bold and provocative (Interview ACJ96-2, May 6, 1996, 8:30). As one of the participants in the CUP put it, "A true 'dark legend' has been woven around this commission, that it disposed of extraordinary influence . . . but the truth was very different" (Interview FJ96-2, June 13, 1996, 13:00).

instructing the executive to fill a vacancy in his court, rather than notifying the Supreme Court (which handled nominations) that the post had gone unfilled. Alvarez claimed that these were trumped-up charges, for all he had done was notify the Minister of Justice, whose legitimate concern it was, that the post had remained vacant for five months. The true reason the Court sought to punish him, he argued, was because of his cooperation with the Allende administration in drawing up proposals to democratize the justice system. And indeed, Judge Alvarez and five of his colleagues who had served on Allende's judicial commission, had already been denounced to the Supreme Court by rightwing congressmen.[62] In the end, Alvarez was suspended for only five days,[63] but the action taken against him had a chilling effect on the rest of the judicial hierarchy. It became clear to lower-court judges that if they expressed excessive enthusiasm for Allende's reform proposals, they would be subject to disciplinary measures. As Alvarez claimed in a magazine interview, after this "what else could we do [but remain silent]?" (Harnecker and Vaccaro 1973: 29 and 32).[64]

The reluctance of judges to do anything that might cross their superiors was evident in the low level of participation in Allende's *audiencias populares* initiative. In order to put the judiciary at the service of ordinary people,[65] Allende had proposed, among other things, the creation of neighborhood courts to mediate or arbitrate community disputes that fell outside of the jurisdiction of the regular courts (see *Mensaje Presidencial*, May 21, 1971).[66] These courts were to be run by lay judges elected from the community, and the only requirement for office would be literacy (Spence 1979: 39; see also Soto and Aróstica 1993: 60). Faced with vehement opposition from both the Center and the Right

---

[62] Among the denouncers was Senator Raúl Morales Adriazola and lawyer Pablo Rodríguez Grez, both notorious members of the far Right.

[63] Although after the coup, the Supreme Court expelled him from the judiciary.

[64] In their presentation of his statements, the journalists who interviewed him claimed that Alvarez had fallen victim to the "legal dictatorship" exercised from the Supreme Court. They also noted that the situation in which he found himself was not surprising, given that the hierarchical structure of the judiciary "is the negation of democracy. This is the only [branch of the state] in which the maximum authorites are self-generating, have life tenure, and don't have to answer to anybody for their acts."

[65] Allende assumed the presidency having run on a platform that promised to replace "class justice" with "popular justice."

[66] For a fuller description of the UP stance on neighborhood courts, see Spence 1979: 41–45.

to this proposal, the Allende government suggested, as an alternative, that the Supreme Court encourage members of the judiciary to spend one day a week providing services in special *audiencias populares* (A.P.s) in poor neighborhoods. The Supreme Court acceded to the proposal in theory; however, the program engaged "an extremely low level of participation" (Soto and Aróstica 1993: 59). As Jack Spence explains, the institutional incentives within the judiciary simply did not favor participation in this project. Because the Supreme Court possessed such strong control over the careers of subordinate judges, conducting regular reviews of their performance, maintaining the right to dismiss them for bad behavior, and drafting the lists of nominees for promotions to higher-court positions, only a clear signal from the Supreme Court would effectively encourage participation of lower judges in this new program. "Given the benign views of any of the Supreme Court to the traditional system of justice and the lack of energy with which it promoted the idea of the A.P.s, it would not be hard for the lower court judges to assume that, at the least, no professional credit would come from participating in the A.P.s" (Spence 1979: 60–61).[67]

Moreover, it became increasingly clear that the Supreme Court was doing its best to give "professional credit" to those who followed its ideological lead. Interviewees claimed and archival research confirmed that, under Allende, the Supreme Court began stacking the nomination lists for vacancies in the higher courts with the most conservative candidates. As a former judge who had been part of the advisory committee to Allende's Ministry of Justice[68] explained, the nomination lists formed by the Supreme Court were so obviously stacked with conservatives that the administration ended up appointing the nominee who made the list based on seniority alone, even if that person lacked other qualifications (Interview FJ96-1, June 11, 1996, 9:00). My review of the plenary sessions of the Supreme Court for this period, in which the votes received by each candidate and the final nomination lists are recorded, confirmed this: Whereas under Frei, the government selected the nominee who made the list based on seniority only once, under Allende, the government appointed exclusively seniority-based nominees.[69]

[67] Indeed, "'volunteers for the A.P.s had to perform the additional tasks without cutting into their normal tasks" (Spence 1979: 97). For a discussion of how one of these A.P.s actually functioned, see Spence 1979: Ch. 4.
[68] Refer to note 61.
[69] Records of the plenary sessions of the Supreme Court, Vols. 14–18, covering years 1964–1973.

Independent evidence of the effects of institutional ideology from the period are more difficult to come by, since many of the actors from the period are long since deceased, and since no surveys or interview-based studies of judges were conducted during this period.[70] However, that this ideology was at work in the 1964–1973 period is supported by both judicial speeches and declarations from that era, as well as by a number of my interviews.

In his speeches inaugurating the judicial year in both 1970 and 1971, for example, then president of the Supreme Court Ramiro Méndez Brañas claimed that the Left's charge of class bias in the judiciary was unreasonable; judges could not be blamed for the outcomes of the cases they decided, as they simply applied the laws in force in the country.[71] Ironically, he felt so strongly about this that in 1970 he appeared with a fellow justice on a national television program to rebut the charge that the courts administered "class justice." In his 1972 speech, Méndez defended this action as an effort to protect the judiciary from insidious efforts from the Left to "politicize" the judicial system. Any remarks that he had made in the previous year's speech, he noted, were merely responses to the defamatory and often obscene attacks the judiciary had suffered, and were not "political" assertions. Judges should have the right to defend themselves without being accused of "taking sides" in current political battles, he argued. Judges neither desire nor are able to intervene in current politics, "because [such intervention] affects independence and impartiality, without which any concept of justice disappears." He thus issued a warning against those "outside influences that are attempting to infiltrate the administration of justice with their political proselytizing." The Supreme Court, he announced, would "adopt the appropriate measures to prevent members of the judiciary from listening" to such voices, bent on "destroying our crystalline tradition of respect for the rule of law." Finally, Méndez reiterated the opposition of the Supreme Court to Allende's proposal for neighborhood courts. Again, he claimed, this official expression of opposition was not "political," but rather technical. "Just as doctors opine on issues of public health or engineers on the problems of the nation's bridges and

---

[70] Indeed, as noted earlier, the judiciary in general received very little press coverage before the 1990s.

[71] See the speeches printed in the opening pages of *RDJ* 67 (1970) and 68 (1971). Note that in April of 1970, the plenary of the Supreme Court issued a collective statement reiterating Méndez's arguments (*El Mercurio*, 15 April, 1970, p. 25).

roads, it is the business of judges to opine on [juridical] matters," he asserted.[72]

As is evident in these statements and the acts that accompanied them, the Supreme Court made it clear to the rest of the judiciary, and to the public, that adjudication was and must remain apolitical. Judges that stuck with traditional legal interpretations, that ruled to protect the status quo, or that acted to defend the judiciary from critique were behaving appropriately, that is in a strictly professional-legal manner. Only those who demonstrated sympathy with or lent legitimacy to left-wing causes and critiques merited the derogatory "political" label. As one former judge explained, "In the judiciary, they always tell you, 'You are a judge; you can't get involved in politics,' and they accused those of us who were leftists [and were legal advisers to the Allende government] of meddling in politics. But the people of the Right who get involved in politics, by participating in television programs or writing press editorials [as several judges did under Allende], aren't 'meddling in politics because they're intervening in favor of the Right. In other words, to the degree that judges favor positions of the Right, they aren't being political!" (Interview FJ96-1, June 11, 1996, 9:00).[73]

Although it is impossible to separate the influence of ideational factors from that of more material structural incentives, my claim is that institutional structure alone does not provide the whole explanation for Chilean judicial behavior in this period or in those that followed. As Rogers Smith has argued, institutions are "not only fairly concrete organizations, . . . but also cognitive structures, such as patterns of rhetorical legitimation characteristic of certain traditions of political discourse," which give people functioning within them a sense of professional duty and integrity (1988: 91). Like individuals in any institutionalized setting, then, judges in Chile did not simply "ask the question 'how do I maximize my interests in this situation?' but instead 'what is the appropriate response to this situation given my position and responsibilities?'" (Koelble 1995: 233). And my claim is that the ideological premium on remaining apart from and above "politics" set clear parameters for acceptable professional conduct, leading judges either to defer, in the traditional manner, to the executive, or to take more active stands to defend (established) law and justice from "political" machinations.

[72] *RDJ* 69 (197) 1: xv and xvii.
[73] Similar sentiments were expressed by FJ96-2, June 13, 1996, 13:00, and FJ96-6, June 19, 1996, 20:00.

CONCLUSION

In sum, the reason that Chilean courts played such a conservative role in the period 1964–1973 is that institutional features of the judiciary – namely, the autonomous bureaucratic structure and the antipolitics professional ideology – encouraged and reproduced conservative and conformist behavior among judges. Although the personal conservatism of certain members of the Supreme Court is a relevant factor, it alone cannot explain judicial performance either during this period or in the seventeen years of dictatorship that followed. Indeed, my point has been to show that most Chilean judges were not born conservatives, committed to a right-wing agenda because of ties of blood, marriage, or childhood socialization. Rather, their conservative behavior was a response – sincere, strategic, or a bit of both – to institutional dynamics. Despite the high levels of independence and professionalism of the Chilean judiciary, the understandings and incentives transmitted and enforced within the institution rendered most judges unwilling or unable to take independent stands in defense of liberal-democratic principles – long before the military seized power.

CHAPTER FOUR

LEGITIMIZING AUTHORITARIANISM, 1973–1990

The dissolution or mass resignation of the Supreme Court would have been better from the point of view of clarifying what was happening in Chile. At least it would have been clear to the people, clear in the conscience of the country, and clear internationally. I think that one of the tremendous things that happened in Chile is that the dictatorship cloaked itself nationally and internationally with the legality that the judiciary gave it.

Chilean Human Rights Lawyer[1]

When the generals overthrew the Allende government and seized power on September 11, 1973, they did so in the name of the rule of law (*el estado de derecho*). In its first official statement justifying the coup, Edict No. 5 (*Bando No. 5*), the governing junta declared that the Allende administration had "placed itself outside the law on multiple occasions, resorting to arbitrary, dubious, ill-intentioned, and even flagrantly erroneous [legal] interpretations;" and had "repeatedly failed to observe the mutual respect which one power of the state owes to another." For these reasons, the Allende government had "fallen into flagrant illegitimacy," and the armed forces had "taken upon themselves the moral duty . . . of deposing the government, . . . [and] assuming power" with the objective of reestablishing "normal economic and social conditions in the country, with peace, tranquillity, and security for all."[2]

---

[1] Interview HRL96-5, August 2, 1996, 12:00.
[2] Cited in Loveman and Davies 1997: 181.

At first, many Chileans believed that the military was intervening on a temporary basis and would call elections within a few months. However, it soon became apparent that this was not the junta's intention. Although the new leaders claimed they had come to power to restore both order and Chilean national identity (*chilenidad*), their approach rejected the values of civilian politicians, particularly those who had been at the helm for the past ten years.[3] Indeed, for General Pinochet and his supporters, "liberal democracy was a showcase for irresponsible, selfish demagogues that had proven itself a failure" (Constable and Valenzuela 1991: 69).

With the goal of building a new, apolitical order, Pinochet thus "turned for inspiration to [nineteenth-century Chilean statebuilder] Diego Portales...who believed the best government was an 'impersonal' semidictatorship with limited concessions to popular representation" (Constable and Valenzuela 1991: 70).[4] In so doing, he "inevitably had recourse to that political group which represents the most conservative sectors of the Chilean society," a group that "thinks that it has no politics, and believes that it upholds the eternal interests of the Chilean nation, manifested in the institutions it has inherited from a previous century."[5] Among such institutions was the judiciary.

This chapter analyzes the political role of the judiciary during the years of the military regime, highlighting continuities with the preauthoritarian past. In particular, the chapter demonstrates how the institutional characteristics of the judiciary (its structure and ideology) facilitated judicial capitulation to and cooperation with the military regime. To begin, these institutional factors had produced a Supreme Court whose members, despite having been appointed in the majority (eight of thirteen) by the progressive governments of Eduardo Frei and Salvador Allende, were very conservative in their professional orientation. From the earliest days of the dictatorship, the high court justices demonstrated a clear willingness to support the military government's

---

[3] As Jorge Nef argued in 1974, "the military is attempting to convince the population that it is the incarnation of Derecho (not quite the same thing as 'law') and that they impartially rule in the name of eternal principles which transcend legality and other civilian formulas" (Nef 1974: 74).

[4] Loveman emphasizes the deliberate links drawn by leaders of the military regime between their political vision and Chile's Portalian legacy (1988: 312–313).

[5] *The Manchester Guardian* of October 6, 1973, cited in Nef 1974: 73.

"antipolitics" agenda (Loveman and Davies 1997). Second, the Supreme Court continued to hold tremendous power over the judicial hierarchy, through which it induced conservatism and conformity among appellate and district court judges. Not only did the Supreme Court quickly disqualify from service those judges that had demonstrated sympathy with the Allende administration, but it also set a tone for the judiciary in which anyone who questioned the legitimacy of the military regime's tactics was suspect of wanting to "politicize" justice and upset the rule of law. The Supreme Court continually discouraged any such efforts via the diversion of cases into the military justice system, the overturning of nonconformist decisions, and disciplinary action against the few judges who refused to fall in line. Their efforts were facilitated by the long-standing ideology of the Chilean judiciary, according to which judges were to remain "apolitical." Any judge desiring to preserve his/her professional integrity and standing needed to take care to demonstrate his/her fidelity to law alone, and law was to remain distinct from and superior to politics.

In this institutional setting, even democratic-minded judges were, with few exceptions, unwilling to take public principled stands in cases brought against authoritarian laws and practices. Challenging the decisions of the military junta, self-proclaimed guardians of the national interest, would both violate their professional duty to remain apolitical and imperil their chances of professional advancement. The Chilean judiciary thus not only failed to contribute to the defense of human rights when that defense was most needed, but it provided a mantle of legitimacy to the Pinochet regime. Far from reflecting and demanding respect for the liberal principles and practices that support democratic – or simply humane – politics, the judiciary, led by the Supreme Court, accepted, endorsed, and helped to perpetuate the brutal and often arbitrary rule of a privileged minority.

To make these points, this chapter is organized into three parts. Although there are many possible ways to break down the authoritarian period for analytical purposes, the logical division for any work focusing on legal aspects of the regime is around the 1980 Constitution. Thus, Part I of the chapter covers the period 1973–1980, when the 1925 Constitution was (nominally) still in place, and Part II discusses the 1981–1990 period, after the 1980 Constitution came into force. In both of these sections, I first offer an overview of the military government's laws and policies, highlighting those developments that were most relevant for the courts in deciding rights cases. This provides a context for my discussion of the jurisprudential record in each period, in which I focus on habeas corpus and constitutional review decisions, as well as review of military court decisions (for the 1973–1980 period) and some other high profile human rights cases that don't fit in these other categories (for both periods). In Part III of the chapter, I provide an analysis of judicial behavior throughout the authoritarian era, discussing the evidence for the competing hypotheses presented in Chapter 1 and making the case for my institutional argument.

PART I

1973–1980: "THE RULE OF LAW SHOW"

THE MILITARY GOVERNMENT'S APPROACH
TO LAW (1973–1980)

As noted in the introduction to this chapter, the armed forces seized power in 1973 in the name of the rule of law. However, it was clear from the start that although the generals often sought to rule *through* law, they did not rule *under* law.[6] Immediately after the coup had begun, they issued Decree Law No. 1, which announced that the governing junta would "guarantee the full effectiveness of the judiciary's attributes" and would "respect the Constitution and the laws of the Republic, *insofar as the country's present situation permits*" (see Frühling, Portales, and Varas 1982:85 [my emphasis]). As this last clause suggests, under the military regime in Chile, "policy was law and law was policy" (Gardner 1980: 272). Moreover, all policy (and hence all law) was rooted in national security doctrine, that is, in the belief that the primary mission of the armed forces, "singular representatives of the Nation and of the State" (Frühling 1982: 51; see also Munizaga 1988), was to protect society from internal "enemies."[7] Indeed, Pinochet used the war on communism to justify the regime's permanent restrictions on civil and political liberties, as well as the construction of a "new institutional order." In this war, anyone who was not with the armed forces was against them, and thus the military's definition of the enemy "grew broader by the day" (Constable and Valenzuela 1991: 38).

Torture was the major tool of repression for the military government. Both of the regime's secret police forces, the DINA (Directorate

---

[6] Barros characterizes the military government's approach as rule *by* law, as opposed to the rule *of* law (2002).

[7] National security doctrine generally refers to the ideology with which the United States trained Latin American militaries during the Cold War, broadening the military mission to maintaining internal social order (i.e., counterinsurgency) as well as to security from external threats. However, such a mission was not simply an import from abroad, as a number of works suggest. Indeed, the idea of the military as the guardian of the national interest and essence has a much longer history in Latin America. See particularly Frühling 1982 and Loveman and Davies 1997.

for National Intelligence), which operated until August 1977, and the CNI (National Center for Information), which replaced it, operated clandestine torture centers where tens of thousands of detainees, often kidnapped from their homes or off the streets, were subjected to a variety of barbaric treatments.[8] A total of 3,197 individuals were murdered or disappeared at the hands of state agents during the dictatorship,[9] and another 5,000 were disappeared for weeks and months, "provoking terror among their families and friends" (Verdugo 1990: 296). Between 1973 and 1975, the government detained 42,486 persons for political reasons, and from 1976 to 1988, it carried out 12,134 individual arrests and 26,431 collective arrests.[10]

Although the regime clearly targeted leftist groups that had supported Allende (first the MIR, then Socialists, and then Communists), nearly half of the victims of the regime had no formal political affiliation. They thus became targets of the government because of known or presumed political views, "guilt" by association, or just bad luck.[11] In addition, although "the vast majority of affluent and comfortable families were never touched by repression," the "harshest treatment of all was reserved for the most vulnerable supporters of Allende: small-town peasant and labor leaders who had no international contacts and no place to hide from official and personal vengeance" (Constable and Valenzuela 1991: 34 and 144).[12]

---

[8] Forms of torture included severe beatings, sequential rapes, cigarette burns, electric shock treatments (often on the genitals), near drowning, forced ingestion of urine and feces, the use of drugs like pentothal to inhibit resistance, and psychological tortures such as mock execution, forced witnessing or listening to the torture of others (including relatives), and threats of harassment of family members. See Organization of American States 1985: 90–91. The Chilean government finally issued an official report on torture in 2004, available online at http://www.latinamericanstudies. org/chile/informe.htm.

[9] This is the official figure of the National Corporation for Reparation and Reconciliation, which continued the work of the Rettig Commission from 1991 to 1996. From http://www.derechoschile.com/english/victims.htm, accessed October 5, 1999.

[10] From http://www.derechoschile.com/english/victims.htm, accessed October 5, 1999.

[11] See the table in the Ministerio Secretaria General de Gobierno de Chile 1991: Vol. II, 885, which states that 46 percent of victims were "not political activists" ("sin militancia política").

[12] See also Secretaria General de Gobierno de Chile 1991: Vol. II, 887, which gives a breakdown of victims according to occupation.

The regime sought to give formal legal cover to pursuit of this "enemy" by producing a constant stream of decree laws. Decree Laws Nos. 3 and 4, issued on September 11, 1973, and published on September 18,[13] declared the entire country to be in both a state of siege and a state of emergency. Decree Law No. 5, issued on September 12 and published on September 22, announced that the state of siege should be understood as a state of war, calling for the application of harsher penalties for certain political crimes. Moreover, it revised the Law of Internal State Security to establish the jurisdiction of military courts over violations of that law during wartime.[14] What this meant was that all those found guilty of the political crimes in question were to be considered traitors to the nation and sentenced accordingly (and oftentimes retroactively!) by courts whose members answered to the junta.[15] It was not until late 1974 that the state of war was pronounced officially over and not until 1978 that jurisdiction over political crimes was formally returned to ordinary courts (R. Garretón 1987: 36).

In the early months of the regime, the government issued several decree laws that would figure prominently in many rights cases brought before the courts. Decree Law No. 81, published on November 6, 1973, declared the government's power to expel citizens from the country. It required previous authorization for those exiled or expelled to re-enter the country, established punishment for clandestine entry, and gave jurisdiction for violations of the decree to military courts. On November 26, 1973, Decree Law No. 128 was published to clarify Decree Law No. 1. Decree Law No. 128 stated: "The Constituent Power and the Legislative Power are exercised by the governing junta through decree laws with the signature of all of its members and when these former deem it appropriate, with the signature of relevant cabinet ministers. The dispositions of the decree laws which modify the Constitution will form part of its text and should be considered incorporated therein." With respect to the judiciary, Decree Law No. 128 provided that the

[13] Because of the prominence of formalism in Chilean legal reasoning, the date on which any given law is published in the *Diario Oficial*, the government's official record, is of great significance for legal reasoning.

[14] Previously, such violations fell under the jurisdiction of an appellate court judge. See the text of the decree law in Frühling, Portales, and Varas 1982: 126–127.

[15] On the exercise and expansion of military justice under the Pinochet regime more generally, see Organization of American States 1985: 175–192; López Dawson 1995a; Pereira 2005: Ch. 4.

courts would discharge their functions in the manner and with the independence and authority specified in the Constitution of 1925. The next year, after the Supreme Court signaled, in a constitutional review decision,[16] that it would not automatically consider decree laws to be tacit amendments to the Constitution, the military government issued Decree Law No. 788. This decree, published in December 1974, declared explicitly that any previous decree laws found to conflict with the 1925 Constitution were to be considered amendments thereof.[17] It also stated that future decree laws intended to modify the Constitution would be issued as express exercises of the junta's constituent power. This rendered it technically impossible to challenge in court the constitutionality of any early military regime legislation, and it meant that, until the enactment of Constitutional Act No. 3 in September 1976, "there was no specific instrument that embodied all the rights [allegedly] protected, since the exercise of those rights had to be adapted to the decrees of the political power" (Organization of American States 1985: 26).

Several other decree laws issued in 1974 had crucial consequences for future legal battles. On January 17, 1974, Decree Law No. 247 declared that to be legally binding in Chile, international treaties must not only be signed and ratified, but also officially promulgated and published in the *Diario Oficial*. Clearly responding to appeals by human rights lawyers to international human rights treaties, this decree had significant consequences for future judicial rulings. On June 18, 1974, the government published Decree Law No. 521, which created the DINA as a legal entity. This law was significant above all in that several of its provisions were explicitly "secret"; that is, they were published in a special issue of the *Diario Oficial* with (very) limited circulation.[18]

Decree Law No. 527, published June 26, 1974, reiterated the powers of the junta established in Decree Law No. 128 and specified the powers of the executive, exercised by the President of the Junta, General

---

[16] The case was *Federico Dunker Biggs*. For further discussion, see Barros 2002 at 96–97.

[17] Mónica Madariaga, who was Minister of Justice at the time, said the government privately called this the "Varsol law," referring to a household detergent (Constable and Valenzuela 1991: 128). Barros notes that Decree Law No. 788 "was totally at odds with the junta's stated commitment to restore the rule of law" (2002: 103).

[18] See "artículo único transitorio" in the text of the law, reproduced in Frühling, Portales, and Varas 1982: 100–101.

Pinochet.[19] It gave him the exclusive power to declare a state of siege in one or more parts of the country "in case of danger of foreign attack or of invasion" (Frühling, Portales, and Varas 1982: 88). Crucially, this decree added the words "danger of" and "or of invasion" to a clause that was otherwise taken *verbatim* from the 1925 Constitution. This allowed Pinochet to perpetuate indefinitely the state of siege, despite the relative peace and order that had been established within the country. Because of the vagueness of the terms "danger" and "invasion," Pinochet had only to assert that the communist threat was alive and well and clandestinely organized within Chile in order to have legal cover for the permanent restriction on civil and political rights. This prerogative was further codified and extended by Decree Law No. 640, of September 10, 1974, which specified different "regimes of emergency" in accordance with different types of threat to public order. Decree Law No. 640 also extended wartime procedure and punishment to all but one of the various degrees of the state of siege, meaning that military tribunals would continue to have jurisdiction over most civilian political crimes.[20]

It should be noted that, with these decree laws, the state of siege took on characteristics unprecedented in Chile. Based on Pinochet's subjective perception and exclusive interpretation of any threat to "national security," a state of siege could be declared for the entire national territory, for any length of time, and with no restrictions on its renewal. This, particularly in combination with the expanded internal powers of the military and the existence of the secret police, meant that basic civil and political rights such as the right to life and physical integrity, due process, the inviolability of the home, and the freedoms of expression, of the press, and of assembly, had very restricted formal legal protection and were routinely and grossly violated.[21]

As criticisms from the human rights community, both domestic and international, mounted,[22] the military pronounced, in September 1976,

---

[19] The decree pronounced Pinochet the "Supreme Chief of the Nation." Six months later, he forced the junta to sign another decree that officially made him President of the Republic.

[20] From an analysis by the staff of the *Vicaría de la Solidaridad*, on file at the Fundación de Documentación y Archivo de la Vicaría de la Solidaridad (FDAVS). See also Organization of American States 1985: 29–30.

[21] From the *Vicaría* analysis mentioned in the previous note.

[22] The DINA made 1976 a particularly bad public relations year for the regime. In mid-July, Spanish diplomat Carmelo Soria was found dead inside his car in Santiago's Mapocho River. The government claimed the ECLA employee had had an accident

four "Constitutional Acts" designed to demonstrate the regime's alleged commitment to the rule of law, democracy, and "Christian humanism." Constitutional Act No. One was devoted to the Council of State, a high-level advisory body composed of former presidents of the Republic and prominent persons appointed by Pinochet.[23] The Council's main role was to review and approve the new Constitution then being drafted. Act No. Two repealed Chapter I of the 1925 Constitution and replaced it with the structure of the state which had been established by decree laws after the coup. Act No. Three listed and explained the rights of the human person, very similar to those found in the 1925 Constitution, and asserted that these are prior to the rights of the state. However, it also incorporated a set of "constitutional duties," including the duty to "help preserve national security" and the duty to "obey the orders that are given by the constituted authorities, in accordance with their attributions."

In addition to stipulating the remedy of *amparo* (habeas corpus), Constitutional Act No. Three also established a new mechanism for the judicial defense of civil and political rights: the writ of protection (*recurso de protección*). A petition for a writ of protection could be filed in an appellate court by any individual or group which believed that a third party, public or private, had violated one or more of their civil or political rights. It required that the court issue a ruling within forty-eight hours, and allowed for an appeal to the Supreme Court. As one analyst observes, this new writ effectively expanded the judiciary's power of constitutional review, for it explicitly authorized judges to "assume

---

and driven himself into the river, but evidence of foul play was abundant. In early August, two well-known Christian Democratic human rights lawyers were kidnapped and expelled from the country. The details that these distinguished individuals offered of the experience in their legal battle to return to Chile made an important impression on public opinion. Perhaps most dramatic, however, was the assassination of Allende's Defense Minister, Orlando Letelier, carried out in Washington, DC, on September 21, 1976. A car bomb planted by DINA agents killed both Letelier and a young colleague, Ronni Moffitt, and significantly strained Chile's relations with the U.S. government.

[23] Former Presidents Jorge Alessandri and Gabriel González Videla both participated in the Council of State, but Eduardo Frei Montalva refused. Alessandri resigned from the Council after Pinochet and his advisors reversed many of the changes he and the other Council members had made to the draft of the 1980 Constitution. However, he did not make the reasons for his resignation public at the time, nor did he openly oppose the Constitution in the 1980 plebiscite. See Cavallo, Salazar and Sepúlveda 1997.

an active, dynamic, creative and imaginative role," and "adopt all the provisions [they] deem necessary to re-establish the rule of law (*el imperio de Derecho*), ensuring proper protection to the affected party" (Soto 1986).

It should be noted, however, that Constitutional Act No. Four placed additional and significant formal limitations on the rights and remedies so augustly proclaimed in Act No. Three. It established four new classes of states of emergency and catalogued the restrictions that the president could place on citizens' rights during such states. In addition, Article 6 empowered the president to suspend the right to personal freedom and the right of assembly, and to restrict freedom of opinion and of association when "he deems it essential for preventing subversion." Article 13 extended the period during which a person could be detained without being brought before a court to ten days. And Article 14 stated that both the *recurso de amparo* and the *recurso de protección* "will only be viable [in states of emergency] insofar as they are compatible with the legal requirements of such situations" (Organization of American States 1985: 26–31).[24]

Moreover, within months of the publication of the Constitutional Acts, the government issued Decree Law No. 1,684, declaring unequivocally that the *recurso de protección* was inadmissible (*improcedente*), under any circumstances, during a state of emergency. The decree, issued "without consulting the Council of State, the Constitutional Commission, or the legislative committees of the junta" (Valenzuela 1995: 48), was announced on the same day (January 28, 1977) that the government forcibly shut down the Christian Democratic–owned Radio Balmaceda. The shutdown came as part of the move to repress the Christian Democratic Party and eliminate the possibility that the future of the regime would be controlled by the political Center. On its heels came Decree Law No. 1,967, of March 11, 1977, which dissolved all those parties that had previously only been "in recess" (Constable and Valenzuela 1991: 129; Cavallo, Salazar, and Sepúlveda 1997: 159–160).[25]

---

[24] For one analyst, the four Acts read together "like a tongue-in-cheek Orwellian invention" (Loveman 1988: 322).

[25] Note that all Marxist parties or movements were banned by Decree Law No. 77, of October 13, 1973, whereas Decree Law No. 78, issued four days later, declared all other parties or movements in recess.

In December 1977, the U.N. General Assembly, for the fourth time in as many years, condemned Chile for human rights abuses.[26] Pinochet was furious, and in reaction, decided to call a plebiscite on his rule. Preparation for the "National Consultation" was rushed and lacking in even the most basic legal foundation.[27] There were no voter registration rolls, no electoral court, and virtually no opposition press coverage. The vote was held "under the state of siege, without organized political parties, [and] with severe restrictions on the right to assembly and the freedom of information" (Organization of American States 1985: 269). Asked whether they "support President Pinochet in his defense of the dignity of Chile" and the construction of a new institutional order, voters could check a Chilean flag to vote "yes" or a black box to vote "no." Blank ballots were counted as "yes," and Pinochet declared victory with an alleged 75 percent of the vote (Organization of American States 1985; Constable and Valenzuela 1991; Angell 1993). Buoyed by his victory, Pinochet proceeded to detain and then internally banish a series of Christian Democratic figures who had publicly denounced the "consultation" (Badilla 1990a: 32).

Meanwhile, however, the United States had stepped up pressure on the regime to investigate the army's alleged involvement in the Washington, DC, murder (by car bombing) of Orlando Letelier.[28] On April 8, 1978, the government acceded to the United States' extradition request for the civilian DINA agent, Michael Vernon Townley, and on April 17, after a brief but tenacious resistance, agent Townley confessed his participation in the crime to U.S. prosecutors, claiming that he had acted on the orders of his superiors in the DINA, who themselves answered directly to Pinochet.[29]

In the midst of this crisis, Pinochet named a trusted aide, Sergio Fernández, to the Ministry of the Interior. Just one week later, Minister Fernández oversaw the promulgation of the now infamous amnesty law. Decree Law No. 2,191, of April 19, 1978, offered an official amnesty

---

[26] The vote in 1977, very similar to previous years, was ninety-six to fourteen, with twenty-five abstentions.

[27] Indeed, this is why, at the advice of Jaime Guzmán, the general called the referendum a "consultation," which was more informal and thus did not have to meet the same legal standards as a "plebiscite." (Organization of American States 1985: 269; Cavallo, Salazar, and Sepúlveda 1997: 181).

[28] On the Letelier assassination, see Matus and Artaza 1996.

[29] "La Farsa de la Justicia," *ANALISIS*, extraordinary edition, September 1991, 26.

for all "authors, accomplices, or concealers" of politically connected crimes committed between September 11, 1973, and March 10, 1978.[30] Whereas the law was clearly designed to benefit military and police officials who had perpetrated innumerable human rights abuses since the coup, and to reassure them in the wake of the anxiety caused by the active American investigation of the Letelier case, it also offered amnesty to several hundred leftist prisoners.[31] The government thus presented the amnesty law as a gesture of humanitarian goodwill designed to promote national reconciliation.[32]

THE JUDICIAL RESPONSE TO MILITARY LAW AND POLICY (1973–1980)

As the preceding account demonstrates, Chile's military government was keenly attentive to questions of formal legality, seeking to portray itself, however disingenuously, as committed to the rule of law. To bolster this image, of course, the junta needed the support of the judiciary, whose dignity and independence it pledged to (and did, at least formally) respect. To the dismay of democracy and human rights supporters, the judges gave them exactly what they were looking for.

Immediately following the coup, the President of the Supreme Court, Enrique Urrutia Manzano, expressed, in the name of Chile's administration of justice, his "most intimate satisfaction" with the new government's pledge to respect and enforce the decisions of the judiciary. The entire Court, transported to the court building in a military bus, ratified this statement (*El Mercurio*, September 13, 1973). On September 18, one week following the coup, the Supreme Court justices were among a handful of high-ranking state officials to attend a religious ceremony to bless the new government (Cavallo, Salazar, and Sepúlveda 1997: 19). On September 25, the members of the junta paid a special visit to the Supreme Court, during which the President of the Court hailed them for "all of their historic and juridic value," claiming that the activities

---

[30] Pinochet had declared an end to the state of siege on March 10, 1978. However, it had been immediately replaced with a state of emergency, which offered little change in the formal protection of civil and political rights.

[31] On release, however, most of these were sent directly into exile (Constable and Valenzuela 1991: 130).

[32] Note that eight months earlier, the DINA had been dissolved and replaced by the CNI, marking the government's effort to reign in the activities of the secret police forces.

of the justice system would now be "not only respected, but dignified." With no reference to the alleged state of war or state of siege which had been declared, he wished the *de facto* authorities, "the best of success in your actions, for the well-being of our fellow citizens and for the country as a whole" (R. Garretón n.d.: 13).

These were the first of many acts through which the judiciary offered public legitimation of the military regime and influenced the public's perception of the entire judiciary as obsequious to the will of the junta.[33] Moreover, as the atrocities of the security forces became known and the willingness of the Pinochet government to twist, evade, or simply rewrite the law to its benefit became obvious, the judiciary's acceptance, passive or active, of the regime's illegalities stood in stark contrast to the strong and vocal stance it had taken against the Allende government.

The following sections summarize judicial performance in four areas central to the rule of law and rights protection: habeas corpus, or as it is known in Chile, *amparo*; Supreme Court review of military court decisions; constitutional review of laws (*inaplicabilidad por inconstitucionalidad*); and the constitutional review mechanism introduced by the military government in 1976 with the explicit goal of protecting certain rights, the *recurso de protección*.

Habeas Corpus (*Amparo*)

Perhaps the most notorious category of judicial decisions under Pinochet is that of habeas corpus, or as it is known in Chile, *amparo*. As Barros (2002: 141) notes, "Personal liberty was sacrosanct in the many texts that form Chile's constitutional and legal tradition – under no circumstance could an individual be deprived of his or her freedom without legal justification." On coming to power, the junta did nothing formally to alter these norms. Yet, according to a 1985 report of the Inter-American Commission of Human Rights, Chilean courts accepted only ten of the fifty-four hundred *recursos de amparo* filed by human rights lawyers between 1973 and 1983 (Constable and Valenzuela 1991: 122). In the remaining seven years of the military regime, only twenty more such *recursos* prospered, leaving the total at thirty out of almost nine thousand (Rigby 2001: 92, n. 34). This means that the courts only

---

[33] Another important moment came on June 27, 1974, when Urrutia Manzano participated in the stealthily planned ceremony to declare Pinochet "Supreme Chief of the Nation." Urrutia himself placed the presidential sash on the general (Cavallo, Salazar, and Sepúlveda 1997: 31–32).

Table 4.1. Published decisions in *amparo* cases,
1973–1980

	Apellate court	Supreme court
Amparo Granted	3	0
Amparo Denied	15	19

challenged the legality of the military regime's detentions in *two or three tenths of a percent* of cases.

My own sample, consisting of published decisions in *amparo* cases from the 1973–1980 period, looks good by comparison: in three of thirty-seven total decisions (or 8 percent), *amparo* was granted (see Table 4.1). However, in all three cases, the decision was subsequently overturned by the Supreme Court, which itself accepted zero such petitions. Therefore, no citizen secured even formal judicial protection.[34]

The pattern of behavior in habeas corpus decisions was reminiscent of that of the 1930s and 1940s discussed in Chapter 2. As in that earlier period, the courts took extraordinarily long to process *amparo* petitions, in many cases a month or more, despite the fact that they were legally obligated to rule on them within twenty-four hours.[35] In some cases, the Supreme Court added formalistic impediments to filing such writs, although the law designed the writ to be totally informal and easy to file.[36] In most cases, the courts didn't challenge the legality of detention orders issued under the state of exception, nor did judges use their powers to check that detainees were being treated lawfully, either by visiting detention centers or demanding that individual detainees be brought before the court.[37] Complaints of torture thus went ignored or

[34] I fully acknowledge the probable ineffectiveness of the *amparo* under a police state (Barros 2002), but the point is that the judiciary never even attempted to defend the most basic legal principles and procedures.

[35] In mid-1980, when human rights lawyers at the *Vicaría de la Solidaridad* asked the Supreme Court to instruct appellate courts to rule on writs of habeas corpus within twenty-four hours, as mandated by law, the Court sent a memo asking that they do so only "insofar as the relevant paperwork is in order and as the evidence permits." In other words, "the highest court in the land gave express authorization to the inferior courts to disregard the express text of the law" (R. Garretón 1989: 20).

[36] See, for example, *Hernán Santos Pérez*, 28 April, 1978; *Fallos del Mes* No. 234: 87–88.

[37] See, for example, *Luis Alejandro Fuentes Díaz*, April 8, 1975, *Fallos del Mes* No. 197: 31, or *Luis Corvalán Lepe*, July 30, 1974, *Fallos del Mes* No. 188: 132.

uninvestigated, and confessions offered under torture were accepted. Moreover, if no decree ordering an individual's arrest could be proven to have been issued, judges ruled that the person must not have been detained, and denied *amparo* on the grounds that the writ had been filed on insufficient evidence or with the intention of causing concern or alarm (Amnesty International 1986). In other words, from the beginning, the decisions of the high courts, and especially the Supreme Court, reflected a willingness "not simply to accept the government's version of things, but to go out of their way to eliminate all possibility of studying the merit of the cases and [instead] to justify the government" (Interview HRL96–8, October 17, 1996, 16:00).

On September 14, 1973, for example, a former official of the Frei government, Bernardo Leighton, submitted a *recurso de amparo* by telephone for seven Popular Unity leaders being held "in some regiment." The police claimed the individuals in question were not in their custody, and that they didn't have contact with the Ministry of Interior. Nonetheless, the Santiago Appeals Court quickly rejected the writ, arguing that since the country was clearly under a state of siege, the executive could legally detain people in places other than jails for common criminals.[38] This decision clearly overlooked several legal facts. First, Article 72 of the 1925 Constitution specified that a declaration of state of siege can only be made by the president in cases of external attack, or by Congress in cases of internal disturbance, and that even during a state of siege the constitutional rights of public officials must be maintained.[39] Moreover, the decree declaring the state of siege had not yet been published in the *Diario Oficial*, meaning that technically it was not yet law when the decision was issued.[40] Worst of all, the court issued the decision without even having seen an arrest warrant, thereby signalling that in a state of siege anybody could be arrested at any time by any official for any reason (R. Garretón 1987: 32–33). Despite all of

---

[38] *ANALISIS*, special edition, November 1982, 60.

[39] These rights were laid out in Article 33 of the 1925 Constitution: "No Deputy or Senator from the day of his election can be indicted, prosecuted, or arrested, except in a case *in flagrante delicto*, unless the Court of Appeals of the respective jurisdiction, in open session, has previously authorized the indictment by declaring that there exist grounds for prosecution by declaring that there exist grounds for prosecution. From this decision an appeal may be taken to the Supreme Court."

[40] In addition, the Court mistakenly cited Decree Law No. 1 rather than Decree Law No. 3 in the decision, the latter of which actually declared the state of siege.

this, the Supreme Court confirmed the decision and set a crucial and disheartening precedent for the months and years to follow.

Even the kidnapping and forced exile of two prominent centrist lawyers, Jaime Castillo and Eugenio Velasco, around which a large percentage of the legal community rallied, seemed not to sway judicial authorities. On August 6, 1976, Castillo and Velasco were seized from their workplaces by DINA operatives – Velasco in the court building itself. The agents transported them directly to the airport, from which they were flown immediately to Buenos Aires. That same day, lawyers filed *recursos de amparo* on their behalf, and the Santiago Appeals Court accepted a petition requesting that their expulsion be suspended until the *recursos* had been resolved. By that time, however, Castillo and Velasco had already arrived in Argentina.

Ten days later, the Santiago Appeals Court heard arguments from both the lawyers, represented by (future President) Patricio Aylwin and Juan Agustín Figueroa, and from the government, represented by (future Minister of Justice) Hugo Rosende. The following day, the court rejected the writs by a vote of two to one.[41] As Velasco himself explains, "the heart of their reasoning [was] that Decree Law 81 [of 1973], which authorized the junta to expel Chileans, didn't require that any explanation or justification be given regarding why the persons affected by the measure 'constitute a danger for national security'" (Velasco 1986: 136). The petitioners' lawyers had argued that according to both the Constitution and the International Covenant on Civil and Political Rights, to which Chile was a signatory, the executive did not have the right to expel Chileans from the country, even under a state of siege.[42] Moreover, even if Decree Law No. 81 was accepted as legitimate, the government had not abided by its requisites: Castillo and Velasco had not been presented with a decree signed by the Minister of the Interior offering a justification for their expulsion (*un decreto fundado*), nor had they been allowed to "choose freely their country of destination."[43] The majority appeals court decision rejected both sets of arguments,

[41] Judges Eduardo Araya and Sergio Dunlop argued the expulsion was legal and legitimate. Judge Rubén Galecio dissented.

[42] Note that having been ratified by thirty-five countries, the Covenant had become binding as of March 23, 1976.

[43] These arguments were accepted and strongly asserted in the dissent of Rubén Galecio Gómez.

recognizing Decree Law No. 788 over and above the Constitution and any international treaty, and asserting, in traditional fashion, that judges did not have the right to evaluate or question the reasoning of the executive for its actions under a state of siege.[44]

The case was immediately appealed to the Supreme Court, which subsequently received a number of letters: one signed by ten respected law professors from a variety of political backgrounds, another signed by former President Eduardo Frei Montalva and three hundred other leading intellectuals and former political leaders, and a third from the nation's religious leaders.[45] Despite this lobbying, on August 25, 1976, the Court upheld the appeals court decision,[46] arguing, first, that the International Covenant on Civil and Political Rights couldn't apply because it had never been promulgated and published in the *Diario Oficial*, as required by Decree Law No. 247 of January 17, 1974.[47] Second, the Court asserted that it did, in fact, have the right to "ponder the justification given for the decree of expulsion," since this was "indispensable to resolving the acceptability of a petition for habeas corpus"; however, without further explanation, it stated that "this had been done."[48] This latter argument outraged the two exiles and the legal community supporting them, for it invoked the need for scrutinizing the rationality of the expulsions, yet accepted the expulsions on the basis of no scrutiny whatsoever (Velasco 1986: 170–171). The Court seemed simply to have accepted the government's argument that the reasons behind the expulsions were a matter of national security, and that a ruling in favor of Castillo and Velasco "could create problems of public order" (Cavallo, Salazar, and Sepúlveda 1997: 113). Indeed, the president of the Supreme Court, José María Eyzaguirre, stated,

---

[44] The full text of the decision was reprinted in the monthly report of the *Vicaría de la Solidaridad* for July 1976, on file at the FDAVS.

[45] The public statement of the religious leaders outraged the editors of the newspapers supporting the regime. Both *El Mercurio* and *La Segunda* denounced the illegitimate meddling of the ecclesiasts in the judicial process (Velasco 1986: 148–149).

[46] The case was decided unanimously by Justices Eyzaguirre, Erbetta, Correa, Retamal, and Pomés.

[47] Ever trying to improve his image abroad, Pinochet promulgated the treaty on November 30, 1976, via Decree Law No. 778 but, crucially, did *not* have the decree law published in the *Diario Oficial*.

[48] See the monthly report of the *Vicaría de la Solidaridad* for August 1976, on file at the FDAVS. The decision is also discussed in Detzner 1988 and Velasco 1986.

"I don't believe Velasco is a terrorist, but he is acting against other legal dispositions," such as the "political recess."[49]

Review of Military Court Decisions

The willingness of the Supreme Court to abandon established legal principles and procedures and, thereby, extend carte blanche to the military's "war on terror," was also evident in its abdication of review power over the decisions of military tribunals. Its first major decision in this regard was issued soon after the coup, in a *recurso de queja* brought against the members of a Valparaíso war tribunal for for their life sentence against an alleged leftist spy.[50] On November 13, 1973, the Court not only refused the appeal but also renounced altogether its power to review the decisions of wartime military courts. The decision argued that because Decree Law Nos. 3 and 5 had declared the country to be in a state of war, the Military Code of Justice was in effect and war tribunals were in operation. It was the general in charge of the territory in question who had the exclusive power to approve, revoke, or modify the decisions of the wartime tribunals and discipline its members. The Court claimed that, "for obvious reasons," it could not exercise jurisdictional power over the military line of command, and thus could not intervene to alter the decision.[51]

The Supreme Court handed down this ruling despite the fact that it had traditionally exercised – and, indeed, jealously demanded – supervision over all of the nation's tribunals, including wartime military tribunals.[52] In 1882, during the War of the Pacific, for example, the Supreme Court had annulled a sentence handed down by the General in Chief of the Chilean Occupying Army in Peru (Tavolari 1995: 79).[53] This power was so widely accepted that "even some high officials

[49] See monthly report of the *Vicaría de la Solidaridad* for August 1976, on file at the FDAVS.
[50] The defendant was Juan Fernando Silva Riveros.
[51] See *Fallos del Mes* No. 180: 222–225. The decision was rendered by the first chamber of the Supreme Court, whose members were Eduardo Ortiz, Rafael Retamal, Luis Maldonado, Victor M. Rivas, Enrique Munita, and Osvaldo Salas.
[52] This power was stipulated in Article 86 of the 1925 Constitution, as well as in Article 53 and Article 98, No. 5 of the Judicial Code.
[53] As law professor Daniel Schweitzer stated, "The interpretation and application that [legal] doctrine and jurisprudence, especially that of the Supreme Court, had always given such precepts was, until November of 1973, invariable, both before and after the writing of the *Ley Orgánica* [*de Tribunales*]; before and after the constitutional

of the armed forces were alarmed" by the Court's decision to renounce it (Velasco 1986: 156).

The Court stuck firmly to its position, however, reiterating it in the months and years that followed. In a nearly identical case brought by Sergio Roubillard González against the members of the Arica war tribunal in August 1974, a completely different set of justices used identical reasoning to conclude again that the Supreme Court lacked jurisdiction over wartime tribunals.[54] This time, however, there was one dissent, that of future Supreme Court president, José Maria Eyzaguirre. Eyzaguirre argued that Article 74 of the Military Justice Code, which grants broad powers to the commander-in-chief for the full exercise of military jurisdiction, cannot take precedence over the Constitution. The Constitution, he reminded his colleagues, states that the Supreme Court has review power over all the courts of the country, "without any differentiation or exception," and "in case of a contradiction between the [Military Justice Code and the Constitution], this Court must apply [the latter]."[55]

Unfortunately, Eyzaguirre was alone in his legal interpretation,[56] and the result was that several thousand Chileans were subjected to trial by tribunals whose judges "often had no legal training and who were mid-level officials, filled with hatred and with the desire to demonstrate their 'toughness' in order to earn merit in the eyes of the junta" (Velasco 1986: 156).[57] Between 1973 and 1976, approximately two hundred individuals were sentenced to death and executed, and thousands of others received harsh, disproportionate prison sentences (Luque 1984: 26–29; see also Ministerio Secretaría General de Gobierno de Chile 1991: Vol. I, Ch. 3; Pereira 2005). Long after the state of war was formally declared to have ended, the concepts of "potential states of war" and of the "internal enemy" persisted in the doctrine of National Security,

reforms of 1874; under the 1833 Constitution as well as under the 1925 Constitution . . ." (1975: 6).

[54] *Sergio Roubillard González (queja)*, August 21, 1974, *Fallos del Mes* No. 189: 156–157.

[55] Eyzaguirre was clearly aware of the legal aberrations occurring in the war tribunals, for later, in session 251 of the Commission in charge of drafting the new (1980) constitution (October 19, 1976), he admitted that the military courts had handed down some "dreadful" decisions (Tavolari 1995: 79).

[56] In October 1977, Rafael Retamal reversed his 1973 position and dissented, but also was alone in doing so.

[57] Pereira reports that the average acquittal rate in Chile's military courts was only 12.42 percent (2005: 267).

which was incorporated into the 1980 Constitution. Claiming what was among the broadest jurisdiction in the world, Chile's military justice system tried approximately four civilians for every military defendant, without basic due process (Verdugo 1990; see also López 1995a; Pereira 2005). Moreover, the military courts shielded members of the armed forces and their civilian collaborators from prosecution. As Barros notes, "Montesquieu's description of justice in despotic regimes – 'the prince himself can judge' – applies to the war tribunals, since justice was being dispensed by officers hierarchically subordinate to the commanders in chief, who were creating the law" (2002: 138). The Supreme Court's abdication of its jurisdiction over appeals of decisions by wartime tribunals, and its willingness to hand cases over to the military justice system on demand, thus permitted, under a patina of formal legality, a practice that was fundamentally at odds with even the most basic definition of the rule of law.

Constitutional Review (Inaplicabilidad por Inconstitucionalidad)

As noted earlier, on coming to power, the junta left the 1925 Constitution in place, leaving it theoretically possible for citizens to challenge in court the constitutionality of military government policies. In some areas of the law, the Supreme Court did stand by the Constitution, at least early on.[58] Although the junta had established, in Decree Law No. 128, that it had both legislative and constituent powers, the government did not always make clear when it was exercising which of these powers. In several rent and labor law cases, the Supreme Court thus asserted its continued acceptance of the 1925 Constitution as a controlling document, and its own power to declare part or all of a decree law unconstitutional (Precht 1987).[59]

The Court never came close to doing this in more politically sensitive cases, however. In my sample from the 1973–1980 period, the justices rejected the petition for inconstitucionalidad in twenty-nine of thirty-two instances, and the three accepted were not particularly sensitive

---

[58] This made the judges more vulnerable to critique. As one analyst argues, if the Court was willing and able to stand up in defense of judicial review via the recurso de inaplicabilidad, "what reason would there be for not doing the same with the writ of habeas corpus, which has such an honorable and long tradition and is as important and essential, if not more so, than the former" (Amunátegui 1989: 11)?

[59] See, for example, the decision of July 24, 1974, in the case of Federico Dunker Biggs, Fallos del Mes No. 188: 118–121.

cases. Despite the fact that human rights lawyers constantly appealed to the Constitution in their defense of regime victims, the justices never embraced these ready examples of more liberal reasoning. Indeed, in December 1974, when the junta issued Decree Law No. 788, stating that all previous decree laws in contradiction with the Constitution should be considered modifications thereof, the Court quickly accepted the proposition.[60] In subsequent *recursos de inaplicabilidad* and in other cases in which arguments were presented regarding the unconstitutionality of early decree laws, the Court stated simply that any decree law issued between September 11, 1973, and the day that Decree Law No. 788 was issued could not conflict with the 1925 Constitution, as "it must be necessarily accepted that [these laws] have had and have the quality of tacit and partial modifications" to the Constitution.[61] That Decree Law No. 788 itself made a mockery of the Constitution, judicial review, and the rule of law seemed either to elude or simply not to bother the justices.[62]

Later, when the regime issued the four Constitutional Acts to replace the 1925 Constitution, the justices waffled on the effects of Decree Law No. 788. When lawyers attempted to argue that the provisions in Decree Law Nos. 81 and 604 (regarding expulsion) were in conflict with the protections offered by Constitutional Act No. Three and should be declared unconstitutional, the Supreme Court declared that Decree Law Nos. 81 and 604 had acquired constitutional rank via Decree Law No. 788 and thus could only complement and not conflict with other constitutional precepts. When defense lawyers accepted that Decree Law Nos. 81 and 604 had, by means of Decree Law No. 788, modified the 1925 Constitution, and argued that they should thus be considered

---

[60] Decree Law No. 788 was issued while a *recurso de inaplicabilidad* filed by former Senator Renán Fuentealba was pending before the Supreme Court. Fuentealba's lawyers were arguing that his expulsion, based on Decree Law No. 81, was unconstitutional.

[61] *Luis Corvalán Lepe* (*amparo*), *Fallos del Mes* No. 203: 202–205. See also *Alfonso Salvat M.* (*inaplicabilidad*), January 8, 1975, *Fallos del Mes* No. 194: 300–303, where sixteen similar decisions are also listed, and *Luis Fernández Fernández* (*inaplicabilidad*), March 11, 1977, *Fallos del Mes* No. 220: 1–5.

[62] Note that subsequent to the publication of the four "Constitutional Acts" in September 1976, the Court began deferring many rulings on the constitutionality of laws issued previous to the Acts to lower courts, arguing that such cases were simply a matter of the supercession or survival of laws. See, for example, *Empresa Nacional de Electricidad S.A.* (*inaplicabilidad*), June 9, 1978, *Fallos del Mes* No. 235: 116–124. See also Precht 1987.

to have been tacitly repealed and replaced by the Constitutional Acts, the Court claimed that Decree Law No. 81 and 604 had *not* in fact acquired constitutional rank and were thus simply laws which helped to clarify the provisions of the Constitutional Acts.[63] The justices seemed determined to give the military government a constitutional blessing to defend "national security."

It should be noted, however, that in doing so, the Court was simply continuing a longstanding pattern in inapplicability rulings, one that predated the authoritarian regime (see Couso 2002: 177). As discussed in Chapter 2, although the 1925 Constitution gave the judiciary specific new powers to check the excesses of the other branches, judges chose only to assert this power in cases related to property rights. In more traditional "public law" cases, the Courts tended to circumscribe their own authority and defer to the executive. "Both before and after the coup, ... the Supreme Court's review did not uphold the spirit, values, nor principles of the constitution" (Barros 2002: 112).

The New Constitutional Review Mechanism: *Recurso de Protección*

In the late 1970s, the courts were presented with some of the first *recursos de protección*, which had been created by the Constitutional Acts of September 1976. As noted earlier, the *recurso de protección* offered the courts a new and explicit means to defend individual rights. However, Decree Law No. 1,684, published on January 31, 1977, had declared the writ inadmissible (*improcedente*) during states of emergency. Sometimes the courts interpreted Decree Law No. 1,684 sweepingly, arguing that it precluded them from ruling on the substance of any petitions for writs of protection. In these instances they rejected the petitions outright.[64]

---

[63] See, for example, *María Eugenia Soto Verscheure y otro* (*amparo*), March 20, 1980, *RDJ* 77 (1980) 2.4:37–38; *David Benavente G.* (*amparo*), July 8, 1980, *Fallos del Mes* No. 260: 208–209; *Silvia Costa Espinoza* (*amparo*), July 8, 1980, *Fallos del Mes* No. 260: 206–208; *José Ormeño V.* (*amparo*), August 5, 1980, *Fallos del Mes* No. 261: 254–257; *Rosaura Mendoza C.* (*amparo*), December 31, 1980, *Fallos del Mes* No. 265: 445–448; *Andrés Zaldívar Larraín* (*amparo*), January 26, 1981, *Fallos del Mes* No. 266: 499–505.

[64] See, for example, *José Mora Escalona* (*protección*), June 1, 1977, *Fallos del Mes* No. 223: 122–123, *Ricardo Cifuentes Iturra* (*protección*), September 8, 1977, *Fallos del Mes* No. 226: 240–241, *Ormeño e hijos Ltda.* (*protección*), March 10, 1980, *RDJ* 77 (1980) 2.1: 15–16, all Supreme Court decisions; and *Fernando Palma Montenegro*

Other times, though, the courts argued that Decree Law No. 1,684 only applied to writs involving the rights which were explicitly subject to restrictions under states of emergency (speech, association, assembly, etc.); thus, petitions filed to protect the right to life or the right to property, for example, were admissible even under a state of emergency and had to be ruled on on their merits.[65]

Unfortunately, this more liberal interpretation did not produce greater judicial protection for regime opponents. In the case of *José Miguel Benado Medwinsky*, for example, the petitioner filed a *recurso de protección* to "restore the rule of law" and have the courts send help to "save the life" of a CNI prisoner who claimed he was being tortured.[66] In the first instance, the Santiago Appeals Court (Judges Cereceda, Ossa, and Alvarez) rejected the petition on grounds that it was inadmissible in a state of emergency. In an unusual twist, the Supreme Court (Justices Retamal, Maldonado, Rivas, Correa, and Urrutia) reviewed the decision and remanded the case to the Appeals Court, arguing that although a *recurso de protección* could not be brought against an arrest under a state of exception, torture was not authorized by such an exception, and, hence, the Appeals Court was obliged to rule of the merits of the case. Rather than seize the opportunity to assert its authority in cases involving bodily integrity, the Appeals Court swiftly ended the matter by declaring that the petitioner had already attempted to get protection via the *recurso de amparo*, and was denied at both the appellate and Supreme Court levels; thus, there was nothing further to investigate.[67]

(*protección*), December 18, 1980, *RDJ* 77 (1980) 2.2: 138–140 (Santiago Appeals Court).

[65] See, for example, *Rubén Waisman Davidovich* (*protección*), July 10, 1980, *RDJ* 77 (1980) 2.2: 82–85; *José Miguel Benado Medwinsky* (*protección*), August 13, 1980, *RDJ* 77 (1980) 2.4: 124–126; *Aída del Carmen Cerro Saavedra* (*protección*) October 13, 1980, *RDJ* 77 (1980) 2.2: 178–186.

[66] September 12, 1980, *RDJ* 2.4: 180–184.

[67] A reverse process occurred in the case of *Emilio Filippi Murato y otros* (*protección*), October 17, 1980 (*RDJ* 77 (1980) 2.1: 131–135). In this case, the Supreme Court overruled the Santiago Appeals Court (Judges Libedinsky, Gálvez, and Faúndez), which had accepted a *recurso de protección* filed by an opposition press agency denied authorization for a new publication. The appellate judges argued that the military officer in charge of a territory under a state of emergency did not have the right to deny this authorization. The Supreme Court, however, contended that the Law of Internal State Security authorized military leaders to issue any orders deemed necessary to maintain public order, including limitation or suspension of the freedom of press.

High-Profile Public Law Cases

No analysis of the role of the judiciary in the authoritarian period would be complete without a discussion of some of the era's most high-profile cases, many of which carried over into the new democratic regime after 1990. It should be noted, however, both here and later in this chapter (1981–1990 section), that only some of these decisions were published in the country's jurisprudential journals. Therefore, the discussion of these cases is based primarily on information from the archives of the *Vicaría de la Solidaridad* (the human rights organization sponsored by the Catholic Church), press accounts, books published after 1990, and, where possible, the published decisions themselves. My objective in presenting these is twofold: to provide specific information on how the courts dealt with cases of which the mass public was very aware, and to introduce legal issues and debates that continued to be of central relevance in the postauthoritarian period.

At the end of 1978, the earth-shaking discovery of fifteen cadavers, apparently buried alive in an old mine oven at Lonquén, held promise that, at last, the Supreme Court might recognize and take action regarding the disappeared. On December 1, representatives from the *Vicaría de la Solidaridad* held a meeting with the new president of the Supreme Court, Israel Bórquez, who reacted by saying he was "tired of the fabrications of the Church." Despite his negative reaction, they finally persuaded him to raise the issue to the plenary of the Court. The report presented to the Court was carefully crafted so as to keep the exact location of the discovery secret. The greatest fear of human rights defenders was that the DINA would get access to the information and somehow destroy the evidence (Atria 1989 Vol. II: 153). The Court thus ordered the local judge, Juana Godoy, to confirm the report.

Five days later, after the bodies had been exhumed, the Court appointed Santiago Appeals Court judge Adolfo Bañados Cuadra as *ministro en visita* to the case. Bañados began his investigation immediately. Meanwhile, the Minister of the Interior declared that the government did not "discard the possibility that, in the struggle that inevitably had to be waged after September 11, 1973, in order to repel attacks by armed groups and destroy an organized subversion with the magnitude of a civil war, there could have been people of that side who died without being opportunely identified." In addition, *El Mercurio* editorialized that the public should understand clearly "the unfortunately inevitable character of past repressive acts" that were not crimes but were simply "the carrying out of military duties, in a period of commotion and conflict which was very much like a civil war." For his part, Bañados clarified that "there had not been a war in Chile" (P. Verdugo 1990: 154).

Within four months, Bañados had completed his investigation, con-cluding that the bodies corresponded to fifteen individuals from Isla de Maipo who had been murdered in a single act on or about October 7, 1973, and for which police Captain Lautaro Castro and his subordinates appeared responsible. Because uniformed personnel were thus clearly implicated in the crime, Bañados declared himself without jurisdiction and passed the case to the Santiago military court. In August 1979, in a statement explicitly recognizing the guilt of eight policemen in the crime, the military judge, general Enrique Morel Donoso, applied the 1978 Amnesty Law and definitively closed the case.

When the Martial Court upheld the definitive closure of the case, lawyers for the victim's families filed a *recurso de queja* with the Supreme Court, arguing that the provisions of the 1949 Geneva Conventions, to which Chile was a signatory, trumped the amnesty law and obligated the country to prosecute war crimes. Not only had the junta declared the country to be in a "state of war" between September 1973 and September 1974, but the Supreme Court itself had invoked this reason to abdicate jurisdiction over military tribunals. Thus, the acts committed by military officials during this period were subject to the regulations established by the Geneva Conventions, and the country had the duty to try and to punish those accused of violating these regulations.[68] Without entering into a substantive analysis of this argument, the Court rejected the *recurso de queja*.

The Supreme Court also overturned a decision of the Martial Court that had given a small victory to the relatives of Lonquén's victims. On his closure of the case, the first-instance military judge had ordered the removal of the victims' remains from the morgue where they were kept during the investigation. Even as family members were in church awaiting the release of the bodies for a funeral service, the judge had the remains whisked off and buried in a common grave in the Isla de Maipo cemetery. The families thus filed a disciplinary action (*recurso de queja*) against him, which was upheld by the Martial Court. On appeal, how-ever, the Supreme Court overturned the decision, arguing that legally the victims had not been individually identified for the purposes of

---

[68] See the monthly report of the *Vicaría de la Solidaridad* for November 1979, on file at the FDAVS and Pacheco 1985.

burial, and that thus no mistake or abuse had been committed by the military judge (Pacheco 1985; P. Verdugo 1990: 166–168).[69]

For the families of the victims of Lonquén, then, justice had not been served. However, Judge Bañados had proven that horrific crimes had been committed by military personnel and then covered up by the government, and, moreover, that with a decided effort, the truth about such crimes could be discovered. For many, he was thus the "exception that proved the rule" about judicial passivity toward and, hence, complicity in the brutality of military rule.

Bañados's conduct contrasted particularly strongly with that of the Supreme Court in another politically transcendent case decided in 1979: the request from the United States for the extradition of the suspects in the Letelier murder. As noted above, in early 1978 the United States had begun formal inquiries into the Letelier case in Chile. On determining that DINA agents were inculpated in the case, the appellate judge specially appointed to the case had declared a lack of jurisdiction and handed the investigation over to the military justice system. On August 1, 1978, however, on the basis of the confession offered by Michael Vernon Townley (mentioned earlier), the Federal Grand Jury of the District of Columbia was able to indict Townley, five Cubans, and three members of the Chilean army on charges of conspiracy and the first-degree murder of Orlando Letelier and Ronni Moffitt. On September 20, the United States thus formally requested the extradition of General Manuel Contreras, Colonel Pedro Espinoza, and Captain Armando Fernández Larios.

The first extradition decision was handled by Israel Bórquez, who assumed the presidency of the Supreme Court in March of 1979.[70] On May 14, 1979, insisting that the government had not dictated any part of the decision to him, he rejected the extradition request. His decision hinged on the claim that a confession obtained via a plea bargain in

---

[69] See also the monthly report of the *Vicaría de la Solidaridad* for November 1979, on file at the FDAVS.

[70] Soon after his appointment, Bórquez shocked the public by telling journalists that he was "fed up" with hearing about the disappeared (*"lo tenían curco"*). When asked to comment on the U.S. grand jury indictment of DINA officials for the murder of Orlando Letelier, he quipped that a bunch of "little colored people" had been selected for the grand jury, "perhaps to hide the blush" that the indictment should have provoked. The derogatory remark only served to exacerbate the friction between the U.S. and Chilean governments (Luque and Collyer 1986: 26).

the United States was not legally valid in Chile, that is, it did not meet the allegedly strict standards regarding confessions in Chilean law. As a result, there was not enough well-founded evidence to try Contreras, Espinoza, and Fernández in the United States.[71] Bórquez did, however, note the need for further investigation by the military courts into "some of the absurd or counter-factual contradictions" established during his investigation.

Four months later, on October 1, 1979, the first chamber of the Supreme Court upheld Bórquez's decision. Although the Court pointed to specific falsehoods in the testimonies of the suspects and other witnesses, as well as the "absurd" or "suspicious" quality of certain facts surrounding the case, the justices claimed that these could only constitute "suspicions" and not "well-founded evidence" of guilt.[72] Extradition was denied and the case was then passed to the military justice system under the name of "Documental falsehood and other." At the end of 1980, a military court quietly issued a decision absolving the military officers of all wrongdoing. The ruling was based almost entirely on the reasoning of the Supreme Court extradition decision.[73]

Summary, 1973–1980

During the first seven and a half years of authoritarian rule, then, the decisions of Chile's high courts overwhelmingly favored the perspectives and policies of the regime's leadership. Most decisions appeared to reflect an acceptance of the government's argument that concentrated, unchecked power was necessary to save Chile from the permanent communist threat. Gone were the concerns, articulated during the Frei-Allende years, for Chile's "crystalline tradition of the rule of law"[74] or "the primordial obligation that the judiciary has to render justice

---

[71] Bórquez reached this conclusion without any analysis of American law regarding plea bargains, and almost laughably, he issued this claim at a time when procedural violations were the norm in Chile. See Jaime Castillo's prologue in Matus and Artaza 1996: 5–6.

[72] Decisions reprinted in *RDJ* 76 (1979) 2.4: 356–437. See also Matus and Artaza 1996: 222, and note that the decision became the backbone of Contreras's defense in later years.

[73] Castillo's prologue in Matus and Artaza 1996 (1, 5–7) notes that one of the military judges in charge of the case for several years turned out to be a former member of the DINA and a close friend of General Contreras.

[74] *RDJ* 69 (197) 1: xv.

and to secure respect for [citizens'] rights."[75] Rather than take stands in defense of liberal principles, the courts "tied their own hands and submitted themselves to the sad 'rule of law show.' . . . Indeed, they adopted a political position of support for the dictatorship and against Chilean Law" (Velasco 1986: 159).

[75] *RDJ* 64 (1967) 2.1: 109.

PART II

1981–1990: THE "NEW INSTITUTIONAL ORDER"

THE MILITARY GOVERNMENT'S APPROACH TO LAW
(1981–1990)

In early August 1980, the military government announced the completion of the text of a new Constitution and issued Decree Law No. 3,465, convoking a national plebiscite to approve it.[76] Although Pinochet himself had argued, before the 1978 "consultation," that a formal plebiscite required electoral registers, this time he did not bother with such technicalities. All that would be required to vote was the presentation of one's identity card, even an expired one, and those who had voted would have their right thumb stamped with (allegedly) indelible ink. Once again, blank ballots would be counted as "yes" votes. Christian Democratic leaders struggled to organize a movement against the plebiscite, which they deemed blatantly illegal and even violent. However, they were unable to garner the support of the moderate Right, whose leaders feared what might happen should the "no" vote win. Moreover, opposition leaders found themselves prohibited, politically and/or economically, from presenting their arguments on television and on most radio stations (see Cavallo, Salazar, and Sepúlveda 1997: 322–332).

The plebiscite was thus characterized by fraud, intimidation, and the fear of expressing opposition. Official government statistics claimed 93.1 percent participation, with 67 percent in favor, 30 percent against, and the rest null or void. However, the opposition noted irregularities in the appointment and work of polling officers, and in the use of indelible ink to prevent voting fraud. They also established that in at least nine provinces, more than 100 percent of the population voted, and in some municipalities, the numbers voting increased by over 80 or 90 percent from 1978 (Organization of American States 1985: 271–272, 333–336; Angell 1993: 187). Despite these challenges, Pinochet trumpeted victory, and on March 11, 1981, the new Constitution became the law of the land.

---

[76] For a thoroughly researched discussion of the factors leading to the development of the 1980 Constitution, see Barros 2002.

The new charter was called the "Constitution of Liberty" after the book by neoliberal economist and philosopher Friedrich von Hayek. However, although the document enshrined "liberal" (here meaning free-market or libertarian) economic rights, it also sanctified antiliberal political and cultural values and practices. Not only did it "institutionalize antipolitics and anti-Marxism," but it also "explicitly emphasized the role of the patriarchal family as the basic unit of a hierarchically organized society" (Loveman 1988: 343). Like the Constitutional Acts before it, the 1980 Constitution combined noble clauses "guaranteeing" important civil liberties and protections with others that severely limited these protections. In the name of Christian values, patriotism, and "national security," the document strengthened or formalized the state's repressive powers. It was, as two analysts put it, "a masterpiece of legal obfuscation" (Constable and Valenzuela 1991: 137).

The 1980 Constitution was composed of 120 permanent articles and 34 "transitional" articles, which combined to exaggerate the powers of the president and to give extensive privileges to the armed forces. Until the new Congress was convened in 1990, the governing junta was to continue to function as the legislature. The junta retained the power to amend the constitution, but all amendments would have to be approved via plebiscite. Political parties remained banned until such time as the junta issued a new law regarding their organization.[77]

Although many of the Constitution's permanent articles were not to take effect until after 1989,[78] when elections would be held, some became effective immediately. Article 19 presented citizens' constitutional rights. The article's first section or "number" guaranteed the right to life and to physical and psychological integrity, and prohibited torture (*todo apremio ilegítimo*). Its number three promised the equal protection of the law and basic standards of due process. Number four protected the "private and public life and the honor of the individual and his family" against libel. Number five established the inviolability of the home.

---

[77] This summary of the 1980 Constitution is based on the *Constitución Política de la República de Chile, Texto aprobado por la H. Junta de Gobierno y que está sujeta a aprobación por plebiscito del día 11 de Septiembre de 1980.*

[78] Because some of these articles were the subject of reform in 1989, and because their impact came after the transition, the most significant of these will be discussed in the next chapter.

Number eight allowed for the state to restrict some rights in order to protect the environment and the individual's right to live in a clean environment. The right to property, detailed in number twenty-four, eliminated the state's promise, made via amendment to the 1925 Constitution under President Frei Montalva, "to seek a suitable distribution of property," and established strict regulations regarding regulatory takings. Article 20 allowed for the defense of all of these rights via the *recurso de protección*.

Although the basic civil and political rights of the 1925 Constitution were preserved, they were severely qualified by other provisions in the document. For example, Articles 23 and 57 together prohibited formal cooperation between parties and politicians, on the one hand, and labor and community organizations, on the other. Article 22 made it every citizens' duty to "honor the fatherland, defend its sovereignty, and contribute to the preservation of national security and the essential values of the Chilean tradition." And Articles 39–41 established four states of constitutional exception which authorized temporary suspension of basic civil and political rights.

Article 40 empowered the president to decree two different states of exception simultaneously. Article 41, No. 3 suspended the *recurso de amparo* and the *recurso de protección* against measures taken by virtue of the state of siege and the state of emergency, respectively. It also explicitly prohibited the courts from reviewing the criteria invoked by the executive to justify actions taken in virtue of the states of exception. Article 41, No. 7 stated that exile orders would remain in force even after the expiration of the state of exception under which they were issued, and stipulated that in order for an exiled individual to reenter the country, the government must issue a decree explicitly nullifying the previous prohibition on that individual's return.

Article 8 declared unconstitutional all parties and movements that propagate "doctrines which attack the family, support violence, or hold a concept of society or the state that is totalitarian or based on class struggle." Individuals accused of violating the article were to be judged by the (newly created) Constitutional Tribunal and, if found guilty, would be prohibited from all participation in public life for ten years. Article 9 established that any individual found guilty of terrorism would be banned from public life for at least fifteen years. Article 90 established that it was the mission of the armed forces to "guarantee the institutional order of the republic."

As just mentioned, the charter (re-)created the Constitutional Tribunal, a body separate from the ordinary judiciary, which had seen a previous, and inglorious, incarnation in the Allende years.[79] As in this previous period, the Tribunal was charged uniquely with abstract (and *a priori*) review of legislation; that is, at the official request of the president or of one-quarter of the members of either house of Congress (or under the military regime, the junta), the Tribunal was to review the constitutionality of draft laws, decrees with the force of law, ordinary decrees referred by the Comptroller General, constitutional reforms, and international treaties.[80] Article 81 provided that the Tribunal's members would consist of three acting Supreme Court justices, selected by the Court itself, and four lawyers, one appointed by the President of the Republic, one by an absolute majority of the Senate (before 1990, the junta), and two by the National Security Council. The constitution stipulated that the members appointed by the president and the junta/Senate must have served as *abogados integrantes* in the Supreme Court for at least three consecutive years. Members would serve eight-year, staggered terms. In sum, the majority of the Tribunal's members was appointed directly by the government, and did not enjoy the secure and lengthy tenure of ordinary judges. Although one might thus expect the Tribunal to be even more subservient to the government than the Supreme Court, the contrary proved true (as will be discussed later).

In the chapter on the judiciary, meanwhile, Article 79 explicitly excluded wartime military courts from Supreme Court supervision. This meant that the Supreme Court was now officially prohibited from reviewing decisions made in some of the most sensitive political cases. Otherwise, however, the Constitution greatly increased the formal

---

[79] A Constitutional Tribunal was first established in 1970 by President Frei Montalva. It reviewed seventeen cases in the two years it operated, most of which were decided unanimously in favor of the executive. It was abolished shortly after the military coup. Its brief and largely unremarkable history is well captured in Silva Cimma 1977.

[80] Note that the formal role of Chile's Constitutional Tribunal was similar to that of the French *Conseil Constitutionnel*, which is more of a legislative than a judicial body. These institutions exercise what is known as abstract and principal review, meaning the constitutionality of the law is considered in and of itself, apart from any concrete case, and the case is brought to the court uniquely for that purpose by a constitutionally designated party (see Cappelletti 1971).

power of the Supreme Court.[81] The Constitution provided that, beginning in 1989, the Court would elect three of the nine designated senators, two of these from their own ranks; three of the seven members of the Constitutional Tribunal, all from their own ranks; and four of the five members of the Electoral Tribunal, three from their own ranks. In addition, the president of the Supreme Court would hold one of the eight voting positions on the National Security Council (COSENA).[82] The COSENA, for its part, was empowered not only to issue resolutions regarding matters of internal and external state security but also to elect two members of the Constitutional Tribunal and four designated senators.

The Constitution also tightened the political control that higher court judges could exercise over their subordinates. Specfically, Article 75 gave the higher courts more discretion over promotions by practically eliminating the principle of seniority. Whereas under the 1925 Constitution, two nominees on the list of five presented to the executive had to be selected on the basis of seniority alone, the 1980 Constitution required that only one nominee be selected for seniority and stipulated that such an individual have an impeccable evaluation record. The Constitution applied the same rule to nomination lists for district level judgeships.

Added to all of these permanent provisions, the Constitution also included twenty-nine transitional articles to remain in effect for eight years, until the first elections were held. The most radical of these was transitional Article 24, which created a new type of state of emergency, totally the prerogative of the president. The article stated that if "acts of violence aimed at altering the public order are committed or if there is a danger that the public peace will be disturbed," the president could unilaterally declare a state of exception. In such cases, the president was permitted the following powers:

a.   to order the arrest of people for up to five days in their own homes or in other places which are not jails, and up to twenty days in cases of "terrorist acts";

[81] In addition to the formal powers listed here, it should be recalled that the introduction of the *recurso de protección* had given both the appellate courts and the Supreme Court a powerful new mechanism of judicial review.

[82] The other seven belong to the president of the republic, the president of the Senate, the heads of the three branches of the armed forces and the head of the national police, and the Comptroller General.

b. to restrict the right to assembly and the freedom of information, the latter only by withholding authorization for new publications;

c. to prohibit entrance into national territory or expel from the country those who propagate the doctrines prohibited by Article 8 of the Constitution, those who are affiliated with or have the reputation of being activists for such doctrines, and those who carry out acts contrary to the interests of Chile or constitute a danger for internal peace; and

d. to order the internal banishment of certain people to a domestic urban locality for up to three months.

The article also declared that "measures adopted by virtue of this disposition will not be subject to any remedy (*recurso*), except that of reconsideration by the authority that ordered them." In other words, the only remedy available to those who believed their rights had been violated in such cases was a request for grace from the president, and thus, on a strict formalist interpretation, the right to habeas corpus was "effectively abolished" (Valenzuela 1995: 52).

From March 11, 1981, forward, Pinochet kept the country perpetually under both a state of emergency (Articles 39–41) and a state of danger (transitory Article 24). He also declared a state of siege twice, once during the popular protests in late 1984 and once after the attempt on his life in September 1986. Under this constitutional cover, repression of political opposition continued. Between the day the new Constitution went into effect and March 11, 1990, human rights organizations registered more than six thousand incidents of torture and cruel treatment, meaning that approximately three people per day were affected.[83] The *Central Nacional de Información* (CNI) continued, in somewhat modified form, the DINA's work of stamping out leftist subversion through torture and assassination.[84] To squelch political mobilization in urban

---

[83] The ratio of torture cases and cases of cruel treatment is approximately 1:5 According to the same source, all political prisoners were tortured (López Dawson 1995b: 57).

[84] This effort was fueled by the reemergence of the MIR in 1980 and the formation of the *Frente Patriotico Manuel Rodríguez* (FPMR), a guerrilla organization formed by members of the Communist Party, in December 1983. After the 1980 plebiscite, the Communist Party had officially adopted a platform endorsing violence ("all forms of resistance") to bring down the Pinochet regime. "In essence, the Communists had decided that the only sensible recourse to Pinochet's attempt to institutionalize an undemocratic, exclusionary regime was popular rebellion" (Oppenheim 1993: 178). See also Cavallo, Salazar, and Sepúlveda 1997.

shantytowns, the government carried out recurrent night-time raids (*allanamientos*), "combined police-military operations in which entire *poblaciones* [poor neighborhoods] were sealed off and all the men were at least temporarily detained while their papers were checked and their houses searched." Displaying "a complete disregard for even the minimal rights of the urban poor," the government thus cultivated fear among the general population (Oxhorn 1995: 218).[85]

THE JUDICIAL RESPONSE TO MILITARY LAW AND POLICY (1981–1990)

Until March 11, 1981, when the new Constitution went into effect, the work of the courts was still formally governed by the 1925 Constitution, albeit modified by the 1976 Constitutional Acts and other controversial decrees. After March 11, 1981, the courts no longer had the option of appealing to the principles of the 1925 Constitution, at least not as principles of positive law. As Loveman (1988: 342) puts it, the new Constitution "marked the end of the *ad hoc* emergency decrees, defined the institutional character of 'protected democracy,' and established a new juridical framework for national life. Government policy now derived from a constitutional process apparently sanctioned by a majority of the Chilean electorate. Future changes in process or policy depended on modification or elimination of this new legal system" (Loveman 1988: 342).

Judges, for their part, faced a choice, as they always do (Cover 1975), between mechanically applying individual articles of the constitution, which gave only the façade of liberal democracy, or striving to give real meaning to the new "higher law" through a more holistic and substantive interpretation. Consistent with their past performance, all but a handful opted for the former approach, continuing to justify the expansive police powers of the military government, to abdicate constitutional control of legislation, and to offer little protection to the many victims

---

[85] In the early 1980s, the Latin American Institute on Mental Health and Human Rights (ILAS) estimated that at least 10 percent of the Chilean population was affected by a repressive situation, which could include arrests, threats, the imprisonment, disappearance, or death of a relative, or expulsion from school, work, or the country. Of these individuals, some two hundred thousand were suffering extreme trauma as the result of torture, detention in a prison camp, or exile. From http://www.derechoschile.com/english/victims.htm, accessed October 5, 1999.

of repression. As in the past, judges demonstrated flexibility and creativity in defense of the regime's policies. When faced with protecting the rights of the opposition, or with the possibility of promoting liberal-democratic principles and practices, however, they generally claimed that the laws tied their hands. With discourse that echoed that of the government, many judges, especially those on the Supreme Court, made clear that there were virtually no limits on the "reason of state."

Strikingly, this judicial performance persisted despite the fact that societal challenges to the legitimacy of the authoritarian regime multiplied throughout the 1980s, providing ample opportunities for judges to ally with dissidents to critique the regime's twisted legality. In May 1983, in the wake of the economic crash,[86] national protests broke out and continued monthly for the next five months. The government responded with varying levels of repression. The explosion of protests transformed opposition journalists, whom the government had previously licensed to publish news magazines, into "bothersome witnesses."[87] In the years that followed, the opposition press thus waged an almost constant battle with the government. Judges, however, remained on the sidelines.

By August 1983, former leaders of the political Center, along with some "renovated" leftists, had formed the Democratic Alliance (*Alianza Democrática* or AD), which called for Pinochet's resignation, a constitutional convention, and an expedited transition to democracy. This group rejected the use of violence, and somewhat warily agreed to negotiate with the government, through the civilian Minister of the Interior, Sergio Onofre Jarpa. This political opening proved short-lived, however. On the fifth national day of protest (September 8, 1983), despite Jarpa's promises to the contrary, the police fiercely repressed the demonstrations

---

[86] From 1977 to 1981, Chile's economy had grown at an average annual rate of more than 7 percent. The government boasted of having brought about "the Chilean Miracle," despite the fact that unemployment remained over 15 percent and Chile's foreign indebtedness surged. In 1982, a dramatic drop in copper prices and a sudden devaluation of the peso led to a severe economic crisis. Several private banks collapsed and were taken over by the government. Unemployment reached record levels, and family incomes dropped by almost a third. The economy experienced a modest recovery between 1984 and 1986, but, by 1987, household shares of income were comparable to that of the late 1960s (Loveman 1988: 346–349; Falcoff 1989: 301–302).

[87] "Prensa: Censura y Represión," *ANALISIS* (September 7–13, 1987), 60.

(Otano 1995; Cavallo, Salazar, and Sepúlveda 1997). Judges continued to comply with the regime.

Over the course of 1984, Pinochet revamped his cabinet with regime hardliners and clamped down on the opposition. His government tight-ened its leash on the press, broadened legislation defining and punishing terrorism, and expanded the scope of military justice and protections for military personnel (Jiles 1984; Ministerio Secretaría General 1991: 95). Supreme Court President Rafael Retamal, often a lone dissenter in these years, made a brave effort to critique the regime's tactics.[88] But, in short order, his colleagues met in plenary to denounce his state-ments and distance themselves therefrom. Moreover, the justices took the unprecedented action of signing an official censure against their president, arguing that the speech he had made "could lend itself to interpretations of a political nature, [and] the law prohibits justices from engaging in politics" (Matus 1999:143).[89]

Despite setbacks, the regime's opposition continued to organize. In August 1985, eleven political groups signed the "National Accord for a Transition to Full Democracy." They called for an end to the states of exception, an end to exile, and constitutional reforms to eliminate the central elements of the 1980 Constitution (economic neoliberalism, national security doctrine, and "protected democracy"). The regime's claim to majority support was becoming increasingly dubious.

Perhaps for this reason, other legal actors began to show some mettle and take stands in defense of liberal democratic/rule of law principles. In 1985, for example, the Constitutional Tribunal issued the first of a series of crucial decisions that set basic standards for free and fair elections in the 1988 plebiscite and beyond.[90] Appealing to the overall struc-ture and spirit of the fundamental law, which both guaranteed political rights and outlined a return to democracy, the Tribunal insisted on the

---

[88] See, for example, *RDJ* 81 (1984) 1: vii–x.
[89] In July 1984, the Court issued an official prohibition of demonstrations or meetings in or around any of the nation's court buildings (Records of the Plenary of the Supreme Court, Vol. 22).
[90] Subsequent decisions included that of October 1, 1986, that revised the law on electoral registers, that of March 7, 1987, which reduced the constraints on political party organization, and that of April 1988, which set campaign standards and required clear dates for the 1988 plebiscite and for the presidential and parliamentary elections that might follow (and did, as Pinochet lost the plebiscite). See *Fallos del Tribunal Constitucional*, 1993.

establishment of an independent electoral commission – the *Tribunal Calificador de Elecciones* or TRICEL – for the 1988 plebiscite. According to transitory Article 11 of the Constitution, the TRICEL was to begin operating "on the appropriate date" for "the first election of senators and deputies." The bill that the junta presented to the Constitutional Tribunal for review thus established that the TRICEL would begin to function in December 1989. However, Tribunal member Eugenio Valenzuela – who was, it should be noted, one of the four members directly appointed by the junta – appealed to the spirit rather than letter of the law, arguing that if the Constitution itself recognized the existence of a "public electoral system," then there was no reason to exempt the 1988 plebiscite, which would inaugurate the transition process, from the rules of such a system. Valenzuela was able to persuade three other Tribunal members, including two members from the Supreme Court, Luis Maldonado and José María Eyzaguirre, to vote with him. On September 24, the Tribunal thus issued a 4–3 ruling, and the government was forced to revise the legislation.[91]

In 1986, the national bar organization (*Colegio de Abogados*), which had officially supported the military regime in its early years, began publicly criticizing the country's legal situation. In July of that year, the first national congress of lawyers under dictatorship issued a statement declaring that the rule of law did not exist in Chile; that the 1980 Constitution was illegitimate; and that nobody could be obligated to obey unjust laws. The lawyers thus resolved to "assume the moral and patriotic duty of promoting, from this moment, political and social democracy and the exercise of rights and liberties that are universally consecrated." The jurists also strongly criticized the country's judges, contending that "a diligent and responsible judicial labor would have avoided or reduced the impunity of the many crimes which have gone without punishment, saving many lives, [and] avoiding exile, disappearances, torture, and other suffering" (Oliva 1986).

In response to such criticism, which only increased in subsequent months, the Supreme Court offered explanations grounded in formalist reasoning. The justices argued that "we apply the law, which is written reason." If there exists any "silence, obscurity, contradiction, or insufficiency in the law, it falls to other sources to decide and respond." The Civil Code "establishes that when the meaning of the law is clear, [the

---

[91] For an in-depth discussion of the significance of the Constitutional Tribunal in limiting the authoritarian government, see Barros 2002.

judge] will not ignore its literal meaning on the pretext of consulting its spirit." Thus, they claimed, it would appear that "some people believe that the fulfillment of a legal mandate merits censure" (*El Mercurio*, July 8, 1987: 1).

To demonstrate how this dismissive attitude played itself out in the jurisprudence of this period, the following sections summarize judicial performance in three of the four areas discussed for the 1973–1980 period: habeas corpus, or *amparo*; *recursos de protección*; and *inaplicabilidad por inconstitucionalidad*. In addition, I offer a discussion of the most high-profile, and hence most politically salient, cases of the 1981–1990 period.

Habeas Corpus (*Amparo*)

The situation surrounding *recursos de amparo* in the 1981–1990 period remained miserable. As Roberto Garretón reports, only in ten to twelve cases out of ten thousand did the courts order the CNI to bring a detained person to the court (n.d.: 42). Once again, my limited sample of all published decisions from the 1981–1990 period looks good by comparison: the courts granted habeas corpus petitions in seven of sixty-two total decisions (or 11 percent). However, since five of these were at the appellate level, and subsequently appealed, the number of cases in which individuals actually received judicial protection is only *two*. Notably, one of these involved a right-wing lawyer who had been cited (but, crucially, *not* detained) for public libel against one of the witnesses in the Letelier case. The courts ordered that the charges be dropped.[92] The other case involved high-profile members of the Christian Democratic Party who had been arrested on grounds that, by participating in a peaceful protest, they had violated the Law of Internal State Security. Both the Santiago Appeals Court and the Supreme Court held that their "respectful and non-violent social dissidence" did not constitute incitement to subversion of the established order, and that therefore, they must be released.[93]

These isolated rulings, along with the individual dissents that became increasingly common in such cases (twenty-three instances in the sixty-two cases in my sample), indicated that there was an awareness of and concern about rights abuses among some judges. Yet only a few judges

---

[92] *Contra Carlos Cruz Coke-Ossa*, RDJ 78 (1981) 2.4:152–160.
[93] *Gabriel Valdés Subercaseaux; Jorge Lavandero Illanes, y otros*, RDJ 80 (1983) 2.4: 79–84.

Table 4.2. Individual votes of judges in published
amparo cases, 1973–1990*

	Appellate court	Supreme court
Votes to Grant	24 (27%)	30 (15%)
Votes to Deny	65 (73%)	175 (85%)

* Votes of substitute judges (*abogados integrantes*) not included.
They accounted for 17 percent of the total votes and sided
overwhelmingly (95 percent) with the government.

were willing to take stands in defense of rights principles. Table 4.2
gives the total of individual votes to grant or deny *amparo*, both at
the Supreme and appellate levels, in my 1973–1990 sample (the vast
majority of which came after 1981).

The numbers look relatively good, especially at the appellate level,
until one gets inside them. For the Supreme Court, it was two justices
that accounted for more than half of all the votes to grant *amparo*: Rafael
Retamal with eight and Enrique Correa with ten votes, respectively. A
full fourteen of the twenty Supreme Court justices (or 70 percent) that
served under the authoritarian regime never cast a single vote to grant
amparo (at least not in the published cases). At the appellate level, a
single judge, Carlos Cerda Fernández, of the Santiago Appeals Court,
accounts for nine of the twenty-four votes (or 38 percent) to grant
amparo. Thirty-two of the forty-four appellate judges (or 73 percent)
whose names appeared in the published cases never cast a single vote
to grant *amparo*.

Indeed, in general, the courts remained very passive in the face of the
regime's abuses. After the new constitution went into effect, the government issued arrest and exile orders citing either permanent Article
41 or transitory Article 24. In cases in which the government's order
was based on Article 41, the courts generally referenced the clause that
prohibited judicial review of the executive's criteria to justify actions
taken in virtue of the states of exception.[94] In cases in which the administrative act was based on transitory Article 24, the courts often simply

[94] See, for example, *Ricardo Aníbal Ríos Crocco* (*amparo*), December 9, 1986, *RDJ* 83
(1986) 2.4: 200–203; *Ana María Torres Gutiérrez* (*amparo*), March 16, 1985, *RDJ* 82
(1985) 2.4: 67–72. Also see related cases: *Héctor Hugo Cuevas Sandoval* (*amparo*),
November 17, 1983, *Fallos del Mes* No. 300: 687–689; *Tomás Fernando Inostroza
Catalán* (*amparo*), December 26, 1983, *RDJ* 80 (1983) 2.4: 138–148; *Raúl Alejandro
Pinochet Ruiz-Tagle* (*amparo*), March 26, 1984, *Fallos del Mes* No. 304: 41–43.

declared the writs inadmissible, citing the clause that stated that the only remedy available in such cases was reconsideration by the authority that issued the order.[95] Other times, judges claimed that the writs were admissible, but that the courts were limited to verifying that the arrest or expulsion orders had met formal requirements (i.e., had been issued and were being carried out according to the strict letter of the law).[96]

Moreover, because the Supreme Court accepted the CNI's argument that the quarters of the secret police were also military sites to which all civilians had restricted access, the appellate courts were obligated to rely on the "good faith" of the CNI to cooperate in judicial investigations. Not surprisingly, such good faith was not forthcoming. Although in 1980 the Supreme Court had advised the country's appellate courts to solicit reports on detentions from whichever government organ appeared responsible for them, the CNI, like the DINA before it, had insisted that the courts direct all inquiries on detainments to the Ministry of the Interior. In May of 1982, the Supreme Court wrote to President Pinochet protesting the lack of cooperation from the CNI in a case before the Santiago Appeals Court. Pinochet apologized, expressing his government's commitment to the "total reestablishment of the

---

[95] See *Manuel Ramón Almeyda Medina* (*amparo*), June 25, 1981, *RDJ* 78 (1981) 2.4: 83–85; *Gerardo Antonio Espinoza* (*amparo*), July 30, 1981, *Fallos del Mes* No. 272: 308–310; *Héctor Hugo Cuevas Salvador* (*amparo*), January 21, 1983, *RDJ* 80 (1983) 2.5: 9–12; *Cristián Castillo Echeverría* (*amparo*), April 26, 1984, *Fallos del Mes* No. 305: 146–147; *Alfredo Joignant Muñoz* (*amparo*), July 18, 1984, *Fallos del Mes* No. 308: 363–364; *Benedicto Enrique Figueroa Puentes* (*amparo*), August 22, 1984, *RDJ* 81 (1984) 2.4: 122–134; *José Miguel Insulza Salinas* (*amparo*), September 3, 1984, *Fallos del Mes* No. 310: 457–463; *Alejandro Abarca Cáceres y otro* (*amparo*), November 7, 1984, *RDJ* 81 (1984), 2.4: 240–244; *Roberto Tognarelli Barragan* (*amparo*), November 15, 1984, *RDJ* 81 (1984) 2.4: 255–266; *Fernando Salvador Arraño Oyarzún* (*amparo*), September 22, 1986, *RDJ* 83 (1986) 2.4: 219–220; *Edelmira Avila López* (*amparo*), May 28, 1987, *RDJ* 84 (1987) 2.4: 63–64.

[96] See *Martín Hernández Vásquez* (*amparo*), June 10, 1981, *RDJ* 78 (1981) 2.4: 93–94; *Carlos Podlech Micheaud* (*amparo*), January 11, 1983, *Gaceta Jurídica* 31: 34–38; *María Julieta Campusano Chávez* (*amparo*), June 14, 1984, *Fallos del Mes* No. 307: 275–280; *Francisco Márquez Pommiez* (*amparo*), January 14, 1985, *RDJ* 82 (1985) 2.4: 102–106; *Oscar Delfín Moya Muñoz* (*amparo*), April 22, 1986, *Fallos del Mes* No. 329: 169–170; *Leopoldo Ortega Rodríguez* (*amparo*), May 7, 1986, *RDJ* 83 (1986) 2.4: 43–45; *José Miguel Varas Morel* (*amparo*), July 29, 1988, *RDJ* 85 (1988) 2.4: 85–87. See also the Supreme Court's rulings in the Jaime Insunza and Leopoldo Ortega case, July 9, 1984, discussed in the the monthly report of the *Vicaría de la Solidaridad* for July 1984, on file at the FDAVS, 15–19.

rule of law," and promised that it wouldn't happen again.[97] In late 1986, after the courts of San Miguel, Concepción, and Valdivia all complained that the CNI had refused to cooperate with judicial officials and had even sent false or misleading information designed to obstruct justice, the Supreme Court sent another memo to the government. Once again, Pinochet responded by expressing "the profound disturbance that these events caused him" and indicating that he had instructed the Ministries of the Interior and of Defense "to reiterate to [the CNI] orders to proceed at all times in strict accordance to the Constitution and the Laws" (Tavolari 1995: 77; R. Garretón n.d.: 42).[98] Clearly, Pinochet, like Allende before him, was allowing his police force to use discretion in complying with judicial orders. However, these few, polite memos were the only public objections that the Supreme Court raised to the legal abuses of the military regime (Tavolari 1995: 77).

Constitutional Review I: *Recursos de Protección*

Because the *recurso de protección* had been in existence for five years, and because it was given even greater permanence by the 1980 Constitution, after 1981 Chileans increasingly employed this mechanism to claim their rights before the courts (appellate and Supreme). The following summary is based on an analysis of 118 published decisions in *protección* cases involving civil and political rights cases (excluding property) for the 1981–1990 period.[99] Of these, the courts voted to grant the writ in thirty instances, or approximately 25 percent of the cases. However, as I will explain further below, in ten of these cases the ruling actually favored the state or community over the individual, and those that did favor the individual did so only to the extent that the regime's own legal text provided explicitly for this.

As with the *recurso de amparo*, the courts used varying criteria for admitting *recursos de protección*. (Recall that the Constitution stated that the petition for *protección* was inadmissible in a state of emergency.) Sometimes judges claimed that the petition was inadmissible

---

[97] Records of the Plenary of the Supreme Court, Vol. 22. See also monthly report of the *Vicaría de la Solidaridad* for May 1982, on file at the FDAVS, 33–35.

[98] Records of the Plenary of the Supreme Court, Vol. 24.

[99] These include physical and psychological integrity, freedom of expression, freedom of assembly, freedom of conscience, freedom of association, equality before the law, freedom of labor, and the right to work and education.

only if the right or rights in questions were among those that could be restricted under a state of emergency.[100] Other times, they claimed that the petition was admissible if the constitutionally permitted restrictions were exceeded.[101] In addition, judges employed shifting standards regarding whether or not the petitioner was required to identify the offending party specifically or individually in order to secure a writ from the court.[102]

Substantively, decisions on *recursos de protección* tended not to challenge the administrative acts of the regime, although in the rare cases in which the regime's own legislation put some limit on the government, the courts did police the limit. Judges ruled that university rectors had the right to expel students from their institutions for participating in illegal demonstrations, and that wartime tribunals were legally empowered to judge specified acts committed by civilians. In other words, individuals judged by such entities could not claim that their rights to equality before the law and/or due process were infringed.[103] Courts also ruled that the government's cancellation of the "legal personality" (*personalidad jurídica*) of the Hare Krishna – making it impossible for the group to conduct legal transactions as an entity – was not a violation of the freedom of religion, and that the armed forces did not violate

---

[100] See, for example, *María Angélica Ditzel Marín* (*protección*), June 2, 1981, *RDJ* 79 (1981) 2.5: 77–83.

[101] See, for example, *Sociedad Publicitaría y de Servicios Informativos Ltda. con Ministro del Interior* (*protección*), January 5, 1983, *RDJ* 80 (1983) 2.5: 3–7; *Sociedad Editora La República Limitada, Editora de la Revista Cauce contra Director de DINACOS* (*protección*), June 11, 1984, *Gaceta Jurídica* 48: 44–47.

[102] Compare *Juna Morello Peralta* (*protección*), December 28, 1983, *Fallos del Mes* No. 301: 785–787, *Consejo Regional de Concepción del Colegio de Periodistas de Chile A. G.* (*protección*), March 25, 1985, *RDJ* 82 (1985) 2.5: 6–10, *Sindicato de Pilotos Lan* (*protección*), February 20, 1985, *Gaceta Jurídica* 56: 36–37, and *Wilhelmus Van Der Berg Verstrepen* (*protección*), March 29, 1988, *Fallos del Mes* No. 352: 32–35, on the one hand, to *Gustavo Villalobos y otros* (*protección*), April 9, 1985, *Gaceta Jurídica* 58: 46–49, *Carmen Hales* (*protección*), May 10, 1985, *Gaceta Jurídica* 58: 9–52, *Estudiantes de la Universidad Playa Ancha* (*protección*), August 7, 1986, *RDJ* 83 (1986) 2.5: 62–65, on the other.

[103] See *Raúl Acevedo Molina con Vicerrector Académico de la Universidad de Santiago* (*protección*), December 27, 1984, *RDJ* 81 (1984) 2.5: 40–50; *Colón con Vice-rector Universidad de Santiago* (*protección*), March 20, 1985, *Gaceta Jurídica* 57: 68–74; and *Jorge Donoso Quevedo y otro* (*protección*), May 8, 1984, *Fallos del Mes* No.306: 193–199.

the individual's right to association by prohibiting their members from belonging to the Free Masons.[104]

In cases involving the right to assembly, the courts held both the government and the public to the rules of the regime; that is, they upheld the rule that all meetings held in public places had to have previous government authorization but declared that the government could not require authorization for nonpolitical gatherings held in private locales.[105]

Freedom of expression and the press was another area in which the courts did not allow the government to stretch its own (limited) boundaries. For example, judges reminded the government that the Constitution prohibited prior censorship under a state of emergency (although it allowed it under a state of siege), and ruled that the retraction of previous authorization for publication, as well as the indefinite postponement of a decision on such authorization were also unconstitutional.[106] However, they also ruled that police harassment of journalists, in the form of covert infiltration of a reporting site, forced removal of journalists from a news scene, or seizure of journalistic equipment, did not constitute a violation of freedom of the press.[107] In addition, they endorsed the argument that hunger strikes were illegitimate forms of protest on the grounds that they violated the strikers' own right to life.[108]

In sum, in *recurso de protección* cases, judges were sometimes willing to check specific administrative acts via adhesion to the letter of the law, but proved unwilling to challenge the regime's illiberal policies

---

[104] *Círculo Védico (protección)*, March 12, 1984, *Fallos del Mes* No. 304: 9–11; *Renato Verdugo Haz y otros (protección)*, July 29, 1989, *Fallos del Mes* No. 368: 366–371.

[105] See *Presidente del Consejo Regional del Colegio de Matronas y otros (protección)*, March 17, 1986, *Fallos del Mes* No. 328: 35–37, and *Luis Ibacache Silva y otros (protección)*, March 20, 1986, *Fallos del Mes* No. 328: 51–54.

[106] See *Sociedad Publicitaría y de Servicios Informativos Ltda. con Ministro del Interior (protección)*, January 5, 1983, *RDJ* 80 (1983) 2.5: 3–7; *Jorge Lavandero Illanes y otro (protección)*, April 19, 1984, *Fallos del Mes* No. 305: 107–115; *Sociedad Editora La República Limitada, Editora de la Revista Cauce contra Director de DINACOS (protección)*, May 2, 1984, *RDJ* 81 (1984) 2.5: 124–129 (which cites another case decided on the same grounds nine days later); *Sociedad Impresiones y Comunicaciones Ltda. con Ministro del Interior (protección)*, March 31, 1986, *Gaceta Jurídica* 70: 27–31

[107] See *Consejo Regional de Concepción del Colegio de Periodistas de Chile A. G. (protección)*, March 25, 1985, *RDJ* 82 (1985) 2.5: 6–10; *Mario Aravena Méndez (protección)*, October 10, 1985, *Fallos del Mes* No. 323: 667–671.

[108] *Fernando Rozas Vial y otros con Párroco de San Roque y otros (protección)*, August 9, 1984, *RDJ* 81 (1984) 2.5: 161–165; *Intendente de la Región de Atacama con Párroco de El Salvador*, July 3, 1986, *RDJ* 83 (1986) 2.5: 108–111.

by seeking out a democratic spirit in the 1980 Constitution.[109] Their approach to interpretation in *recursos de protección* was thus far from the "active, dynamic, creative and imaginative" role that one prominent (and politically conservative) legal scholar proclaimed it should be (Soto 1986).

Constitutional Review II: *Inaplicabilidad por Inconstitucionalidad*
When presented with *recursos de inaplicabilidad por inconstitucionalidad* brought against laws issued after the 1980 Constitution, the Supreme Court offered interpretations that placed almost no limit on the power of the government to restrict or eliminate individual rights. In my sample of the sixteen published decisions from this period, the Court found constitutional violations in only two cases, both involving a law, passed by the junta, that sought to resolve, in favor of the state, disputes dating to the agrarian reform (Frei-Allende period).[110] In these cases, the Court argued that the law violated Article 73, paragraph 1 of the 1980 constitution, which states that the power to resolve civil and criminal disputes belongs exclusively to the judiciary, and that neither the president nor the Congress can, in any circumstances, revise the content of judicial decisions or revive cases that have closed. As in the past, the Court jealously guarded its authority over civil law matters and the traditional strict separation of powers; when traditional matters of public law were in question, however, the Court refused to challenge the executive.

For example, the Constitution required a "supermajority" (*quórum calificado*) to pass legislation establishing the death penalty for any crime. However, the Court rejected the argument that the governing junta could not form such a supermajority, holding that the constitutional provisions regarding legislative procedure would only apply after a new Congress had been elected in 1989. Until that time, then, the junta could issue virtually any law it pleased, as it maintained both legislative and constituent powers.[111]

---

[109] As noted earlier, some dissenters, as well as members of the Constitutional Tribunal, proved this was possible.

[110] *Sociedad Agrícola y Maderera Neltume Limitada (inaplicabilidad)*, April 19, 1985, RDJ 82 (1985) 2.5: 86–104; and *Jaime Bunster Iñíguez y otros (inaplicabilidad)*, January 29, 1987, RDJ 84 (1987) 2.5: 23–30. Note that in these same cases, the Court rejected the challenges based on formal/procedural unconstitutionality.

[111] See *Hugo Jorge Marchant Moya (inaplicabilidad)*, November 10, 1986, RDJ 83 (1986) 2.5: 139–144.

In another *inaplicabilidad* case, the Court argued that the state had the perfect right to limit the freedom of assembly in the interest of public order, the common good, and the security of the state. Therefore, despite the fact that the Constitution guaranteed the right "to gather peacefully without prior permission and without arms," a law penalizing "those who without authorization foment or convoke public collective acts in the streets, plazas and other public places and those who promote or incite demonstrations of any other type which allow or facilitate the alteration of public tranquility" could not be considered unconstitutional. In a decision largely justifying the expansive police powers of the military regime, the Court found that there were no constitutional limits to the restrictions the government could place on public assembly if the government assessed that the public gatherings in question "altered public tranquility" or otherwise threatened the rights of other members of the society.[112]

Similarly, in a *recurso de inaplicabilidad* brought against the inclusion of "apology for terrorism" as a terrorist act in Decree Law No. 18,314, the Court ruled that the government had the broad and exclusive constitutional right to determine what qualified as a terrorist act and how such an act should be punished.[113] And in another case in which the vagueness of a law limiting the freedom of expression and the freedom of press was challenged, the Court ruled that it was sufficient for the law to signal that "all acts in violation of measures taken by virtue of the president's extraordinary powers" were to be met with specified penalties. In other words, the Court gave the president free reign to determine, as a state of "emergency" unfolded, precisely which acts were violations of the public order and merited the sanctions previously established by law. Moreover, the Court declared that the administrative acts issued under such conditions, that is, those that "complemented" or clarified the law, could not be challenged via a *recurso de inaplicabilidad*, as the petition could only be brought against *laws*, not other administrative edicts.[114]

---

[112] *Rodolfo Seguel Molina y otros (inaplicabilidad)*, January 28, 1986, *Fallos del Mes* No. 326, 980–992. Note that Justice Retamal dissented.

[113] *Clodomiro Almeyda Medina (inaplicabilidad)*, January 26, 1988, *Fallos del Mes* No. 350: 1013–1019. It should be noted that the charge against Almeyda was based on statements he made to the press during his years in exile. In the end, he was sentenced to 541 days in prison.

[114] *Emilio Filippi Murato (inaplicabilidad)*, October 7, 1988, *RDJ* 85 (1988) 2.5: 241–245.

A final example of the Court's leniency toward the government in a *recurso de inaplicabilidad* is the decision in a 1985 case challenging the constitutionality of Decree Law No. 3,655. This decree had expanded wartime military jurisdiction, procedure, and punishments to cover cases of violence against members of the police and armed forces.[115] In this case, the plaintiff claimed that since Decree Law No. 3,655 had been published after the 1980 Constitution, and since it was a law relating to the organization and attributions of the judiciary, it should have been reviewed by the Court before becoming effective, as Article 74 of the 1980 Constitution established. Because the government had not sent the law to the Court for review, its application could not be considered constitutional. In their decision, however, the justices applied a looser standard than they had in the past regarding the requirement of publication for laws to go into effect. The justices claimed that although the law had not been published until March 17, 1981, it had been issued on March 10, 1981. The constitutional status of Decree Law No. 3,655 was thus to be determined in the same way as that of other laws issued before the 1980 Constitution.[116]

Since 1978, however, the Supreme Court had consistently abdicated its power to review the constitutionality of laws issued before new constitutional provisions. The high court's official stance was that the status of decree laws issued prior to the day that the 1980 Constitution went into effect should be determined by lower court judges in concrete cases. From 1981 to 1990, the Court held that because what was at issue in such cases was simply the survival of the laws or their supercession by the Constitution, it was not the role of the Supreme Court to decide whether or not the Constitution had rendered the previous laws null and void. This was something any judge should be able to determine.[117]

---

[115] Decree Law No. 3,655 declared that henceforth cases of violence against members of the police and armed forces would be tried in wartime military tribunals according to wartime procedure and with the application of wartime (i.e., heightened) punishments. Decree Law No. 17,983 of March 28, 1981, clarified that until 1989, the governing junta would continue to exercise both constituent and legislative powers (reiterating transitory Article 28), and explained how bills would be processed in the government.

[116] *Hugo Jorge Marchant Moya (inaplicabilidad)*, January 29, 1985, *RDJ* 82 (1985) 2.4: 51–59. Note that justices Retamal, Erbetta, and Meersohn dissented in this case.

[117] See, for example, *José Guerra Bastías (inaplicabilidad)*, December 31, 1985, *Fallos del Mes* No. 325: 865–867. Again, Retamal and Erbetta dissented. For other examples, see Precht 1987.

The Court also consistently abdicated its power to determine whether the military government's laws had been passed according to constitutional procedural standards, that is, to review laws for formal constitutionality. The justices offered two arguments for this. First, they claimed that a ruling of formal unconstitutionality was a form of abstract review (i.e., unconnected to any concrete case or controversy), and as such did not fall within the power of the Supreme Court.[118] Second, they argued that if procedural errors had been made in passing a bill into law, then the law was simply null and void, that is, it was not a law at all. Since no *recurso de inaplicabilidad* could be brought against something that was not a law, it was the responsibility not of the Supreme Court but of lower-court judges to determine this nonexistence and reject or ignore the faulty disposition in any given case before them.[119] On many issues of constitutional review, then, the Supreme Court justices passed the buck to their subordinates, who, as one analyst notes, "obviously avoided any pronouncement" on such matters (R. Garretón n.d.: 69). As this book elucidates, judges who had been socialized into a professional ideology of antipolitics and whose career prospects were largely in the hands of the conservative Supreme Court were hardly disposed to review matters which their superiors saw no reason to challenge.[120]

High-Profile Public Law Cases

In late March 1985, Chileans were stunned by the brutal roadside murder, by throat-slashing, of three members of the Communist Party. Santiago Appeals Court judge José Cánovas was assigned as *ministro en visita* to the case. Despite death threats, Cánovas was able, in the space of three months, to accumulate a file of some one thousand pages on what became known as the *degollados* (slit-throats) case. Based on a report from the CNI, the judge pinpointed an intelligence unit of the national police (*Carabineros*) called DICOMCAR as the main group of suspects.

---

[118] See *Sociedad Agrícola y Maderera Neltume Limitada* (*inaplicabilidad*), April 19, 1985, *RDJ* 82 (1985) 2.5: 86–104; and *Jaime Bunster Iñíguez y otros* (*inaplicabilidad*), January 29, 1987, *RDJ* 84 (1987) 2.5: 23–30.

[119] See *Arnoldo Wünkhaus Ried* (*inaplicabilidad*), October 13, 1987, *Fallos del Mes* No. 347: 682–684; *Alvaro Zúñiga Benavides y otros* (*inaplicabilidad*), June 15, 1988, *RDJ* 85 (1988) 2.5: 97–109.

[120] Precht says that lower court judges "seem to have viewed this transfer of jurisdiction ... as a 'poisoned gift'" (1987: 101).

Displeased with his rapid progress in the investigation, the government urged his removal from case, but the president of the Supreme Court, Rafael Retamal, insisted that he persevere. On July 30, certain that the crime had been committed by members of the armed forces, Cánovas declared himself without jurisdiction and attempted to pass the case to a military court. Before doing so, however, he issued preliminary indictments and arrest orders on high-ranking police officers. His findings were so damning that their publication rocked the government. "For the first time since the military coup, a member of the judiciary had accused the regime's security forces of a crime."[121] Leading police officials, including junta member César Mendoza, announced their retirement. Not wanting to see the armed forces implicated institutionally in the crimes in question, or to risk having the government accused of cover-up, the government ordered the military courts to refuse jurisdiction on the grounds that the crimes were acts of terrorism (i.e., they fell under the Anti-Terrorist Law).[122] The Supreme Court thus voted to keep Cánovas on. One month later, after indicting more people, Cánovas again attempted to pass the case to the military court, but the Supreme Court ruled a second time to keep the case in Cánovas's hands.[123]

In November 1985, the Santiago Appeals Court released two of the suspects. The following January, the Supreme Court declared there were insufficient grounds for indictment of four more, including DICOMCAR chiefs Luis Fontaine and Julio Omar Michea. The Court reached this conclusion after spending less than a day reviewing the two-thousand-page court record compiled by Cánovas.[124] The decision provoked a strong reaction from the National Bar Association, whose president, Raúl Rettig, resigned in protest. Frustrated by his superiors, Cánovas applied temporary closure to the case. Given that "the higher

[121] From http://derechoschile.com/english/dissidence.htm, accessed October 5, 1999.

[122] The junta had issued Law 18,314, the "Anti-Terrorist Law," on May 17, 1984, as part of the crackdown against the opposition. The law defined terrorist acts in very broad terms and established harsh penalties for both direct and indirect participation. In this case, the government sought to prosecute the crime as an isolated act of "terrorism," so the murders could be pinned on (alleged) rogue elements that acted outside of official orders.

[123] Monthly report of the *Vicaría de la Solidaridad* for August 1985, on file at the FDAVS, 27–38.

[124] Monthly report of the *Vicaría de la Solidaridad* for January–February 1986, on file at the FDAVS, 23–9.

courts have decided" that there is insufficient evidence to accuse a specific person as author, accomplice, or concealer of the crime, Cánovas announced that it was "impossible, for now, to continue the investigation."[125] He retired from the judiciary on March 28, 1989, leaving the unsolved case behind him (see also Cánovas 1988; Caucoto and Salazar 1994).

Although his efforts were frustrated by his superiors, Judge Cánovas's investigation had not been in vain. The detention of one of the individuals he indicted, the civilian Miguel Estay Reyno, allowed another *ministro en visita*, Judge Carlos Cerda Fernández, to subpeona him for testimony.[126] Judge Cerda was investigating a case involving thirteen communists who disappeared in 1976. The case had been briefly investigated by another appellate judge but closed for lack of evidence in 1977. Cerda, a persistent dissenter in these years, had pursued the investigation in earnest and concluded that it was not "excessive repressive zeal" on the part of a few individuals that had caused the 1976 disappearances, as the government maintained. Rather, the disappearances were the methodical work of an organization whose mission was to exterminate the Communist Party, a branch of the DINA known as the *Comando Conjunto Antisubversivo*. On August 14, 1986, Cerda thus indicted forty people, all but eight of whom were members of the armed forces.

The indictment provoked a rapid reaction from defense lawyers, who filed several judicial petitions to paralyze the case. The following month, the Santiago Appeals Court upheld a *recurso de queja*, ordering Cerda to apply the amnesty law and close the case definitively. On October 6, the Supreme Court ratified the decision. Cerda refused and, as will be discussed later, was suspended for two months with half his pay. In Cerda's absence, the high court's order fell upon the judge who temporarily replaced him in the case. This judge complied with his superiors and closed the case definitively (P. Verdugo 1990: 306–309).[127]

Judge Cerda was the first judge to articulate explicitly the thesis that amnesty could not be applied until guilty verdicts had been determined.

---

[125] Monthly report of the *Vicaría de la Solidaridad* for January–February 1987, on file at the FDAVS, 56–8.

[126] Monthly report of the *Vicaría de la Solidaridad* for November 1985, on file at the FDAVS, 51–52.

[127] Monthly report of the *Vicaría de la Solidaridad* for August 1986, on file at the FDAVS, 19–24.

Before this, many first instance judges had closed disappearance cases on the basis of amnesty, but the appeals courts, including (notably) the Martial Court, had always amended the decisions such that the closure was only temporary, that is, such that the cases could be re-opened should new evidence arise. After the Supreme Court ordered definitive closure in this case, however, and punished Cerda for challenging their interpretation of the law, most courts began applying amnesty immediately to cases involving political crimes committed before March 1978 (P. Verdugo 1990: 310–311; Brett 1992: 101).

In July 1986, during a national strike called by the *Asamblea de la Civilidad*, two student demonstrators, both nineteen years of age, were doused with gasoline and burned alive by a military patrol. Rodrígo Rojas Denegri, son of a Chilean exile and resident of Washington, DC, died four days after the incident. His friend Carmen Gloria Quintana Arancibia was severely disfigured. The government deflected denunciations of the crime by labeling them part of a communist conspiracy to distort the international image of Chile, and attempted to portray the youths as victims of their own terrorist plot. When this tactic failed, the government asserted that the event had been an "accident" (P. Verdugo 1986).

Initial investigations into the crime were conducted by district-level judges. However, amidst public uproar over the case and strong reactions from the U.S. government, the Santiago Appeals Court voted to appoint a *ministro en visita*. The appointed judge, Alberto Echavarría, accepted the government's "accident" thesis. He concluded that the crime consisted only of manslaughter, for which a lone individual, Pedro Fernández Dittus, was responsible. He based his resolution solely on the testimony offered by the soldiers who were suspects in the case, neglecting or ignoring altogether the contrary evidence offered by civilian eye witnesses and the victims themselves.[128] The case thus passed to the military courts (P. Verdugo 1986: 15 and 125–127).

Three weeks later, in an unprecedented ruling, the Martial Court revised Echavarría's decision, charging the head of the patrol unit with "unnecessary violence resulting in death and serious injury." In other words, the Martial Court increased the severity of the charge against the soldier (Collyer 1986). The case then passed to a military tribunal, which finally issued a verdict in August 1989. Fernández

---

[128] Rojas had made a declaration to the judge in the hospital before he died.

was given a suspended prison sentence of three hundred days (Brett 1992).[129]

In January 1988, another Santiago Appeals Court judge, Arnoldo Dreyse, shocked the public by sentencing national labor leaders Manuel Bustos and Arturo Martínez to a year and a half in prison, and their colleague Moisés Labraña to sixty-one days in prison, for violating the clause of the Law of Internal State Security prohibiting all strikes that "disturb public order or produce perturbations in public services." The defendants had in fact called a general strike for October 7, 1987, but it had been, by all accounts, a failure. The labor minister had even submitted a report for the case in which he stated categorically that there had been no paralyzation of activities. Nonetheless, in the decision, Judge Dreyse argued that the defendants had "convoked a paralyzation of work and of every manner of activities all over the country," which "effectively... was characterized by violence, the sowing of hate, the stench of resentment, as well as a series of offensive and dangerous demonstrations in public [places], which intensely altered the proper and normal tranquility of the entire country." Moreover, he referred to the organizers as a "subversive narcotrafficking-terrorist spectre" that had called a national strike by "communists, hippies, common delinquents, [and] traffickers of ideas or of drugs."

The defendants and their lawyers were appalled at this inappropriate and offensive language, and they filed a series of appeals against the decision.[130] The panel of judges of the Santiago Appeals Court that processed the appeal overturned the conviction, arguing that the intention of the defendants had not been to disrupt production or disturb public order but simply to demand higher wages. In other words, the judges argued that the strike had been a legal form of protest and a legitimate attempt to influence public policy.[131] In August 1988, however, the Supreme Court overturned this decision and sentenced Bustos and Martínez to a year and a half of internal banishment. The high court argued that any form of union activity other than collective bargaining was illegal and constituted a violation of the Law of Internal State

---

[129] In January 1991, the Martial Court absolved him of any offense against Carmen Quintana.

[130] Monthly report of the *Vicaría de la Solidaridad* for February 1988, on file at the FDAVS, 58–64.

[131] Ibid., 64–65.

Security. The decision also included a "reminder" to Judge Dreyse that resolutions must be written "with juridical language and with serious-ness, without making allusions or using phrases that are unrelated to the issue in question."[132] The Court did not, however, find Dreyse's improprieties grave enough to require official sanction.

In August 1989, in the wake of constitutional reforms that were part of a strong momentum toward formal democracy, the Supreme Court ruled on a *recurso de casación* filed by the families of ten of the Communist Party members whose disappearance had been investigated by Carlos Cerda. Building on the points made by Judge Cerda in his refusal to close the case, lawyers for the family argued that amnesty could not be applied until the investigation had been completed; that kidnapping and conspiracy were ongoing crimes not contained within the time period covered by the amnesty law (Decree Law No. 2,191); that amnesty could only be applied subjectively, that is to individual perpetrators, and not objectively to crimes; and, in any case, that the Geneva Conventions of 1949 obligated the Chilean state to prosecute those responsible for crimes committed during a state of civil war. In short, the victims' lawyers contended that "the national amnesty is rendered null and void in regard to acts which international law qualifies as criminal."[133]

The Supreme Court[134] rejected all of these arguments, emphasizing two points: first, that the courts were obligated to apply and conform with all laws issued by the legislator; and, second, that since amnesty had the effect of "erasing" the crime, "leaving its perpetrator in the same situation as he would be in if he hadn't committed it," there was, in effect, nothing to investigate in cases covered by the amnesty law. In short, judges had no choice legally but to close all such cases defini-tively. In addition, the justices referred to a 1931 decision of the Court that described amnesty as the "forgetting of the past," which aimed at "conserving social harmony." Amnesty is "a law of public interest" whose legal effects are "broader and more satisfactory than absolution."

---

[132] *Ministerio del Interior (queja)*, August 17, 1988, *Fallos del Mes* No. 358: 598–601.

[133] *Miguel Estay Reyno (casación forma y fondo criminal)*, August 11, 1989, *Fallos del Mes* No. 369: 489–505 at 495–496. This is the same argument put forth by the lawyers for the victims in the Lonquén case, discussed earlier.

[134] The unanimous decision was rendered by Justices Ulloa, Zúñiga, and Cereceda, and *abogados integrantes* Ricardo Martín and Juan Colombo.

Appeals in cases covered by the amnesty law were thus pointless.[135] With this reasoning, the Court ordered Carlos Cerda, once again, to permanently close the case. Cerda again refused, and applied only temporary closure. Not only did this signify his assessment that some new piece of evidence would allow future reactiviation of the case, but it also reflected his hope that the Court's stance would change with the transition to democracy (Otano 1992). As the next chapter will show, however, Chile's high court justices were not inclined to promote a transition to greater liberality after the transition to civilian rule. Cerda would remain an isolated modeler of liberal principles and practices.

Summary, 1981–1990

With the official state of war long since ended, a new constitution established, and an increasingly strong public movement for democratization in evidence, one might have expected the behavior of Chilean judges to change after 1981. What the preceding account shows, however, is that while there was "a kind of awakening of conscience among some judges," and, "in isolated cases, a willingness to go further than they had up until then" (Interview HRL96-1, July 4, 1996, 11:00), the overwhelming pattern in judicial decision making was passivity, deference to the executive, and an apparent commitment to order over liberty. Although both the organized Bar and the regime's own Constitutional Tribunal used their professional prestige and institutional weight to help move the country in a liberal-democratic direction, the judiciary continued to display "a willingness to collaborate that bordered on the abject" (Constable and Valenzuela 1991: 134). I turn now to the question of why this behavior persisted.

---

[135] *Miguel Estay Reyno* (*casación forma y fondo criminal*), August 11, 1989, *Fallos del Mes* No. 369: 489–505 at 497–505. In fact, the justices were contradicting much past jurisprudence regarding amnesty. Before the 1973 coup, the courts had held that amnesty erased the criminal punishment but not the offending act itself; amnestied offenders remained liable for the civil damages caused by their actions. See *Marcos Chamúdez contra Alberto Gamboa Soto*, October 13, 1965, *Fallos del Mes* No. 83: 252–253 and *Alberto Gamboa S.* (*inaplicabilidad*), December 7, 1966, *RDJ* 63 (1966) 2.4: 359–366.

PART III

EXPLAINING THE JUDICIAL ROLE UNDER PINOCHET, 1973–1990

REGIME-RELATED FACTORS

In any analysis of judicial behavior under authoritarianism, the first and most obvious hypothesis is that regime-related factors – that is, direct or indirect interference with the courts by the government – explain outcomes. Thus, I begin with a discussion of the evidence for this hypothesis. My argument is that although the military government did use a variety of tactics to make its will known to judges, and changed some rules along the way to strengthen its influence in the judiciary, an explanation that attributed judicial behavior in Chile from 1973 to 1990 solely or primarily to fear of and manipulation by the government would overlook crucial elements of the picture.

To begin, I must emphasize that judicial independence was, on the whole, respected under the authoritarian regime.[136] For reasons explained in Chapter 1, the military government had incentives to refrain from direct interference with judicial functioning. Not only does such an approach have appeal for authoritarian leaders in general (Toharia 1975; Tate 1993; Moustafa 2007), but it was of particular importance in the Chilean case, as one of the central reasons the generals offered for staging the coup was to restore the rule of law. The military did not shut down the ordinary courts even temporarily, nor did they replace sitting judges with their own people. On the contrary, they pledged immediately to respect judicial independence, and received, in return, the blessing of the full Supreme Court.

In the interviews I conducted in 1995–1996, judges generally maintained that they had not been subjected to threats or other types of interference from the military government, insisting on the continuity of judicial independence across time.[137] A full twenty-four of the

---

[136] The exception to this was the regime's treatment of the labor courts, which, it should be noted, went unopposed by the Supreme Court. See Palma González 1998.

[137] Moreover, interviews with retired judges, lawyers, and law professors generally confirmed the idea that the judiciary was, at least at the time of the coup, basically free from the kind of corruption and manipulation common in other Latin American

thirty-six acting high court judges interviewed, or two-thirds, insisted that they had always enjoyed formal independence in their decision making. In fact, some were emphatic about this point: "The military government was very respectful of the judiciary. We never received pressure of any sort from the government" (Interview SCJ96-5, May 23, 1996, 14:00). "We had perfect independence, in all cases. We remained unscathed (*incólume*)"(Interview SCJ96-8, June 11, 1996, 13:30). "I would be lying if I told you I received any pressure at all. The judges were respected, before the transition and after. There has always been independence" (Interview ACJ96-8, May 8, 1996, 15:00). "I even had to judge in cases of people who had held posts in the Allende government, and *never, never, never* did I receive any influence of any kind, either direct or indirect, from the [military] government. Rather, they let me act as I saw fit, and when you talked to other colleagues, they said the same thing" (Interview ACJ96-3, April 29, 1996, 13:00). In short, as one put it, "The judiciary has always remained independent, unshakable (*inquebrantable*)" (Interview SCJ96-14, June 27, 1996, 18:20).[138]

This is not to deny the clear evidence of more subtle forms of pressure or manipulation brought to bear by the military government on the judiciary. Although my review of the records of the plenary sessions of the Supreme Court revealed no instance in which promotions were dictated by the government, nor even any cases in which the Ministry of Justice rejected a list of nominees proposed by the Court, they did indicate that some of the early investigations into judicial behavior, as well as some transfers during the authoritarian regime, were made at the recommendation of the Ministry of Justice (see esp. Vols. 18 and 22).[139] Furthermore, although the new military leaders did not themselves

countries. Indeed, this is why criticisms of the judges' behavior under Pinochet are so strong: People believed in the independence of the judiciary and therefore had high expectations of it.

[138] Similarly, Enrique Correa Labra, who dissented in many human rights cases under Pinochet and served as president of the Supreme Court under Aylwin, "affirmed categorically that the judiciary had enjoyed 'total and absolute' independence under the military government" (Brett 1992: 219).

[139] The case could easily be made, however, that such indirect steering of the judiciary was nothing new. The executive is, for obvious reasons, always going to attempt to exert whatever influence possible on judicial selection and tenure. The organization of the CUP under Allende is one such example. Moreover, Chilean law had long authorized the president to oversee the conduct of judges, although the power to evaluate and remove judges was given exclusively to the Supreme Court (see esp. Article 72, No. 4 and Article 85 of the 1925 Constitution).

conduct a purge of the judiciary, they did pass some laws making it easier for the Supreme Court to dismiss potential troublemakers. Decree Law Nos. 169 and 170, published on December 6, 1973, modified both Article 323 of the Judicial Code and Article 85 of the 1925 Constitution, allowing judicial employees to be removed from service for an annual evaluation of "poor performance" by a simple majority (rather than the previous requirement of two-thirds) vote of the Supreme Court. The vote was to be secret, and the justices were under no obligation to give reasons for the negative evaluation. These decrees facilitated the internal purge conducted by the Supreme Court in January 1974.[140]

In the 1980s, rather less subtle pressure was brought to bear by Pinochet's ideological ally, Hugo Rosende, who was sworn in as the new Minister of Justice in January 1984. Rosende was reportedly obsessed with judges' ideological leanings, and made it clear to the Court that he wanted appointees who "will never meddle in politics," with "politics defined, of course, as the politics of dissidence" (Matus 1999: 180). In 1984, he oversaw the expansion of the Supreme Court from thirteen to seventeen members, which allowed at least one hardline regime supporter, Hernán Cereceda, to rise to the high court. Cereceda allegedly became the main informant for the government on the opinions and activities of judicial personnel (Matus 1999: 158). In 1989, in the wake of Pinochet's loss in the (October 5, 1988) plebiscite, Rosende succeeded in getting the junta to approve what became known as the "candy law" (*ley de caramelo*).[141] The legislation was so called because it allowed justices over seventy-five to retire within ninety days with a sweet financial deal. Seven justices took advantage of the offer, allowing the military regime to make seven new appointments to the Court, albeit drawn (as always) from nomination lists proposed by the Court itself.[142]

---

[140] The internal purge of the judiciary is discussed later in this chapter. Note that these changes were later reversed, first by a modification of the content of Decree Law No. 169 and then with the 1980 Constitution.

[141] This was Decree Law No. 18,805 of June 17, 1989. In addition, just before the transition, the military government added a line to the Judicial Code to prevent those who had been fired from the judiciary from serving as *abogados integrantes*, and to prohibit the future impeachment of government officials for behavior under the military regime.

[142] Democrats accused the government of stacking the Court. However, the editors of *El Mercurio* justified the move, arguing that in passing the law the military government "not only operated legally and legitimately, but also was able to anticipate an eventual

There is thus, not surprisingly, some evidence that the military government tried to exert some control over the judiciary, although the means it used were mostly indirect. Although there were certainly instances in which the government brought direct pressure to bear in specific cases,[143] Chile's did not become a system of "telephone justice." Indeed, as explained earlier, the military government wanted to preserve its image of respect for law and courts, and, thus, rather than interfere in the judicial process, its leaders preferred simply to restrict the scope of jurisdiction of the ordinary courts and expand that of those tribunals over which they (thought they) had more direct control, namely, the military courts and (later) the Constitutional Tribunal. Like governments before and after theirs, they did their best to influence judicial selection and tenure, but they did so within the limits of the established system, in which the Supreme Court continued to play the dominant role.

POLITICAL ATTITUDES AND PREFERENCES

As some observers have noted, the military government did not really need to intervene in the judicial system, because "the Supreme Court was at their service" (Interview HRL96-4, July 23, 1996, 10:00). Given the Court's immediate endorsement of the coup, and their persistently faithful, often vigorous, enforcement of the authoritarian regime's laws

---

attack against the judicial order of the Republic." In their view, the Supreme Court had not been altered: "It is the same, in spirit and even in part of its membership, as that which in a plenary resolution on June 25, 1973, warned the Marxist President of the moment: 'As long as the judiciary is not erased from the Constitution, its independence will never be abrogated'" (*El Mercurio*, September 28, 1989).

[143] One famous example is the *Apsi* case of 1983, in which one chamber of the Supreme Court initially accepted, but then, in an unprecedented "clarifying decision," reversed and rejected a *recurso de protección* on behalf of the editors of the magazine. In this case, the government was attempting to shut down the publication on charges that it had violated the terms of its initial authorization, which restricted it to coverage of international politics. The Court first argued that this complete suspension violated the constitutional protection of free expression. Three weeks later, under clear pressure from the government, three of five justices modified their positions and argued that, while the government could not shut *Apsi* down altogether, it could insist that it cease coverage of domestic politics. See *Sociedad Publicitaria y de Servicios Informativos Ltda. con Ministro del Interior (protección)*, RDJ 80 (1983) 2.5: 3–9.

and policies, it is tempting to conclude that judicial cooperation with the military government was a function of shared political attitudes and policy preferences.

The human rights lawyers I interviewed clearly believed political attitudes were a key factor. As one argued, "I think there was an ideological commitment on the part of the judges – at least of the Supreme Court – with the military government. . . . They thought that the military government was doing the right thing and they felt comfortable in that schema" (Interview HRL96-4, July 23, 1996, 10:00). Most members of the high court "embraced the doctrine of national security," explained another (Interview HRL96-1, July 4, 1996, 11:00). One human rights lawyer recounted the reaction that the president of the Supreme Court at the time of the coup, Enrique Urrutia Manzano, had to his explanation of what human rights lawyers were attempting to accomplish: "He said to me more than once, 'Well, what do you want us to do, if the problem here is either they kill us or we kill them?' You see, it was a complete war mentality!" In another case, in which this lawyer was arguing in defense of a group of disappeared peasants, the president of the chamber called him to the bench and said he did not understand what the lawyer was asking for. "I said, 'we want you to help us locate them!' And the judge said, 'but all these people must be dead!' So you see, they knew what was happening, but they thought it was justified. [Their attitude was that] the military had saved them from communism, so if they killed a few thousand people, [they weren't going to] make problems for them" (Interview HRL96-5, August 2, 1996, 12:00).[144]

Some of the judges I interviewed also emphasized the importance of political preferences. One judge charged, "It was the composition of the Supreme Court – people of the extreme Right, in some cases – which explains the behavior of the judiciary under the military regime. It was a question of shared values" (Interview ACJ96-4, May 2, 1996, 9:00). "The coup was theirs (*El golpe era de ellos*)," affirmed another (Interview ACJ96-12, May 9, 1996, 18:30). A few of them "were ultra-partisans of the military regime; they were in their glory! [And] as long as they kept quiet, they had everything, any favor, they wanted," explained

---

[144] Thus, as the lawyer recounted, "One had the feeling that for the justices, one was a pain, bringing problems, bothering them. . . . Sometimes they'd fall asleep during your arguments! They had a thousand ways of showing that you were disagreeable to them, that you were bringing up issues which annoyed them."

one retired judge (Interview FJ96-4, June 17, 1996, 12:30). "You have to understand the mentality of these people: that human rights are necessarily associated with Marxism, the U.N. is Marxist, the Church is Marxist, and Chile is the only pure, orderly place, an example for the whole world" (Interview AC2, May 6, 1996, 8:30). Thus, as one appellate judge stated in a 1990 magazine interview, "I wouldn't speak of interference [by the military government in the judiciary]. . . . There wasn't interference, but rather a sort of romance, like walking hand in hand" (Rojas 1990).

Notwithstanding these statements, there is evidence that the judiciary was not, at the individual level, monolithic in its enthusiasm for the authoritarian regime. Not only do the statements just cited, as well as the decision data presented earlier, indicate that at least some judges did not sympathize with the Pinochet regime, but the fact that the military government deemed it necessary, even back in 1973, to issue Decree Laws 169 and 170 reveals that the generals were not convinced that they could count on unified and unfailing judicial support, even from the Supreme Court itself. That they sought to restrict the jurisdiction of the ordinary courts, preferring to have politically sensitive cases tried in military courts, or later, the Constitutional Court, also indicates a general lack of confidence that ordinary judges were and would remain solidly behind them.

There is at least some evidence from the period that the military leaders were right to be cautious. In the mid-1980s, a group of younger judges led by Hernán Correa de la Cerda and centered in the newly created appellate court of San Miguel[145] began meeting to read and critically analyze judicial decisions. Eventually, these magistrates produced a "letter of reflection," in which they listed the complaints that citizens had made of the judiciary.[146] Although these judges refused to identify themselves with any movement or political party, and never went public with their views, "it was clear that the changes they aspired to would not come about under dictatorship" (Matus 1999:147). Clearly,

---

[145] The new appellate court was created in 1980 to relieve the caseload of the Santiago Appeals Court.

[146] Several interviewees mentioned this document, but none would allow me access to it. In 1986, this group succeeded in getting their candidate, San Miguel appellate judge Germán Hermosilla, elected to the presidency of the National Association of Magistrates.

then, there existed a pro-democratic contingent, however timid, within the judiciary during the dictatorship.

Moreover, my indirect probing of judges' political views in 1996 interviews revealed *Pinochetistas* to be in the distinct minority.[147] In fact, only six acting high court (AHC) judges demonstrated themselves to be clearly approving of Pinochet's rule, or ideologically aligned with the military regime.[148] These judges made statements such as: "The constitution of 1980 politically organized the country perfectly;" (Interview SCJ96-1, May 16, 1996, 16:00) or "Sure, the military regime leaders committed excesses, but that was a necessary evil. It was like amputating a leg to save the patient. The same thing has happened in every country" (Interview SCJ96-8, June 11, 1996, 13:30). One even greeted me by saying:

> It's good you came now and not before. There were 11,000 armed men in the streets; it was going to be another Cuba! Under Allende, no human rights were respected. They attacked every one, the right to property, even the right to life, and then they come complaining about human rights after the coup! And they carried out a tremendous propaganda campaign in the U.S., all those people in exile. Marxists are great at propaganda. (Interview SCJ96-5, May 23, 1996, 14:00)

---

[147] All of these judges had served under the authoritarian regime, and many of them under Frei and/or Allende, as well. Most of them spoke quite freely about how the regime changes of the past thirty years had affected their work. In addition, they were open about their views on issues such as whether the Allende regime had destroyed the rule of law, or whether the critique made of the judiciary in the *Rettig Report* was fair or unfair (see Chapter 5). Only a few (four) AHC judges refused to answer these questions on the grounds that they were "political." I was thus able to categorize the judges into three groups: antidemocratic, or clearly sympathetic with the Pinochet project; democratic, or clearly at odds with the Pinochet regime and articulate about the nature of democratic politics; and ambiguous, or offering statements which made me uncomfortable classifying them in one of the other two groups. Within this third category, I did separate those whose responses were more democratic from those that were less so.

[148] In general, clearly pro-military regime judges were very forthcoming with their political views. Contrary to what I expected, it was they who generally raised political issues in the interview, before I got to the explicitly political questions. It is interesting that they, like most of the Right in Chile, were proud of and totally unrepentant about military rule. It was, rather, the democrats who walked on eggshells and felt the need to apologize for or whisper their beliefs. This problem was analyzed and critiqued in Moulián 1996.

Among other things, this group fully approved of the existing extent of military jurisdiction.[149] As one explained, the military should judge any and all cases involving their personnel, because they need to "maximally strengthen the principle of authority and discipline." And, in cases in which civilians put in question the honor of the military, "the Army has the right to defend itself" (Interview SCJ96-5, May 23, 1996, 14:00).

In contrast to this group, fourteen AHC judges made it clear that they were ideologically at odds with the military regime and well aware of the historical and international standards of democracy.[150] "I was always against the dictatorship. I've always been against any type of dictatorship, whether of the left or of the right. I like democracy, legitimate authorities elected by the people, not those imposed by force," expressed one of these (Interview ACJ96-8, May 8, 1996, 15:00). These judges strongly insisted that there was no rule of law under the military regime, as the executive clearly answered to no one. "Of course not! The military government itself was illegal!" quipped one (Interview ACJ96-17, May 17, 1996, 13:00). Several of these judges felt the judiciary very well could have done more to defend human rights and the rule of law under Pinochet. As one argued, judges are representatives of the people, and in this capacity, many judges failed, for "they did not defend the essential [lo esencial]" (Interview ACJ96-2, June 10, 1996, 9:00). In addition, these judges strongly rejected the extant scope of military court jurisdiction. As one stated, "The military tribunals have never had the necessary impartiality and independence, and this came to a crisis point in the military regime.... Obviously the decisions and the knowledge of the matter were controlled from above; not one military judge could act without first consulting [his superiors]. I'm for eliminating military courts altogether, or as far as possible allowing military

---

[149] At the time of my interviews, any crimes committed by military personnel, as well as any illegal acts affecting military personnel, committed on military property, or "threatening" the institution of the military, still fell under the jurisdiction of military courts. Thus, a vast majority of those tried in military courts continued to be civilians, whereas military personnel enjoyed special treatment (*fuero*) in the justice system, all of which violated the constitutional principle of equality before the law. See López Dawson 1995a.

[150] I use the term "historical and international standards of democracy" because the *Pinochetistas* often attempt to apply the term "democracy" to the regime they created. Such "new speak," the systematic use of terms such as liberty and democracy to describe their polar opposites, was common to a number of Latin American military regimes in the 1970s, as noted by Alberto Ciria (1986: 57–69).

crimes to be tried by [ordinary] courts of law" (Interview ACJ96-10, May 9, 1996, 10:00).

Finally, there were those (sixteen) AHC judges "in between," who asserted differing levels of disagreement with and distance from the Pinochet regime, but didn't articulate a clear democratic ideology in the course of the interview. Those whom I categorized as ambiguous but antidemocratic leaning were those like the judge who, on the one hand, approved of the military's promotion of Portalian values and asserted that the 1980 constitution was written by a commission of people of "all political tendencies," but, on the other hand, said, "I can't conceive of an authority that sends people to death, and from what I saw, that is what happened" (Interview SCJ96-3, May 20, 1996, 8:30).[151] Also in this category was a judge who claimed he disapproved of "the repression [under the military regime] which didn't respect any norm whatsoever," yet admitted to going along with the regime so as to be promoted (Interview SCJ96-13, June 20, 1996, 11:00), and another who generally used Chilean right-wing discourse, but who expressed strong disapproval of the extent of military court jurisdiction (Interview ACJ96-3, April 29, 1996, 13:00). Those who fall under the rubric of 'ambiguous but more democratically inclined' are those who, for example, justified the military intervention because of the "civil war," on the one hand, but asserted support for and admiration of President Aylwin (1990–1994), on the other (Interview SCJ96-7, June 5, 1996, 18:00), or those who never explicitly articulated a fully democratic vision, but who made it clear they were opposed to the present extent of military court jurisdiction or made references to international human rights treaties (Interviews ACJ96-11, May 9, 1996, 13:00; ACJ7, May 7, 1996, 12:30).

In summary, then, of the thirty-six AHC judges I interviewed in 1996, fourteen can be deemed clearly democratic, six of authoritarian persuasion, and sixteen somewhere in between, with about nine of these making more democratic statements, and seven offering more dubiously democratic responses. This, together with other evidence presented here and in Chapter 3, suggests that an explanation that attributes judicial complicity with the military regime uniquely or even primarily to uniform policy preferences on the part of judges cannot stand.

The claim I advance, then, is not that political preferences had nothing to do with judicial performance under the authoritarian regime, but

[151] As noted earlier, the 1980 constitution was written by a small group of very conservative lawyers who were Pinochet loyalists, and not by a pluralistic commission.

rather that any real "romance" between judges and military leaders was restricted to a powerful bloc on the Supreme Court (led by justices like Bórquez and Urrutia), as well as some zealots in the inferior ranks, whom the former were able to reward through promotion (e.g., Cereceda, Dreyse). Most judges, I contend, were not personally enamored of or committed to the military regime, particularly as time wore on, but they had neither the professional understandings nor incentives to resist authoritarian laws and policies. It was the institutional structure and ideology of the judiciary that rendered them handmaidens of the military rulers.

LEGAL PHILOSOPHY

Before proceeding with my discussion of institutional factors, I must address one other argument that has sometimes been advanced to explain the failure of judges to resist undemocratic rulers,[152] namely, that positivist legal philosophy renders judges insensitive to the substantive content of the laws they apply, and unconcerned about the outcomes of their decisions (Dyzenhaus 1991). As mentioned earlier, Chilean judges did take shelter behind positivist defenses, washing their hands of any responsibility for the brutality and longevity of the authoritarian regime. Yet, as one human rights lawyer protested, the claim that they were only applying the law "is not true, because they rendered decisions that favored the government even against the laws, against norms, against principles!" (Interview HRL96-8, October 17, 1996, 16:00).[153] And, as another remarked, "Judges are very faithful to the letter of the law when it suits their ideas" (Interview FJ96-1, June 11, 1996, 9:00)!

The decision data reported earlier support these claims. From 1973 to 1980, judges ignored long-standing legal norms on habeas corpus and review of military tribunal decisions, granting unchecked discretion to the military in the "antisubversive war." Furthermore, judges put up no protest as the junta proceeded to gut the 1925 Constitution, issuing blanket decrees to amend or supersede any provision that might stand in its way. After 1981, when the regime's new constitution went into effect, judges adhered to the letter of the law, but in a manner that maximized the government's discretion to determine when public order was

---

[152] I do not address the class-based argument here, as the relevant data was presented in Chapter 3.

[153] R. Garretón makes this same point (n.d.: 79).

threatened and, therefore, when constitutional rights could be suspended. In other words, rather than emphasizing those parts of the Constitution that set limits on the exercise of power, the courts perpetually ignored or denied them in favor of the vague clauses which extended executive discretion. Hence, it seems inappropriate – even generous – to attribute judicial behavior in Pinochet's Chile to a professional commitment to legal positivism.

Moreover, my 1996 interviews revealed that a significant number of AHC judges (twenty-three of thirty-six) recognized, at some level, that the judicial decision-making process is not simply "mechanical," as a plain-fact positivist would have it. This view cut across the political lines discussed earlier. Some interviewees spoke openly about how, with experience, they had become less formalistic (Interviews SCJ96-4, May 23, 1996, 11:00; SCJ96-10, June 11, 1996, 18:30; SCJ96-12, June 18, 1996, 18:00; ACJ96-17, May 17, 1996, 13:00), how they grounded their interpretation in the "grand principles of the Chilean system" and in the "national conscience" (Interview SCJ96-5, May 23, 1996, 14:00) or how they had "become conscious of the need to democratize, equalize, or mold (*formar*) society" (Interview SCJ96-6, May 24, 1996, 12:00). One claimed that "Justice is a social concept, and it's natural that one's sense of justice evolves over time. The judge is very sensitive to what is happening in society; he can't divorce himself from society; he is part of it. [And, although] the judges are very much bound by the law, the law always leaves room for interpretation" (Interview SCJ96-7, June 5, 1996, 18:00). Others explained: "[In deciding cases,] one isn't worried about the norms; rather, one searches for the intuitive criteria of justice, and then attempts to reaffirm or justify this in the legal precepts" (Interview SCJ96-10, June 11, 1996, 18:30). "The basic objective of the judge is to render justice . . . and the work of the judge is precisely a work which can even involve creation . . . in the search for that interpretation which represents the general understanding of the community" (Interview ACJ96-6, May 6, 1996, 11:00). "If I believe that the application of the law produces injustice, I don't apply it, or rather, I interpret it to conform to the side of justice" (Interview ACJ96-13, May 10, 1996, 12:00). One judge confessed that his interpretation of the law changed as conditions, such as the level of crime or the degree of pollution in Santiago, changed around him (Interview ACJ96-1, April 26, 1996, 18:00). Another even argued that "interpretations which conflict with the law are in style" (Interview SCJ96-12, June 18, 1996, 18:00).

Thus, it is not legal positivism *per se* that accounts for judicial behavior in Chile. However, part of the explanation does appear to rest in the related, and broader, professional ideology of apoliticism, which, as I have explained in previous chapters and will further sustain later, was transmitted and enforced within the judiciary. The premium on "apoliticism" within the institution meant not that judges ignored altogether the choices they faced in adjudication,[154] or felt some absolute fidelity to the letter of legal text; rather, it meant that, when it came to public law, judges were expected to lend unquestioning support to the executive. The support could be passive or active, but the key was to refrain from second-guessing "political" decisions and, thereby, to stay out of politics. In the case of the military government, this was even more pronounced, I argue, as the military presented its rule as a (superior) *alternative to* politics.

INSTITUTIONAL STRUCTURE AND IDEOLOGY

I turn thus to the development of my institutional argument, which has two parts: one structural and the other ideological. The discussion that follows treats them separately, but I should emphasize that the two were, as in the past, mutually reinforcing.

Evidence of the effects of internal control, that is, of what I am calling the *institutional structure*, on judges is overwhelming. It came up again and again in my interviews – cited by nineteen of thirty-six AHC judges, as well as by all the retired and lower court judges I interviewed[155] – and was clear in the discipline and promotion record as well. As one judge noted, under the military regime, "there were different conceptions of what was happening, but the Supreme Court was very powerful over the hierarchy and controlled the responses" (Interview SC96-7, June 5, 1996, 18:00).

The first and most obvious way in which the Court acted to bring the judicial ranks in line after the coup was through an internal purge of avowed and suspected Allende sympathizers in January 1974. With the legal path prepared by Decree Law Nos. 169 and 170, discussed earlier,

---

[154] Indeed, as Correa notes, in many areas of the law, such as marriage nullification, debt readjustment, and the attenuating circumstances of criminal responsibility, judges have long shown themselves to be creative, flexible, and equity-minded (1992: 90).

[155] I have interspersed quotes from these interviews throughout the book. In addition to those found in this section, see those in Chapters 3 and 5.

the Supreme Court used its power to dismiss or force the retirement of an estimated 12 percent of judicial employees, among them approximately forty judges.[156] For the most part, this was done via poor evaluations for their performance in 1973, although some "early retirements" were achieved via a transfer of "troublemakers" to undesirable (geographically isolated) posts (Interview FJ96-5, June 18, 1996 12:00).[157] All of the members of the CUP, the judicial advisory committee to Allende, were dismissed. One of these individuals remarked in an interview, "Isn't it clear that the Supreme Court [removed us all] for political reasons? For the Supreme Court, it's legitimate for any of their members to make political declarations, and during the military government they did so, but a simple judge isn't allowed that right" (Interview FJ96-2, June 13, 1996, 13:00).

Having observed the internal purge, judges "became afraid to do anything, even if they weren't in agreement with what was taking place" (Interview HRL96-1, July 4, 1996, 11:00). As one retired judge explained, "Because of the hierarchy, there exists a sort of reverential fear of the Supreme Court, such that even when they have a determined opinion on some issue, judges normally wind up resolving it in accordance with what the Supreme Court has ruled. There are very few cases, even under democracy, in which a subordinate judge has maintained his way of thinking on a given matter when the Court has ruled in a different way" (Interview FJ96-2, June 13, 1996, 13:00). Under the military regime, this pressure intensified. Recalling the mood set for the judiciary by the high court before and around the plebiscite on the 1980 Constitution, one judge stated:

> I remember as the plebiscite approached, people were talking about it, and naturally within a logic of the 'yes' vote, as if it were impossible to think that someone there would consider voting 'no.' And I was afraid, I *broke out in a sweat* worrying that someone would ask me which way I was going to vote. Nobody asked me, because nobody thought I was for the 'no,' but if

---

[156] The exact numbers here are difficult to come by. I tabulated these figures using a list of names and posts from a support group for judges expelled for political reasons, checked against the official evaluations ledger at the Supreme Court. However, because of all the possible extenuating circumstances, it is difficult to confirm the exact number. It is interesting to note, however, that out of 260 judges evaluated for their performance during 1973, 82 were put on the "satisfactory" list, or list 2 (out of four), which is basically a slap on the wrist, or a "tomato," as one judge called it. This figure is more than twice the average for list 2 in other years.

[157] These are documented in the records of the plenary of the Supreme Court, Vol. 18.

they had asked me, I probably would've been booted from the judiciary – and that is no exaggeration – for my answer. (Interview AC96-2, May 6, 1996, 8:30)

This fear was not unfounded. In 1983, after Santiago Appeals Court judge and longtime president of the National Association of Magistrates, Sergio Dunlop, made some mild criticisms of the judicial retirement system, the Supreme Court responded first by giving him a warning and then putting him on list 2 (of four) in the annual evaluations. Dunlop, who had been a fierce opponent of Allende, thus resigned from the judiciary in 1983 and became a loud critic of the institution. In public statements over the following years, Dunlop contended that the institutional structure of the judiciary was such that only those willing to "remain prudently silent" could find their way to the top (Constable and Valenzuela 1991: 131). "Although judges have tenure," he argued, "in reality their careers depend on the members of the Supreme Court" and those judges that take stands at odds with that of the Supreme Court become "marked." As regards the role of the judiciary under the military regime he stated: "Those who lead [the institution] are those who must signal the standards and the direction to take.... The Supreme Court justices could have acted peacefully defending a different interpretation without having anything happen to them" (Interview in *La Epoca*, May 9, 1989, 12–13).

This last statement began to appear increasingly valid as the 1980s progressed. Not only did the opposition begin organizing and dissenting ever more openly in the wider society, but elements within the regime began to suggest a need for democratic transition. As discussed earlier, the Constitutional Tribunal played an important role in pressing the government to reconstruct and respect certain democratic legal norms. The Supreme Court, however, did little to nothing in this regard. On the contrary, the Court as a whole actively discouraged judges from challenging or criticizing the military government. As noted earlier, the justices even went so far as to censor their own president, Rafael Retamal, when he expressed his disapproval of the regime's policies.

Lower-court judges observed and took note of Retamal's actions and their consequences. When conferences on human rights began in the mid-1980s, some lower court judges attended, but, as one related, "you couldn't let your superiors know you were participating in such acts" (Interview LCJ96-1, April 25, 1996, 11:00). During this period "lower-court judges were paranoid about being poorly evaluated or expelled from the judiciary if they let slip some commentary or did something which their superiors in the Supreme Court or the government wouldn't like" (Matus 1999: 148). And, indeed, the San Miguel judges who met privately to produce the "letter of reflection," noted earlier, were sub-sequently informed in their yearly evaluations that they "had received votes in favor of putting them on list two." This served as "a signal that their names would not figure on the nomination lists for future promotion" (Matus 1999: 159–160).

More open critics of the regime, meanwhile, suffered more serious repercussions. As noted earlier, in August 1986, Santiago Appeals Court judge, Carlos Cerda Fernández, concluded his tenacious and thorough investigation of the 1976 disappearance of thirteen communist leaders and indicted forty people, including thirty-two members of the armed forces. Having reached this point in the investigation (*sumario*), most expected Cerda either to apply amnesty to close the case or to hand it over to the military courts. However, Cerda announced that he would do neither. He grounded his decision on the brief presented for the case by ex-Minister of Justice, Monica Madariaga, the very author of the 1978 amnesty law. Madariaga, whose views on the human rights issue had changed radically since her tenure as minister, maintained that amnesty was a "social pardon," which could not be applied until the truth about the crime had been established, and the guilt of the perpetrators declared.[158] On appeal, both the Santiago Appeals Court and the Supreme Court rejected this argument. The high court overtur-ned the indictments and ordered Cerda to apply the amnesty law to close the case. Cerda responded that to do so would be "evidently contrary to law (*derecho*)" and that thus, according to Article 226 of the Penal Code, he had the right to refuse the order of his superiors. This act outraged the members of the Court, and, in an extraordinary plenary session, they suspended Cerda from the judiciary for two months with only half pay.[159] On learning of the sanction, Cerda stated, "My actions are in keeping with the oath of allegiance to justice, truth, and peace which judges swear to when they take their offices."[160]

---

[158] Monthly report of the *Vicaría de la Solidaridad* for August 1986, on file at the FDAVS, 21–22. See also, P. Verdugo 1991.

[159] Monthly report of the *Vicaría de la Solidaridad* for October 1986, on file at the FDAVS, 55–59. Interestingly, the president of the Court, Rafael Retamal, was absent from the meeting.

[160] From http://derechoschile.com/english/dissidence.htm, accessed October 5, 1999.

Approximately a year and a half later, in May 1988, the Supreme Court censured another judge, René García Villegas, for having included a statement "disrespectful of military justice" in an official resolution. García, the judge of the twenty-first criminal court of Santiago, had taken on the investigation of more than forty cases of torture committed in his jurisdiction between 1985 and 1989, including one case for which he indicted eight CNI agents. In a November 1987 interview with opposition newspaper, *La Epoca*, García declared, "Torture is always criminal, even if the highest reasons of state are invoked" (*La Epoca*, November 15, 1987: 17–18). He was thus averse to renouncing jurisdiction over crimes committed by the regime's security forces, and in a March 1988 resolution contesting the military's claim to jurisdiction over such cases, he bluntly stated as much. The offending passage read, "As has been evident in previous cases, once the investigations that civilian judges have undertaken related to reported crimes presumably committed by security agents are handed over to the military justice system, they become definitively paralyzed and abandoned, resulting in impunity for those incriminated."[161] For this, as well as for "declarations made to the press about similar cases," the Supreme Court issued García a formal reprimand.

On October 24, 1988, the Court sanctioned García again, this time with fifteen days' suspension at half salary, for having "gotten involved in politics." García's alleged impropriety consisted in a statement offered in a radio interview with Radio Exterior de España that "Torture is practiced in Chile." The excerpt had been used, allegedly without García's authorization, in the public campaign for the "no" vote in the October 5 plebiscite. In annual evaluations for both 1988 and 1989, the Court thus ranked García in list three for "incompetent performance," forcing his resignation from the bench on January 25, 1990.[162] The Court also sanctioned several appellate court judges, including the head of the National Judicial Association, Germán Hermosilla, for having expressed their solidarity with García during his suspension. The punishment was "duly reflected in their annual assessment" (Brett 1992: 232).

[161] Monthly report of the *Vicaría de la Solidaridad* for March 1988, on file at the FDAVS, 78–81.
[162] "Supremazo Final contra Juez García," *ANALISIS* (January 15–21, 1990): 22–24. See also García's autobiography, *Soy Testigo* (1990).

Institutional structure thus goes a long way to explaining why even democratic-minded judges refused to take public stands, personal or professional, against the authoritarian regime. As I noted in Chapter 3, most judges came from very modest social backgrounds, and had chosen the judicial career because it was respectable and secure.[163] They were thus largely predisposed to be risk-averse when it came to professional matters. Once on the judicial career ladder, this tendency was reinforced by the "reverential fear" of the Supreme Court. Judges learned quickly that the best way to get ahead was to avoid making waves, and thereby "avoid getting burnt" by their superiors (Interview FJ96-4, June 17, 1996, 12:30).[164] Although this pattern was evident under the previous democratic regime, it was even more marked under military rule, when the Supreme Court took punitive action against any judge that dared challenge their wisdom and authority.

Of course, fear of punishment and career sabotage by superiors cannot explain the behavior of the Supreme Court judges themselves, who, having reached the pinnacle of the hierarchy, were untouchable within the system. As noted earlier, personal attitudes and preferences were clearly at work in some cases, and the military government did its best to create opportunities for its most devoted supporters to rise in the ranks. But it would be a mistake to treat judicial attitudes and preferences as entirely exogenous to the institution. Supreme Court justices reached their posts after having spent forty or more years in an institutional setting that discouraged creative, innovative, and independent decision making. Those who succeeded in rising in the ranks were not those with bold or fresh perspectives, but rather those who best emulated and pleased their superiors, that is, those who demonstrated conservatism and conformity.

The parallels between this pattern of professional socialization and that of the Chilean military are pronounced. According to Constable and Valenzuela, the typical military officer is characterized by loyalty, discipline, and circumspection, and the "desired military mold" is "competent and plodding, rather than brilliant." Those seeking to reach the rank of general should (as did Pinochet) do "just well enough to advance, but not so well as to arouse suspicion" (1991: 48). Indeed, one of my

---

[163] Carlos Cerda was an at least partial exception to this, as was Juan Guzmán, who features in Chapter 5.

[164] Refer to Chapter 3.

interviewees claimed, "what happens to judges is something like what happens to Chilean military men. They are brainwashed. And he who is independent, intelligent, [and] brave *won't be* promoted. They will bother him and will most likely brand him a 'communist' so that he will be marginalized from the judiciary" (Interview FJ96-2, 13 June, 1996, 13:00). Thus, it could hardly be expected that Chile's Supreme Court justices would, in general, possess the skills and initiative necessary to stand up to the authoritarian leaders.

Moreover, the Supreme Court judges, like all members of the judiciary, were socialized from day one to believe that, to be professional, judges must remain "apolitical." This understanding is what I have labeled the *institutional ideology* of the judiciary, and it was evident in judicial discourse throughout the authoritarian era. What made it particularly relevant in this period, I argue, is the fact that the military government itself claimed to be above politics. On the view that it was politicians, with support from democratic civil society, that had caused the socioeconomic debacle of the Allende years, the generals had seized power with the explicit mission of depoliticizing the country (Nef 1974; Valenzuela 1995; Loveman and Davies 1997). Thus, questioning the policies of the military regime was, by the regime's own definition, political and dangerous, while supporting the military was apolitical, patriotic, and noble. My claim is that the judiciary's traditional commitment to apoliticism fed perfectly into this "antipolitics" project. To prove their commitment to law (and order) over politics (and disorder) judges either refrained from challenging the military's policies or outright endorsed them.

As I noted in Chapter 3, it is difficult to document the independent effect of this ideology on judicial behavior, particularly under the authoritarian regime when Supreme Court justices invoked it to threaten their subordinates or to justify punishing them. Nonetheless, taken together with the evidence I will offer in Chapter 5, as well as the pre-1973 pattern presented in the previous chapters, the examples that follow suggest that for many judges, deferring to the (self-proclaimed "apolitical") military government need not have been a conscious strategic choice but was simply a matter of abiding by professional expectations.

In early 1974, in his speech inaugurating the judicial term, Supreme Court president Enrique Urrutia Manzano explicitly reminded judges of their professional duty to eschew politics. He explained that two months earlier the Supreme Court had transferred or removed from office a number of employees who had participated openly in politics under Allende. He argued that this was necessary in order to guard "the full independence of the judiciary, and that, in consequence, any participation whatsoever of employees in partisan proselytizing impaired the administration of justice and deserved condemnation." Later in the address, he boasted of the active role taken by the Supreme Court against the Allende government, and of its official endorsement of the coup on September 12, 1973, which he clearly viewed as something other than political behavior. In contrast to the Allende government, he argued, the military government had fully respected the judiciary as the symbol of Chilean law and justice. He closed by calling on his audience to aid in the "reconstruction of the Republic ... with the objective of making a better Chile, to which, with a healthy, prudent, opportune, and disinterested administration of justice, the judiciary could contribute so much."[165]

Urrutia thus contrasted the prejudicial, illegitimate politicking of the Allende government and its judicial sympathizers with the impartial, professional, and patriotic action of the Supreme Court. Because the military, too, acted out of "impartiality, professionalism, and patriotism" (Nef 1974; Munizaga 1988),[166] it was both logical and completely legitimate for the judiciary to cooperate with the military government in the "construction of a better Chile." It was thus clear that "the courts should be at the service of the new legality that the military power was creating and at the service of the entire process that began with the coup" (Interview with HRL96-5, August 2, 1996) and that those who would critique or disregard that position might throw into question their professional integrity and fitness for judicial service.

This understanding was also articulated in the 1984 plenary censure of Supreme Court president Rafael Retamal, in which, as noted earlier, the justices reminded their colleague that judges were prohibited by law from engaging in politics. Likewise, the basis for the suspension and, ultimately, the dismissal, of Judge René García in 1988 was his having "gotten involved in politics." Both cases not only served to perpetuate the "reverential fear" of the Supreme Court discussed above, but also to reinforce the notion that the good judge, the true professional, is one who goes along and plays along, who sides with tradition, unity, and order. By contrast, he who dares to challenge the forces of tradition, unity, and order, to speak up in defense of liberal or

[165] *RDJ* 71 (1974) 1: 18–21.
[166] Urrutia's position clearly acccepts this perspective.

democratic principles, is playing "politics" and thereby betraying his lack of professionalism. In such an ideological environment, it is unsurprising that most judges would remain quietest and deferential.

CONCLUSION

To summarize, a complete and accurate explanation of judicial performance under the Pinochet regime requires an understanding of the institutional setting in which judges functioned. On coming to power, the military government did not install its own judges, nor did it subsequently interfere in the judicial decision making process. Nonetheless, the judiciary threw its support behind the regime and lent it a mantle of legal legitimacy for seventeen years and beyond. Even when other juridical actors, such as the bar association and the Constitutional Tribunal, began to take stands that challenged and limited the government's prerogatives, the judiciary remained at the service of the regime. Only a few brave individuals broke ranks with their brethren to take public stands against authoritarianism, and these individuals were duly punished by the Supreme Court. My argument, then, is that the longstanding institutional features of the judiciary, namely, its autonomous bureaucratic structure and its ideology of apoliticism, gave it a conservative bias that made it an ideal ally for the military regime. The effective policing of the judicial hierarchy by the Supreme Court, as well as the constant reinforcement of the notion that to take independent or unconventional stands was to behave in an illegitimate "political" manner, ensured that all but the most exceptional judges would refrain from asserting themselves in defense of liberal democratic principles and practices.

CHAPTER FIVE

CONTINUITY AND CHANGE AFTER THE RETURN TO DEMOCRACY, 1990–2000

On March 11, 1990, General Augusto Pinochet transferred the presidential sash to Patricio Aylwin Azócar, thereby bringing military rule to a formal end. Aylwin had been elected as the candidate of the *Concertación de Partidos para la Democracia*, which had formed out of the *Concertación por el No* organized for the 1988 plebiscite.[1] He won the presidency with 55 percent of the popular vote, and the *Concertación* won 72 of 120 seats in the Chamber of Deputies and 22 of the 38 elected seats in the Senate.[2]

On coming to power, the *Concertación*'s top priority was to "reconstruct and consolidate democracy to ensure that the rule of law would be secured" (Oppenheim 1993: 206). As one Chilean author observes, "During the years of resistance to the dictatorship, the concepts of democracy and human rights had been forged into a single, indivisible ideal" (Otano 1995: 161). Therefore, important sectors of the population held that "to do justice is to build democracy" (Badilla 1990b).

---

[1] Despite Pinochet's efforts, the clean October 5, 1988, plebiscite had resulted in a vote of no confidence in the military regime. The opposition political parties succeeded in mobilizing 55 percent of Chile's six million voters to cast ballots against Pinochet. The 44 percent support for the '*Sí*' was significant, but not enough to allow the government to contest the vote. With pressure from his peers and his aides, Pinochet was forced to acknowledge defeat. For accounts of the plebiscite and its aftermath, see Constable and Valenzuela 1991, Oppenheim 1993, Otano 1995, Drake and Jaksic 1995, and Barros 2002.

[2] There were also nine designated senators, so the *Concertación* did not have a majority in the Senate.

The judiciary was thus to be a central focus of the continuing transition to democracy.

As this chapter will show, however, the judiciary proved to be an obstacle to the deepening of democracy well into the 1990s. During the first eight years of the new democratic regime, judges as a whole continued to support the ideology and interests of the military and the undemocratic Right. Despite the prosecution of a few important figures from the military regime and sporadic decisions recognizing human rights principles, the judiciary, led by the Supreme Court, generally endorsed the legal edifice constructed by the leaders of the authoritarian regime and left largely unchallenged the principles and values embodied therein. As in the past, those judges who attempted to break publicly from this pattern were reprimanded by their superiors in the Supreme Court. In addition, the justices of the Supreme Court, with explicit support from their subordinates, resisted most of the reform proposals put forth by democratic administrations, and cast themselves, as they had for decades, as above all forms of politics.

By the end of the decade, judges had begun to change their tune somewhat. Indeed, by the end of 2000, Chilean courts had convicted twenty-eight individuals for authoritarian-era human rights violations,[3] and revoked General Pinochet's immunity from prosecution in the infamous Caravan of Death case.[4] Many observers attributed this to the exogenous shock of Pinochet's detention in London, from October 1998 to March 2000, and, to be sure, "Londres" had a significant impact on Chilean judges. Yet, as this chapter will show, institutional reform had set the stage for these changes, enhancing the effectiveness of the external push to punish past abuses. With the groundwork laid domestically, the foreign judicial action emboldened, challenged, and impelled Chilean judges to depart decisively from their previous pattern of conservative rulings upholding the military government's blanket amnesty law.

---

[3] Figure is from http://www.derechos.org/nizkor/chile/doc/codepu00/cap1.html. Note, however, that most of these were for violations that occurred after the period covered by the amnesty law. The first convictions for violations that occurred under the amnestied period did not come until 2002.

[4] In January 2001, Santiago Appeals Court Judge, Juan Guzmán, indicted Pinochet in this case. However, the general subsequently escaped conviction when Judge Guzmán's colleagues and superiors determined he was, by law, mentally unfit to stand trial.

In a more general sense, however, the institutional practices of the Chilean judiciary proved remarkably sticky, even after the Pinochet arrest. Although the stance of judges toward authoritarian-era rights violations evolved over the course of the 1990s, in rights cases that post-dated the authoritarian regime, judges proved persistently conformist and conservative. Judges showed little interest in seizing the opportunities presented to them, whether in the law or in the broader political context, to defend and promote citizens' rights. Thus, at the dawn of the new millennium there was still no evidence of a more general rights revolution in Chile (Epp 1998; Couso 2004b).

The chapter proceeds in three sections. The first section discusses post-1990 judicial reform efforts, as well as other developments in the legal and political spheres that provided the context for judicial performance. The next section summarizes judicial performance during the 1990–2000 period, examining first the trajectory of decisions in cases involving authoritarian-era rights abuses and then the record of decisions in rights cases that postdate the return to democracy. As in preceding chapters, the third and final section offers an explanation for the patterns highlighted earlier, bringing to bear, in particular, evidence from interviews in both 1996 and 2001.

DEMOCRATIC-ERA EFFORTS TO LIBERALIZE LAW AND JUSTICE

President Aylwin, constitutional lawyer and son of a former Supreme Court president, was elected on a strong human rights platform.[5] Although the *Concertación*'s acceptance of the 1978 amnesty law and the (partially reformed) 1980 Constitution as conditions for the transition itself limited significantly what his government could accomplish,[6]

[5] The *Concertación* platform included both a proposal to overturn the amnesty law and legal reforms to impede future rights violations, among them modifications of the internal state security law, the arms control law, and antiterrorist laws. It also proposed extensive reforms of the judicial system and penal codes, and an overhaul of the military justice.

[6] In anticipation of the transition, a reform package in 1989 had abolished constitutional restrictions on political parties and party membership, prohibited exile as a sanction, repealed restrictions on habeas corpus petitions, expanded the number of elected senators (from twenty-six to thirty-eight), and added a line to Article 5 making it a duty of the state to respect and promote the human rights guaranteed

Aylwin remained officially committed to "bring[ing] to trial anyone who had committed particularly atrocious abuses under the old regime" (Correa 1997: 132), and to securing full investigation of all major human rights violations (Brett 1992: 193–194).[7]

Knowing he was unlikely to get cooperation from the judiciary, which he declared to be "in crisis" (Badilla 1990a: 31), Aylwin moved early in his tenure to create the Commission for Truth and Reconciliation, also known as the Rettig Commission after its chairman, Raúl Rettig.[8] The commission was charged with investigating human rights abuses under the military government, preparing an official report, and presenting the findings to the courts for possible prosecutions. The objective was to have a group of persons "of recognized prestige and moral authority" prepare a "report in conscience" that would offer the public "a rational and well-founded conception of what took place" under the military regime (Supreme Decree No. 355, cited in Brett 1992: 130). They were given one year to complete this task.

The group's mission explicitly excluded the investigation of torture, exile, and other abuses; only deaths and disappearances were to be documented.[9] The names of perpetrators were not to be published, and the commission was not given the mandate to pass judgment on the possible guilt of individuals. The commission investigated both government violations and left- and right-wing terrorism, the latter so as

by the Constitution and by international treaties ratified by Chile. In addition, the outgoing government had finally published the International Covenant on Civil and Political Rights in the *Diario Oficial*, rendering it formally binding on Chile.

[7] Through a legislative package dubbed the "Cumplido Laws" after Minister of Justice, Francisco Cumplido, Aylwin sought to adapt existing legislation to meet the standards of the major international human rights conventions to which Chile was a signatory. The administration proposed to abolish the death penalty, to restrict the jurisdiction of military courts, to strengthen guarantees of due process, to release political prisoners from the authoritarian period, and to reactivate the investigation of the Letelier-Moffitt assassinations. It was not until 1991 that the Congress partially approved the package, although military jurisdiction remained largely unchanged.

[8] Rettig was a distinguished former president of the Chilean bar association and a former Radical Party senator. On the work of the commission in general, see Otano 1995: Ch. 11.

[9] It was not until November 28, 2004, that a report on torture prepared by The National Commission on Political Imprisonment and Torture was released by President Ricardo Lagos. The twelve-hundred-page report confirmed more than twenty-seven thousand cases of imprisonment and torture. It was followed by a compensation package and free health care for the victims.

to appease the armed forces, who viewed casualties suffered by military and police members as "human rights violations." In February 1991, the Rettig Commission delivered its final report accounting for 2,115 victims of human rights violations, of which 1,068 were disappeared, as well as the fate of another 164 victims of political violence.[10]

The Rettig Report devoted a full chapter to a critique of judicial performance under the military regime.[11] It stated that the ineffectiveness of the courts in protecting human rights had been caused by "weakness and a lack of vigor" on the part of many judges. Specifically, the chapter scolded the judges for having denied judicial protection to victims of illegal arrest, for having failed to pursue energetic investigations of human rights crimes and bring those responsible to justice; and for having abdicated review of the decisions of war tribunals. It noted that judges had not respected legal time-limits for ruling on habeas corpus petitions, had not challenged arrests carried out without arrest warrants, had routinely accepted postdated arrest orders, and had taken no action to prevent either the use of clandestine detention centers or prolonged incommunicado detention. By contrast, in cases in which state officials were implicated, judges had used overly rigorous formal standards of evidence, had accepted statements given by the accused with no effort to corroborate official information, and had applied the amnesty law precipitously to cover cases in which the investigation of the facts had not yet been completed. In short, the *Report* accused the country's judges of having aggravated the human rights situation under the military regime.

Around the same time that the Rettig Report was published, Aylwin publicly stated that in dealing with human rights abuses under the military regime, the judges had "lacked moral courage" (*El Mercurio*, March 9, 1991). To make up for their previous failing, President Aylwin urged the courts to "carry out their function and pursue exhaustive investigations" in the 220 some cases on which the Commission had uncovered new evidence. He made clear that, in the view of the government,

---

[10] See *Summary of the Truth and Reconciliation Commission Report* (1991: 92). Note that in February 1992, the *Corporación Nacional de Reparación y Reconciliación* was formed to continue investigations and archive the relevant material. This organization remained in operation until 1996, documenting approximately 1,000 more deaths and disappearances to bring the official total to 3,197.

[11] See *Report of the Chilean National Commission on Truth and Reconciliation* (1991: vol. 1, Ch. 4, 117–126).

the amnesty law could not limit investigation, an interpretation that became known as the "Aylwin doctrine."

Aylwin recognized, however, that liberalizing the role the judiciary played in the polity would take more than a simple purge of authoritarian elements or the public cajoling of moral weaklings. In order to renovate the judicial vocation, and thereby to increase judges' democratic legitimacy and accountability, a variety of changes to judicial structure, procedure, and training were needed. As one Chilean legal scholar put it, in the 1990s, the judiciary was the "Cinderella" of the Chilean state: long neglected, poor, and atrophied, and in need of serious attention in order that she might stay and dance at the national democratic ball (Correa 1999).

Hence, on April 1, 1991, Aylwin sent a comprehensive set of judicial reform bills to Congress.[12] Based on analyses conducted by opposition jurists known as the *Grupo de los 24* and subsequently adopted by the national bar association, the bills consisted of two "organic constitutional laws" and one amending the Constitution (all requiring supramajority approval).[13] Specifically, the reform package called for:

- Creation of a National Justice Council, to be composed of representatives of the legislature, the executive, and the judiciary, as well as members of the bar association and university law faculties. The Council, modeled after those in Italy and Spain, was to be charged with planning, administration and budgetary control of the judiciary, thereby permitting the Supreme Court, which devotes a significant percentage of its time to such matters, to focus on strictly judicial tasks. Crucially, the Council was also to take over responsibility for composing the nomination lists for vacancies on the Court.[14]
- Expansion of the Supreme Court from seventeen to twenty-one members, along with jurisdictional changes to promote the unification of legal interpretation. These changes included division of the Court into specialized chambers and alteration of the rules

---

[12] It should be noted that many similar reforms (e.g., National Judicial Councils, ombudsmen, penal procedure reforms) were being adopted around Latin America at the time. On this see Hammergren 2002 and Langer 2004.

[13] On the proposed reforms, see Guzmán Vial 1991, Peña 1991, Valenzuela Somarriva 1991b; Valenzuela Somarriva 1991a, Guzmán Vial 1992, and Correa 1999.

[14] For an exhaustive account of why the National Justice Council was rejected in Chile, see Hammergren 2002.

governing the *recurso de queja* to encourage the Court to focus on *recursos de casación*.

- Alteration of the evaluations process to make it more objective and transparent.
- Establishment of a judicial school (*Academia Judicial*) to improve the caliber of incoming judges, to promote continuing education as they climb the hierarchy, and generally to improve the prestige of the judicial profession.
- Creation of the office of ombudsman (*defensor del pueblo*) as an additional mechanism against abuses by public officials.
- Expansion of the Judicial Assistance Service and the creation of family and community courts to provide free and accessible legal advice and more effective institutions for the resolution of community disputes.
- Alteration of the penal procedure code and the creation of a *Ministerio Público* staffed with public prosecutors, such that the investigation and sentencing functions in criminal courts would no longer be carried out by a single person.

These proposals were "moderate from the perspective of the government [but] in the eyes of both the opposition and the Supreme Court itself, appeared to be the revolutionary agenda of a Marxist government" (Matus 1999: 66). Without the requisite supramajority support, Aylwin was thus forced to withdraw the proposals for a National Judicial Council and an Ombudsman (*defensor del pueblo*). In the end, only the specialization of the Supreme Court, changes to the procedural rules for *recursos de queja*, modification of the evaluation system, and the Judicial School were approved. None of these changes took effect, however, until after Aylwin left office.[15]

---

[15] Specialization of Supreme Court chambers commenced in 1995. The *Academia Judicial* began functioning in April 1996. The entrance examination was open to anyone with a law degree. In the first year, twenty of one hundred examinees were accepted. The new evaluations system was first used in the evaluation process of 1996 (for the year 1995). The system requires judges to rate their subordinates on a scale of 1–7 in several areas. These totals are then averaged for each person evaluated. Evaluators must identify themselves with the grades they give, but they do not have to justify them. Judges interviewed for this study felt the new system was even more unfair than the former, because there was no agreement within the judiciary on what the different numbers meant (e.g., does a decent employee deserve a 5 or a 7?), and because one very low evaluation could bring down an individual's average.

In December 1992, members of the *Concertación* coalition launched an impeachment attempt against three justices of the Supreme Court, Lionel Beraud, Hernán Cereceda, and Germán Valenzuela. The action was sparked by the judges' decision to wrest a disappearance case from the hands of a judge whose investigation was bearing fruit and pass it to the military courts, where it was promptly closed.[16] A group of representatives from the Chamber of Deputies charged the judges with "gross neglect of duty," claiming that the *Chanfreau* decision was merely the culmination of a pattern of "reiterated and inexcusable neglect . . . to do justice in the face of violence and extreme cruelties experienced within Chilean society." The decision, they argued, demonstrated a clear will to procure impunity and deny justice in cases of grave human rights violations, since it is publicly known . . . that when such cases pass to military justice, they cease to advance and end by being closed."[17] The Chamber of Deputies approved the impeachment charges, but the Senate voted, largely along coalition lines, that judges could not be dismissed for their legal interpretations. However, in the case of Justice Hernán Cereceda, who was charged additionally with inexcusable and illegal delay in rendering a decision (in a separate case), three right-wing senators broke ranks and voted with the Concertación to dismiss him from office.[18]

Although only partially successful, then, the impeachment effort sent a strong message to the judiciary. On assuming his post, the new president of the Supreme Court, Marcos Aburto, suddenly declared that the amnesty law should not impede investigation. By mid-1993, a considerable number of lower-court judges had thus begun following the "Aylwin doctrine," reopening human rights cases in an attempt to clarify the facts before applying the amnesty law.

Infuriated by this and other government policies, on May 28, 1993, Pinochet staged a military show of force. While President Aylwin was on a state visit to Scandinavia, heavily armed soldiers appeared in the streets of Santiago bearing black berets, or *boinas*. Pinochet and his

---

[16] This case, known as the *Chanfreau* case after the disappeared individual, will be discussed further later in the chapter.

[17] See *Diario de Sesiones de la Camara de Diputados*, Session 37, January 8, 1993.

[18] See the debate and vote in the *Diario de Sesiones del Senado*, Sessions 24–27, January 19–20, 1993. The three swing votes against Cereceda are said to have been motivated by a desire to punish him not for his conduct in the cited case, but for other unspecified "irregularities."

colleagues claimed that the *boinazo* was a response to the government-led "smear campaign against the armed forces." Among the specific "insults" the military leaders cited were the prosecution of Pinochet's son for a fraudulent business transaction, the subpoenaing of officers on active duty to testify in human rights cases, the government's pardoning of leftist political prisoners, the lack of full cooperation from the Ministry of Defense, and Aylwin's proposed reforms of the military appointment system. Pinochet was particularly enraged by the negative coverage of these matters in *La Nación*, the official government paper.[19]

Aylwin's response, once he had controlled the immediate threat, was to attempt a legislative resolution to human rights cases, which some labeled a *punto final* law. The goal was to accelerate investigation of human rights cases so as to clarify unsolved crimes, and the proposed means was to provide anonymity to those who offered testimony and to those identified as perpetrators. Once the cases were resolved, amnesty would be applied and the cases closed. Because of opposition within the governing coalition, however, Aylwin finally withdrew the bill in September 1993.

Between April and September 1993, the government was able to appoint two new justices to the Supreme Court, bringing the total of new appointments under Aylwin to six. However, because of the institutional factors discussed in this book, the presence of these new justices did not necessarily signify an imminent change in judicial performance in Chile. Indeed, it was not until 1998, after Aylwin's successor, Eduardo Frei Ruiz-Tagle,[20] succeeded in passing a major reform to the Supreme Court, that judicial performance began to change notably.

Bearing in mind the (largely failed) experience of the Aylwin government, the Frei administration opted to take a subtler and more gradual approach to judicial reform (Correa 1999). Although Frei sought to remove human rights from the political spotlight and focus instead on socioeconomic matters (Correa 1997: 142), reform of the courts did not disappear from the government's agenda. With support from non-governmental organizations associated with both the *Concertación* and the opposition, Frei's Ministry of Justice centered its efforts on one piece

---

[19] See Human Rights Watch/Americas 1994: 8–9, and Otano 1995: Ch. 22.

[20] This President Frei was the son of Eduardo Frei Montalva, who was president from 1964–1970 (see Chapter 3). A Christian Democrat, Frei Ruiz-Tagle was the candidate of the *Concertación* coalition. He served from 1994 to 2000, when he was replaced by a third *Concertación* president, Socialist Ricardo Lagos.

of Aylwin's earlier package: criminal procedure reform. This reform, which was finally approved by Congress in August 1997, called for a transition of the criminal justice system from a written, inquisitory system to an oral, accusatory one. In other words, judges in criminal cases were no longer to have both prosecutorial (investigatory) and judicial functions, but would reach a decision based on the evidence and legal arguments presented by public prosecutors and defense lawyers. Moreover, criminal trials were to be conducted orally and publicly, introducing new procedural guarantees for defendants that were absent under the closed written system (*Ministerio de Justicia de Chile* 1996).[21] As will be discussed later, judges reacted negatively to the reform initiatives, but, after a sustained effort on the part of the reform coalition to educate judges about the virtues of the system, a majority of the Supreme Court finally voted in favor of what was billed "the reform of the century" (Correa 1999).

Later that year, the Frei government was able to capitalize on an alleged corruption scandal involving members of the Supreme Court to push a major reform of the Court through Congress. The scandal arose out of the case against accused drug dealer and money launderer Mario Silva Leiva, or "Cabro Carrera," who was allegedly protected for years by a network of government officials and public employees. Representatives from the opposition party UDI (*Unión Democrática Independiente*) took advantage of the political uproar over the case to file impeachment charges against Supreme Court president Servando Jordán for undue intervention or interference in the Cabro Carrera case and in the case of another suspected drug dealer, Rita Romero. Not to be outdone, members of the *Concertación* filed a separate accusation against four justices, including Jordán, for misconduct in the 1991 case of convicted Colombian drug dealer Luis Correa Ramirez.[22]

Claiming that it wanted to address the root of the problem, and confident after its successful cooperation with the opposition on criminal procedure reform, the government seized the moment to propose

---

[21] As noted earlier, this sort of reform was occurring across the region in the 1990s. See Langer 2004.

[22] Correa Ramirez had been convicted and imprisoned after smuggling a half ton of cocaine into Chile in 1989, and on April 17, 1991, the Third Chamber of the Supreme Court denied him parole. One month later, however, the justices unanimously and inexplicably paroled him on a bond of about U.S.$1,100, after he had served only one-quarter of his sentence. Correa Ramirez then fled the country. See ChIP News, for July 1, 1997.

fundamental structural changes to the Supreme Court. With support from the leading opposition party, *Renovación Nacional* (RN), the Frei administration proposed a new nomination system for Supreme Court justices, reserving five posts on the Court for lawyers from outside the judiciary and requiring ratification of any appointee by two-thirds of the Senate. The bill also expanded Supreme Court membership from seventeen to twenty-one, provided for the (comfortable) retirement of all judges over the age of seventy-five, and shortened the term of Supreme Court president from three to two years. Although, or perhaps because, all of the Supreme Court justices in question survived impeachment attempts,[23] the judicial reform effort gathered momentum. Even the far-Right UDI expressed support for most aspects of the reform package. Despite opposition from the judiciary, the reforms prospered and 1998 brought eleven new faces to the Court, including five lawyers from outside the judicial hierarchy (Lagos 1998).[24]

Pressure for change was already being brought to bear on the judiciary, then, when British Home Secretary Jack Straw ordered General Pinochet's arrest on October 16, 1998.[25] The arrest had a dramatic effect on Chilean political life. The heretofore untouchable *caudillo*, who had maintained hero status among a significant minority of Chileans, was suddenly and dramatically knocked from his pedestal. Detained in Great Britain, a country for which many Chileans had a special admiration and affinity,[26] and denied immune status by that nation's highest court,[27] Pinochet could no longer claim that the long-standing

---

[23] For the charges brought by the UDI, Servando Jordán narrowly escaped impeachment: The July 25 vote in the Chamber of Deputies was fifty-two to fifty-two. In the other case, in which charges were brought against Jordán and three others, only twenty-four deputies voted to impeach the judges, whereas forty-nine voted to absolve.

[24] See Article 75 of the Constitution, as modified by this reform.

[25] The arrest came at the request of Spanish judge Baltasar Garzón, who sought the extradition of General Pinochet to Spain to stand trial, under universal jurisdiction, for crimes against humanity. The final ruling of the Law Lords, Britain's highest court, came in March 1999, and stated that the general could be extradited to Spain, but only on charges of torture committed after the International Convention against Torture became part of British law in 1988. For more details, see Davis 2003.

[26] Chileans have long fancied themselves the "British of Latin America" (Blakemore 1993) and the two countries had an especially close relationship during the Thatcher years, when Chile backed Britain in the Falklands/Malvinas war.

[27] For a good summary of the trials in London and the legal debates, see Human Rights Watch 1999.

accusations against him were the fabrications of isolated extremists. Moreover, because he was off the scene and unable to respond directly, Chileans felt free to engage in public debate about the dictatorship with a degree of openness that had been impossible for the past twenty-five years (Human Rights Watch 2003).[28] Important figures on the political Right distanced themselves from Pinochet, and some individuals issued confessions or apologies (e.g., Editorial, *Qué Pasa*, April 17, 1999). Even the military, under the new leadership of General Ricardo Izurieta, seemed to give only lukewarm support to the embattled former general.[29]

The Frei government, for its part, broke with its formerly lackadaisical stance on the human rights issue and organized the *Mesa de Diálogo*, or Human Rights Roundtable. The Roundtable brought human rights lawyers and military officials together for the first time to discuss the past and to seek information regarding the fate of the disappeared. Although critics dismissed the talks as a cynical move to locate bodies and, thereby, turn disappearances into amnestiable murders, the Roundtable did lead, in mid-2000, to the first official recognition on the part of the military that state officials had committed atrocities under the military regime (Zalaquett 2001: 40–47).

Meanwhile, the Frei government demanded Pinochet's return to Chile on grounds of national sovereignty and for humanitarian reasons (the general was eighty-four and ailing). Challenging the view of human rights activists, who had pursued the foreign prosecution out of frustration with domestic courts (Brett 2000), Chilean government officials insisted that Pinochet could and would be tried in Chile, that is, that the Chilean judiciary was both willing and able to hold human rights violators accountable. Although Britain's highest court did find grounds for extradition, ultimately, the British government succumbed to pressure from the Chileans, releasing Pinochet and returning him to Chile on humanitarian grounds in March of 2000 (just before the inauguration of Socialist president Ricardo Lagos).[30]

---

[28] One indication of this loosening of the public debate was the founding of the satirical weekly newspaper, "The Clinic," whose headlines were regularly critical of Pinochet.

[29] Pinochet had stepped down as Commander-in-Chief of the Armed Forces in March of 1998. Izurrieta served for three years, after which he was replaced by General Juan Emilio Cheyre, who was even more forward-looking (see Human Rights Watch 2003: 13–14).

[30] I offer a limited treatment here, but extensive discussion of the national and international trials of Pinochet can be found in Davis 2003 and Roht-Arriaza 2005.

THE JUDICIAL ROLE IN THE 1990S

Given the dramatic changes in the domestic and international political context just described, one might expect to see equally dramatic changes in the behavior of Chilean judges in this period. However, as I will demonstrate in this section, there was surprising continuity in much of the rights jurisprudence of the courts during these years. In the pages that follow, I document and describe the pattern of judicial decision making in (published) rights cases of the 1990s, first in cases from the authoritarian era and then in cases that postdate the transition. I demonstrate that the judiciary's treatment of authoritarian-era human rights abuses – at least those covered by the 1978 amnesty law – remained predictably passive, until after the 1997 reforms and Pinochet's detention abroad. In rights cases that postdate the return to democracy, by contrast, the more traditional conservative and conformist pattern persisted.

Decisions in Authoritarian-Era Rights Cases

Just as they had under military rule, human rights lawyers fought tirelessly in the 1990s to keep disappearance and murder cases open. Their hope was that, in a new political context, judges would rise to meet the expectations of the democratic majority and the requirements of international law. The desired response was long in coming.

Table 5.1 summarizes the outcomes of all published rights cases in terms of the party that they favored (the military/authoritarian legality or citizen/liberal legality).[31] The main issues in these cases were whether the investigation of an alleged crime had reached a point where the amnesty law could be applied; whether the amnesty was legitimate under the constitution and under international law; and whether a case involving military personnel must automatically be transferred to military courts, which had no independence from the military chain of command.

As this table indicates, the European judicial action against Pinochet did correlate with a change in judicial treatment of past human rights violations, although, as I argue throughout this chapter, the groundwork

---

[31] The same caveats apply as in earlier chapters as to the representativeness of this sample. If anything, it exaggerates the percentage of liberal decisions, because they were unusual and, for that reason, sure to be published, whereas the others were simply a sampling of a far more common set.

Table 5.1. Published decisions in authoritarian-era rights cases, 1990–2000[a]

	Favor military/ authoritarian legality	Favor citizen/ liberal legality
Before Pinochet's arrest in London	29	6
After Pinochet's arrest in London	1	5

[a] All are appellate and Supreme Court decisions, with the latter comprising the bulk thereof.

had already been laid and some movement in a liberal direction was already in evidence before the general's arrest. The brief narrative that follows traces this evolution through a discussion of some of the cases contained in Table 5.1.

In the first highly anticipated ruling after the transition, delivered on August 24, 1990, the Supreme Court ruled *unanimously* that the application of amnesty was constitutional in disappearance cases, validating the practice of applying amnesty before the facts of the case had been clarified.[32] The petition for *inaplicabilidad* had been filed for a case involving the disappearance of seventy people between 1973 and 1974, the evidence for which pointed to the guilt of (ret.) General Manuel Contreras and other DINA agents. Petitioners argued that the amnesty law (DL 2,191) was unconstitutional on three grounds. First, it violated the human rights guaranteed by both the Constitution and the international treaties and covenants which had been incorporated into Chilean law via the reform to Article 5 of the Constitution. Second, the law denied the judiciary its constitutional right and duty to investigate crimes and to identify the culprits. And, third, the law violated the principle of equality of the law by granting amnesty only to those who had not yet been prosecuted for political crimes committed during the period in question (Etcheberry 1990).

In the decision, the Supreme Court offered a detailed defense of the amnesty law.[33] The justices argued that the amnesty was "essentially

[32] The case was *Iván Sergio Insunza Bascuñán* (*recurso de inaplicabilidad*), RDJ 87 (1990) 2.4: 64–86.

[33] Before ruling on the merits of the case, the Court affirmed its right and duty to rule on the constitutionality of laws issued before the 1980 Constitution. This was a major shift in jurisprudence, as under the military regime, the Court had consistently argued that such cases were a simple matter of supercession, to be determined by lower courts. "In other words, [the Court claimed] that it couldn't inconvenience the military government, but that it could inconvenience a democratic government..." (Garretón n.d.: 69). Subsequently, the Court's position on this matter

general and equal in regard to the punishable facts" that it covered, and that it had been issued by a legitimate legislative power in the general interest of society.[34] The law was neither arbitrary nor contrary to the constitutional order because Article 60, Number 16 of the Constitution expressly permitted legislation of this nature as part of the "legitimate exercise of sovereignty." The Court thus not only justified the amnesty law but reasserted the legitimacy of the military regime.

Equally important, the Court offered a long analysis of the juridical concept of amnesty and explicitly established that "once it is verified that the facts in question are covered by the amnesty law, judges must declare amnesty... [and] are not bound by article 413 of the Penal Procedure Code which requires the completion of the investigation in order to permanently close a case."

In regard to the place of international law, the Court argued that the Convention for the Prevention and Sanction of the Crime of Genocide, although part of Chilean law since 1953, did not apply because "no specific sanctions had been established in the national legislation to punish such a crime." The International Covenant on Civil and Political Rights, for its part, did not apply because the decree incorporating it into Chilean law had not been issued until April 29, 1989; that is, it could not have retroactive effects.

Finally, and perhaps most controversially, the Court said that although Chile had been bound by the terms of the Geneva Conventions since 1951, they were not applicable in this case because there had been no internal armed conflict in Chile. "Although [the criminal facts under investigation in this case] took place during the state of siege period covered by the amnesty law, they do not appear to be the consequence... of a state of internal conflict bearing the characteristics [defined by the Convention]." This argument blatantly contradicted both the legal facts and the Court's previous criteria. Decree Law 5 had explicitly declared that the state of siege should be understood as a "state of war," as established in Article 418 of the Military Justice Code. Article 418 of the Military Justice Code, for its part, established that war is

oscillated. Compare, for example, *Viola Dimter Brandau* (*inaplicabilidad*), December 18, 1990, *Gaceta Jurídica* 125: 47–53; *Miguel Vera Bascur* (*inaplicabilidad*), October 31, 1991, *RDJ* 88 (1991) 2.5:263–9; *Sociedad Benefactora y Educacional Dignidad* (*inaplicabilidad*), September 16, 1992, *RDJ* 89 (1992) 2.5: 270–291.

[34] Decree laws 126 and 527 were cited as proof of the "legitimacy" of the legislative power of the junta.

either declared via a law or via the decree of a state of siege. Moreover, the Court had repeatedly recognized the existence of a state of internal war in its decisions, even going so far as to renounce its power to review the decisions of war tribunals.

Although this particular ruling was, "technically speaking . . . binding only to the case under review, the message to the judiciary [regarding interpretation of the amnesty law] was clear" (Brett 1992: 200). Moreover, subsequent decisions reinforced the Court's position. For example, in June 1992, the Supreme Court overturned a decision of the Puerto Montt Appeals Court[35] and granted *amparo* to a military officer arrested for a 1973 political murder. The Court stated that because it had been established that the crime had occurred on September 16, 1973, and because the suspect had not been on trial or convicted at the time the amnesty law was issued, he was clearly a beneficiary of amnesty and had to be released immediately.[36] Similarly, in September 1993, the plenary of the Supreme Court denied requests for information filed by lower-court judges on four cases closed by virtue of the amnesty law, arguing that because they had occurred in the period covered by the amnesty law, and because the statute of limitations had also expired, there was no justification for reviving them.[37]

Meanwhile, on October 30, 1992, the Court also issued its infamous ruling on the *Chanfreau* case. The Santiago Appeals Court had named Gloria Olivares as *ministro en visita* to investigate the kidnapping and disappearance of MIR leader, Alfonso Chanfreau, and her ongoing investigation was clearly pointing to the culpability of military personnel (Camus 1992; Hidalgo 1992). The Martial Court thus filed a jurisdictional challenge with the Supreme Court. The latter ruled that the alleged crimes had been committed during a state of (internal) war (as established by Decree Laws 3 and 5 of 1973) and had taken place in a location where the DINA had operated. This implied that DINA agents were responsible for Chanfreau's disappearance, and because (according to DL521) DINA agents were considered military personnel, suspects in

---

[35] The decision was signed by one sitting judge, Manuel Barría, and one *abogado integrante*.

[36] *Raúl Gajardo Leopold* (*amparo*), June 2, 1992, *Gaceta Jurídica* 144: 82–85. The decision was signed by Justices Jordan, Faúndez, Araya, all appointed under Pinochet, and two *abogados integrantes* appointed by Aylwin.

[37] *Vicente Blanco Sarmiento* (*contienda de competencia*), *Fallos del Mes* 418: 768–9. Note, however, that five of thirteen justices, all appointees of the Aylwin government, dissented.

the case could only be tried in military courts. The Court thus ruled for the immediate transfer of the case to the military courts, where amnesty was swiftly applied.[38]

As discussed earlier, the ruling shocked the public and provoked an impeachment motion in Congress. The fact that the Court had (again) changed its opinion regarding the state of war in 1973–1974, directly contradicting the position taken in the 1990 *inaplicabilidad* case (*Insunza Bascuñán*), particularly incensed many Chileans. In addition, because Judge Olivares had not even arrested or indicted anyone, the decision was based on the most minimal evidence (Aylwin 1992; Young Debeuf 1992).

Another case that captured much public attention was that of Carmelo Soria, a Spanish national murdered by the DINA in 1976. At the time of his death, Soria was employed by CEPAL, the United Nation's Economic Commission for Latin America, and thus ostensibly enjoyed the diplomatic immunity and protections extended to all U.N. employees by a treaty to which Chile was a signatory. If international law was to apply in any case, it was certainly in this one.

The case followed a labyrinthine legal path. It was first reopened in March 1991, after the publication of the *Rettig Report*. Under pressure from Spain and the U.N., the Chilean Ministry of Foreign Affairs requested, in May 1992, that the Santiago Appeals Court appoint a *ministro en visita* to the case. Judge Violeta Guzmán was assigned, and she refused to apply amnesty before the investigation was complete. On July 28, 1993, the Supreme Court rejected a *recurso de queja* against Judge Guzmán's handling of the case.

However, four months later, when the military court filed a jurisdictional dispute claim, the Supreme Court wrested the case from Judge Guzmán.[39] The decision stated, in terms now familiar, that the evidence gathered by Judge Guzmán suggested that DINA agents had committed

---

[38] *Contienda de competencia*, October 30, 1992, *RDJ* 89 (1992) 2.4: 235–237. In this case, the justices who signed the majority opinion were Cereceda, Béraud, and Valenzuela, all Pinochet-era appointees, with Aylwin appointees Carrasco and Garrido dissenting. However, it should be noted that precisely the same reasoning had been offered by a different set of judges in an earlier decision rendered on April 28, 1992. See *Fallos del Mes* 402: 234–236. In that case, the ruling was 5–0, with Justice Correa Bulo and *abogado integrante* Eugenio Valenzuela (both appointed by Aylwin) included.

[39] In this case, two *abogados integrantes* joined Justice Germán Valenzuela and Auditor General Fernando Torres Silva in the majority, with Justices Correa Bulo and Carrasco, both Aylwin appointees, dissenting.

the murder in the line of duty, and so the case clearly fell under military jurisdiction.[40] However, the decision went even further to emphasize, unnecessarily and uncritically, that the mission of the DINA as a military service was to defend national security and that Soria had been "an activist of the Communist Party, an illicit association that, at the time that the events occurred, was acting clandestinely."[41] As with the Chanfreau case, then, the military judge applied amnesty and closed the case within a matter of days.

The case did not die there, however. While the case was pending, the Spanish government had appealed to the Chilean Foreign Ministry for the appointment of a Supreme Court *ministro en visita*, as provided for by the Cumplido Laws in cases that affected diplomatic relations.[42] The Chilean government agreed, but the Supreme Court initially refused the government's request. Spain recalled its ambassador in protest, and the Chilean Foreign Ministry asked the Court to reconsider. This time, the Court acceded. On December 10, Justice Marcos Libedinsky, an Aylwin appointee, was assigned to the case.

To the dismay of the human rights community, as well as the government, Justice Libedinsky confirmed the military court's decision to amnesty the case. He argued that because the DINA's involvement was established by the evidence in the court's possession, the amnesty was applicable even though the identity of the individuals had not been established or any formal charges made. He upheld the military court's argument that the amnesty law applied to crimes not to the perpetrators, and that the obligation of the courts to investigate ended once it had been determined that the crimes in question fell within

---

[40] The decision noted that "in any state ruled by law, such as Chile . . . the principle of legality must prevail, that is: what the law commands, prohibits, or permits must be complied with in its clearest meaning." By this same reasoning, the courts inevitably respected the expansive (and highly illiberal) jurisdiction of the military justice system after 1990. See, for example, the decisions on the *contiendas de competencia* of May 5, 1992, in *Fallos del Mes* 402: 241–244; of March 22, 1993, in Gaceta Jurídica 153: 77–79; and of December 30, 1993, in *Fallos del Mes* 421: 1125–1127. All three decisions included votes from both Pinochet and post-Pinochet appointees, with no dissents.

[41] *Homicidio de Carmelo Soria Espinoza* (*contienda de competencia*), November 16, 1993, *Fallos del Mes* 420: 988–998.

[42] See the summary of these laws in note 7. Information regarding *ministros en visita* is provided in Appendix A.

the general terms of the law (*El Mercurio*, Jan. 9, 1994; Human Rights Watch/Americas 1994: 13–15).

The Soria family appealed the decision, invoking Article 2 of the Convention of Vienna, ratified by Chile in 1977, which requires states to punish those responsible for crimes against international civil servants and diplomatic officials. Soon after President Frei assumed office in 1994, then, a new justice was assigned to the case – Frei's first appointee to the Court, Eleodoro Ortiz. But after two years, in June 1996, Ortiz also applied amnesty to the case. He argued (among other things) that Soria did not meet the criteria of the U.N. treaty for diplomatic protection, and that because Chile's constitution only officially recognized the binding legal nature of international human rights treaties by a 1989 reform,[43] such treaties could not apply retroactively to extinguish the effects of the amnesty law. Two months later, the criminal chamber of the Supreme Court unanimously upheld Ortiz's decision and the case was closed.[44]

Despite this predominant pattern during the early to mid-1990s, there were occasional glimmers of hope. In September 1994, for example, two separate chambers of the Santiago Appeals Court, in both cases led by Humberto Nogueira, a constitutional law scholar serving as a "substitute judge" (*abogado integrante*), rendered two decisions denying the validity of the amnesty law.[45] They argued that, according to the claims of Pinochet himself and to numerous rulings of the Supreme Court, Chile had been in a state of war in 1974, and that hence the state was bound by the terms of the Geneva Conventions, to which Chile had become a signatory in 1951. The Conventions prohibit murder of prisoners, mutilation, cruel treatment, torture, and hostage-taking in war time, and explicitly preclude amnesty for such war crimes.[46] Both decisions were drafted by Nogueira, and for a few weeks after they were issued,

---

[43] Refer to note 6.

[44] The judges in question were Pinochet-era appointees Zurita and Alvarez, Aylwin-appointee Navas, and two *abogados integrantes*. This decision provoked an impeachment attempt against these justices, but the motion did not prosper in Congress.

[45] The cases were the 1974 disappearances of Lumi Videla, on the one hand, and Barbara Uribe and Edwin VanYurick, on the other. The decisions were rendered on September 26 and September 30, 1994, respectively. See *Gaceta Jurídica* 171: 126–135.

[46] Note that lawyers for human rights victims had offered these arguments beginning in the Lonquén case in 1978, discussed in Chapter 4.

the human rights community was optimistic that the "Nogueira effect" would undermine the amnesty law in the courts. But when the Supreme Court reviewed the decisions on appeal more than one year later, the justices dismissed the arguments based in international law, upheld the validity of the amnesty law, and closed the cases.[47]

Additionally, in two cases not covered by the amnesty law, outcomes were more favorable to human rights. Most significant were the rulings in the Letelier/Moffitt case, which had been explicitly excepted from the amnesty law in 1978 as a result of pressure from the United States government. The case featured prominently in the political life of the new democratic regime from the start, but it took more than a year for the Supreme Court to agree to appoint one of its own, as a *ministro en visita*, to the case. The task fell on the Court's newest member; Aylwin appointee Adolfo Bañados. Because prosecuting lawyers were up against the statute of limitations, they immediately gave Bañados detailed dossiers requesting preliminary indictments of the main suspects. On September 20, 1991, with less than a day to spare, Bañados issued these indictments against (ret.) General Manuel Contreras and Brigadier Pedro Espinoza, charging them with murder and with the malicious use of false passports. The Supreme Court upheld the ruling, but granted the defendants bail.[48]

In October 1992, Bañados closed the *sumario* part of the trial, definitively indicting Contreras and Espinoza, and on November 11, 1993, two years after beginning the investigation, Bañados rendered his verdict. He sentenced Contreras to seven years and Espinoza to six years in prison, respectively, for the assassinations of Orlando Letelier and Ronnie Moffitt.[49] However, citing the statute of limitations, he absolved them on charges of issuing false passports.

The decision was then appealed to the wider Supreme Court. In January of 1995, oral arguments before the Court were televised. Political party leaders and generals of the armed forces were all present, and the broadcast attracted a huge audience. The Court's decision was

[47] The rulings came on October 26, 1995, and January 30, 1996 (see Table 5.2). Note that Nogueira had already been removed from all *abogado integrante* lists.

[48] *Contra Juan Manuel Contreras Sepúlveda y otros* (*apelación encargatorio de reos*), November 18, 1991, *Fallos del Mes* 396: 689–699.

[49] See *Fallos del Mes*, November 1993, Supplementary Edition. See also Matus and Artaza 1996.

anticipated for months, and no party was sure what the outcome would be. Finally, on May 30, 1995, the Supreme Court upheld Bañados's sentences.[50]

Meanwhile, Santiago Appeals Court judge Milton Juica, who had taken over the *degollados* case from José Cánovas in May 1989, also made substantial progress toward justice.[51] The 1990 assassination of DICOMCAR chief, Luis Fontaine, had made it difficult to determine who ordered the 1985 killings of the three Communist Party members. Nonetheless, by March 1992, Judge Juica was able to preliminarily indict eleven people under the Anti-Terrorist Law on the charge of having formed an "illegal association" for the purpose of carrying out kidnapping and murder. Among the eleven charged was former junta member, César Mendoza, for cover-up of the crime.

Mendoza's lawyers filed a *recurso de amparo*, arguing that his arrest had been made on the basis of insufficient evidence. Both the Santiago Appeals Court and the Supreme Court rejected the writ.[52] "Within days of this decision, *Carabineros* announced that it was discontinuing legal aid to the prisoners, and issued a public statement repudiating the 'execrable crimes' and declaring the police force to have been 'betrayed and deceived'" (Brett 1992: 249). The police were thus able to cast the crime as the work of renegades, as they had sought to from the beginning, denying any institutional responsibility whatsoever.

Two months later, in May 1992, the case was blown open by the confession of a former member of DICOMCAR, Santiago San Martín Riquelme. A new plea-bargaining law, known as the "Efficient Repentence" law, encouraged San Martín and nine other suspects to confess. Based on this new evidence, Juica concluded that the chief author of

[50] That evening, Contreras announced from his farm that he was "not going to any prison," beginning a nearly five month game of cat and mouse with the executive. It was not until October 21, 1995, that the government finally managed to get him behind bars at the Punto Peuco prison. See the chapter entitled "Rumbo a la Cárcel," in Matus and Artaza 1996. Note that Espinoza, although maintaining his innocence, had agreed to abide by the judicial ruling and had entered prison several months before. Also note that the prison had been specially outfitted for Contreras and Espinoza with such comforts as cellular telephones, computers, and a fully stocked bar.
[51] Refer to Chapter 4.
[52] However, Mendoza's lawyers were later able to have the indictment revoked.

the crimes had been Colonel Luis Fontaine, chief of DICOMCAR. Juica closed the *sumario* on July 15, 1993, and issued the convictions on March 31, 1994, nine years after the crime was committed. He sentenced fifteen ex-members of *Carabineros* and one civilian to prison terms ranging from forty-one days to life.[53]

These two cases revealed that the courts were capable of investigating human rights abuses and convicting perpetrators. Judges remained unwilling, however, to challenge the legitimacy of the legal edifice that protected most authoritarian regime officials from prosecution. Indeed, the clear trend in 1995 and 1996 was toward applying amnesty and declaring authoritarian-era cases closed.[54]

In mid-1997, however, the Frei government moved ahead with reform of the judiciary, and soon thereafter, the doctrinal commitment to automatic application of the amnesty law began to crumble. This shift is documented in Table 5.2.

Several things should be noted about this table. To begin, although justices appointed in the postauthoritarian era (those in italics), including *abogados integrantes*, could have formed majorities against the amnesty law in 1995 and 1996, they did not. Indeed, it wasn't until late 1997, around the time of Frei's reforms, that signs of a shift (noted in bold) began to appear.[55] The change was led by two individuals: Luis Correa Bulo, who was appointed to the Court under Aylwin,[56] and José Luis Pérez, who was first a substitute judge (*abogado integrante*) and, in 1998, became a full-fledged member of the Court, as one of the external

---

[53] On the conclusion of the case, lawyers for the victims argued that "in the person of Milton Juica Arancibia, the judiciary has regained some of its honor and prestige.... [He] demonstrated that with determination, courage, and wisdom, great crimes committed during the dictatorship ... can be illuminated and solved" (Caucoto and Salazar 1994: 166). Note that the Supreme Court upheld the sentences with only minor modifications in October 1995.

[54] See "La Amnistia," in the Temas section of *La Epoca*, October 29, 1995. Note that in August, the Frei government proposed a bill to expedite investigations into human rights abuses and bring pending cases to a final (and hopefully conclusive) close. However, because the necessary opposition support for the reforms could only be secured via amendments which were unacceptable to members of the *Concertación*, the legislation died in Congress.

[55] Bear in mind that dates are of publication of the decision, but actual debate and drafting may have taken place weeks, even months, earlier.

[56] Justice Correa Bulo has since been removed from the Court by his peers for (apparently) unrelated ethical misconduct. For more information on his discharge, see *La Tercera*, April 20, 2001.

appointees (*ministros desde afuera*).[57] These two judges first advanced alternative interpretations of the amnesty law in dissents, and, later, were able to persuade a majority of justices to join them (Interview ACJ01–3, June 22, 2001, 14:00; Interview SCJ01–9, 28 June, 2001, 13:00). This shift began before Pinochet stepped down as commander-in-chief and before his arrest in London, although it did not cement until after the latter event.

In the first of these decisions (those issued in 1997), the justices in question simply claimed that amnesty could not be applied until the guilt of specific parties for the alleged crimes had been determined. In other words, they insisted that amnesty extinguishes the criminal responsibility of particular individuals whose guilt has been established in court, but cannot offer a blanket exoneration for the acts themselves. By 1998 (even before Pinochet's arrest), they also began invoking the Geneva conventions, as Humberto Nogueira had attempted four years earlier, to declare the (self-) amnesty law illegitimate. This was the basis for the 5–1 ruling of September 9, 1998, in the *Poblete Córdova* disappearance case,[58] which marked the first time that the Court accepted the binding nature of international humanitarian law.[59] In the same decision, the justices noted that because no body had been found, the alleged disappearance should be classified as a kidnapping, which was, in any case, an ongoing crime that continued beyond the period covered by the amnesty law. The Court relied more on this latter argument in its decisions postdating Pinochet's arrest.

Emboldened by these rulings, in June 1999, a Santiago Appeals Court judge, Juan Guzmán Tapia, indicted the five army officials who led the so-called Caravan of Death operation in the weeks immediately following the 1973 military coup.[60] The operation resulted in the deaths of

---

[57] Pérez's service as a substitute judge in various courts in Santiago dates to the authoritarian regime. In interviews in both 1996 and 2001, it was clear that he his political views were right of center, but he was no conservative ideologue.

[58] The chamber was composed of one prereform justice, two of the new "external" appointees, and two substitute judges (*abogados integrantes*). Their names appear in Table 5.2.

[59] "Por Primera Vez Suprema Aplicó Convenios de Ginebra," *La Tercera*, September 11, 1998 (online). The decision itself can be found in *Fallos del Mes* 478: 1760–1769. See especially considerando no. 9, at 1763–1765.

[60] The so-called Caravan of Death refers to the operation, carried out in October 1973, in which a military death squad traveled the length of the country executing leftist detainees. See P. Verdugo 2001.

Table 5.2. Published Supreme Court rulings in cases involving the amnesty law, 1995–2000[a]

Date[b]	Case name	Amnesty granted?	Justices in majority[c]	Justices in dissent
26-10-1995	Osvaldo Romo Mena	Yes	Dávila, Bañados, Navas, Ortíz, Pfeffer (AI)	—
30-1-1996	Osvaldo Romo Mena	Yes	Dávila, Bañados, Navas, Ortíz, Pfeffer (AI)	—
24-7-1996	Basclay H. Zapata Reyes	Yes	Dávila, Bañados, Libedinsky, Pfeffer (AI), Bullemore (AI), Torres S. (AGE)	—
22-8-1996	Contra G. Salinas Torres	Yes	Zurita, H. Álvarez, Navas, Fernández (AI), Bullemore (AI)	—
3-9-1996	Desaparición de Alfonso Chanfreau	Yes	Dávila, Bañados, Navas, Pfeffer (AI), Verdugo (AI), Torres S. (AGE)	—
27-1-1997	Detención illegal de Rodolfo González P.	Yes	Dávila, Bañados, Navas, Correa B., Verdugo (AI), Torres S. (AGE)	—
June 1997	**Judicial reform law introduced**			
7-8-1997	Contra Osvaldo Romo Mena y otros	Yes	Dávila, Bañados, Rencoret (AI), Torres S. (AGE)	*Correa B., Bullemore (AI)*
19-11-1997	Presunta Desgracia de R. Espejo Gómez y G. Farías	No	*Correa B., Navas, Montes (AI), Castro (AI)*	Bañados, Torres S. (AGE)
January 1998	**Judicial reform implemented**			
10-3-1998	**Pinochet steps down as commander-in-chief**			
19-8-1998	Osvaldo Romo y otros	Yes[d]	O. Álvarez, Rencoret (AI), Torres S. (AGE)	*Chaigneau, Cury, Bullemore (AI)*
20-8-1998	Presunta Desgracia de Juan Paredes B.	Yes	Dávila, Bañados, Navas, Torres S. (AGE)	*Correa B., Pérez*

Date	Case	Decision[a]	Majority	Other
8-9-1998	Fernando Laureani y Osvaldo Romo	Yes	Dávila, *Pérez, Navas, Correa B., Bullemore* (AI), Torres S. (AGE)	—
9-9-1998	Detención Ilegal de P. Poblete Córdova	No	***Pérez, Cury, Navas, Montes (AI), Castro*** (AI)	Torres S. (AGE)
16-9-1998	Detención illegal de H. Ziede Gómez	Yes	Dávila, *Bañados, Navas, Correa B., Ortíz, Bullemore* (AI), Torres S. (AGE)	—
6-10-1998	Presunta Desgracia de Marcos Quiñones	Yes	*Navas, Chaigneau, Cury, Bullemore* (AI), Torres S. (AGE)	***Pérez***
16-10-1998	**Pinochet's arrest in London****			
26-10-1998	Presunta Desgracia de Carlos H. Contreras	No	***Correa B., Pérez, Chaigneau, Bullemore*** (AI)	*Navas*, Torres S. (AGE)
11-11-1998	Samuel Eduardo Gutiérrez S.	Yes	Dávila, *Navas, Bullemore* (AI), Gómez (ASE)	***Correa B., Pérez***
29-12-1998	Detención Ilegal de A. Barrios Duque	No	***Correa B., Pérez, Cury, Bullemore (AI)***	*Navas*, Torres S. (AGE)
7-1-1999	Fernando Gómez Segovia y otros	No	***Pérez, Chaigneau, Cury, Bullemore (AI), Castro*** (AI)	Torres S. (AGE)
20-7-1999	Caravan of Death	No	***Correa B., Pérez, Chaigneau, Cury, Navas***	—

[a] All information is from the jurisprudential journals *Revista de Derecho y Jurisprudencia, Fallos del Mes*, and *Gaceta Jurídica*.
[b] Dates are given in day-month-year form. Note that these refer to the date the decision was published, not necessarily to when it was debated and decided in chambers.
[c] Figures appointed in the authoritarian era are in regular type, whereas those appointed after the transition are in italics. AI = "abogado integrante" (substitute judge). AGE = Auditor General del Ejército (chief judge advocate of the army), who, since 1987, joins the Supreme Court as a voting member in cases involving the military justice system. ASE = Auditor Subrogante del Ejército, who filled in for the AGE.
[d] Because the vote in this case was a tie (3–3), the *principio pro reo* (a principle that gives the benefit of the doubt to the defendant) was applied.

some seventy-five individuals, nineteen of whose remains had yet to be located. Although recognizing and applying amnesty for the confirmed deaths, Judge Guzmán argued that the remaining nineteen were victims of "aggravated kidnapping," which, as the Supreme Court had ruled, extended beyond the time frame of the amnesty law.[61] Both the Santiago Appeals Court and the Supreme Court, in turn, upheld the indictments.[62]

These rulings helped give credibility to the government's claims that Chile's judiciary was willing and able to prosecute authoritarian-era abuses and that, hence, Pinochet should be sent home to face trial (e.g., ChIP News, July 21, 1999). And, indeed, soon after the general's return, both the Santiago Appeals Court and the Supreme Court ruled that there were sufficient grounds in the Caravan of Death case[63] to revoke Pinochet's senatorial immunity.[64] Both courts acknowledged that, at the very least, there was enough evidence to suggest that Pinochet had illegally covered up or sought to protect the generals directly involved with the crimes, and that the existence of this "well-founded suspicion" was sufficient to revoke his immunity and require that he stand trial.

The revocation of Pinochet's immunity in turn permitted Judge Guzmán to indict the general in January 2001. And although the former dictator subsequently escaped conviction on grounds that he was "mentally unfit" to stand trial, many of his subordinates did not. By September 2003 (the thirty-year anniversary of the coup), the courts had convicted 22 individuals and over 330 more were facing charges (Human Rights Watch 2003: 6).

---

[61] ChIP News, June 9, 1999.

[62] ChIP News, July 6, 1999, and July 21, 1999. The indicted officers were retired General Sergio Arellano Stark, retired Brigadier Pedro Espinoza, and retired Colonels Marcelo Moren Brito, Sergio Arrendono Gonzalez, and Patricio Diaz Araneda.

[63] For more information on the rulings, see "El Fallo que Desaforó a Pinochet en Primera Instancia, La Tercera, on line; "En cuanto a los requisitos que hacen procedente la Declaración de Desafuero," La Tercera, August 8, 2000; and "Fallo Histórico," Qué Pasa, August 12, 2000.

[64] According to Article 45 of the 1980 Constitution, any president that served at least six years may subsequently serve as a senator for life. Pinochet had assumed this office in March 1998, after stepping down as Commander-in-Chief of the Armed Forces. Although he retired from the Senate in July 2002, as an ex-President, he continued, until his death, to enjoy legal immunity, which would have required a separate recovation in each and every case against him.

Decisions in Postauthoritarian Rights Cases

The previous section demonstrates that an important change took place during the 1990s in judicial treatment of rights cases dating to the dictatorship. It is thus tempting to conclude that the role of the Chilean judiciary underwent a major shift in this period towards more "positive independence."[65] However, such a conclusion would be incorrect. As I show in the following pages, judicial treatment of rights cases that postdate the transition to democracy remained remarkably consistent with the past in two major respects. First, judges tended to neglect analysis of the constitutionality of acts challenged in court in favor of a more narrow assessment of their conformity to ordinary law. In other words, they displayed little desire or capacity to defend or promote citizens' constitutional rights or constitutionalism in general. Second, even where they did rule in favor of parties bringing constitutional claims, their decisions were as likely to limit constitutionalist principles as they were to uphold them.

The data to support these claims comes from judicial decisions in two kinds of cases: *recursos de inaplicabilidad por inconstitucionalidad* and *recursos de protección*.[66] Although the published record held only a handful of decisions on *inaplicabilidad*, an exhaustive study of all *inaplicabilidad* cases by Chilean legal scholar Gastón Gómez revealed that between 1990 and 1996, the Supreme Court only ruled in favor of the petitioner in 15 of the 530 cases filed, or 2.83 percent (Gómez 1999: 10). Moreover, based on a content analysis of the decisions, Gómez concluded that the Court largely failed to resolve questions of constitutional supremacy in a unified and consistent manner, to protect fundamental rights with integrity and coherence, and to develop a coherent approach to the interpretation of constitutional principles and values (Gómez 1999: 28).

The same basic conclusions apply to the judicial treatment of *recursos de protección* during the 1990s. By the time of the transition, this constitutional review mechanism was well established and more familiar to

---

[65] Widner (2001) refers to the concept of "positive independence" as part of an attempt to define what judicial independence is in the context of Africa. She borrows the concept from Simpson 1989.

[66] Because the transition to democracy meant an end to policies of arbitrary arrest, detention, torture, and killing, petitions for *amparo* no longer flooded the courts. Although I found twenty *amparo* decisions in the published records (eight granted and twelve denied), there was no discernible pattern therein, and I was unable to find secondary studies that treated a broader sample.

the public, so citizens increasingly petitioned for judicial intervention when public or private parties infringed upon constitutionally protected rights. Indeed, between 1990 and 1999, a total of approximately 16,000 petitions for *protección* were filed in Chilean courts. Sixty percent of these were directed to the Santiago Appeals Court, and these became the subject of two sophisticated studies. The first (Correa and Gómez 2000, cited in Couso 2004a: 78–79) analyzed over five thousand decisions issued between 1990 and 1998, and concluded that in over 98 percent of these, judges never reviewed the constitutionality of the challenged action, but focused merely on its legality. In other words, if the court could cite an ordinary law authorizing or prohibiting a challenged action, it would make that the basis of its ruling, rather than deciding whether or not the law itself was consistent with or violative of the constitution. The second study (Couso 2002; Couso 2004a) focused on a subset of these decisions that were filed against the government or state agencies for violations of the constitutional right to property.[67] In these 781 cases, the Santiago Appeals Court ruled in favor of the government 76 percent of the time (597 decisions), and for the plaintiffs 22.5 percent of the time (176 cases). Moreover, when the challenged government official or agency was "centralized and prominent," as opposed to "decentralized and politically minor," the success rate for the plaintiffs fell to 13 percent.(Couso 2002: 292–293; Couso 2004a: 80–81). Couso (2002: 82) concludes that "in the area of property rights, Chile's judges have not sought to defend constitutional rights. Instead, they have upheld the laws and administrative acts of the government, giving greater weight to current law and policy than to constitutional principles."

My own data, which includes all published decisions in *protección* cases involving civil and political rights (excluding property) for the 1990–1999 period, supports the general conclusion that Chilean judges continued to have a "weak commitment to constitutionalism" (Couso 2004a: 82). Although, as Table 5.3 shows, the courts granted *protección* in more than 50 percent of these cases, in more than half of these seemingly "pro-rights" cases, the decisions in fact ignored or distorted constitutionalist principles.[68]

---

[67] Note that the *recurso de protección* can be filed against private parties for violations of constitutional rights, as well as against government officials or agencies.

[68] By constitutionalist principles, I mean limiting state power and favoring individual rights.

Table 5.3. Published decisions on *protección*, 1990–1999 (civil and political rights cases)[a]

| | Granted | | | |
	Constitutionalist	Not Constitutionalist	Denied/ Dismissed	Total
Courts of Appeal	7	12	18	37
Supreme Court	6	10	12	28
Total	13	22	30	65

[a] I do not offer a breakdown of the cases in which the courts refused *protección*, since the reasons for dismissals or denials were almost as numerous as the cases themselves. Instead, I dissect the decisions that favored the plaintiff.

As noted in Table 5.3, there were thirteen published instances in civil and political rights cases in which courts ruled to grant *protección* and, thereby, supported constitutionalist principles.[69] However, in only six of these instances (that is, 9 percent of the sixty-five decisions in the sample) was the challenged actor a government official or agency.[70] In the other seven cases, it was private entities (schools and a hospital) that were found to have violated a constitutional right of the petitioner, and the rights in question were the right to life, due process, and equal treatment.

Strikingly, in twenty-two of the thirty-five decisions (or 63 percent) granting *protección*, the courts actually demonstrated ignorance of or hostility to constitutionalist principles. In the area of the right to life/personal security, for example, petitions were no longer brought against governmental action, as they had been under the dictatorship;

---

[69] *Sociedad Agrícola Melico Ltda. Con Secretario Regional Ministerial de Bienes Nacionales IX Región (protección)*, December 19, 1990, and April 15, 1991, *RDJ* 88; *Luis Angel Rosas Diaz contra Director general de Investigaciones (protección)* January 25 and May 16, 1991, *Fallos del Mes* 390; *Independent Fisheries Chile S.A. con Fiscalizadores de la Dirección del Trabajo – Unidad de Inspección de Coronel (protección)*, September 30 and October 23, 1991, *RDJ* 88; *Constanza Pellegrino Garrido con Directora del Colegio Compañía de María/ Santiago Seminario (protección)*, January 6 and March 7, 1994, *RDJ* 91; *Carlos Muller Reyes (protección)*, March 9 and May 17, 1995, *Gaceta Jurídica* 179; *Augusto Palma Galvez (protección)*, October 24, 1995, *Gaceta Jurídica* 184; *Sergio Zañartu Valenzuela con Clínica Indisa y Hospital de la Universidad Católica de Chile (protección)* March 25, 1997, *Gaceta Jurídica* 201; *Patricia Avello Avila, contra Liceo San Francisco de Asis de Arauco*, February 24 and March 23, 1999, *Gaceta Jurídica* 225.

[70] In all but one of these cases, the issue in question was due process.

instead, cases were filed by public or private authorities against individuals who opted to put their own life in danger for political or religious reasons. In such cases, the courts decided for the petitioners but *against* the individuals. They repeatedly ruled that prisoners' hunger strikes violated the strikers' own right to life and that the constitution thereby required authorities to force-feed the strikers.[71] Similarly, in cases involving the refusal of Jehovah's Witnesses to accept blood transfusions, the court ruled that "in a conflict between the right to life and the right of conscience/religion, the former must prevail."[72] Thus, the constitution required hospital authorities to administer the blood transfusions against the will of the patients.[73]

In the area of free speech, the courts handed down similarly illiberal rulings. For example, in 1993, the courts granted *protección* to several public figures who claimed that a book about to be published in Chile revealed unflattering, and in some cases damning, information about their private lives. Release of the book in Chile, they claimed, would violate their right to honor and privacy, protected by Article 20 of the Constitution, and thus they asked for, and got, the court to issue an injunction against distribution.[74] In 1996–1997, both the Santiago Appeals Court and the Supreme Court granted petitioners *protección*

---

[71] *Director Nacional de Gendarmería* (*protección*), November 8, 1991, *Fallos del Mes* 397: 785–787 (confirming appellate decision); *Max Díaz Trujillo* (*protección*), November 12, 1992, *Fallos del Mes* 408: 844–846, overturning appellate decision; *Director Nacional de Gendarmería* (*protección*), March 24, 1994, *Gaceta Jurídica* 165: 77–78.

[72] *Luis Muñoz Bravo* (*protección*), May 9, 1992, *Fallos del Mes* 402: 227–231.

[73] *Jorge Carabantes Cárcamo contra Director de Salud Metropolitano Occidente* (*protección*), November 9, 1991, *RDJ* 88; *Luis Muñoz Bravo* (*protección*), March 24 and May 9, 1992, *Fallos del Mes* 402: 227–31; *Jorge Reyes Ibarra* (*protección*), August 22 and October 2, 1995, *Gaceta Jurídica* 184; *Patricia Castillo Castillo* (*protección*), December 1, 1995 and January 18, 1996, *Gaceta Jurídica* 187; *Daniela Gaona* (*protección*), March 8, 1997, *Gaceta Jurídica* 201. It should be noted that the *Carabantes Cárcamos* and *Daniela Gaona* cases involved minors, making the argument for intervention notably stronger.

[74] *Andrónico Luksic Craig,* (*protección*), May 31 and June 15, 1993, *Fallos del Mes,* 415: 347–360. The Santiago Appeals Court argued that in both the Constitution and the International Covenant on Civil and Political Rights, the right to privacy was listed, ordenally, before the right to free expression. According to the court, this signaled that the former ranked higher in importance than the latter. Despite the lack of support for such reasoning in regard to the Chilean Constitution, and the fact that international law explicitly establishes that all internationally protected rights are interdependent and nonhierarchical, the Supreme Court endorsed and upheld the

in order to ban public, adult showings of the Martin Scorsese film *The Last Temptation of Christ*.[75] The courts agreed with petitioners that the film attacked the honor of Jesus Christ and the Catholic Church, ignoring arguments regarding the constitutional centrality of the freedom of expression and religion.[76]

In another series of decisions, the courts granted *protección* to individuals who claimed that, as beneficiaries of the 1978 amnesty law, they should be exempt from the constitutional requirement that they go through the Senate to have their political rights (citizenship or voting rights) restored. In most of these cases, the courts ruled that such individuals should not have to appeal to the Senate, as the amnesty had erased the crime, the punishment, and all related effects thereof. Consequently, the rights once taken away should be restored, without question, at the simple request of the affected individuals.[77] Although this might be interpreted as favorable to constitutionalism, it is in fact somewhat ambiguous, since it rests on a particular interpretation of the amnesty law, the legal legitimacy of which had itself been challenged.

In sum, Chilean judges did not seize on the opportunities presented by the new political context of the 1990s to chart a broadly liberal constitutionalist course. Although over the course of the decade they began to take rights more seriously in cases dating to the authoritarian-regime, in cases that postdated the transition, the old patterns persisted. Judges demonstrated little proclivity to enforce – much less develop – constitutional limits on the exercise of public power. As in the past, their rulings, mostly passively but sometimes actively, favored order over liberty, and the state or society over the individual.

ruling. Moreover, the Court added that honor and privacy are such important values that there is no conception of the common good that could permit their sacrifice.

[75] *Abogados en representación de Nuestro Señor Jesucristo de la Santa Iglesia Católica contra el Consejo de Calificación Cinematográfica*, January 20 and June 17, 1997, *Gaceta Jurídica* 204: 37–54.

[76] For more details on these and other examples of illiberal rulings in freedom of expression cases, see Human Rights Watch 1998; Hilbink 1999; and Matus 2002.

[77] *Máximo Fuller Guíñez con Director del Registro Electoral* (*protección*), September 20, 1990, RDJ 87 (1990) 2.5: 157–162; *Herminio Osorio Vergara con Director del Registro Electoral* (*protección*), September 24, 1991, RDJ 88 (1991) 2.5: 321–327; *Luis Fuentealba Medina con Director del Registro Electoral y Directora del Servicio Nacional del Registro Civil y Identificación* (*protección*), November 3, 1992, RDJ 89 (1992) 2.5: 333–340. *Ulises Heisohn Westermeier contra Servicio Electoral de la República de Chile* (*protección*), December 1998, *Gaceta Jurídica* 222.

EXPLAINING THE JUDICIAL ROLE
IN THE NEW DEMOCRACY

What factors explain the behavior described above? I maintain that the record of the 1990s reflects the continuing influence of the institutional structure and ideology that I have highlighted throughout the book. As in the past, the top-down career control exerted by the Supreme Court over the judicial hierarchy and the emphasis on remaining "apolitical" produced judicial behavior that was largely conformist and conservative. Judges had neither the understandings nor the incentives to promote a rights revolution (Epp 1998) in Chile. Indeed, it was only when a combination of domestic institutional reform and transnational judicial action brought sufficient pressure to bear on them that Chilean judges changed their approach to dealing with authoritarian-era rights abuses. Where such pressure was absent however, as in post-1990 rights cases, judges proved unequipped or disinclined to take stands in defense of constitutionalist principles.

Before elaborating this argument, I must address alternative hypotheses, such as the possibility that *regime-related factors* were the key determinants in judicial behavior during the 1990s. As numerous scholars have noted (M. Garretón 1989; Valenzuela 1995; Moulián 1997), the regime change that took place in 1990 in Chile remained incomplete in several key respects, leaving the military with a number of tutelary powers over the new democratic government. The so-called authoritarian enclaves (M. Garretón 1990) included the National Security Council (COSENA), which gave the Armed Forces formal veto power over democratic decision making; the designated senators, who were appointed by unelected state officials (from the military and judicial bodies) and who lent conservative forces disproportionate power in the legislative process; and the insulation of the commanders-in-chief of the army and the uniformed police from potential dismissal by the President of the Republic. Perhaps most significantly, Pinochet himself retained his position as Commander-in-Chief of the Armed Forces until March 1998, and his faithful servant, Auditor General Fernando Torres Silva, remained entitled to a vote on any Supreme Court decision involving military personnel.[78] Thus, authoritarian leaders remained in a position

---

[78] Since 1987, the Auditor General del Ejército (chief judge advocate of the army) joins the Supreme Court as a voting member in cases involving the military justice system. Fernando Torres Silva served in this position until April 1999, when he resigned

to try to intimidate officials of the new regime into compliance with their wishes, and, in fact, they were not shy about issuing verbal threats, and, on at least two occasions, engaging in outright saber-rattling. Although such events may have scared at least some judges off from pursuing human rights violators (Human Rights Watch 1994), two points can be made against fear or intimidation as the key variable to explain judicial behavior during the 1990s. First, the record of published decisions reveals no blanket silencing effect for events like the *boinazo*, or a sudden liberation when Pinochet stepped down as commander-in-chief. Indeed, if one takes into account dissents, the *boinazo* appears to have strengthened the resolve of some justices to keep authoritarian-era cases open.[79] Furthermore, as shown in Table 5.2, Supreme Court judges began taking stands against automatic application of amnesty despite the continued presence of Auditor General Torres Silva in such cases and many months before Pinochet retired as head of the military.[80] Second, the continuity in postauthoritarian rights cases, which were of no concern to the military, indicates that something other than fear of provoking the military was shaping judicial behavior in rights cases during the 1990s.

More plausible, then, is the argument that judges were simply acting on their *personal policy preferences* or *political attitudes*. This is, without question, the most common explanation one finds in journalistic accounts of Chilean judicial behavior (e.g., Pozo 1983; Luque and Collyer 1986). Some accounts highlight the effects of the 1989 *ley de caramelo*, which provided sweet retirement packages to justices over seventy-five and allowed Pinochet to appoint seven justices to the Court just before the transition.[81] Although the appointments respected established procedure, meaning appointees were selected from lists drawn up by the Supreme Court itself, there is no doubt that the Pinochet government made sure to promote the most conservative and/or compliant individuals possible.

To be sure, in my 1996 interviews, I found a very vocal contingent of *Pinochetistas* on the Supreme Court (four solidly so, and three

abruptly (and was rumored to have been forced out by the new Commander-in-Chief of the Army, Ricardo Izurieta).

[79] See, for example, the breakdown of votes in the cases discussed in notes 37 and 39.
[80] This point was emphasized by one of the judges in these cases (Interview SCJ01–9, June 28, 2001, 13:00).
[81] See Chapter 4.

ambiguously so). These individuals revealed their political attitudes in answers to, among other things,[82] questions regarding the *Rettig Report*: "Much of the *Rettig Report* was incorrect. Many of the people they listed were just exiled, not disappeared," one argued (Interview SCJ96–2, May 16, 1996, 18:00). "Those people didn't want democracy touched in any way, and that wasn't possible. What happened was an indispensable remedy. It was like cleaning house, getting rid of the garbage," responded another (Interview SCJ96–8, June 11, 1996, 13:30). "The commission was totally biased in favor of the radical parties," several complained (Interviews SCJ96–5, May 23, 1996, 14:00; ACJ96–15, May 15, 1996, 12:30; SCJ96–2, May 16, 1996, 18:00).[83] Not surprisingly, the individuals who made these statements voted consistently in favor of amnesty and the transfer of cases to military jurisdiction.

Moreover, when I returned for interviews in 2001, and asked what had changed and why, eleven of fourteen judges pointed to the new faces on the Supreme Court. As one stated, "Judges don't seek out cases, they just respond to what is brought before them. That the response to these issues is different has to do with the change in personnel" (Interview ACJ01–3, June 22, 2001, 15:30). And he continued:

> The judiciary may have experienced some changes in structure and procedure, but in my view what is key is the people that are making decisions. There are now new individuals with different criteria in positions of power. Ten years ago, the situation was different, and in 5–10 years, it may also be different, because it all depends on who is in control of important cases (Interview ACJ01–3, June 22, 2001, 15:30).

As one of this judge's colleagues put it, "the penal chamber of the Supreme Court is now much more in line with the times. They are concerned about and capable of offering a better image of the judiciary" (Interview ACJ01–2, June 25, 2001, 15:30). This was affirmed by one of the very members of the penal chamber, who said, "The change really has to do with the way of thinking of the new justices" (Interview SCJ01–8, June 18, 2001, 13:00).

---

[82] For more, see Chapter 4.

[83] It should be noted that the Rettig Commission was carefully composed of people from across the political spectrum (with the exception of the far Right), and would better be described as liberal than "radical." In fact, one of its members was a former Supreme Court justice, who had served on the official Commission of Human Rights under the military government. See Brett 1992: 132.

Clearly, then, political attitudes are an important part of the expla-nation for judicial treatment of rights cases during the 1990s; however, they fail to account for two things: the timing of the change in treat-ment of authoritarian-era human rights cases, and the continuity in postauthoritarian cases. First, the timing: As can be seen by tracing the italicized names in Table 5.2, post-Pinochet appointees (be they jus-tices or *abogados integrantes*) made up majorities in the penal chamber of the Court long before the change in interpretation took place. It was not until late 1997, around the time that the judicial reform law was proposed and passed, that the shift began, and not until after Pinochet's detention in London that it solidified. Second, as discussed earlier in the chapter, no concomitant shift took place in judicial treatment of posttransition rights cases. What's more, in these cases, there was very little variation among individual judges. Out of the 246 total votes cast in the 65 *recurso de protección* cases in Table 5.3, only 18 (or 7 percent) were dissenting votes. This seems to indicate that, notwithstanding their diverging views on the authoritarian regime, Chilean judges share something that leads them to behave in a strikingly uniform manner in other rights cases.

My claim is that this "something" is institutional factors, which con-tinued to be of overarching importance to explaining judicial behavior in Chile during the 1990s. As in the past, *institutional structure and ideol-ogy* combined to preclude or discourage judges from asserting themselves in defense of constitutionalist principles. Only in the area where intense domestic and international pressure was brought to bear, namely, regard-ing the treatment of authoritarian-era human rights abuses, did judges display greater energy and commitment to upholding rights.

In earlier chapters, I provided evidence from the disciplinary record to demonstrate the constraints placed on appellate and lower-court judges who might demonstrate positive independence. This continued in the post-Pinochet era. For example, in July 1990, the Supreme Court turned down a request by Aylwin's Ministry of Justice to have Judge Nelson Muñoz serve on the Ministry's advisory committee for judicial reform. To justify their refusal, they cited the judge's poor annual eval-uations.[84] Muñoz's "differences" with his superiors had begun in 1984, when he demanded entrance to the military government's concentra-tion camp at Pisagua (Rojas 1990). He was verbally reprimanded by the Iquique Appeals Court and his annual grading "suffered accordingly"

---

[84] Muñoz had been placed on List Three in several previous years.

(Brett 1992: 232). His participation in the uncovering of a secret grave of human rights victims at Pisagua early in 1990, and his vigorous investigation of the case also displeased his superiors. Believing that his dismissal was imminent, he thus resigned his post in October 1990.

In August 1990, appellate judge Carlos Cerda Fernández challenged the Supreme Court's definitive application of the amnesty law to the case of the disappeared communist leaders.[85] He claimed that the amnesty law blatantly contradicted the 1980 Constitution, which had been reformed in 1989 expressly to incorporate international human rights conventions into Chilean law (Article 5). To close the case, he argued, would be to go against the democratic sovereign will. In the justification for his refusal, Cerda declared,

> What is a judge to do when he is confronted with a routine order which he perceives to violate openly what the majority of society, in a first glimpse of democracy after a long period of juridical exception, has charged him with preserving? . . .
>
> The judge must always know himself and feel himself to be an authority that exercises sovereignty which resides essentially in the Nation, above all in a Rule of Law. . . . I [feel] protected by the oath [that I took when I was sworn in as a judge], an oath deeply rooted in my conscience. I [have] no doubts regarding how I must proceed.[86]

For this, the Supreme Court suspended Cerda (for the second time) for two months, and in the annual evaluations conducted in January 1991, the Court gave him a rating that expelled him from the judiciary. Cerda appealed the dismissal and, although he did not retract his previous statements, successfully supplicated to keep his post. However, "the message that the Supreme Court would not accept acts of insubordination even under a new political scenario was clearly heard by the rest of the magistracy, as was the idea that amnesty must be applied to cases involving human rights violations, just at the moment when they were being reactivated" (Matus 1999: 53).

In April 1992, Judge Beltrami of Quillota (near Valparaiso) began an active investigation of the alleged 1974 secret burial of victims of extrajudicial executions. As part of the process, he demanded entrance into a military barracks. Because he was denied entry, he filed charges

---

[85] On this case, see Chapter 4.
[86] For excerpts of his dramatic defense, which even invoked passages from the bible, see Otano 1992 at 22.

against the commanding officer for obstructing justice. For this, he was formally reprimanded by the Supreme Court for exceeding his functions (Brett 1992: 259).

In late 1992, Santiago Appeals Court Judge Gloria Olivares was the target of criticism by her superiors for "excessive protagonism" in the *Chanfreau* case, discussed earlier in the chapter (Hidalgo 1992). Like Cerda before her, Olivares had asserted her duty to pursue all leads and had called key figures from the military regime to testify. The Supreme Court not only reprimanded her, but also took the case away from her and handed it to the military justice system.

Thus, in the first half of the 1990s, lower- and appellate court judges were actively discouraged by their superiors from charting a new liberal course. As one lawyer who worked on judicial reform put it, "district-level and appellate court judges aren't free; they are afraid to act in accordance with their own opinions.... They don't dare experiment because they fear not being able to rise in the hierarchy" (Interview OL96–3, July 25, 1996, 10:00). This was abundantly clear in my 1996 interviews, when more than half of judges expressed criticism of the discipline and promotion system.[87] In the words of one of these:

> The structure of our judiciary is very out-dated, Napoleonic. It works to transform a given personality, to produce a judge with a certain profile, one who tries to resolve always in accordance with what the Supreme Court says.... The judge from day one is sent messages that tell him, 'Look, you need always to go along with your hierarchical superior.' This is something quite negative, I think, and something which is always somewhat present,...for when the training of the judge causes him to identify with something other than the constitution, [such as the view of his superiors], he loses his independence. (Interview ACJ96–12, May 9, 1996, 18:30)

With this concern in mind, President Aylwin had proposed the National Judicial Council, but it failed. The Supreme Court remained empowered not only to evaluate and discipline subordinates but also to control nominations for promotions to all higher courts, including itself.[88] It was not until after the 1997 reform, under President Frei,

---

[87] Many of these statements were reported in earlier chapters.

[88] In an interview with the magazine *ANALISIS* in 1991, Aylwin's Minister of Justice, Francisco Cumplido, said he had discovered that "it is common practice for the Supreme Court to telephone appellate court judges and order them to compose a nomination list with one individual favored by the Supreme Court and two "bad" judges, so that the government will be forced to elect the one they want. I

that the system was (modestly) altered. The reform, described earlier in the chapter, had two immediate effects. First, and as indicated earlier, it got rid of some of the oldest and most conservative judges on the high court; and second, it injected some new (extrabureaucratic) blood directly into the Supreme Court. With five Supreme Court posts now occupied by lawyers whose professional views had not been forged inside the judicial bureaucracy, the judicial cupola could be exposed to fresh ideas.[89] This, in combination with the fact that the Senate was brought into the judicial appointment process, meant that the "reference group" from which judges take their cues on professional standards was set to change (Guarnieri and Pederzoli 2002:166–167). Whereas in the past, the judiciary was a closed, autonomous bureaucracy, whose institutional structure encouraged judges to play primarily to the conservative Supreme Court, the reforms offered judges opportunities and incentives to consider a (somewhat) wider range of perspectives on legal interpretation and the judicial role.

In addition, the reform process itself encouraged (and, at times, forced) judges to reflect upon and reassess their role in democracy. Policy makers realized fairly early on that, to be successful, reforms could not be foisted on judges but rather required their acquiescence and participation. They thus organized extensive seminars, roundtable discussions, and state-sponsored trips abroad designed to expose judges to new ideas and alternative models (Interview OL96–17, June 28, 1996, 12:15; Interview OL96–2, July 22, 1996, 17:00; Interview OL96–15, October 18, 1996, 10:30). Meanwhile, the reform initiatives brought increased journalistic coverage of the judiciary. As well as finding themselves frequently in the media spotlight over human rights rulings, judges saw journalists devote unprecedented attention to the evaluation and promotion process within the judiciary.[90] That this mattered was clear

returned such nomination lists [and] I was thus visited by the acting president of the Supreme Court, who upbraided me for my audacity, saying that 'not even in Pinochet's dictatorship' had such situations occurred" (from Camus 1991: 20–21).

[89] This was limited somewhat by the fact that it was the Court itself that conducted the competition for nominations to the "external" slots, meaning there was a strong likelihood they would choose lawyers they knew and trusted (i.e., that were similar to them) (Interview OL01–04, June 14, 2001, 10:00; Interview SCJ01–08, June 18, 2001, 13:00.)

[90] See "Desafuero cruza elección de quina para la Suprema," *La Tercera*, June 1, 2000, available online at http://www.ua.es/up/pinochet/noticias/junio/01-junio-tercera.html.

in interviews, where one judge stated, "The times are really changing. In the past, judges had a minimal role to play in the system, but now there is a greater popular consciousness about law, courts, and about rights and remedies. People have high expectations for the courts" (Interview SCJ01–2, June 15, 2001, 12:30). Similarly, another claimed, "There has been a cultural change in Chile, as in the whole world. People value things that they didn't value before, and so they are bringing problems to the court that they never brought before (Interview ACJ01–2, June 22, 2001, 15:30).

Perhaps even more immediate in effect than the reform, however, was Pinochet's detention and trials in London. This brought the judiciary under intense international scrutiny and domestic political pressure. Human rights advocates claimed that Chilean courts had proven themselves incapable of prosecuting authoritarian-era human rights abuses, much less those implicating Pinochet himself, and that this made foreign action under universal jurisdiction legitimate and necessary.[91] Determined to save national face, the Frei government insisted Chilean judges were up to the task (Human Rights Watch 2000: 110; Golob 2002). Table 5.2 shows the Supreme Court proved the latter at least partially right.

In interviews in 2001, more than half of the judges I spoke with cited *Londres* as an important influence on judicial behavior. As one clearly conservative judge argued, Pinochet's trial in London

> was a milestone in history and they [the Spanish and English judges] inflicted serious damage. They should've let us resolve our affairs in our own way, let us deal with OUR problems, internal problems. [Instead,] the Supreme Court was forced to change its criteria. Those two foreign countries obliged us, as if we were one of their colonies, to change our criteria. (Interview SCJ01–10, June 19, 2001, 8:00)

A more progressive judge also saw Pinochet's detention as crucial:

> The arrest and trial of Pinochet in London was key because [before] Chilean judges felt uncomfortable with serving as arbitrator in the political sphere, but with the force of the circumstances in London, they lost that feeling of discomfort, which was often laced with fear, because they were put on the spot. The fact that Pinochet was being judged abroad was a judgment of Chilean judges; they looked shameless. So it was a question of identity. Moreover, the

---

[91] See, for example, comments by human rights attorney, Roberto Garretón cited in Brett 2000: 35.

political discourse of this country – even of the [right-wing] opposition was "Pinochet should be tried at home." So the judges felt themselves to be in a more favorable or convenient position. The situation removed the restraints on the Chilean judge. (Interview ACJ01–2, June 25, 2001, 15:30)

As yet another judge put it,

> Pinochet's arrest in London served as a vaccination for the Armed Forces and the population. It prepared the environment for his prosecution here. The effects would have been much stronger, more violent, the opposition much stronger, if London hadn't happened. The events in London helped show that it wasn't just certain Chilean groups who believed the military government had committed crimes against humanity that begged punishment, but in fact the whole world thought this. (Interview ACJ01–4, June 19, 2001, 17:00)

When I asked their opinion about Garzón and universal jurisdiction, many judges stated strongly that Pinochet should be judged at home because Chilean judges were perfectly capable of judging him. One judge known for his work in human rights cases said:

> No, I don't agree with Garzón. He has the competence to rule on events that occurred in Spain or Europe, but Chilean judges are the ones who should rule on crimes committed here in Chile, and they are perfectly capable of doing so. (Interview SCJ01–3, June 19, 2001, 13:00)

Another judge who had ruled against amnesty said,

> I have not read Garzón's rulings, but I think that it's not necessary for Spanish courts to intervene in the affairs of the Chilean judiciary. We are perfectly capable of ruling on human rights matters. I don't think our judges have been influenced by Garzón; rather, I think there is more a sense of rejection or resistance to Garzón's actions. (Interview SCJ01–8, June 18, 2001, 13:00)

These statements, taken together with evidence from judicial rulings offered above, indicate that Pinochet's arrest and trials in London served as an important catalyst to strengthen and expedite a process of change that had already begun within the judiciary. It can't be said that Pinochet and others would have remained judicially untouched (and untouchable) without *Londres*, but it is clear that the foreign judicial action helped to *secure* an important change in the Chilean judiciary's treatment of human rights cases (Lutz and Sikkink 2001).[92]

---

[92] As Chilean human rights lawyer José Zalaquett wrote in October 2000, "increasing efforts to call Pinochet to account in Chile would have taken place at any rate ... had

Having said this, it is also important to emphasize that the effect of this "exogenous shock" was not only enhanced but also limited by domestic conditions. Although clearly impacting judicial treatment of authoritarian-era cases, the international attention and pressure was not strong enough to set off a more comprehensive liberal or constitutionalist turn. Even partially reformed, the institutional structure continued to provide incentives for conservative and comformist behavior, and the institutional ideology, which equated professionalism with apoliticism, persisted.

In the latter part of the decade, the Supreme Court did not react as heavy-handedly to judicial assertiveness in human rights cases as they had in the 1980s and early 1990s, but the Court did continue to monitor and call attention to unorthodox behavior of subordinates. Most notably, during his investigation into the Caravan of Death and other cases in which Pinochet was implicated, Santiago Appeals Court Judge Juan Guzmán repeatedly came under fire from his superiors. He received three "severe alerts" (*severas llamadas de atención*) and one written censure from the Court, reprimanding him for being "overly communicative with the press," for not showing sufficient discretion in his professional conduct, and for not showing the requisite respect for decisions of his superiors (Guzmán Tapia 2005: 176–180). In one instance, they reacted to his statement in a newspaper interview that judges "were not slaves to the law" and "maintained the authority to interpret legislation."[93]

Not surprisingly, then, Guzmán was among the judges that I interviewed in 2001 who continued to express frustration and concern with the control exerted by the Supreme Court over the hierarchy. As one declared, "In the current system, the justices of the Supreme Court can control the lower judges, so there is no real independence. Judges shouldn't be allowed to evaluate and appoint judges because they don't reward independence. When judges reach the Supreme Court, they seem to forget everything they saw and experienced as first instance judges. They act like gods, untouchable" (Interview ACJ01–4, June 19, 2001, 17:00). One of his superiors agreed: "Many people don't even publish work in legal journals because it might be dangerous for one's

the former dictator never traveled to London"; however, these would have "most likely [come] in a different shape or on a lesser scale or at a slower pace."
[93] See, for example, "Suprema Sancionó a Guzmán," *El Mostrador*, December 6, 2000, available online at http://www.elmostrador.cl/modulos/noticias/constructor/detalle_noticia.asp?id_noticia=16330.

career to do so. If I could change one thing about the judiciary, it would be the evaluations system. It doesn't matter to us up here in the Supreme Court, but those down below are always wondering how their superiors will evaluate them, and this robs the judge of his tranquility" (Interview SCJ01–1, June 14, 2001, 16:00). A third judge echoed this sentiment, stating: "The evaluations system distorts judicial independence, because it forces judges to operate always with a certain level of fear. A lower-ranking judge will always want to satisfy the criteria of his superiors, but the judge shouldn't have to think about what others might to do to him personally, how his decision will affect his career" (Interview SCJ01–5, June 25, 2001, 13:00). Thus, although the 1997 reform wrested some control from the Supreme Court, at least in terms of its autonomy to select its own members, it continued to have a felt power over the judicial hierarchy, one whose effect is clearly conservatizing.

This effect was enhanced, moreover, by the continuing weight of the institutional ideology of the judiciary, which is grounded in the notion that adjudication is and must remain completely separate from and above politics. This understanding not only deters judges from taking stands in defense of constitutionalist principles, particularly those that depart from the conservative past but also discourages them from engaging in public dialogue with nonjudicial actors regarding legal interpretation and reform.

To support this claim, I point first to the reaction of judges to the critique and reform proposals mounted after the transition to democracy. For example, the Supreme Court reacted very strongly to the criticism made of the judiciary in the 1991 *Rettig Report*. While, as mentioned above, some of this derived from the attitudes of the justices at the time, it is noteworthy that in my 1996 interviews, dismissiveness of the *Report* was not limited to Pinochet supporters. One Supreme Court justice, appointed by Aylwin, argued that the *Rettig Report*'s critique of the judiciary was "a partial and impassioned response," which was inappropriate because "the judiciary must be judged with rationality and tranquility" (Interview SCJ96–11, June 12, 1996, 18:30.) One of his colleagues, also an Aylwin appointee, contended that the critique "doesn't correspond to us [judges]. . . . It wasn't developed within a judicial analysis, [rather] it was conducted using a different logic, a political logic" (Interview SCJ96–7, June 5, 1996, 12:30). In a similar vein, one appellate judge stated, "If a doctor gives an opinion on cancer, it's very important to note whether or not he is a specialist in cancer, if the opinion is scientific, professional, because we [judges] and they [politicians] are motivated by different impulses and objectives" (Interview ACJ96–7, May 7, 1996, 12:30). All three seemed to echo the view of a Pinochet-era appointee to the Supreme Court, who stated that the *Rettig Report* critique, as a "political critique of a non-political power," was "impertinent," "had nothing to do with us (*nada que ver*)," and was "like a pig in mass (*chancho en misa*)" (Interview SCJ96–3, May 20, 1996, 8:30).[94]

More generally, interviews revealed that most judges conceived of politics as the dirty and divisive activity of politicians and the masses.[95] By contrast, they described their own work as pure, honest, and unifying. In their view, politicians act out of passion and self-interest alone, whereas judges use reason, wisdom, and objectivity, and look only to the common good. Judges thus interpreted the reform proposals of the democratic governments, aimed at the debureaucratization and democratization of the judiciary, as attempts to instrumentalize the judiciary and undermine law. In 1992, the plenary of the Supreme Court voted 10–5 (with two Aylwin appointees in the majority) to reject Aylwin's judicial reform proposals. The president of the Supreme Court, Enrique Correa Labra, who had frequently dissented in human rights cases under the military regime and was expected to be an ally of the new democratic government, declared himself to be "an absolute enemy" of the reforms (Matus 1999: 62). He maintained that the judiciary was "pure and independent," without any defect whatsoever, and when reminded that public opinion did not agree with him, he answered, "I'm not interested in public opinion" but only in the opinion "of those trained in law" (Matus 1999: 63).[96]

Such views were still in evidence in 1996, when judges I interviewed reacted strongly to the idea of having increased democratic oversight of the judiciary via a National Justice Council. Like Correa Labra, they contended that the proposal for such a Council was an attempt to "politically influence," "politically control" or "politicize" the judiciary

[94] It should be noted that the idiom "*chancho en misa*" is used in common parlance to mean irrelevant or totally off-base. However, the literal imagery in this case is worth noting: The porcine politicians interfering irreverently in the pristine, transcendent realm of the judiciary.

[95] Elements of such a perspective emerged in twenty-two of thirty-six of my 1996 interviews with acting high court judges.

[96] Thirteen appeals courts also officially expressed their support for Correa's views, as did the National Association of Magistrates (Brett 1992: 246; Matus 1999: 68).

(Interviews SCJ96–8, June 11, 1996, 13:30; SCJ96–13, June 20, 1996, 11:00; SCJ96–5, May 23, 1996, 14:00; SCJ96–10, June 11, 1996, 18:30; SCJ96–11, June 12, 1996, 18:30; ACJ96–3, April 29, 1996, 13:00), and that it would "rob judges of all independence" (Interviews SCJ96–1, May 16, 1996, 16:00; SCJ96–4, May 23, 1996, 11:00). One judge equated the idea to bringing civilians into the army, slapping uniforms on them, and making them generals (Interview ACJ96–18, May 29, 1996, 13:30). Two others explained frankly: "The Supreme Court is the head of the judiciary, and it should stay that way. The Court needs to be able to oversee (*fiscalizar*) the judiciary as a whole" (Interview SCJ96–9, June 11, 1996, 17:30; SCJ96–10, June 11, 1996, 18:30). For, as another claimed, "The judiciary is above politics" (Interview SCJ96–11, June 12, 1996, 18:30).[97]

One year later, when the Frei government pushed its judicial reform through Congress, the reaction that came from the judicial ranks was less hostile and somewhat more varied. However, there was still significant judicial resistance to the public criticism aroused by the impeachment scandal that provoked the legislative action. For example, on July 30, 1997, the National Association of Magistrates staged a day of "judicial mourning" to protest the "unusual and unjust smear campaign against the judiciary and the proposed reforms to its structure." A majority of judicial employees participated, dressing in black and even attending special masses.[98] The Supreme Court, for its part, roundly rejected the proposals for incorporation of lawyers from outside the judicial career into the Supreme Court, for participation of the Senate in ratification of appointments to the Court, and for obligatory retirement of those over seventy-five.[99]

Of course, the reform did happen, and, as noted earlier, by 2001, judges seemed somewhat more open to engagement with civil and political society.[100] However, interviews revealed that traditional views on

---

[97] There also were those who refused to answer a number of questions which they felt "fell in the realm of the political." These made statements such as, "As a judge, I'd prefer to abstain from formulating judgments regarding issues which fall outside the boundaries of judicial business, or cross into the boundaries of the political" (Interview ACJ96–6, May 6, 1996, 11:00).

[98] "Inédita Protesta del Poder Judicial," *La Tercera,* July 31, 1997 (online).

[99] "Corte Suprema: Un Rotundo No a la Reforma," *La Epoca,* August 29, 1997 (online).

[100] It should be noted, however, that following the release of the Report on Torture in 2004, the "renovated" Court reacted with the same sort of hostility as it had to the *Rettig Report* (see Kornbluh 2005).

appropriate professional conduct still prevailed. As one appellate judge stated:

> In Chile, independent judges are [still] not rewarded. The criterion used for deciding who should ascend in the judicial hierarchy is the judge's *ponderación* [roughly translated: calmness, steadiness, or balance]. The best judge is s/he who is most *ponderado*. But to be considered *ponderado*, a judge must not offend anyone. *Ponderado* winds up meaning "domesticated." And a "domesticated" judge does not provide rights guarantees. (Interview ACJ 01–3, June 22, 2001, 14:00)

Such a view was echoed by a Supreme Court justice, who explained that he had been very involved with an international Judges for Democracy group:[101]

> We tried to start such a group here, but it failed. In Chile, one cannot realize this type of activity because . . . it is not accepted that a judge can manifest publicly which utopia he identifies with; rather, it is considered preferable that that is kept hidden, under the table. (Compare this to Spain, Brazil, or Argentina, where each magistrate is free to express his views without reproach.) So while there are an important number of judges in Chile who are more progressive, our culture impedes them from organizing. (Interview SCJ01–5, June 25, 2001, 13:00)

Broadening the argument slightly, another judge lamented:

> The Supreme Court has maintained its iron control over the judiciary and squelched any hint of liberalization. But more than this, there is the cultural problem. . . . People here don't accept that the way the judge resolves a case . . . depends on how s/he understands the law. In the orthodox sectors of the legal community, this idea is rejected, on the grounds that admitting and allowing judicial discretion would destroy legal security. . . . And so, ultimately, institutional change is not enough. This legal culture (or lack of legal culture) would have to change. In Europe, one can observe such a change. The effort to integrate [the EU legally] is not just formal, but substantive;

---

[101] During the past thirty to forty years, associations of Judges for Democracy have sprung up across continental Europe and in some Latin American countries. These organizations have had an active role in transitions to democracy, and/or, where democracy was established, they have sought to make judges aware of the important, and explicitly political, role they have in liberal-democratic regimes, defending and promoting the principles embodied in the constitutions and international treaties that bind their countries. For an analysis of the emergence of the Spanish Judges for Democracy, see Hilbink forthcoming.

there is a historic commitment [to rights protection.] Here, there's some initiative, but there's no commitment comparable to that in Europe. (Interview ACJ01–2, June 25, 2001, 15:30)

CONCLUSION

In conclusion, just as judicial performance did not change markedly with the military coup in 1973, nor did the transition back to democracy in 1990 usher in a new era of judicial assertiveness in defense of rights and rule of law principles. Rather, as this chapter demonstrates, there continued to be substantial continuity in judicial behavior well into the 1990s. Only after a combination of institutional reform and external pressure began to alter judges' understandings and incentives did a liberal shift become apparent, but, even then, it was limited largely to authoritarian-era issues. In postauthoritarian rights cases, and in the face of judicial reform proposals, judges continued to behave in conservative and conformist ways. The few who were interested in advancing a broader liberal turn found themselves frustrated by the institutional setting in which they worked.

CHAPTER SIX

CONCLUSIONS AND IMPLICATIONS

For many years, comparative politics scholars largely ignored how law and courts functioned in different countries, writing them off as, at best, powerless institutions in most places (Tate 1987).[1] Because courts lack the power of purse and sword (Hamilton 1788), and because politicians often are thought to be self-interested power maximizers (e.g., Geddes 1994), political scientists (along with many citizens) gave little credence to the notion that judges, armed only with legal argument, could make a difference in political outcomes, save (perhaps) in the "exceptional" U.S. case (Tocqueville 1969; Lipset 1996).

Such a dismissive stance is no longer sustainable. People around the world are increasingly looking to judges to hold rulers to the liberal principles enshrined in their constitutions and/or in international treaties that their countries have ratified. In authoritarian regimes, such as Egypt and China, lawyers and average citizens have sought to take advantage of their governments' moves to increase judicial independence and professionalism to advance civil and political rights (Diamant, Lubman, and O'Brien 2005; Moustafa 2007). In new (or renewed) democracies, such as Argentina, Hungary, and South Africa, groups and individuals have turned to courts for everything from addressing past human rights abuses to securing long-held or newly granted social rights (Smulovitz 1995; Klug 2000; Scheppele 2003; Gloppen 2005). And in established democracies, courts remain (as in the United States) or have become (as in Canada, Israel, Italy, and the United Kingdom) a central focus for

[1] For a good example of this for Latin America, see Wiarda and Kline 1985.

those working to protect minority rights, battle official corruption, or hold the executive accountable in the war on terror (Della Porta 2001; Lester 2004; Scheppele 2005; Woods 2005).

Clearly, then, people around the globe have high hopes for what they might achieve through judicial channels. Yet theorists have yet to determine when and why judges will or will not prove willing and able to live up to such expectations. Through an analysis of judicial behavior in Chile under democratic and authoritarian regimes, this book has sought to contribute to the blossoming literature on this question (see, e.g., Epp 1998; Stone Sweet 2000; Russell and O'Brien 2001; Scheppele 2001; Widner 2001; Ginsburg 2003; Maravall and Przeworski 2003; Chavez 2004; Gloppen, Gargarella, and Skaar 2004; Hirschl 2004; Helmke 2005; Moustafa 2007). It has assessed the applicability of competing hypotheses regarding the roots of judicial behavior in both democratic and undemocratic contexts, and has brought to bear evidence that, in the Chilean case, institutional factors explain the persistent failure of judges to take stands in defense of liberal democratic principles. This final chapter will summarize the book's conclusions, marshal support for the argument from other country cases, and explore the implications of the findings for debates in comparative politics and public law.

INSTITUTIONALIZED APOLITICISM

This book began with a question: Why did Chilean judges, who had been trained under and appointed by democratic governments and were steeped in a long-standing legalist tradition, facilitate and condone authoritarian policies? For seventeen years of dictatorship (and beyond), Chilean courts not only failed to defend human rights, but they legitimated, sometimes passively, sometimes actively, the laws and practices of the military regime. As the Report of Chile's National Commission on Truth and Reconciliation noted, and as this book amply documents, judges acted weakly or with insufficient energy, particularly in areas where the law allowed them a significant margin to give protection to individuals persecuted by the regime. By contrast, in cases implicating state officials, judges found myriad reasons to dismiss charges or otherwise exonerate the accused (Ministerio Secretaría General 1991). Thus, far from reflecting and demanding respect for the constitutionalist principles and practices that support democratic – or simply humane – politics, the judiciary, led by the Supreme Court, accepted, endorsed, and helped to perpetuate the brutal and arbitrary rule of a privileged minority.

The explanation I have offered for this performance is that the institutional characteristics of the judiciary, grounded in the ideal of apoliticism, furnished judges with understandings and incentives that discouraged assertive behavior in defense of rights and rule of law principles. Through an analysis of judicial decisions in civil and political rights cases before, during, and after the Pinochet regime, as well as of interviews and other archival data, I have shown the limits of rival propositions, such as those that attribute the performance of Chilean judges to personal policy preferences, class interests, positivist legal philosophy, or regime-related factors. Although each of these alternatives captures some aspects of the story, only the institutional explanation can account for behavior that cut across individual attitudinal and objective class lines, went far beyond a simple "plain-fact" application of Chilean law, and remained quite consistent before, during, and after the authoritarian interlude.

The details of the judicial role in the Pinochet era were captured in Chapter 4, which examined judicial behavior both before and after the introduction of the 1980 Constitution. The chapter documented how, in the name of the rule of law, Chilean courts overwhelmingly supported the military government's argument that concentrated, unchecked power was necessary to save Chile from the permanent communist threat. Even after the government declared an end to the official state of war and leaders of other legal institutions began pushing (along with other social forces) for more liberal interpretation of the country's new constitution, judges continued to rule consistently in favor of the state over the individual citizen. The chapter contended that although regime-related factors and personal political attitudes were part of the equation, this judicial legitimation of the military regime was, above all, facilitated and maintained by the institutional structure and ideology of the judiciary. The Supreme Court held tremendous power over the judicial hierarchy, through which it induced conservatism and conformity among appellate and district court judges. It was able to do so by dismissing or taking disciplinary action against the few judges who refused to fall in line with its servile stance vis-à-vis the military government. These efforts were facilitated by the long-standing ideology of the judiciary, according to which judges were to remain "apolitical."

Any judge desiring to preserve their professional integrity and stand-ing needed to take care to demonstrate their fidelity to "law" alone, and "law" was to remain distinct from and superior to "politics." Challenging the decisions of the military junta, self-proclaimed apolitical guardians of the national interest, would both violate judges' professional duty to remain apolitical and imperil their chances of professional advance-ment. Thus, as the chapter underscores, even democratic-minded judges were, with few exceptions, unwilling to take public principled stands in cases brought against authoritarian laws and practices.

As established in Chapters 2 and 3, this performance did not mark a significant break with the past. Indeed, these chapters revealed that the judiciary had long had a conservative bias, and, moreover, that this bias was institutionally constructed and reproduced. Chapter 2 explained how, from early in the country's republican history, Chilean judges were trained to be "slaves of the law," but in a context in which law, partic-ularly public law, was understood as the will of the executive. Rather than defend legal principles embodied in the constitution, or in the idea of constitutionalism, then, in public law cases, judges were expected to defer to the other ("political") branches of government. Later, institu-tional reforms designed to insulate judges from political (that is, exec-utive and legislative) control rendered the judiciary an autonomous bureaucracy in which conservative elites on the higher courts, and in particular the Supreme Court, were empowered to reinforce and repro-duce their own views through discipline and promotions within the institution. This served to freeze a nineteenth-century understanding of the law, society, and the judicial role into the institution. Hence, in the decades that followed, even as the social composition of the judiciary became overwhelmingly middle (indeed, lower-middle) class, judges acted energetically to defend private property and contract from increasing levels of state regulation, but refused to challenge elected officials in traditional matters of public law. As Chapter 3 explained, when progressives Frei Montalva and Allende came to power, some judges, particularly at the Supreme Court level, did begin taking stands in defense of civil and political rights. However, they did so almost exclusively in cases involving conservative interests, the protection of which was deemed natural and necessary, not "political." The courts thus manifested a weak and inconsistent commitment to rights protec-tion, as well as to the principle of equality before the law central to both liberalism and democracy.

Moreover, as demonstrated in Chapter 5, this pattern of confor- mity and conservatism continued well beyond the return to formal democracy. Indeed, the chapter revealed that it was not until after judi- cial reforms took effect and Pinochet was detained in London that the judiciary's treatment of authoritarian-era human rights abuses began to change. In rights cases that postdated the return to democracy, by con- trast, the more traditional behavior continued. As in the past, judges displayed little desire or capacity to defend or promote citizens' consti- tutional rights or constitutionalism in general, and where they did rule in favor of parties bringing constitutional claims, their decisions were as likely to limit individual rights as they were to uphold them. Extend- ing the argument developed throughout the book, the chapter claimed that this behavior was institutionally conditioned. Although partially reformed, the institutional structure of the Chilean judiciary continued to provide incentives for conservative and conformist behavior, and the institutional ideology, which equated professionalism with apoliticism, persisted. Most judges remained sincerely committed to a passive and conservativizing role in the system, concerned above all with appearing aloof from and impervious to politics. Those with a stronger sense of mission to defend and promote the principles embodied in the constitu- tion and international human rights treaties continued to feel frustrated and constrained by their institutional setting.

In sum, without dismissing altogether the relevance of other fac- tors that contributed to Chilean judicial conservatism, this analysis has shown that institutional characteristics go furthest in explaining the very persistent patterns discussed in Chapters 2 through 5. Long before and well after Pinochet was on the scene, the institutional setting of the judiciary in Chile systematically inhibited the development and expression of liberal, but not conservative, judicial preferences. On the one hand, the Supreme Court's vertical control of the judicial hierarchy and the institution's hegemonic antipolitics ideology discouraged judges from professionally exercising liberal qualities of mind: openness, inde- pendence, creativity, and a sense of "humane skepticism" (Shklar 1986). Indeed, the display of such characteristics was considered "political" and hence unprofessional. On the other hand, the judiciary's institutional features embodied and fostered conservative values and professional attitudes: hierarchy and paternalism, an elitist disdain for politics, and a preference for uniformity and order over pluralism and toleration. These characteristics were deemed timeless, natural, or necessary, and not "political." In a word, illiberal institutional dynamics account largely for illiberal judicial performance in Chile.

The most obvious and immediate implication of this argument is that no one should be surprised by the performance of the Chilean judiciary under Pinochet. Given the historical-institutional characteristics of the judiciary highlighted in this book, Chilean judges could not have been expected to behave in any other manner. Contrary to what many critics have asserted or implied, then, Chilean judges did not betray their vocation;[2] rather, from a democratic perspective, the judicial vocation had been misconstructed in Chile. An institution with a long-standing autonomous bureaucratic structure and antipolitics ideology could hardly be expected to produce judges willing and able to defend liberal democratic principles. Hence, although Chile may have been more democratic than her neighbors, in the sense of having gradually achieved a high level of inclusiveness and participation in the system, and may have been more rule-bound, orderly, and politically stable than other societies in the region, the country was not more constitutionalist. Rather, very much like neighboring countries, Chile's tradition is one of constitutions without constitutionalism (Borón 1993). As this book has confirmed, Chilean constitutions were designed to offer a "tool for governing society," not to set limits on government power (Frühling 1993). Chilean leaders constructed the judiciary to serve more as "ballast for the executive" than as a defense against the abuse of citizens' rights (Adelman 1999: 292), and Chilean judges have generally been true to this role. As I have argued elsewhere (Hilbink 2003), then, at least as regards constitutionalism, Chile is less "exceptional" in Latin America than some have portrayed it.

---

[2] For example, the father of military regime victim Carlos Contreras Maluje told a journalist, "When I turned to the tribunals, I told the judges that the life of my son was in their hands, and that only they could respond to his cries for help ... [but] apart from the two judges of the appeals court [who upheld his writ of habeas corpus], they all betrayed their duty, making themselves co-participants in the barbarity" (cited in P. Verdugo 1990: 98). Similarly, in his speech justifying his impeachment vote against three Supreme Court judges in January of 1993 (see Chapter 5), Senate president Gabriel Valdés stated, "I have profound respect for judges ... because it is they who, definitively, have the mission to protect persons.... The judiciary is the last protection for a human being in defense of his rights.... I firmly believe that the verdict [in question here] is a manifestation and symbol of a system of thought and judicial practice that cannot continue to be accepted from the perspective of judicial duties" (see *Diario de Sesiones del Senado*, Session 27, January 20, 1993, at 3625).

INSTITUTIONALIZED APOLITICISM IN COMPARATIVE
PERSPECTIVE

The conclusions of this book are not merely of relevance for scholars of Chile, however. Although the institutional features on which my argument rests have specific and demonstrable roots in Chilean history, neither the structure nor the ideology I highlight are unique to Chile. Indeed, the institutional structure I describe is (or has been) quite typical in the civil law world, and the conservatizing effects thereof have been documented in numerous cases. The institutional ideology I describe is also, to differing degrees, present among judges in many countries, not only in the civil law world, but in common-law countries as well. Therefore, when I claim that the institutional features constructed around the ideal of apoliticism in Chile rendered judges unwilling or unable to take stands in defense of liberal-democratic principles, I implicate many other possible cases.

As regards the institutional structure, perhaps the closest analogs are Italy's pre–World War II and Spain's pre-1978 judiciaries. In Italy, the judiciary was until the 1960s, "an exemplification of Weber's ideal type of bureaucracy" (Di Federico 1976: 42). Once having passed the state exam required for entrance into the career (usually between the ages of twenty-three and twenty-six), judges moved up the ranks of the hierarchy on some combination of merit and seniority. However, in the name of "apolitical" professionalism, promotions to higher positions were under the discretionary control of the judicial elite. The judges of the highest court (called the Court of Cassation [CC]) based promotions on secret evaluations of their subordinates, evaluations that touched on both the official and private conduct of the personnel.[3] CC members also had the power to discipline their subordinates for failure to fulfill official duties, or for any behavior (official or private) that eroded community trust in the judge or undermined the prestige of the judiciary. Judges thus had an "anxious dependence on the higher echelons of the judicial hierarchy, and [a] need [to] anticipate[] in their behavior and performance the expectations of the judicial elite in order to attain organizational gratifications" (Di Federico and Guarnieri 1988: 169). This system of internal behavioral control not only helped to induce among judges "conformity to a style of work and life detached and aloof

---

[3] It was not the entire high court that controlled promotions but, rather, a subdivision thereof, called the *Consiglio Superiore della Magistratura* (CSM).

from the social and political context" (Di Federico and Guarnieri 1988: 167) but also led, according to critics, to a "'conservative' and even 'reactionary'" political orientation among judges (Di Federico 1976: 54; Pepino 2001).[4] To be sure, judges did not come to play an active role in defense of liberal-democratic rule-of-law principles until the bureaucratic institutional structure was reformed in the 1960s and 1970s (Pederzoli and Guarnieri 1997; Guarnieri 2003).

Similarly, before recent reforms in Spain, the unbroken bureaucratic tradition of the judiciary led judges to be overwhelmingly detached, passive, and/or conservative with regard to social reality (Beirich 1998). Discipline and promotions within the Spanish judicial hierarchy were controlled (from 1870 until 1980) by members of the country's highest court, the Supreme Tribunal (TS), who used their power to "exercise explicit ideological control" over all judges (Andrés Ibáñez 1988: 42). A 1952 law made it obligatory for every hierarchical superior to provide an annual report on the "honesty, intelligence, work ethic, professional aptitude, tact, discretion, public and private conduct, and [when relevant] management" of each of his subordinates (Andrés Ibáñez 1988: 67). These secret reports were then transmitted to the Ministry of Justice and used by the Judicial Council (essentially a subdivision of the TS) to decide who qualified to appear on the lists of three nominees for vacancies in higher ranks (including the TS itself).[5] The process was complemented by reports from the *Inspección de Tribunales*, a group composed of the president of the TS and ten magistrates (that is, judges who had already been promoted once) that were nominated by the president of the TS and approved by the Ministry of Justice. This group conducted "periodic, routine inspection of the nation's courts" aimed primarily at "preventing than really correcting irregularities." In the name of professionalism, the judicial elite thus exercised "formidable social control" over their subordinates and gave the judiciary a clearly quietist and conservative orientation (Toharia 1975: 59–60; Beirich, 1998: 69).

---

[4] Indeed, an analysis of the CC's use of these discretionary powers by a well-respected scholar of the Italian judiciary found that they showed "a rather benevolent attitude in the evaluation of those aspects pertaining to the lack of diligence in the performance of official duties," but "an almost unfailing tendency to penalize" private conduct that produced negative gossiping, non-technical criticism of judicial pronouncements, or involvement in political activities, "especially if connected with parties of the moderate or extreme left" (Di Federico 1976: 47).

[5] Only the president of the Supreme Tribunal was selected directly by the executive (Toharia 1975: 58).

The structure encouraged a contemplation of the past rather than of the present or the future, such that the formally independent judges were unlikely to take stands critical of traditional values and principles, or of any government that claimed to embody those (Toharia 1974–1975; Toharia 1975: 107). The Spanish judiciary thus served Franco well, not simply capitulating to his rule, but, legitimizing his ideology and treating expressions of pluralism as crimes against state security (Bastida 1986: 185–187; Andrés Ibáñez 1988).

Another case that lends credence to the argument regarding the effects of an autonomous bureaucratic structure is post–World War II Japan, where lower-court judges "are closely monitored" and their careers "carefully manipulated" by judicial elites (O'Brien and Ohkoshi 1996: 65).[6] With the objective of securing judicial independence (i.e., depoliticizing control of the judiciary), the 1947 Constitution (Article 77) shifted "authority over the training, nomination, assignment, and oversight of lower court judges and other judicial personnel" from the Ministry of Justice to the Supreme Court (O'Brien and Ohkoshi 1996: 70), or, in practice to the General Secretariat of the Supreme Court, which is staffed by a carefully and institutionally groomed judicial elite (Miyazawa 1991: 48–50). At the same time, the Constitution gave judges the new power of judicial review over legislation and administrative actions. As in Chile in the 1920s (see Chapter 2), a purge of judicial personnel did not accompany these reforms. Thus, prewar judges "continued to exercise influence and arguably wielded greater power due to the reorganization of the courts. They were positioned to conserve as much as possible of the past and to rebuff efforts to enforce new constitutional guarantees for civil rights and liberties" (O'Brien and Ohkoshi 1996: 71). Because lower-court judges are subject to repeated review by the General Secretariat during the course of their careers, "it [has been] difficult for those lower court judges who seek better positions within the judiciary to deviate from what the General

---

[6] It should be noted that a competing argument used to explain the passivity and conservatism of Japanese judges is the dominance of one party, the LDP, in postwar Japan (Ramseyer 1994; Ramseyer and Rasmusen 2003). Without the alternation of parties in power, the argument goes, politicians have no incentive to permit real judicial independence, and therefore they are willing and able to control judicial behavior (i.e., intervene to make judges their agents), even if indirectly. My analysis of Chilean judicial behavior in both the pre- and post-Pinochet eras, when there was plenty of party competition, poses a challenge to the generalizability of this rival proposition.

Secretariat expects of them (Abe 1995: 304). Indeed, as various authors have demonstrated, the General Secretariat has a record of rewarding conformist and conservative judges through promotion and desirable transfers, while discriminating against those who have advocated or ruled in accordance with more liberal understandings of constitutional guarantees (Miyazawa 1991: 55–57; Abe 1995: 314–317; O'Brien and Ohkoshi 1996: 74–76; Ramseyer and Rasmusen 2003). Even in selection to the Supreme Court itself, whose members need not be career judges (but often are), the chief justice and the General Secretariat "exercise extraordinary influence over the appointments" (O'Brien and Ohkoshi 2001: 51). There is no "advice and consent" process, the media pays little attention to the appointments, and the Cabinet, which has the final say over appointments, defers to the recommendation of the Supreme Court (O'Brien and Ohkoshi 2001: 46 and 51). The result has been a notorious passivity on the part of Japanese judges, who refuse to assert their independence in defense of rights and other constitutionalist principles. As O'Brien and Ohkoshi put it, "Dialogue and debate over constitutional politics remains constrained in the Supreme Court, the lower courts, and the country" (1996: 83). Although those who administer the system justify it "in terms of the need of political neutrality of the judiciary" (Miyazawa 1991: 59) or the need to preserve judicial independence (Abe 1995: 315), in fact the "alienation from democratic process allows internal elites to promote a single political perspective and deprive independence of a vast majority of judges" (Miyazawa 1991: 59).

There is thus good comparative support for my claim that an autonomous bureaucratic structure, which is supposed to insulate the judiciary from politics, tends to reproduce conservatism and conformity, rendering it unlikely that judges will assert themselves in defense of liberal principles. Nonetheless, the other part of my argument, namely, that an institutional ideology of apoliticism is as important in explaining judicial conformity and conservatism as judicial structure – that is, that judicial role conceptions are as important to judicial behavior as more material incentives – should not be deemed superfluous. On the one hand, such an ideology was or is present in all of the cases discussed above (Italy, Spain, and Japan). On the other hand, variants of this ideology are apparent even in cases with very different judicial structures, and are clearly associated with judicial passivity in the face of violations of constitutionalist principles.

As Guarnieri notes, "Judicial interventions in the political process require not only an independent and powerful judiciary but also judges *willing* to intervene. Thus we have to consider . . . the judicial culture and . . . the way judges tend to define their role" (2003: 235, my emphasis). In Italy, until at least the 1960s, a "dogma . . . of neutrality and apoliticism" characterized the judiciary, and, "like all dogmas . . . was fueled by obsessive repetition and by unconditional and often sincere adhesion" (Pepino 2001: 18). This "dogma" offered "decisive cultural support" to the autonomous bureaucratic structure described above, reinforcing the tendency of even liberal-minded judges to refrain from taking stands in defense of constitutional principles (Pepino 2001: 18–19). It has only been in the last few decades, when "a different conception of the role of the judge has gained ground," recognizing and advocating judicial creativity, that judges have become "more likely to assert their independence when on the bench" (Guarnieri 2003: 235; see also Della Porta 2001).

The same applies to Spain, where, until at least the 1970s, a "notable absence of a critical spirit" persisted among judges (Andrés Ibáñez 1988: 66). Historically, judges were never authorized to exercise any real discretion or independent power, but were expected to maintain "an attitude of blind submission and obedience" to the sovereign will as embodied in the law (Toharia 1975: 26–27). For judges, "a questioning of the 'rightness' of a law was seen to be politicization. From their perspective, the idea of reinterpreting laws passed by the parliament would make them political by involving them in the legislative process" (Beirich 1998: 71). In accordance with the 1870 Organic Law of the Judiciary, the judge, like any good civil servant, was expected to be 'apolitical,' or strictly 'professional.' And judges lived up to these expectations. As former President of Spain's Constitutional Tribunal, Francisco Tomás y Valiente, noted:

> The system wanted conformist judges, and it got them. [It] produced judges more jealous of the appearance of being apolitical than an effective independence. The result was not a norm of corruption; rather it was the predominance of an obedient judge, often competent, highly cognizant ideologically of the regime, apolitical and highly conscious of his position in the Administration of Justice, but not a true judicial power (cited in Beirich 1998: 69).

As in Italy, it was only through purposive challenges to this ideology that judicial behavior began to change (Hilbink forthcoming).

In Japan, by contrast, such an ideology has persisted, despite efforts to critique and change it (Miyazawa 1991: 59–60; Abe 1995: 319). Miyazawa emphasizes the roots of this ideology in the prewar conception of the judiciary as a mere agency of the executive, whose role it was to unquestioningly carry out the will of the government (1991: 57). This has persisted, he argues, because of the commitment of the judicial elite to a "conception of neutrality [that] appears to mean simply the sharing of the perspectives of the dominant political group." Indeed, he notes that "elite judges seem to find . . . satisfaction in their role as a rear guard of the status quo" (Miyazawa 1991: 59). Similarly, Abe argues that there is an unwritten norm which requires judges to regulate their behavior so as to preserve organizational autonomy (1995: 314–316). In other words, judges are expected to "refrain from behaving in such a way as to generate doubt that the judiciary might be biased against the will of the political majority" (Abe 1995: 314). As he underscores, "those judges who perfectly internalize [such] criteria" and behave accordingly are those who "succeed to responsible positions in judicial administration" (Abe 1995: 318).[7]

The parallels in these four cases (Chile, Italy, Spain, and Japan) might easily be chalked up to their shared participation in the "civil law tradition" (Merryman 1985). As Martin Shapiro notes, in most civil law countries, "the judiciary is a hierarchically organized civil service, more or less cut off from private practitioners, and with relatively close affinities and connections [and, I would add, role conceptions] with the rest of the higher levels of the career government bureaucracy." This, he notes, "may systematically bias the judiciary" in favor of the state in a broad range of politically significant cases (1981: 156). However, a professional commitment to apoliticism is not limited to judges in civil law countries. Indeed, invocations of a strict law/politics distinction to justify judicial passivity in constitutional cases are frequent in common law countries, as well.

For example, Dyzenhaus has made a strong case that it was South African judges' view that they must remain apolitical which prevented them from placing the apartheid government "in the rule of law dilemma" (1998: 160).[8] In other words, rather than engage in the "deeply political act" of "requiring [the] government [to] live up

---

[7] Another case that appears to support my argument about ideology is Weimar Germany. See Kahn-Freund 1981.

[8] By the "rule of law dilemma," he means having to choose "between accepting the costs as well as the benefits of operation under the rule of law or doing without the legitimacy which attaches to government under the rule of law" (Dyzenhaus 1998: 159).

to ideals which itself, however cynically, professe[d]," judges opted to remain passive and implement "without protest, and often with zeal," laws that clearly violated the principles underlying the rule of law idea (Dyzenhaus 1998: 160 and 27).[9]

Similarly, Gloppen argues that "'the un-political judge' is a central *norm of appropriateness*" among judges in both Tanzania and Zambia, "explaining a reluctance to challenge the government if they can avoid it" (2004: 123, emphasis in the original). Notably, she reveals a link between this norm and the identification of judges in these countries with the British common law tradition. As she explains, the judges in her study "emphasize that, in the common law tradition, courts are reactive, rather than proactive," and that some "explicitly distance themselves from activist colleagues who fail to comply with the proper judicial role" (Gloppen 2004: 122).

Widner devotes an entire chapter of her analysis of how judges sought to build judicial independence in common-law African states to how and why judicial interpretation of rights grew more assertive in the late 1980s and 1990s (2001: Ch. 9). Although she downplays the idea that the legal culture of the bench was the most significant limitation on assertions of judicial independence (2001: 55), she emphasizes the ways in which judicial leaders such as Francis Nyalali (Chief Justice of Tanzania) worked to recast the "proper role" of the judge to include more political/less narrowly legal considerations. Among such considerations were "the principles and values which motivated the great leaders of the African liberation movement," principles and presumptions implicit in the common law, positive and customary international law, and policy concerns (Widner 2001: 183–186). In other words, she illustrates that an important part of building "positive" judicial independence (Widner 2001: 29) in Africa involved the crafting and dissemination of a new and more political judicial role conception.

Even in the United States, where liberalism has a stronger history, analysts concerned with the preservation of constitutionalist principles have remarked on the tendency of judges to conceive their role, or assert the boundaries thereof, in terms of a duty to leave clearly "political" matters to the elected branches. For example, Franck (1992) critiques the tendency of American judges to invoke the "political questions"

---

[9] Although Dyzenhaus associates the conception of the rule of law as anti-politics more directly with legal positivism than I do here (e.g., 1998: 16–17; see also Dyzenhaus 1991), his argument remains compatible with mine.

doctrine – that is, the notion that certain matters are outside the (strictly legal) judicial purview – to avoid review of the foreign policy decisions of the elected branches. Citing Jefferson and Madison (among others), Franck argues that this judicial "abdicationist phenomenon" is "not only not required by but wholly incompatible with American constitutional theory." In order to be true to the constitutionalist principles on which the American polity was founded, the executive should "not be the judges of its own cause in a clash between political policy and the rule of law" (Franck 1992: 4–5 and 156). Those concerned about executive discretion in the war on terror are now expressing similar points (e.g., Cole 2004).[10] To the extent that judges hold that executive decisions regarding national security are "political questions" not appropriate for judicial review, they will not be willing and able to serve constitutionalism.

All of these examples appear to support my theoretical claim that judicial institutions constructed around the ideal of apoliticism tend to produce conservative and conformist judicial behavior, and render it unlikely that judges will assert themselves in defense of rights and rule of law principles. But what about cases in which judges *have* taken such stands? In the Introduction to this book, I highlighted the fact that, in contrast to Chile, judges in Brazil and Argentina did demonstrate some mettle in the face of gross abuses of power by military governments. The question is: can institutional factors account, at least in part, for this variation? I believe they can.[11]

In some aspects of its structure, the Brazilian judiciary is similar to the Chilean: It is organized as a civil service bureaucracy in which judges enter by examination and ascend in the ranks according to seniority and merit, as evaluated by their superiors (Brinks 2005: 614).[12] There are, however, a number of important differences. First, Brazil has a federal system, in which courts administered at the state level have

---

[10] See, for example, the editorial, "A Judicial Green Light for Torture," from the *New York Times*, February 26, 2006.

[11] Note that my claim here is not that institutional conditions in these cases provoked the judicial resistance but, rather, that they permitted, even facilitated, behavior that was institutionally precluded in Chile. For an interesting diachronic analysis that appears to support this claim, see Solomon 1996.

[12] This may have limited the autonomy of lower-court judges in the past, but under the terms of the 1988 Constitution, "upper courts [have] little influence over professional development of lower court judges" and "lower courts judges are largely free agents in the decision making process" (Taylor 2006: 341).

always played a key role. Second, since the first republican constitution (1891), judicial review has been decentralized, meaning that, as in the United States, all Brazilian judges enjoy judicial review powers.[13] Third, the members of the highest court, the *Supremo Tribunal Federal* (STF), which has the final say on constitutional matters, have always been nominated by the President of the Republic and approved by the Senate, as in the United States (Arantes 1997).[14] This renders them "more sensitive to political concerns" and more "politically accountable" than other judges in the system (Brinks 2005: 614). Perhaps for this reason, they "ruled consistently against military actions" in the first four years after the 1964 coup, upholding the habeas corpus petitions of civilian political figures, challenging the military's definition of threats to national security, and resisting the effort to strip the Tribunal of jurisdiction over constitutional challenges to executive action (Osiel 1995: 531 and 533–535). Even after the military government tried to reign in the STF by expanding its size and packing it with its own appointees (Institutional Act 2 of October 1965),[15] the justices continued to challenge the legitimacy of the regime's illiberal laws and policies and to appeal to the broader public in their rulings (Osiel 1995: 534–536). The government's solution, at the end of 1968 and early 1969, was to purge the STF of its most critical members and restrict the jurisdiction of ordinary courts over politically sensitive matters, diverting them instead to the military justice system (Ballard 1999; Pereira 2005).

As Pereira shows, however, a fidelity to peacetime legal procedure and an openness to more liberal legal interpretation and case outcomes also characterized the military courts in Brazil's authoritarian regime, where "civilian judges [who] were career civil servants often dominated legal judgments because their colleagues on the bench were military officers shuffled in and out on three-month terms" (2005: 75). This appears to indicate that the institutional ideology of Brazilian judges, even those below the level of the STF, did not include the same taboo against ruling on "political" matters as did that in Chile. As Pereira notes, the high acquittal rates of Brazil's military courts "represent the courts' formal

---

[13] The constitutional jurisdiction of different courts under the 1988 Constitution is complex and varied, but the general point holds. See Arantes 1997.

[14] Under the military regime, however, the executive maintained exclusive appointment powers.

[15] Note that this act also suspended tenure and salary guarantees for all lower court judges.

recognition of the rights of individuals over and above the claims of the state for security." Although it requires independent research to support it, it thus seems safe to say that the Brazilian conception of judicial professionalism and independence does not require judges to be "apolitical," or, at least, does not define the defense of rights, even those of regime critics, to be "political" and hence off limits to judges.[16] To be sure, the notable activism of the Brazilian judiciary since the return to democracy in 1988 indicates a strong openness on the part of judges to exercising their constitutional review powers in even the most sensitive political matters (Arantes 1997; Ballard 1999; Brinks 2005; Taylor 2006).

In Argentina, for its part, the institutional features of the judiciary are completely different from those in Chile. As in Brazil, there exist both state and federal courts, and judicial review is diffuse. Moreover, no portion of the judiciary is a career bureaucracy. Instead, as in the United States, all federal judges were, until 1994, nominated by the President of the Republic and approved by a simple majority of the Senate.[17] What this means is that, as in the United States, judges have always had strong ties to political parties (Larkins 1996; Peretti 1999). Also, following quite explicitly its U.S. counterpart, the Argentine Supreme Court asserted early on the power to resolve "important and contentious" political issues (Helmke 2005: 63; see also Miller 1997 and Chavez 2004: 42–44).[18] In the 1940s, however, Argentine presidents began reacting to what they perceived as political meddling by the Court and instituted an informal practice of removing potentially unreliable

---

[16] As both Daniel Brinks and Tony Pereira pointed out to me in personal communications, Brazilian judges nonetheless had the reputation, at least prior to the transition in 1988, of being excessively formalistic and bureaucratic. To be sure, the critical discourse of the judicial association *Juízes para a Democracia*, indicates this still applies to some degree. Given the size and diversity of the country, however, the reality is probably that there are, and have long been, competing conceptions of the appropriate judicial role available for adoption by individual judges.

[17] Reforms of 1994 increased the Senate approval rule for the Supreme Court to a two-thirds majority, and added the requirement that the approval process be public. In addition, the reforms created a National Judicial Council, whose various members are appointed by the executive, legislature, judiciary, bar, and law schools, and it is this body that now draws up binding lists of nominees for lower judicial posts. The president selects appointees from these lists, and the Senate maintains approval power.

[18] Contrast this to Chile, where the Supreme Court tended historically to avoid constitutional review (refer to Chapter 2).

justices and replacing them with loyal supporters (Chavez 2004; Helmke 2005: 63–67). Not surprisingly, it was in this period that the Court developed its version of the American "political questions doctrine," asserting it frequently to refuse challenges to military seizures of power and declarations of states of emergency.[19]

Helmke (2005) has argued quite persuasively that, from this point forward, judicial behavior in Argentina (at least at the level of the Supreme Court) is best understood as strategic, that is, as driven primarily by the justices' desire to stay in office, or at least to salvage their reputations when they anticipated imminent removal. Accordingly, when judges in the most recent authoritarian period perceived that the military was losing its grip on power, they began taking consistent stands in defense of rights and rule of law principles (Helmke 2005: 128). Although this is not a general pattern one would wish to see emulated, it is clear that, so long as the broader context permitted it, the institutional structure and ideology of the Argentine judiciary offered plenty of space for judges to assert themselves in defense of liberal-democratic principles, before, during, and after authoritarian interludes. Indeed, as Brysk notes, "judicial support for human rights [after the transition to democracy] derived from an autonomous institutional environment that facilitated the expression of personal and professional convictions" (1994: 114). Unfortunately, since the 1990s, respect for judicial independence on the part of elected officials has been uneven, limiting the authority and legitimacy of Argentina's courts.

BROADER IMPLICATIONS OF THE ARGUMENT

Having established the comparative empirical support for the book's argument, I now step back to assess the implications of the findings for broader debates in comparative politics and public law. In this closing section, I make three claims: First, my study of Chile reinforces the point made by numerous scholars of judicial behavior that formal judicial autonomy in no way guarantees that judges will assert their authority to limit the power of government actors or advance liberal-democratic principles. In other words, formal judicial independence is not in itself enough to produce judicial action in defense of rights and the rule of

---

[19] As Larkins (1996: 619) argues, broad application of the political questions doctrine often implies a low level of judicial independence, which was certainly the case in Argentina.

law; other conditions must obtain. Second, and relatedly, the analysis bolsters the claim made by new institutionalists that institutional conditions strongly shape judges' behavior, including their proclivity to take stands against public officials. Moreover, it underscores that institutions act both to constitute and constrain judicial preferences, and suggests that the institutional origins and impact of judicial role conceptions merit more attention from scholars. Finally, the Chilean case, along with the other examples cited in the preceding section, demonstrates not just the impossibility but the undesirability of striving for an "apolitical" judiciary. Indeed, judicial institutions designed to keep judges beyond politics leave judges lacking in precisely those attributes necessary for them to assert themselves against abuses of official power and defend liberal-democratic values and practices. Those concerned with promoting the judicial protection of rights and the rule of law, then, must acknowledge the fundamentally *political* nature of such a judicial role, and advance institutional reforms that foster democratic political sensibility and responsibility among judges.

The Limits of Judicial Independence

For emerging democracies today, building the rule of law and improving rights protection are common, though often elusive, goals. Although courts are by no means the only institutions that can or should provide these goods, many scholars and policy makers agree that if judges are to contribute to the realization of these goals, they must enjoy a strong measure of formal autonomy or independence. Without a professional and independent judiciary in place, the argument goes, rulers are free to distort or ignore the law, rendering the quality of governance overly dependent on the virtue and good will of rulers. The existence of an independent judiciary, outside the control of sitting government officials, provides both opposition leaders and average citizens the possibility of challenging the decisions of those in power, of bringing them to account for their actions. As MacCormick puts it, "a legal order that is working according to the ideal of the rule of law . . . insists on the production by governments of an appropriate warrant in law for all that they do, coupled with the right of the individual to challenge the warrant produced by the government," (1999: 175) and there can clearly be "no security against arbitrary government unless such challenges are freely permitted" and have the potential to prevail (1999: 176). In order for that possibility to obtain, however, particularly in any case to which the government is a party, judges must not be subject to control by other public officials. Citizens can never expect to win challenges to the legitimacy of governmental action (or private action endorsed by sitting government officers) unless such challenges are "subjected to adjudication by officers of state separate from and distanced from those officers who run prosecutions" (MacCormick 1999: 176) Judicial reformers thus seek, above all, to find ways of preventing executive or legislative interference with or manipulation of courts, that is, of achieving judicial independence.

Yet one of the central lessons that can be taken from the Chilean case is that such formal judicial independence does not necessarily produce assertions of judicial authority against abuses of official power or in favor of citizens' rights. As the preceding chapters have amply demonstrated, judicial autonomy has long been respected in Chile, but judges have overwhelmingly refused to assert themselves in defense of rule of law and rights principles, whether under democratic or authoritarian regimes. Moreover, as noted in Chapter 4, it was the formally less independent Constitutional Tribunal, created and staffed directly by the military rulers, that ultimately took stands in favor of liberal-democratic principles and facilitated a return to democracy.

My analysis thus supports two points, one conceptual and one theoretical, made in recent literature in the field of law and courts. First, it underscores the need to make a clear distinction between formal judicial autonomy or "negative" judicial independence, on the one hand, and independent judicial behavior or "positive" independence, on the other (e.g., Russell 2001; Widner 2001; Burbank and Friedman 2002). Although the former concept refers largely to the norms (formal and informal) governing judicial appointment, discipline, tenure, and procedure, the latter is defined as "a recognition of the importance of giving the actions of the other branches of government a sober second thought, of restraining practices that violate the dignity of community members" (Widner 2001: 41), and making a distinct "contribution to the business of government by championing the virtues associated with the ideal of the rule of law" (Simpson 1989: 147). Although there are clearly advantages to limiting our object of inquiry to the formal or "negative" type of judicial independence (Russell 2001), ultimately it is positive independence that many scholars and citizens of (liberal-) democracies seek to explain or promote. It might thus be helpful to find a term other than "independence" to capture this dependent variable.

Second, and relatedly, the Chilean example bolsters the claim made by new institutionalists that judicial behavior is a product neither of legal formalism – that is, simply applying the laws on the books – nor of individual policy preferences (Ginsburg 2003: 69). Both the legalist and attitudinalist theories proceed on the assumption that formally independent judges are free to assert themselves against (perceived or real) abuses of power by other state actors (Lovell and McCann 2005: 258–259). To the extent that they do not, either the law or the (exogenous) preferences of the judges are to blame. If this assumption were correct, however, one would not find the very uniform absence of such action in the (ordinary) judiciary across regimes in the Chilean case. The analysis thus suggests that those interested in understanding or encouraging particular forms of judicial behavior should turn their attention to features of the institutional context that impede or enable the assertion of judicial authority, whether under authoritarian or democratic regimes (Burbank and Friedman 2002; Ginsburg 2003; Moustafa 2007).

INSTITUTIONS AS RULES *AND* ROLES

As I explained in Chapter 1 and as is clear in the preceding section, the argument of this book fits in the "new institutionalist" literature in (American) public law. Although it is certain that judges bring (exogenous) personal policy preferences with them to the bench, as attitudinalists emphasize, there is now growing agreement among scholars that a judge's inclination and ability to let those determine his/her rulings are influenced by institutional factors. The remaining disagreement appears to be over how to define institutions (formal or informal? materialist or norm-oriented?) and how to explain their effects on behavior (constraining or constituting of preferences?). The argument I offer in this book attempts to transcend the "either/or" nature of these debates, acknowledging the relevance of the formal and the informal, the more material and the more ideational, and both the constituting and constraining nature of institutional factors in the Chilean judiciary. Although at first blush this may sound wishy-washy, in fact, such a syncretic approach is frequently advocated in political science today (see, e.g., Thelen 1999; Maveety 2003b). Moreover, leading lights in judicial behavior studies have long recognized that "judges' decisions are a function of what they prefer to do, tempered by what they think they ought to do, but constrained by what they perceive is feasible to do" (Gibson 1986: 150).

Having established that, I want to highlight the part of the argument that takes seriously the "what they think they ought to do" part of the

equation.[20] So much of social behavior is conditioned by understandings that people have internalized, through both formal training and
often less formal socialization, about what is appropriate and inappropriate to their role in any given setting. As Migdal puts it, "Institutions
create routines, and, even with coercion only a distant threat, those
routines ensure significant obedience" to implicit and explicit norms
(2001: 255). Yet many political scientists tend to overlook or down-
play the importance of roles in political life, emphasizing instead more
tangible and quantifiable factors. Role theory has certainly not been
absent in judicial studies (see, e.g., Becker 1966; Grossman 1968; Glick
and Vines 1969; Gibson 1981; Paterson 1982; Kenney 2000), but with
the predominance of the attitudinalist model for many years, it never
gained a wide following. Based on my findings in the Chilean case and
the supporting evidence I cite from other country cases on the importance of institutional ideology, I contend that the time is ripe for a return
to considerations of role in the judicial arena, and of the mechanisms
by which role conceptions are instilled, maintained, or modified.[21] As
Baum has recently noted, both consciously and subconsciously, judges
are motivated by a desire for respect and approval from their reference
groups or audiences (2006: 43–48), and among the audiences that will be
most salient for judges are professional colleagues and superiors (2006:
171). To understand judicial behavior, then, it is imperative that we
consider the institutional settings in which different judges work, and
the impact these have on the way they understand both what they can
and *ought* to do. Institutions alone may not determine judicial behavior,
but we need to understand the ways that different institutional factors,
including those that are ideational, "refract and constrain" outcomes
(Thelen and Steinmo 1992: 3).

In Defense of Political Courts[22]

Having argued for the importance of institutional variables to explaining judicial behavior, in general, I turn now to the more specific normative question of which kinds of institutional features are more or
less likely to foster judicial assertiveness in favor of rights and the rule

---

[20] I am indebted to Phil Shively for stimulating my thinking on much of what I say in
this paragraph.
[21] This might well fit in the research agenda on "informal institutions" proposed by
Helmke and Levitsky (2004).
[22] The title of this section deliberately echoes the title of Peretti 1999.

of law. Drawing on the analysis presented in this book, as well as the other cases discussed in this chapter, I contend that if the goal is to produce courts whose members are willing and able to assert themselves in defense of rights and rule of law principles, the political nature of the judicial role must be acknowledged and institutionally cultivated. Indeed, the most important lesson that can be taken from the Chilean case is that constructing a judiciary around the ideal of apoliticism is not simply misleading and impossible, but in fact discourages some of the key professional understandings and practices necessary for judges to support a liberal-democratic rule of law.

As noted in Chapter 2, early Chilean state-builders believed, as do many modern-day social scientists (e.g., De Soto 2000; Zakaria 2003), that there could be no political and economic development without the rule of law; and, like some contemporary legal scholars (e.g., Mattei 1997), they believed there could be no rule of law without apolitical judges. They thus (gradually) built and institutionalized a professional, independent judiciary whose structure and ideology were grounded in a strict law/politics distinction: judges were to be "slaves of the law," eschewing any involvement in political affairs, and politicians were prohibited from interfering with judicial matters. Yet, as this book amply documents, this formally apolitical institution played a clearly political, and often illiberal, role before, during, and after the authoritarian regime. Indeed, it was in the name of apoliticism that Chilean judges rendered some of their most deeply political decisions, providing direct and indirect legitimation of authoritarianism.

This insight has both theoretical and practical relevance. Theoretically speaking, it reinforces the notion that courts are never independent in the sense of being removed from and impervious to politics (Shapiro 1981; Rubin 2002). Judges may enjoy formal autonomy in their decision making, but, as suggested earlier in this chapter, the role they play in the polity will be "inevitably intertwined with other strands of politics" (Lovell and McCann 2005: 257). Practically speaking, the analysis suggests that judicial reformers should rethink the guiding conception of judicial professionalism or independence as apoliticism.[23] Although

---

[23] As former US-AID and current World Bank analyst Linn Hammergren notes, external supporters and national participants in judicial reform have tended to work around the theme of an apolitical judiciary, even as the judiciary (worldwide) is confronting a new level of political involvement (1998: 26–27). They have preferred to

it is true that in many places courts are thoroughly and destructively politicized (Mattei 1997), such that judicial offices are filled with politicians' cronies or partisan hacks, the Chilean case shows that the solution is not to insist that a properly reformed judiciary, particularly one with constitutional jurisdiction, be "apolitical." To be sure, it is a worthy aspiration to construct a judicial corps staffed with people who have solid legal training, who can perform relatively efficiently and effectively, and who will not be susceptible to bribery or other forms of manipulation by parties to the cases they hear (see MacCormick 1999; Rubin 2002; Brinks 2005). However, state institutions, even when they are highly professionalized, are not and can never be politically neutral.[24] Institutions embody and transmit "values and visions of the world"; that is, they shape the mentalities of the actors that function within them (Rial 1990: 9; Hammergren 1998: 28). These values and visions will, by definition, have a political (that is, ideological) content. As Dyzenhaus puts it, even an "antipolitical" conception of the judicial role is driven by politics, "by the argument that it is politically appropriate that judges adopt that conception" (1998: 22). Hence, if the goal is to produce courts in the service of liberal democracy, reform programs aimed at professionalizing judicial institutions should take special care to articulate the specific liberal-democratic values and visions that are informing the effort and to design mechanisms to help transmit these to judges (Correa 1993).

To repeat, my point here is not to dismiss the importance of formal judicial independence. Such autonomy can, and should, be effected through various mechanisms that forbid or attenuate signals from nonjudicial units: general mechanisms, such as appointing only legally trained people to the judiciary and providing tenure and salary protection; and specific mechanisms, such as the formal prohibition of performative, informative, and expressive signals from government officers and private parties (Rubin 2002: 70–75; see also Brinks 2005). My argument is, rather, that judicial assertiveness in defense of rights and rule of law principles requires more than formal independence. It requires a

focus on "modernizing" existing structures rather than working "to give the institution a new identity and the internal organization, leadership, and incentive structures to realize it" (Hammergren 2000: 18).

[24] A similar point has been made by critics of Huntington's (1957) idea that a professional military will, by definition, be an apolitical military. See, for example, Bustamente 1998; Fitch 1998.

particular set of professional attributes from judges, attributes that are actively discouraged when adjudication is constructed as apolitical.

What are those attributes? First, in order for judges to "give the actions of the other branches of government a sober second thought" (Widner 2001: 41), judges must be able to find "some critical distance" on matters before them (Scheppele 2002: 227). Judges cannot be expected to serve as a "countervailing force within the larger governmental system" (Fiss 1993: 56) if they do not have enough independence of mind, and the associated confidence, to entertain perspectives that challenge the legal arguments of government officials (which, if unchallengeable, are essentially "political commands" [Scheppele 2002]). If constitutionalism is to work, judges must have the leeway in their professional role "to make at least some of the law themselves" (Scheppele 2002: 270), and making law is a quintessentially *political* function (Dyzenhaus 2000).[25]

Second, and relatedly, if judges are ever to interpret the law to favor arguments advanced by average citizens over those of government officials, they must have a sense of professional connection and responsibility to the citizenry. They should not stand aloof from the political community, handing down authoritative and unassailable pronouncements (Shklar 1986) but should, rather, understand themselves as representative of and responsible to the people (Peretti 1999; Eisgruber 2001). This does not mean that judges should be elected. Elective judiciaries create incentives for judges to cater to particular views or constituencies in cases before them, thereby compromising the functional independence discussed earlier (Croley 1995; Rubin 2002: 87–88). Instead, judges must be encouraged to engage with the people by offering good and accessible reasoning in their decisions, such that citizens will view them as "generally fair, impartial, and trustworthy" (Gillman 2001: 8, citing Lind and Tyler 1988) and that their rulings might "provoke constructive conversations and spirited debates" in the wider polity (Carter and Burke

---

[25] At the same time, of course, judges must take care to demonstrate that their independent-minded rulings are not "arbitrary and random power-plays" (Hutchinson 1999: 211), based solely on intuition or the dictates of personal conscience. They must show their decisions to be guided and bound (although not necessarily determined) by rule(s) or principle(s) located somewhere in the legal system. In cases in which judges see fit to challenge a statute in some way, they should appeal to the constitution, or, where relevant, the common law (Scheppele 2002: 245). Whatever the case, judges must act in good faith – that is, "make some genuine effort" (Hutchinson 1999: 212) – to link their decisions to professed commitments of the political community.

2002: 155). Otherwise put, judges must understand and present their function as an integral part of the democratic *political* process.

Of course, a court's democratic legitimacy will be "threatened if it appears, because of its own narrow membership, to lack an understanding of the broad range of people who come before it" (Minow 1992: 1206). In a diverse society, fair judgment – or impartiality – is not simply a matter of securing judge(s) that are not too close to the accused but also of ensuring that the judges are not too distant from the conflicts and perspectives that they must adjudicate. Moreover, because there is no such thing as perfect impartiality or neutrality in human society, because basic categories such as sex, race, and ethnicity implicate all people, judges must be not only as "objective" as possible about "the facts and the questions of guilt and innocence," but also "committed to building upon what they already know about the world," such that their (inescapable) working assumptions are out in the open and, hence, open to challenge and reconsideration (Minow 1992: 1209 and 1217). The legitimate assertion of judicial authority thus requires that judges be open, sensitive and thoughtfully receptive to competing and evolving perspectives on the law, particularly those coming from (relatively) weak and potentially unpopular individuals or minorities. Such an openness to difference, debate, persuasion, and adaptation is very much part of a democratic *political* vocation (Michelman 1998).

The construction of a judiciary around the ideal of apoliticism is thus not only illusory, but is also fundamentally at odds with advancing a liberal-democratic rule of law. As this book has shown, walling judges off structurally and/or ideologically from politics denies them precisely those professional understandings and incentives necessary for them to serve liberal-democratic constitutionalism. This does not mean that judges whose vocation is constructed around the ideal of apoliticism will be programmed to become *Pinochetista*-style conservatives; rather, my claim is that those who operate under such institutional conditions will be unlikely to possess the professional attitudes and capacities necessary to question or challenge authoritarian acts or policies and will be more likely to block than to support legal innovation.

To begin, when a judiciary is structured so as to separate and insulate judges from politics, adjudication becomes a bureaucratic or technocratic function. Under the vertical control of institutional superiors, judges are discouraged from listening to any voices from outside the judiciary, and from expressing doubts or criticisms regarding the prevailing judicial wisdom. Instead, they have incentives to conform, blend in, take

the path of least resistance.[26] As Damaska explains, professionals "strat-
ified in a chain of subordination" are "under pressure toward unity and
obedience." Those who "desire to make a special impact" interfere with
the "harmonious functioning of the organization," and are thus "likely
to be bypassed for advancement" (1986: 21). Moreover, because they
have no incentive to invest themselves personally in their work, they
are unlikely to take personal responsibility for its effects. The routiniza-
tion of their work permits "emotional disengagement," and the squelch-
ing of internal dissent deepens this detachment (Damaska 1986: 19).
In typical Weberian bureaucratic style, then, judges in such an institution will "*Sine ira et studio*, 'without scorn and bias,' . . . administer [their]
office . . . [without doing] precisely what the politician, the leader as well
as his following, must always and necessarily do, namely, fight . . . take a
stand" (Weber 1946: 95).[27]

An "apolitical" institutional structure thus works against the cul-
tivation of the professional understandings and capacities that allow
judges to assert themselves against abuses of power or tradition. Rather
than promoting independent- and critical-mindedness, such a structure fosters servile and mechanical mentalities and practices. Rather
than cultivating a sense of connection and responsibility to the citizenry, it encourages an inward orientation and a refusal to engage with
"non-experts." And rather than breeding openness to difference, debate,
and interpretive innovation, an "apolitical" judicial structure serves to
enforce unity and repress dissent.[28] In short, within such an institutional
structure, closed-mindedness and conservatism prevail.[29]

Likewise, when the institutional ideology of the judiciary is anchored
by an imperative to remain apolitical, judges are generally discouraged

---

[26] For an interesting account of how the professionalization/bureaucratization of the
Soviet criminal justice system brought an end to judicial resistance to legal excesses,
see Solomon 1996.

[27] This is not to say that judges should have complete freedom from vertical legal
controls, such as cassation rulings or binding precedent. Rather, the point is they
should not be subject to vertical career controls.

[28] As Miyazawa writes about the Japanese judiciary, "Our judiciary may . . . appear to
be more independent from political influences [than other democracies]. However,
this also means a lack of democratic control, and this alienation from democratic
process allows internal elites to promote a single political perspective and deprive
independence of a vast majority of judges" (1991: 59).

[29] Moreover, as Pepino notes, a vertically organized judiciary is always easier to control
from outside, because it is far easier to control such a body than it is a diffuse power
(Pepino 2001: 37).

from taking principled stands against members of a sitting government, from engaging deliberately and responsibly in polity-wide debates, and from taking seriously unconventional or unpopular perspectives. First, and most obviously, judges wary of appearing political will seek to avoid any conflict with members of the other branches. Their tendency will be, in hard cases, to "retreat to a mechanistic formalism" (Cover 1975: 232) and defer completely to the sitting government. Second, because the demand that adjudication be "apolitical" implies that there is an objective position – that is, a correct or true understanding of the meaning of the law – on which professionally trained legal technicians should agree, judges committed to apoliticism are unequipped to face the "conflicting but valid demands made upon [them] by diverse groups and by the vices of conscience and of public necessity," and "accept the responsibilities the community has placed upon their shoulders . . . " (Shklar 1986: 104). They are thus unlikely to represent effectively the competing understandings of law within society, or even to justify their decisions in a language that is accessible to and resonates with average citizens (Peretti 1999; Eisgruber 2001). Finally, judges who are duty-bound to behave apolitically will tend to favor established interests (whether public or private) in their decisions, as questioning traditional legal interpretations is likely to appear "political" (i.e., partisan), while accepting the status quo will generally not (see, e.g., Sunstein 1987).[30] Thus, an insistence that judicial decisions be "apolitical" translates essentially to an imperative that they be conservative – that is, that they preserve the status quo, whatever it may be. In sum, judges who function in a setting where professionalism is equated with "apoliticism" are unlikely to develop or display the attributes that make assertiveness in defense of rights and the rule of law possible.

I thus contend that in order to promote the kind of judicial understandings and capacities necessary to meet the demands and expectations placed on judges in a liberal democracy, the fundamentally *political* nature of the judicial role must be recognized, and judicial institutions must be built or reformed around that recognition.[31] This argument

---

[30] Indeed, conservative rhetoric characteristically portrays existing social relations and understandings as natural, necessary, and timeless phenomena, rather than as political constructs (Foster 1986: 66).

[31] As Solomon notes, it is logical that an authoritarian regime would cultivate a thoroughly bureaucratized judicial system, cut off from wider influences and assessments, but such a model "contradicts democratic values and institutions" (1996: 469).

is not new; indeed, I join a chorus of contemporary authors making similar claims (e.g., Dyzenhaus 1998; Feeley and Rubin 1998; Peretti 1999; Eisgruber 2001; Schor 2003). Nor is it untested, for in numerous countries where constitutional adjudication has been recently intro-duced (i.e., since World War II), the fundamentally political nature of the enterprise has been recognized and reformers have constructed institutional mechanisms to make sure courts, particularly those with constitutional jurisdiction, are embedded in and contained by the demo-cratic political process (Stone Sweet 2000; Scheppele 2003; Hilbink 2006). Although there will always be complexities and contingencies that affect whether and how judges assert their authority across time and space (Burbank and Friedman 2002; Lovell and McCann 2005; Baum 2006), the Chilean experience makes clear that judges institu-tionally conditioned to remain beyond politics will be neither equipped nor inclined to take constitutionalist stands, whether in democracy or dictatorship.

ORIENTING INFORMATION ON CHILEAN LAW AND COURTS[1]

Chile, like all Latin American countries, has a legal and judicial system constructed primarily in the civil law tradition. The judiciary is thus organized much like a state bureaucracy, which judges enter at the bottom rung and work their way up via the promotion process discussed in Chapter 1.

Chile is a unitary (i.e., not federal) state and thus has a single judicial hierarchy. At the bottom are the approximately 450 district-level courts, most of which specialize in civil, criminal, labor, or family cases (some have mixed jurisdiction). Each is presided over by a single judge and a judicial secretary.[2] These courts have no constitutional jurisdiction. Above these are the seventeen courts of appeal, which are divided into chambers in which three judges preside. These courts handle *recursos de apelación*, general appeals that call for the review of both the facts and the law of a case decided in a lower court, or of any significant procedural decisions made by the lower court judge in her treatment of the case. Appellate courts also have first instance constitutional jurisdiction for *recursos de amparo* (writs of habeas corpus) and *recursos de protección*

---

[1] For greater detail, see the *Constitución Política de la República de Chile*; the *Código Organico de Tribunales*; Peña 1993; Vargas Viancos and Correa 1995; and www.poderjudicial.cl.

[2] Interesting to note is that women now fill more than 50 percent of lower-court posts, although their representation decreases dramatically at the appellate level. The first woman was named to the Supreme Court in 2001.

(equivalent writs which cover rights other than those covered by *amparo* and excluding socioeconomic or "third-generation" rights), as well as first-instance jurisdiction[3] in cases involving violations of the Law of Internal State Security. The *recurso de amparo* has a long history in Chile, but the *recurso de protección* dates only to a 1976 "Constitutional Act," which was incorporated into the 1980 Constitution (see Chapter 4). Individuals may petition for a *recurso de amparo* either to regain their liberty or personal security or to prevent a threatened violation thereof.

At the top of the judicial hierarchy sits the twenty-one-member Supreme Court (expanded from seventeen members in 1997), divided (as of 1995) into four specialized chambers (civil, criminal, constitutional, and mixed). The Court is responsible for rendering final judgment on *recursos de amparo* and *recursos de protección*. It also handles *recursos de queja*, appeals for the review of both the facts and the law of a case decided by a lower court, and implying judicial misconduct (*falta o abuso*) of some nature, as well as *recursos de casación*, review, by petition or *de oficio*, of the legal interpretation made by the appellate court, which has stricter requirements than a *recurso de queja*.[4] Unlike its American counterpart, the Chilean Supreme Court does not have the power of *certiorari*, that is, it cannot pick and choose the cases it deems critical enough for review, and therefore it has little control over its caseload.

From 1925 to 2005, the Chilean Supreme Court had powers of judicial review of legislation, which it shared with the Comptroller General of the Republic and the Constitutional Tribunal.[5] The Comptroller, or *Contraloría General de la República*, reviews the legality and constitutionality of all executive decrees and ministerial resolutions within thirty days of their issue, and supervises the use of public funds.[6] The Constitutional Tribunal, which is not a part of the judicial hierarchy

---

[3] "First instance" refers to the first level at which a case may be heard. When cases are appealed in the Chilean system, they are said to go to another "instance."

[4] The Supreme Court also administers the budget of the judiciary via a body called the Administrative Corporation of the Judiciary.

[5] An August 2005 reform of the 1980 Constitution transferred jurisdiction over *recursos de inaplicabilidad por inconstitucionalidad* to the Constitutional Tribunal.

[6] The office of Comptroller is filled by presidential appointment, with majority approval by the Senate. The Comptroller has life tenure, with a required retirement age of seventy-five.

and hence not considered part of the judiciary in Chile, was (re-)created by the 1980 Constitution.[7] Since its creation, it has been responsible for abstract review of legislation; that is, at the official request of the president or one-quarter of the members of either house of Congress, the Tribunal reviews the constitutionality of draft laws, decrees with the force of law or simple presidential decrees that the Comptroller has deemed unconstitutional, constitutional reforms, and international treaties. The Tribunal has recently taken over jurisdiction of *recursos de inaplicabilidad por inconstitucionalidad*, which challenge the constitutional legitimacy of an existing law as applied in a concrete case, but these used to fall under the exclusive jurisdiction of the Supreme Court. Cases brought via this concrete review mechanism were ruled on in plenary, and the rulings had only *inter partes*, not *erga omnes* effects – that is, the decision affected only the individual(s) that were parties in the case (as opposed to nullifying the law in question).[8]

The decisions of ordinary courts at any level in Chile are technically binding only for the case in question, that is, the principle of *stare decisis* does not apply in the system. However, as emphasized in this book, judges have strong incentives to follow the lead of their superiors in adjudicating like cases. Judges can keep up on the decisions of superior courts in various jurisprudential journals published by law schools or the Supreme Court library. Case proceedings are almost exclusively written, meaning that the facts and testimony for each case, as well as the arguments and petitions from lawyers, are gathered in a written dossier that judges can review without the presence of litigants, witnesses, and lawyers.

The details of procedure for all the different kinds of cases are too burdensome for this brief summary. However, because most of what is in question in this book is judicial conduct in the areas of criminal cases and habeas corpus, I briefly review procedure for those cases here.

---

[7] For the original structure of the Constitutional Tribunal, see Chapter 4. The 2005 reforms expanded the Tribunal's membership from seven to ten, revamped appointment rules, extended tenure from eight to nine years, and prohibited members from simultaneously exercising either private legal practice or judicial functions. Now, the president appoints three members, the Congress appoints four, and the Supreme Court appoints three.

[8] The Constitutional Tribunal now has the power to review for its general constitutionality a law previously declared inapplicable in a particular case.

Following a gradual reform of criminal procedure that began in 1998 (the so-called "reform of the century" discussed in Chapter 5), Chile's criminal justice system now resembles those of other Western democracies, with an oral and adversarial trial and full guarantees of due process. However, because all of the criminal cases discussed in this book were processed under the old system, I offer a description of that procedure here.

Under the old system, there were two parts to a criminal trial[9] in Chile: the *sumario* and the *plenario*. In the *sumario*, the judge undertook the investigation to determine whether a crime had been committed and if so, to identify the people deemed responsible, and to determine what the possible punishment should be. This part of the process was secret, and even the suspect(s) and defense lawyers were given limited information about the evidence which was being gathered against them. Note that victims of a crime, including the state, had the right to hire lawyers to intervene on their behalf, but the judge remained in charge of the investigation. If the judge developed well-founded suspicions regarding the involvement of a person in a crime, the judge could detain him for up to five days. During the *sumario*, if the judge had sufficient evidence, s/he could declare an *auto de procesamiento* (a preliminary indictment), which allowed for preventive imprisonment. When the court deemed the investigation complete, it closed the *sumario* and if at that stage there was not enough evidence to try someone or if it became clear there was no crime, the judge was obligated to close the case (*sobreseer la causa*). This closure could be temporary in cases in which new evidence might emerge in the future to allow for indictment, or definitive if the evidence proved that there was no crime or that the suspect in question was not involved. If there was an indictment, the trial passed to the *plenario* stage.[10] In this stage, the defense had access to the case dossier and could submit counterevidence of either innocence or attenuated guilt. In other words, at this stage, either new evidence was presented, or the *sumario* was ratified. Finally, the judge rendered the decision (*dictar el fallo*).

---

[9] "Trial" is really the wrong word, as, before the criminal procedure reform that began in 1998, there was no equivalent to the public presentation of evidence for and against a defendant, precisely identifiable in time, as there is in the United States.

[10] It should be noted that the official "indictment" issued at the close of the *sumario* stage is in fact more than an indictment; it is a formal accusation issued by the judge, which implies strong evidence that the defendant is in fact guilty.

During the "trial," it was possible to appeal against judicial resolutions believed to infringe on the rights of the accused, and all serious privations of liberty were to be reviewed by the superior court. In addition, it was and still is possible for individuals to petition for a *recurso de amparo* (writ of habeas corpus) if they believe they have been arbitrarily deprived of their liberty. *Recursos de amparo* must be processed within forty-eight hours, and it is the duty of the appellate judges, who have jurisdiction in the first instance, to demand that such detainees be brought before the court. Judges also have the duty to visit jails to confirm the incarceration of suspected criminals in public institutions of detention, as well as the humane and legal treatment of suspects and convicted criminals therein.

It should be noted that although the investigation of most criminal cases was conducted by district level judges, in cases affecting foreign relations, that could produce public alarm or that demanded prompt repression because of their severity, or that involved judicial personnel or institutions, an appellate court justice could be assigned to the case as a *ministro en visita*. His or her findings could then be appealed to the appellate court to which he or she belonged. The same applied to such cases that fell under the Supreme Court's jurisdiction, in which case a single justice worked toward a decision, which could then be appealed to the Court as a whole.

Another important characteristic of the Chilean judicial system that should be mentioned is its inclusion of *abogados integrantes* (lawyers who serve as substitute judges) in appellate and Supreme Court chambers to replace judges who are absent as a result of illness or alternative professional duties. These lawyers are appointed by the executive from lists drawn up by the respective courts on which they will serve, lists that are reviewed and trimmed by the Supreme Court. (Until 1981, these lists were drawn up by the bar association [*Colegio de Abogados*], but this was changed by law under the military government.) *Abogados integrantes* in the appellate courts are appointed annually and those for the Supreme Court, every three years. There is no limit to the number of "terms" they can serve, and they can continue in private practice throughout. They are paid on a "per diem" basis, but because the lists for each court are ordenal, the top two to three lawyers may be called in every week, whereas the others are called only occasionally, when the higher-ranked lawyers are busy or when there are an inordinate number of judges absent. *Abogados integrantes* enjoy all the powers of judges and are frequently responsible for drafting decisions. However, on the Supreme Court, decisions must bear the signature of three (of five) permanent judges.

Finally, a word must be said regarding the military justice system, which figures prominently in Chile's post-1973 history. In the first instance, cases under military jurisdiction are handled in secret by a military *fiscal*, who (like a civilian judge) serves as investigator, prosecutor, and judge. When the *fiscal* has reached a verdict on the case, he proposes it to a military judge, who generally has no legal training. The judge can accept the *fiscal's* proposal or adapt the sentence as he sees fit. Throughout the text, I refer to *fiscales* and military judges as "military courts." The military court of appeals is called the *Corte Marcial*, or Martial Court. It is staffed by three military judges and two civilian judges from the Santiago Appeals Court. The prosecution has, in practice, an unlimited amount of time to prepare its case, which is presented in secret to the Martial Court, and the defense is given only five days to respond to charges. The 1980 Constitution limited the control of the Supreme Court over military courts to peacetime courts only, formalizing a practice initiated by the Supreme Court itself after the military takeover in 1973. Also, since 1987, a place on the Supreme Court is reserved for the *Auditor General* of the army, who may cast a vote in any decision affecting military interests. It should be noted that military judges at any level do not enjoy any guarantees of tenure and are not expected to rule impartially; they must represent the interests of the military. Because of this, and a host of procedural rules at odds with international standards on the matter, due process is completely lacking in the military justice system (see also CHILE 1988; López Dawson 1995a). In wartime tribunals, the standards are even more lax and the punishments are yet more severe (see *Report of the Chilean National Commission on Truth and Reconciliation* 1991: Vol. I, Ch. 3; Pereira 2005).

LIST OF INTERVIEWEES (ALPHABETICAL BY CATEGORY)*

SUPREME COURT JUDGES

Marcos Aburto Ochoa (1996)
Orlando Alvarez (2001)
Efren Araya Vergara (1996)
Adolfo Bañados Cuadra (1996)
José Benquis Camhi (2001)
Lionel Beraud Poblete (1996)
Oscar Carrasco Acuña (1996)
Luis Correa Bulo (1996)
Enrique Cury Urzúa (2001)
Humberto Espejo Zuñiga (2001)
Osvaldo Faúndez Vallejos (1996)
Mario Garrido Montt (1996)
Servando Jordán López (1996)
Milton Juica Arancibia (2001)
Domingo Kokisch Mourgues (2001)
Marcos Libedinsky Tschorne (1996, 2001)
Urbano Marín Vallejo (2001)
Jorge Medina Cuevas (2001)
José Luis Pérez Zañartu (2001)
Guillermo Navas Bustamente (1996)

* I am grateful to each and every one of these individuals for giving generously of their time and perspectives to this study.

Eleodoro Ortíz Sepúlveda (1996)
Arnaldo Toro Leiva (1996)
Germán Valenzuela Erazo (1996)
Enrique Zurita Camps (1996)

APPELLATE COURT JUDGES

Juan Araya Elizalde (1996)
Haroldo Brito Cruz (1996)
Raquel Camposano Echegaray (1996)
Hector Carreño Seaman (1996)
Carlos Cerda Fernández (1996, 2001)
Alberto Chaigneau del Campo (1996)
Raimundo Díaz Gamboa (1996)
Humberto Espejo Zuñiga (1996)
Ricardo Gálvez Blanco (1996)
Violeta Guzmán Farren (1996)
Juan Guzmán Tapia (1996, 2001)
Juan González Zuñiga (1996)
Milton Juica Arancibia (1996)
Domingo Kokisch Mourgues (1996)
Hernán Matus Valencia (1996)
Jorge Medina Cuevas (1996)
Sergio Muñoz Gajardo (2001)
Enrique Paillas Peña (1996)
Jorge Pizarro Almarza (1996)
Alejandro Solís Muñoz (1996)
Sergio Valenzuela Patiño (1996)
Cornelio Villarroel Ramírez (1996, 2001)

LOWER COURT AND FORMER JUDGES

Rodolfo Aldea Moscoso (1996)
Carmen Carvajal Maureira (1996)
Sergio Dunlop Rudolffi (1996)
Juan Manuel Escandón (1996)
René Farías Roja (1996)
Rubén Galecio Gómez (1996)
Raúl Gutierrez Varas (1996)
Alicia Herrera Rivera (1996)

Fernando Román Díaz (1996)
Cesar Toledo Fuentes (1996)

ABOGADOS INTEGRANTES

Juan Colombo Campbell (1996)
Claudio Illanes Rios (1996)
Carlos Künsemüller Loebenfelder (1996)
José Luis Pérez (1996)
Fernando Román Díaz (1996)
Mario Verdugo Marinkovic (1996)

HUMAN RIGHTS LAWYERS AND ACTIVISTS

Andrés Aylwin Azócar (1996)
Pedro Aylwin (1996)
Sebastian Brett (1996)
Mario Bugueño (1996, 2001)
Adolfo Castillo (1996)
Jaime Castillo Velasco (1996, 2001)
Francisco Estévez (1996)
Lorena Fries (1996)
Roberto Garretón (1996)
Fabiola Letelier del Solar (1996)
Pamela Pereira (1996)
Marta Pérez (1996)
Alfonso Insunza (1996)
Manuel Jacques (1996)
Marco Ruíz (1996)
Hector Salazar Ardiles (1996)
Hiram Villagra (1996)
José Zalaquett (1996)

OTHER LAWYERS AND LAW PROFESSORS

Rodolfo Aldea Moscoso (2001)
Raúl Bertelsen (1996)
María Luisa Brahm (1996)
Bernardino Bravo Lira (1996)
Gonzalo Cañales (1996)

José Luis Cea (1996)
Jorge Correa Sutil (1996, 2001)
Francisco Cumplido (1996)
Andrés Cúneo Machiavello (1996)
Pedro Daza (1996)
Jaime Del Valle (1996)
Mauricio Duce (1996, 2001)
Patricio Dusaellant (1996)
Leonor Etcheberry (2001)
Hugo Frühling (1996, 2001)
Consuelo Gazmuri (1996)
Gastón Gómez (1996)
Felipe González (1996, 2001)
María Pía Guzmán (1996)
María Angélica Jiménez (1996)
Juan Carlos Manss (2001)
Cecilia Medina (1996)
Jorge Mera (1996)
Mario Mosquera (1996)
Carlos Peña González (1996)
Cristian Riego (1996, 2001)
José María Saavedra (1996)
Gonzalo Sánchez (2001)
Miguel Schweitzer (1996)
Eduardo Soto Kloss (1996)
Roberto Trejo (1996)
Juan Enrique Vargas Viancos (1996)

REFERENCES

Abe, Masaki. 1995. "The Internal Control of a Bureaucratic Judiciary: The Case of Japan." *International Journal of the Sociology of Law* 23: 303–320.

Ackerman, Bruce. 1984. "The Storrs Lectures: Discovering the Constitution." *Yale Law Journal* 93: 1013–1072.

———. 1997. "The Rise of World Constitutionalism." *Virginia Law Review* 83 (May): 771–797.

Adelman, Jeremy. 1999. *The Republic of Capital: Buenos Aires and the Legal Transformation of the Atlantic World*. Stanford, CA: Stanford University Press.

Amnesty International. 1986. "The Role of the Judiciary and the Legal Profession in the Protection of Human Rights in Chile." September.

Amunátegui, Miguel Luis. 1989. "El Poder Judicial en Chile y la Protección de los Derechos Humanos: Situación Actual y Proposiciones." Documento de Trabajo No. 29/89, Corporación de Promoción Universitaria, October.

Andrés Ibáñez, Perfecto. 1988. *Justicia/Conflicto*. Madrid: Editorial Tecnos.

Angell, Alan. 1993. "Chile since 1958." In *Chile since Independence*, ed. Leslie Bethell. New York: Cambridge University Press.

Arantes, Rogério Bastos. 1997. *Judiciário & Política no Brasil*. São Paulo: IDESP.

Arriagada, Genaro. 1974. *De la 'Vía Chilena' a la 'Vía Insurrecional'*. Santiago: Editorial del Pacífico.

Athey, Lois Edwards. 1978. "Government and Opposition in Chile during the Allende Years: 1970–1973." Ph.D. diss., Columbia University.

Atria, Rodrigo y otros. 1989. *Chile: La Memoria Prohibida*. Santiago: Editores Pehuén.

Aylwin, Andrés. 1992. "Guerra Que Sí, Guerra Que No." *La Epoca*, November 12.

Aylwin, Mariana, Carlos Bascuñán, Sofía Correa, Cristián Gazmuri, Sol Serrano, and Matías Tagle. 1996. *Chile en el Siglo XX*. Santiago: Editorial Planeta.

Badilla, Ivan. 1990a. "Corte Suprema: Misión Cumplida." *ANALISIS* (April 23): 31–34.

1990b. "Hacer Justicia Es Hacer Democracia." *ANALISIS* (January 15): 9–11.

Ballard, Megan. 1999. "The Clash between Local Courts and Global Economics: The Politics of Judicial Reform in Brazil." *Berkeley International Law Journal* 17: 230–276.

Barros, Robert. 2002. *Constitutionalism and Dictatorship: Pinochet, the Junta, and the 1980 Constitution*. New York: Cambridge University Press.

Bastida, Francisco. 1986. *Jueces y Franquismo*. Barcelona: Editorial Ariel.

Baum, Lawrence. 1997. *The Puzzle of Judicial Behavior*. Ann Arbor: University of Michigan Press.

2006. *Judges and Their Audiences: A Perspective on Judicial Behavior*. Princeton, NJ: Princeton University Press.

Beatty, David. 1994. "Human Rights and the Rules of Law." In *Human Rights and Judicial Review: A Comparative Perspective*, ed. David Beatty. Boston: Martinus Nijhoff.

Becker, Theodore L. 1966. "A Survey Study of Hawaiian Judges: The Effect on Decisions of Judicial Role Variation." *American Political Science Review* 60: 677–680.

Beirich, Heidi L. 1998. "The Role of the Constitutional Tribunal in Spanish Politics (1980–1995)." Ph.D. diss., Purdue University.

Bellamy, Richard. 1996. "The Political Form of the Constitution: Separation of Powers, Rights, and Representative Democracy." In *Constitutionalism in Transformation: European and Theoretical Perspectives*, ed. Richard Bellamy and Dario Castiglione. Cambridge, MA: Blackwell Publishers.

Bertelsen Repetto, Raúl. 1969. *Control de Constitucionalidad de la Ley*. Santiago: Editorial Jurídica.

Bickel, Alexander M. 1962. *The Least Dangerous Branch*. New Haven, CT: Yale University Press.

Blakemore, Harold. 1993. "From the War of the Pacific to 1930." In *Chile since Independence*, ed. Leslie Bethell. New York: Cambridge University Press.

Bobbio, Norberto. 1987. *The Future of Democracy*. Minneapolis: University of Minnesota Press.

Bollen, Kenneth. 1980. "Issues in the Comparative Measurement of Political Democracy." *American Sociological Review* 45 (June): 370–390.

Borón, Atilio A. 1993. "Latin America: Constitutionalism and the Political Traditions of Liberalism and Socialism." In *Constitutionalism and Democracy: Transitions in the Contemporary World*, ed. Douglas Greenberg,

Stanley N. Katz, Melanie Beth Oliviero, and Steven C. Wheatley. New York: Oxford University Press.

Bravo Lira, Bernardino. 1976. "Los Estudios sobre la Judicatura Chilena de los Siglos XIX y XX." *Revista de Derecho Público* 19–20: 89–116.

———. 1990. "Raiz y Razón del Estado de Derecho en Chile." *Revista de Derecho Público* 47–48: 27–63.

———. 1991. "Bello y la Judicatura: La Reforma Judicial." *Revista de Derecho y Jurisprudencia* 88 (1): 49–58.

———. 1992. "La Judicatura Chilena en el Siglo XX: Raíces de su Crisis y Vías para su Consolidación." *Revista de Derecho Público* 51/52: 87–102.

Brett, Sebastian. 1992. *Chile: A Time of Reckoning*. Geneva: International Commission of Jurists.

———. 2000. "Impunity on Trial in Chile." *NACLA Report on the Americas*. July–August.

Brinks, Daniel. 2005. "Judicial Reform and Independence in Brazil and Argentina: The Beginning of a New Millennium?" *Texas International Law Journal* 40: 595–622.

Brysk, Alison. 1994. *The Politics of Human Rights in Argentina: Protest, Change, and Democratization*. Stanford, CA: Stanford University Press.

Burbank, Stephen B., and Barry Friedman. 2002. "Reconsidering Judicial Independence." In *Judicial Independence at the Crossroads: An Interdisciplinary Approach*, ed. Stephen B. Burbank and Barry Friedman. Thousand Oaks, CA: SAGE Publications.

Bustamente, Fernando. 1998. "Democracy, Civilizational Change, and the Latin American Military." In *Fault Lines of Democracy in Post-Transition Latin America*, eds. Felipe Agüero and Jeffrey Stara. Miami: North-South Center Press.

Caffarena de Jiles, Elena. 1957. *El Recurso de Amparo frente a los Regimenes de Emergencia*. Santiago: Editorial Jurídica.

Camenisch, Paul F. 1983. "On Being a Professional, Morally Speaking." In *Moral Responsibility and the Professions*, ed. Bernard Baumrin and Benjamin Freedman. New York: Haven Publications.

Camus, María Eugenia. 1991. "Existe Consenso respecto a la Crisis del Poder Judicial." *ANALISIS* (January 21): 20–21.

———. 1992. "El Juicio a los Intocables." *Apsi* (October 19): 10–15.

Cánovas Robles, José. 1988. *Memorias de un Magistrado*. Santiago: Emisión.

Cappelletti, Mauro. 1971. *Judicial Review in the Contemporary World*. New York: Bobbs-Merrill.

———. 1985. "Repudiating Montesquieu? The Expansion and Legitimacy of 'Constitutional Justice.'" *The Catholic University Law Review* 35: 672–703.

Carter, Lief H., and Thomas F. Burke. 2002. *Reason in Law*. New York: Longman.

Caucoto Pereira, Nelson, and Héctor Salazar Ardiles. 1994. *Un Verde Manto de Impunidad*. Santiago: Ediciones Academia.

Cavallo Castro, Ascanio, Manuel Salazar Salvo, and Oscar Sepúlveda Pacheco. 1989. *La Historia Oculta del Régimen Militar*. Santiago: Antártica.

Cea, José Luis. 1978. "Law and Socialism in Chile, 1970–1973." Ph.D. diss., University of Wisconsin–Madison.

——— 1987. "Rasgos de la Experiencia Democrática y Constitucional de Chile." *Revista Chilena de Derecho* 14:1: 25–35.

Chavez, Rebecca Bill. 2004. *The Rule of Law in Nascent Democracies: Judicial Politics in Argentina*. Stanford, CA: Stanford University Press.

CHILE: Human Rights and the Plebiscite. 1988. New York: Americas Watch: 55–60.

Ciria, Alberto. 1986. "Argentina in 1983: Reflections on the Language of the Military and Orwell." *North South: Canadian Journal of Latin American and Caribbean Studies* 11: 57–69.

Clayton, Cornell, and Howard Gillman. 1999. "Introduction." In *The Supreme Court in American Politics*, eds. Howard Gillman and Cornell Clayton. Lawrence: University Press of Kansas.

Cole, David. 2004. "Judging the Next Emergency: Judicial Review and Individual Rights in Times of Crisis." *Michigan Law Review*, 101:8 (August): 2565–2594.

Collier, Simon. 1967. *Ideas and Politics of Chilean Independence: 1808–1833*. New York: Cambridge University Press.

——— 1993. "From Independence to the War of the Pacific." In *Chile since Independence*, ed. Leslie Bethell. New York: Cambridge University Press.

Collier, Simon, and William F. Slater. 1996. *A History of Chile: 1808–1994*. New York: Cambridge University Press.

Collyer, Patricia. 1986. "Corte Marcial Destruyó Versión del Gobierno." *ANALISIS* (August 19): 13–16.

Constable, Pamela, and Arturo Valenzuela. 1991. *A Nation of Enemies*. New York: W. W. Norton.

Correa Sutil, Jorge. 1990. "Formación de Jueces para la Democracia." *Revista de Ciencias Sociales (Valparaíso, Chile)* 34–35: 271–320.

——— 1992. "Diagnósticos acerca del Sistema Judicial Chileno." In *Justicia y Libertad en Chile*, ed. Guillermo Martínez. Santiago: Corporación Libertas.

——— 1993. "The Judiciary and the Political System in Chile." In *Transition to Democracy in Latin America: The Role of the Judiciary*, ed. Irwin P. Stotsky. Boulder, CO: Westview Press.

——— 1997. "'No Victorious Army Has Ever Been Prosecuted . . .': The Unsettled Story of Transitional Justice in Chile." In *Transitional Justice and the Rule of Law in New Democracies*, ed. A. James McAdams. Notre Dame: University of Notre Dame Press.

1999. "Cenicienta Se Queda en la Fiesta: El Poder Judicial Chileno en la Década de los 90." In *El Modelo Chileno: Democracia y desarrollo en los noventa*, ed. Paul Drake and Iván Jaksic. Santiago: LOM.

Correa Sutil, Jorge, and Gastón Gómez. 2000. "Informe de Investigación del Recurso de Protección." Unpublished manuscript on file with Gastón Gómez at the Universidad Diego Portales, Santiago, Chile.

Correa Sutil, Jorge, and Marcelo Montero. 1992. "Formación y Perfeccionamiento de Jueces." In *El Poder Judicial en la Encrucijada*, ed. Carlos Peña González. Santiago: Universidad Diego Portales, Escuela de Derecho.

Couso, Javier. 2002. "The Politics of Judicial Review in Latin America: Chile in Comparative Perspective." Ph.D. diss., University of California, Berkeley.

2004a. "The Politics of Judicial Review in Chile in the Era of Democratic Transition, 1990–2002." In *Democratization and the Judiciary: The Accountability Function of Courts in the New Democracies*, ed. Siri Gloppen, Roberto Gargarella and Elin Skaar. Portland, OR: Frank Cass.

2004b. "The Judicialization of Chilean Politics: The Rights Revolution That Never Was." Unpublished manuscript. Photocopy.

Cover, Robert. 1975. *Justice Accused: Antislavery and the Judicial Process*. New Haven, CT: Yale University Press.

Croley, Stephen P. 1995. "The Majoritarian Difficulty: Elective Judiciaries and the Rule of Law." *University of Chicago Law Review* 62: 689–789.

Cumplido, Francisco, and Hugo Frühling. 1980. "Problemas Jurídico-Políticos del Transito hacia la Democracia. Chile: 1924–1932." *Estudios Sociales* 21: 71–113.

Cúneo Machiavello, Andrés. 1980. "La Corte Suprema de Chile: Sus Percepciones acerca del Derecho, Su Rol en el Sistema Legal y la Relación de Este con el Sistema Política." In *La Administración de Justicia en América Latina*, ed. Javier de Belaúnde L. de R. Lima: Consejo Latinoamericano de Derecho y Desarrollo.

Dahl, Robert. 1957. "Decision-Making in a Democracy: The Supreme Court as a National Policy-Maker." *Journal of Public Law* 6: 279–295.

1971. *Polyarchy: Participation and Opposition*. New Haven, CT: Yale University Press.

1989. *Democracy and Its Critics*. New Haven, CT: Yale University Press.

2001. *How Democratic Is the U.S. Constitution?* New Haven, CT: Yale University Press.

Damaska, Mirjan R. 1986. *The Faces of Justice and State Authority*. New Haven, CT: Yale University Press.

Davis, Madeleine. 2003. *The Pinochet Case: Origins, Progress and Implications*. London: Institute of Latin American Studies.

de Ramón, Armando. 1989. "La Justicia Chilena entre 1875 y 1924." *Cuadernos de Análisis Jurídico*, Monograph 12 (October).

1999. *Biografías de Chilenos, 1876–1973, Miembros de los Poderes Ejecutivo, Legislativo, y Judicial*. Santiago: Ediciones Universidad Católica de Chile.

De Soto, Hernando. 2000. *The Mystery of Capital: Why Capitalism Triumphs in the West and Fails Everywhere Else*. New York: Basic Books.

Dean, Howard. 1967. *The Judiciary and Democracy*. New York: Random House.

Della Porta, Donatella. 2001. "A Judges' Revolution? Political Corruption and the Judiciary in Italy," *European Journal of Political Research* 39: 1–21.

Detzner, John A. 1988. *Tribunales Chilenos y Derecho Internacional de Derechos Humanos*. Santiago: Comisión Chilena de Derechos Humanos.

DeVylder, Stefan. 1974. *The Political Economy of the Rise and Fall of the Unidad Popular*. New York: Cambridge University Press.

Dezalay, Yves, and Bryant Garth. 2002. *The Internationalization of Palace Wars: Lawyers, Economists, and the Contest to Transform Latin American States*. Chicago: University of Chicago.

Di Federico, Giuseppe. 1976. "The Italian Judicial Profession and Its Bureaucratic Setting," *The Juridical Review* 21: 40–57.

Di Federico, Giuseppe, and Carlo Guarnieri. 1988. "The Courts in Italy." In *The Political Role of Law Courts in Modern Democracies*, ed. J. L. Waltman and K. M. Holland. Hong Kong: Macmillan.

Diamant, Neil, Stanley Lubman, and Kevin O'Brien, eds. 2005. *Engaging the Law in China: State, Society, and Possibilities for Justice*. Stanford, CA: Stanford University Press.

Diamond, Larry, and Juan J. Linz. 1989. "Introduction: Politics, Society, and Democracy in Latin America." In *Democracy in Developing Countries: Latin America*, ed. Larry Diamond, Juan J. Linz, and Seymour Martin Lipset. Boulder, CO: Lynne Rienner.

Domingo, Pilar. 1999. "Judicial Independence and Judicial Reform in Latin America." In *The Self Restraining State: Power and Accountability in New Democracies*, ed. Andreas Schedler, Larry Diamond, and Marc F. Plattner. Boulder, CO: Lynne Reiner: 151–175.

2000. "Judicial Independence: The Politics of the Supreme Court in Mexico." *Journal of Latin American Studies* 32: 705–735.

Drake, Paul W. 1978. *Socialism and Populism in Chile, 1932–52*. Urbana: University of Illinois Press.

1993. "Chile, 1930–1958." In *Chile since Independence*, ed. Leslie Bethell. New York: Cambridge University Press.

Drake, Paul W., and Iván Jaksic. 1995. "Introduction: Transformation and Transition in Chile, 1982–1990." In *The Struggle for Democracy in Chile*, ed. Paul W. Drake and Iván Jaksic. Revised ed. Lincoln: University of Nebraska Press.

Dubber, Markus Dirk. 1993. "Judicial Positivism and Hitler's Injustice." *Columbia Law Review* 93:7 (Nov.): 1807–1831.

Dworkin, Ronald. 1978. *Taking Rights Seriously*. Cambridge, MA: Harvard University Press.

Dyzenhaus, David. 1991. *Hard Cases in Wicked Legal Systems: South African Law in the Perspective of Legal Philosophy*. New York: Oxford University Press.

1998. *Judging the Judges, Judging Ourselves: Truth, Reconciliation and the Apartheid Legal Order*. Portland, OR: Hart Publishing.

1999. "Recrafting the Rule of Law." In *Recrafting the Rule of Law: The Limits of Legal Order*, ed. David Dyzenhaus. Portland, OR: Hart Publishing.

2000. "Form and Substance in the Rule of Law; A Democratic Justification for Judicial Review?" *Judicial Review and the Constitution*. Portland, OR: Hart Publishing.

Echeverría, Andrés, and Luis Frei, eds. 1974. *1970–1973: La Lucha por la Juridicidad en Chile*. Santiago: Editorial Jurídica.

Eckstein, Harry. 1992. "Case Study and Theory in Political Science." In *Regarding Politics*, ed. Harry Eckstein. Berkeley: University of CA Press.

Edelman, Martin. 1994. *Courts, Politics, and Culture in Israel*. Charlottesville: University Press of Virginia.

Eisgruber, Christopher. 2001. *Constitutional Self-Government*. Cambridge, MA: Harvard University Press.

Ely, John Hart. 1980. *Democracy and Distrust: A Theory of Judicial Review*. Cambridge, MA: Harvard University Press.

Epp, Charles R. 1998. *The Rights Revolution: Lawyers, Activists, and Supreme Courts in Comparative Perspective*. Chicago: University of Chicago Press.

Epstein, Lee, and Jack Knight. 1998. *The Choices Justices Make*. Washington, DC: Congressional Quarterly Inc.

2000. "Toward a Strategic Revolution in Judicial Politics: A Look Back, A Look Ahead." *Political Research Quarterly* 53:3 (Sept.): 625–661.

Etcheberry, Alfredo. 1990. "Amnistía, Derecho y Justicia." *Mensaje* 393 (October): 369–372.

Falcoff, Mark. 1989. *Modern Chile, 1970–1989: A Critical History*. New Brunswick: Transaction.

Fallos del Tribunal Constitucional Pronunciados entre el 23 de diciembre de 1985 y el 23 de junio de 1992. 1993. Santiago: Editorial Jurídica.

Faundez, Julio. 1997. "In Defense of Presidentialism: The Case of Chile, 1932–1970." In *Presidentialism and Democracy in Latin America*, ed. Scott Mainwaring and Matthew Shugart. New York: Cambridge University Press.

Feeley, Malcolm M., and Edward L. Rubin. 1998. *Judicial Policymaking and the Modern State*. New York: Cambridge University Press.

Feinrider, Martin. 1981. "Judicial Review and the Protection of Human Rights under Military Governments in Brazil and Argentina." *Suffolk Transnational Law Journal* 5: 171–199.

Finkel, Jodi. Forthcoming. *Judicial Reform as Political Insurance: Latin America in the 1990s*. Notre Dame: Notre Dame University Press.

Fiss, Owen. 1993. "The Limits of Judicial Independence." *University of Miami Inter-American Law Review* 25(1): 57–76.

Fitch, J. Samuel. 1998. *The Armed Forces and Democracy in Latin America.* Baltimore: Johns Hopkins University Press.

Foster, James C. 1986. *The Ideology of Apolitical Politics.* New York: Associated Faculty Press.

Franck, Thomas M. 1992. *Political Questions/Judicial Answers.* Princeton, NJ: Princeton University Press.

Frühling, Hugo. 1980. "Poder Judicial y Política en Chile." In *La Administración de Justicia en America Latina,* ed. Javier de Belaúnde L. de R. Lima: Consejo Latinoamericano de Derecho y Desarrollo.

——— 1982. "Fuerzas Armadas, Orden Interno, y Derechos Humanos." In *Estado y Fuerzas Armadas,* ed. Hugo Frühling, Carlos Portales, and Augusto Varas. Santiago: Stichting Rechtshulp Chili and FLACSO.

——— 1984. "Law in Society: Social Transformation and the Crisis of Law in Chile, 1830–1970." Ph.D. diss., Harvard University School of Law.

——— 1993. "Human Rights in Constitutional Order and in Political Practice in Latin America." In *Constitutionalism and Democracy: Transitions in the Contemporary World,* ed. Douglas Greenberg, Stanley N. Katz, Melanie Beth Oliviero, and Steven C. Wheatley. New York: Oxford University Press.

——— 1998. "Judicial Reform and Democratization in Latin America." In *Fault Lines of Democracy in Post-Transition Latin America,* ed. Felipe Agüero and Jeffrey Stark. Miami: North-South Center Press.

Frühling, Hugo, Carlos Portales, and Augusto Varas. 1982. *Estado y Fuerzas Armadas.* Santiago: Stichting Rechtshulp Chili and FLACSO.

Fuller, Lon L. 1958. "Positivism and the Fidelity to Law – A Reply to Professor Hart." *Harvard Law Review* 71 (February): 630–672.

· Garapon, Antoine. 1996. *Le Gardien des Promesses.* Paris: Editions Odile Jacob.

——— 1999. "La démocratie à l'épreuve de la justice." In *JUSTICES: Ce qui a changé dans la justice depuis 20 ans.* Paris: Éditions Dalloz.

Garcés, Joan. 1973. *El Estado y Problemas Tácticos en el Gobierno de Allende.* Buenos Aires: Siglo Veintiuno.

Gardner, James. 1980. *Legal Imperialism: American Lawyers and Foreign Aid in Latin America.* Madison: University of Wisconsin Press.

Garretón, Manuel Antonio. 1989. "La Posibilidad Democrática en Chile." Santiago: FLACSO, Cuadernos de Difusión.

——— 1990. "Las Condiciones Sociopolíticas de la Inauguración Democrática en Chile." Working Paper No. 142. Notre Dame: The Kellogg Institute.

Garretón, Roberto. n.d. "El Poder Judicial y los Derechos Humanos." Unpublished manuscript. On file at the Fundación de Documentación y Archivo de la Vicaría de la Solidaridad.

1987. "El Poder Judicial en la Dictadura." *Encuentro Internacional de Magistrados, "Poder Judicial y Derechos Humanos."* Santiago: Comisión Chilena de Derechos Humanos.

1989. "El Poder Judicial Chileno y la Violación de los Derechos Humanos." Documento de Trabajo No. 28/29 (October). Santiago: Corporación de Promoción Universitaria.

Garth, Bryant, and Yves Dezalay. 1997. "Chile: Law and the Legitimation of Transitions." Manuscript, American Bar Foundation. Photocopy.

Gazmuri, Cristián. 2000. *Eduardo Frei Montalva y su Epoca*, Vol. II. Santiago: Aguilar.

Geddes, Barbara. 1994. *Politician's Dilemma: Building State Capacity in Latin America*. Berkeley: University of California Press.

Gerring, John. 2004. "What Is a Case Study and What Is It Good for?" *American Political Science Review* 98 (2): 341–354.

Gibson, James L. 1981. "The Role Concept in Judicial Research." *Law and Policy Quarterly* 3: 291–311.

1986. "The Social Science of Judicial Politics." In *Political Science: The Science of Politics*, ed. Herbert F. Weisberg. New York: Agathon Press.

Gibson, James L., Gregory A. Caldeira, and Vanessa Baird. 1998. "On the Legitimacy of National High Courts." *American Political Science Review* 92:2 (June): 343–358.

Gil, Federico. 1966. *The Political System of Chile*. Boston: Houghton Mifflin.

Giles, Michael, and Thomas Lancaster. 1989. "Political Transition, Social Development, and Legal Mobilization in Spain." *American Political Science Review* 83:3 (September): 817–833.

Gillman, Howard. 1993. *The Constitution Besieged: The Rise and Demise of Lochner Era Police Powers Jurisprudence*. Durham, NC: Duke University Press.

1999. "The Court as an Idea, Not a Building (or a Game): Interpretive Institutionalism and the Analysis of Supreme Court Decision-Making." In *Supreme Court Decision-Making: New Institutional Approaches*, ed. Cornell W. Clayton and Howard Gillman. Chicago: University of Chicago Press.

2001. *The Votes That Counted: How the Court Decided the 2000 Presidential Election*. Chicago: University of Chicago Press.

2004. "Martin Shapiro and the Movement from 'Old' to 'New' Institutionalist Studies in Public Law Scholarship." *Annual Review of Political Science* 7: 363–382.

Gillman, Howard, and Cornell Clayton, eds. 1999. *The Supreme Court in American Politics: New Institutionalist Interpretations*. Lawrence: University Press of Kansas.

Ginsburg, Tom. 2003. *Judicial Review in New Democracies: Constitutional Courts in Asian Cases*. New York: Cambridge University Press.

Glick, Henry Robert, and Kenneth N. Vines. 1969. "Law-Making in the State Judiciary: A Comparative Study of the Judicial Role in Four States." *Polity* 2: 142–59.

Gloppen, Siri. 2004. "The Accountability Function of the Courts in Tanzania and Zambia." In *Democratization and the Judiciary: The Accountability Function of Courts in the New Democracies*, ed. S. Gloppen, R. Gargarella, and E. Skaar. Portland: Frank Cass.

2005. "Social Rights Litigation as Transformation: South African Perspectives." Working Paper 2005: 3, Development Studies and Human Rights. Bergen, Norway: Chr. Michelsen Institute.

Gloppen, Siri, Roberto Gargarella, and Elin Skaar, eds. 2004. *Democratization and the Judiciary: The Accountability Function of Courts in the New Democracies*. Portland, OR: Frank Cass.

Golob, Stephanie R. 2002. "The Pinochet Case: 'Forced to be Free' Abroad and at Home." *Democratization* 9:4 (Winter): 25–57.

Gómez, Gastón. 1999. "El Recurso de Inaplicabilidad." Informes de Investigación No. 4 (November). Santiago: Universidad Diego Portales.

González Bermejo, Ernesto, and Victor Vaccaro. 1972. "Eduardo Novoa: No Solo No Le Dan Armas Legales al Gobierno, Sino que Se Las Quitan." *Chile HOY* 1:19 (October 20): 30–32.

González M., Felipe. 1989. "Modelos Legislativos de Seguridad Interior: 1925–1989." *Revista Chilena de Derechos Humanos* 11 (November): 18–24.

Grossman, Joel B. 1968. "Dissenting Blocs on the Warren Court: A Study in Judicial Role Behavior." *Journal of Politics* 30: 1068–1090.

Guarnieri, Carlo. 2003. "Courts as an Instrument of Horizontal Accountability: The Case of Latin Europe." In *Democracy and the Rule of Law*, eds. José María Maravall and Adam Przeworski. Cambridge: Cambridge University Press.

Guarnieri, Carlo, and Patrizia Pederzoli. 2002. *The Power of Judges*. London: Oxford University Press.

Guzmán Tapia, Juan. 2005. *En el Borde del Mundo: Memorias del Juez que Procesó a Pinochet*. Barcelona: Editorial Anagrama.

Guzmán Vial, Manuel. 1991. "La Modernización del Sistema Judicial." *Mensaje* 40, no. 400 (July): 240–242.

1992. "Análisis de los Proyectos de la Ley de Reformas de la Administración de la Justicia." In *Justicia y Libertad en Chile*, ed. Guillermo Martínez. Santiago: Corporación LIBERTAS.

Habermas, Jürgen. 1996. *Between Facts and Norms: Contributions to a Discourse Theory of Law and Democracy*. Cambridge, MA: MIT Press.

Hamilton, Alexander. 1788. "Federalist Paper 78: The Judiciary Department." In *The Federalist Papers*, Alexander Hamilton, John Jay, and James Madison, New York: The Modern Library (1937).

Hammergren, Linn A. 1998. *The Politics of Justice and Justice Reform in Latin America: The Peruvian Case in Comparative Perspective.* Boulder, CO: Westview Press.

———. 2000. "The Fujimori Judicial Reforms: Finally Cutting the Gordian Knot or Just Another Trojan Horse?" Paper delivered at the 2000 meeting of the Latin American Studies Association, Hyatt Regency Miami, March 16–18.

———. 2002. "Do Judicial Councils Further Judicial Reform? Lessons from Latin America," Working Paper No. 28, Rule of Law Series, Democracy and Rule of Law Project. Washington, DC: Carnegie Endowment for International Peace.

Harnecker, Marta, and Victor Vaccaro. 1973. "Oscar Alvarez (Magistrado): 'La Justicia Es Necesariamente Clasista.'" *Chile HOY* 1:36 (February 16): 29–32.

Hart, H. L. A. 1958. "Positivism and the Separation of Law and Morals." *Harvard Law Review* 71 (February): 593–629.

Held, David. 1987. *Models of Democracy.* Cambridge: Polity Press.

Helmke, Gretchen. 2002. "The Logic of Strategic Defection: Court-Executive Relations in Argentina Under Dictatorship and Democracy." *American Political Science Review.* 96:2 (June): 291–303.

———. 2005. *Courts under Constraints: Judges, Generals, and Presidents in Argentina.* New York: Cambridge University Press.

Helmke, Gretchen, and Steven Levitsky. 2004. "Informal Institutions and Comparative Politics: A Research Agenda." *Perspectives on Politics* 2(4): 725–740.

Henríquez, Helia. 1980. "La Crisis del Estado y el Poder Judicial en Chile." Unpublished manuscript. On file with Jorge Correa Sutil, Universidad Diego Portales, Facultad de Derecho.

Herzog, Don. 1989. *Happy Slaves: A Critique of Consent Theory.* Chicago: University of Chicago Press.

Hidalgo, Guillermo. 1992. "Ministra Locuaz." *Qué Pasa* (October 12): 16–17.

Hilbink, Lisa. 1999. "Un Estado de Derecho No Liberal: La Actuación del Poder Judicial durante los 90." In *El Modelo Chileno: Democracia y Desarrollo en los Noventa*, ed. Paul Drake and Iván Jaksic. Santiago: Ediciones LOM.

———. 2003. "An Exception to Chilean Exceptionalism?" In *What Justice? Whose Justice? Fighting for Fairness in Latin America*, ed. Susan Eva Eckstein and Timothy P. Wickham-Crowley. Berkeley: University of California Press.

———. 2006. "Beyond Manicheanism: Assessing the New Constitutionalism." *Maryland Law Review* 65: 101–115.

———. Forthcoming. "Politicizing Law to Liberalize Politics: Anti-Francoist Judges and Prosecutors in Spain's Democratic Transition." In *Fighting for Political*

Freedom: Comparative Studies of the Legal Complex and Political Change, ed. Terrence Halliday, Lucien Karpik, and Malcolm Feeley. Oxford: Hart Publishing.

Hirschl, Ran. 2004. *Towards Juristocracy: The Origins and Consequences of the New Constitutionalsim.* Cambridge, MA: Harvard University Press.

Holland, Kenneth, ed. 1991. *Judicial Activism in Comparative Perspective.* London: Macmillan.

Holmes, Stephen. 1988. "Precommitment and the Paradox of Democracy." In *Constitutionalism and Democracy*, ed. Jon Elster and Rune Slagstad. New York: Cambridge University Press.

1995. *Passions & Constraint: On the Theory of Liberal Democracy.* Chicago: University of Chicago Press.

Howard, Robert M., and Jeffrey A. Segal. 2002. "An Original Look at Originalism." *Law & Society Review* 36: 113–138.

Hull, Adrian Prentice. 1999. "Comparative Political Science: An Inventory and Assessment since the 1980's." *PS: Political Science & Politics* 32:1 (March): 121–124.

Human Rights Watch/Americas. 1994. "Chile, Unsettled Business: Human Rights in Chile at the Start of the Frei Presidency." *News from HRW/Americas* VI, No. 6 (May).

Human Rights Watch. 1998. *The Limits of Tolerance: Freedom of Expression and the Public Debate in Chile.* New York: Human Rights Watch.

1999. "When Tyrants Tremble: The Pinochet Case." October, Vol. 11, No. 1 (B).

2003. "Discreet Path to Justice?: Chile, Thirty Years After the Military Coup." Available at: http://hrw.org/backgrounder/americas/chile/chile0903-1.htm.

Huntington, Samuel P. 1957. *The Soldier and the State.* Cambridge, MA: Belknap Press.

Hutchinson, Allan. 1999. "The Rule of Law Revisited: Democracy and Courts." In *Recrafting the Rule of Law: The Limits of Legal Order*, ed. David Dyzenhaus. Portland, OR: Hart Publishing.

Illanes Benítez, Osvaldo. 1966. "La Corte Suprema de Justicia de Chile." *Revista de la Comisión Internacional de Juristas* 7:2: 309–318.

Jackson, Donald W., and C. Neal Tate, eds. 1992. *Comparative Judicial Review and Public Policy.* Westport, CT: Greenwood Press.

Jacobsohn, Gary J. 1993. *Apple of Gold : Constitutionalism in Israel and the United States.* Princeton, NJ: Princeton University Press.

Jaksic, Iván, ed. 1997. *Selected Writings of Andrés Bello.* New York: Oxford University Press.

2001. *Andrés Bello: Scholarship and Nation-Building in Nineteenth-Century Latin America.* New York: Cambridge University Press.

Jelin, Elizabeth, and Eric Hershberg. 1996. "Introduction: Human Rights and the Construction of Democracy." In *Constructing Democracy: Human Rights, Citizenship, and Society in Latin America*, ed. Elizabeth Jelin and Eric Hershberg. Boulder, CO: Westview Press.

Jiles, Pamela. 1984. "¡Censura! Embestida contra la Prensa." *ANALISIS* (April 24): 5–11.

Jocelyn-Holt, Alfredo. 1997. *El Peso de la Noche*. Santiago: Planeta/Ariel.

1999. *La Independencia de Chile: Tradición, Modernización y Mito*. Santiago: Planeta/Ariel.

Kahn, Ronald. 1994. *The Supreme Court and Constitutional Theory, 1953–1993*. Lawrence: University Press of Kansas.

Kahn-Freund, Otto. 1981. *Labour Law and Politics in the Weimar Republic*, eds. Roy Lewis and Jon Clark. Oxford: Basil Blackwell.

Kairys, David. 1982. *The Politics of Law: A Progressive Critique*. New York: Pantheon.

Karst, Kenneth, and Keith Rosenn. 1975. *Law and Development in Latin America*. Los Angeles: University of California Press.

Kateb, George. 1992. *The Inner Ocean: Individualism and Democratic Culture*. Ithaca, NY: Cornell University Press.

Kaufman, Edy. 1988. *Crisis in Allende's Chile*. New York: Praeger.

Kennedy, Duncan. 1997. *A Critique of Adjudication*. Cambridge, MA: Harvard University Press.

Kenney, Sally J. 2000. "Beyond Principals and Agents: Seeing Courts as Organizations by Comparing *Référendaires* at the European Court of Justice and Law Clerks at the U.S. Supreme Court." *Comparative Political Studies* (June): 593–625.

King, Gary, Robert O. Keohane, and Sidney Verba. 1984. *Designing Social Inquiry: Scientific Inquiry in Qualitative Research*. Princeton, NJ: Princeton University Press.

Kinsbrunner, Jay. 1967. *Diego Portales: Interpretive Essays on the Man and Times*. The Hague: Martinus Nijhoff.

1973. *Chile: A Historical Interpretation*. New York: Harper and Row.

Klug, Heinz. 2000. *Constituting Democracy: Law, Globalism and South Africa's Political Reconstruction*. New York: Cambridge University Press.

Koelble, Thomas A. 1995. "The New Institutionalism in Political Science and Sociology." *Comparative Politics* 27:2 (January): 231–243.

Kommers, Donald P. 1976. *Judicial Politics in West Germany*. Beverly Hills, CA: Sage Publications.

Kornbluh, Peter. 2004. *The Pinochet File: A Declassified Dossier on Atrocity and Accountability*. New York: New Press.

2005. "Letter from Chile." *The Nation*, January 31, 2005, available online at http://www.thenation.com/doc/20050131/kornbluh.

"La Farsa de la Justicia" 1991. *ANALISIS*. Extraordinary edition, September 26.

Labarca Fuentes, Osvaldo. 1932. *Los Enanos de la Libertad*. Santiago: Editorial Lefax.

Laclau, Ernesto, and Chantal Mouffe. 1985. *Hegemony and Socialist Strategy*. New York: Verso.

Lagos, Andrea. 1998. "Revolución en la Corte Suprema." *La Tercera en Internet*. November 1. Available at: http://www.tercera.cl/diario/1998/01/11/1. html (accessed November 2, 1998).

Langer, Máximo. 2004. "From Legal Transplants to Legal Translations: The Globalization of Plea Bargaining and the Americanization Thesis in Criminal Procedure." *Harvard International Law Journal* 45: 1–64.

Larkins, Christopher. 1996. "Judicial Independence and Democratization: A Theoretical and Conceptual Analysis." *The American Journal of Comparative Law* 44(4): 605–626.

Lastarria, J.V. 1856. *La Constitución Política de la República de Chile Comentada*. Valparaiso: Imprenta Del Comercio.

Lester, Anthony. 2004. "The Human Rights Act 1998 – Five Years On." *European Human Rights Law Review* 3 (2004): 258–271.

Libro Blanco del Cambio de Gobierno en Chile. 1973. Santiago: Editorial Lord Cochrane.

Lijphart, Arend. 1971. "Comparative Politics and the Comparative Method." *American Political Science Review* 65: 682–693.

Linz, Juan, and Alfred Stepan. 1996. *Problems of Democratic Transition and Consolidation: Southern Europe, South America, and Post-Communist Europe*. Baltimore: Johns Hopkins University Press.

Lipset, Seymour Martin. 1996. *American Exceptionalism: A Double-Edged Sword*. New York: W. W. Norton.

Lira, Elizabeth, and Brian Loveman. 2006. "Comisión Investigadora de los Actos de la Dictadura, 1931." Paper presented at the Internacional Colloquium "Justicia, Poder y Sociedad: Recorridos Históricos," Universidad Diego Portales, Facultad de Ciencias Sociales e Historia. Santiago, 19–20 October.

Lomnitz, Larissa Adler and Ana Melnick. 2000. *Chile's Political Culture and Parties*. Notre Dame: University of Notre Dame Press.

López Dawson, Carlos. 1986. *Justicia y Derechos Humanos*. Santiago: Editorial Documentas.

1995a. *Justicia Militar: Una Nueva Mirada*. Santiago: Comisión Chilena de Derechos Humanos.

1995b. "La Corte Suprema y los Derechos Humanos." Manuscript. Photocopy.

Lovell, George I. and Michael McCann. 2005. "A Tangled Legacy: Federal Courts and Struggles for Democratic Inclusion." In *The Politics of*

Democratic Inclusion, ed. Christina Wolbrecht and Rodney E. Hero. Philadelphia: Temple University Press.

Loveman, Brian. 1976. *Struggle in the Countryside: Politics and Rural Labor in Chile, 1919–1973*. Bloomington, Indiana University Press.

1988. *Chile: The Legacy of Hispanic Capitalism*. New York: Oxford University Press.

1993. *The Constitution of Tyranny*. Pittsburgh: University of Pittsburgh Press.

Loveman, Brian, and Thomas M. Davies, Jr., eds. 1997. *The Politics of Anti-Politics: The Military in Latin America*, rev. and updated. Wilmington, DE: Scholarly Resources.

Loveman, Brian, and Elizabeth Lira. 1999. *Las Suaves Cenizas del Olvido: Vía Chilena de Reconciliación Política, 1814–1932*. Santiago: LOM.

2002. *Arquitectura Política y Seguridad Interior del Estado, 1811–1990*. Santiago: Centro Nacional de Conservación y Restauración.

Lowenstein, Steven. 1978. "El Abogado y El Desarrollo." In *Derecho y Sociedad*, ed. Gonzalo Figueroa. Santiago: Corporación de Promoción Universitaria.

Luque, María José. 1984. "Consejos de Guerra: Justicia o Venganza?" *ANALISIS* (June 5): 26–29.

Luque, María José, and Patricia Collyer. 1986. "Proceso a la Corte Suprema." *ANALISIS* (July 1): 23–27.

Lutz, Ellen and Kathryn Sikkink. 2001. "The Justice Cascade: The Evolution and Impact of Foreign Human Rights Trials in Latin America." *Chicago Journal of International Law* 2(1): 1–33.

MacCormick, Neil. 1993. "Constitutionalism and Democracy." In *Theories and Concepts of Politics*, ed. Richard Bellamy. New York: Manchester University Press.

1999. "Rhetoric and the Rule of Law." In *Recrafting the Rule of Law: The Limits of Legal Order*, ed. David Dyzenhaus. Portland, OR: Hart Publishing.

Macedo, Stephen. 1988. "Liberal Virtues, Constitutional Community." *The Review of Politics* 50: 215–240.

Mandel, Michael. 1994. *The Charter of Rights and the Legalization of Politics in Canada*. Toronto: Thompson.

Maravall, José María, and Adam Przeworski. 2003. *Democracy and the Rule of Law*. New York: Cambridge University Press.

Mattei, Ugo. 1997. "Three Patterns of Law: Taxonomy and Change in the World's Legal Systems." *American Journal of Comparative Law* 45: 5–43.

Matus Acuña, Alejandra. 1999. *El Libro Negro de la Justicia Chilena*. Santiago: Editorial Planeta.

2002. *Injusticia Duradera: Libro Blanco de "El Libro Negro de la Justicia Chilena."* Santiago: Editorial Planeta.

Matus Acuña, Alejandra, and Francisco Javier Artaza. 1996. *Crimen con Castigo*. Santiago: Ediciones Diario La Nación.

Maveety, Nancy, ed. 2003a. *The Pioneers of Judicial Behavior*. Ann Arbor: University of Michigan Press.

2003b. "The Study of Judicial Behavior and the Discipline of Political Science." In *The Pioneers of Judicial Behavior*, ed. Nancy Maveety. Ann Arbor: University of Michigan.

Melnick, R. Shep. 2005. "'One Government Agency Among Many': The Political Juris-Prudence (sic) of Martin Shapiro." In *Institutions and Public Law: Comparative Approaches*, ed. Tom Ginsburg and Robert A. Kagan. New York: Peter Lang.

Mera F., Jorge, Felipe González M., and Juan Enrique Vargas V. 1987a. "Función Judicial, Seguridad Interior del Estado y Orden Público: El Caso de la 'Ley de Defensa de la Democracia.'" Cuaderno de Trabajo No. 5, Academia de Humanismo Cristiano, Programa de Derechos Humanos, Santiago.

1987b. "Los Regímenes de Excepción en Chile durante el Período 1925–1973." Cuaderno de Trabajo No. 4, Academia de Humanismo Cristiano, Programa de Derechos Humanos, Santiago.

1988. "Ley de Seguridad Interior del Estado y Derechos Humanos 1958–1973." Cuaderno de Trabajo No. 8, Academia de Humanismo Cristiano, Programa de Derechos Humanos, Santiago.

Merryman, John Henry. 1985. *The Civil Law Tradition*. Stanford: Stanford University Press.

Michelman, Frank I. 1998. "Brennan and Democracy: The 1996–97 Brennan Center Symposium Lecture." *California Law Review* 86: 399–427.

Midal, Joel. 2001. *State in Society: Studying How States and Societies Transform and Constitute One Another*. New York: Cambridge University Press.

Miller, Jonathan M. 1997. "Courts and the Creation of a 'Spirit of Moderation': Judicial Protection of Revolutionaries in Argentina, 1863–1929." *Hastings International and Comparative Law Review* 20: 231–329.

Ministerio de Justicia de Chile. 1996. *Lineamientos Generales de la Reforma Procesal Penal*. Informational pamphlet.

Ministerio Secretaría General de Gobierno de Chile. 1991. *Informe de la Comisión Nacional de Verdad y Reconciliación*. Santiago, Chile.

Minow, Martha. 1992. "Stripped Down Like a Runner or Enriched by Experience: Bias and Impartiality of Judges and Jurors." *William and Mary Law Review* 33: 1201–1218.

Miyazawa, Setsuo. 1991. "Administrative Control of Japanese Judges." *Kobe University Law Review* 25: 45–61.

Mouffe, Chantal. 1993. *The Return of the Political*. New York: Verso.

Moulián, Tomás. 1996. *Chile Actual: Anatomía de un Mito*. Santiago: LOM-ARCIS.

Moustafa, Tamir. 2003. "Law versus the State: The Judicialization of Politics in Egypt." *Law and Social Inquiry* 28: 883–930.

2007. *The Struggle for Constitutional Power: Law, Politics, and Economic Development in Egypt*. New York: Cambridge University Press.

Müller, Ingo. 1991. *Hitler's Justice*. Cambridge, MA: Harvard University Press.

Munizaga, Giselle. 1988. *El Discurso Público de Pinochet*. Santiago: CESOC/CENECA.

Murphy, Walter F. 1993. "Constitutions, Constitutionalism, and Democracy." In *Constitutionalism and Democracy: Transitions in the Contemporary World*, ed. Douglas Greenberg, Stanley N. Katz, Melanie Beth Oliviero, and Steven C. Wheatley. New York: Oxford University Press.

Nadorff, Norman J. 1982. "Habeas Corpus and the Protection of Political and Civil Rights in Brazil: 1964–1978." *Lawyer of the Americas* 14: 297–336.

Navarro Beltrán, Enrique. 1988. *La Judicatura Chilena del Absolutismo Ilustrado al Estado Constitucional*. Santiago: Universidad de Chile, Facultad de Derecho.

Nef, Jorge. 1974. "The Politics of Repression: The Social Pathology of the Chilean Military." *Latin American Perspectives* 1: 58–77.

Nino, Carlos Santiago. 1996. *The Constitution of Deliberative Democracy*. New Haven, CT: Yale University Press.

Nonet, Philippe, and Philip Selznick. 1978. *Law & Society in Transition*. New Brusnwick, NJ: Transaction Publishers.

Novoa Monreal, Eduardo. 1964. "La Crisis del Sistema Legal Chileno." *Mensaje* 13 (1964): 559–566.

1993. "Justicia de Clase (1970)." Reprinted in *Obras Escogidas: Una Crítica al Derecho Tradicional*, compiled by Eduardo Novoa Monreal. Santiago: Centro de Estudios Políticos Latinoamericanos Simón Bolívar.

Nozick, Robert. 1974. *Anarchy, State, and Utopia*. New York: Basic Books.

O'Brien, David M., and Yasuo Ohkoshi. 1996. *To Dream of Dreams: Religious Freedom and Constitutional Politics in Postwar Japan*. Honolulu: University of Hawaii Press.

2001. "Stifling Judicial Independence from Within: The Japanese Judiciary." In *Judicial Independence in the Age of Democracy: Critical Perspectives from Around the World*, eds. Peter H. Russell and David M. O'Brien. Charlottesville: University Press of Virginia.

O'Donnell, Guillermo. 1999. "Horizontal Accountability in New Democracies." In *The Self-Restraining State: Power and Accountability in New Democracies*, ed. Andreas Schedler, Larry Diamond, and Marc F. Plattner. Boulder, CO: Lynne Rienner.

Oliva, Alicia. 1986. "Nadie Está Obligado a Obedecer Leyes Injustas." *ANALISIS* (August 29): 16–17.

Oppenheim, Lois Hecht. 1993. *Politics in Chile: Democracy, Authoritarianism, and the Search for Development*. Boulder, CO: Westview Press.

Organization of American States, Inter-American Commission on Human Rights. 1985. *Report on the Human Rights Situation in Chile*. Washington, DC: General Secretariat, O.A.S.

Osiel, Mark J. 1995. "Dialogue with Dictators: Judicial Resistance in Argentina and Brazil." *Law and Social Inquiry* 20: 481–560.

Otano, Rafael. 1992. "El Juez sin Miedo." *Apsi* (February 24): 18–22.

———. 1995. *Crónica de la Transición*. Santiago: Editorial Planeta.

Ott, Walter, and Franziska Buob. 1993. "Did Legal Positivism Render German Jurists Defenceless during the Third Reich?" *Social & Legal Studies (SAGE, London)* 2: 91–104.

Oxhorn, Philip D. 1995. *Organizing Civil Society: The Popular Sectors and the Struggle for Democracy in Chile*. University Park: Pennsylvania State University Press.

Pacheco G., Máximo. 1985. *Lonquén*. Santiago: Aconcagua.

Palma González, Eric Eduardo. 1998. "Sobre la intervención del poder judicial en Chile luego del 11 de septiembre de 1973." *Revista Jueces para la Democracia* 32 (July): 89–92.

Parry, J. H. 1966. *The Spanish Seaborne Empire*. New York: Alfred A. Knopf.

Paterson, Alan. 1982. *The Law Lords*. Toronto: University of Toronto Press.

Pederzoli, Patricia, and Carlo Guarnieri. 1997. "Italy: A Case of Judicial Democracy?" *International Social Science Journal* 152: 253–270.

Peña González, Carlos. 1991. "¿A Qué Nos Obliga la Democracia? Notas para el Debate sobre la Reforma." *Mensaje* 400: 245–247.

———. 1993. "Informe sobre Chile." In *Situación y Políticas Judiciales en América Latina*, ed. Jorge Correa Sutil. Santiago: Escuela de Derecho, Universidad Diego Portales.

———. 1994. "Hacia una Caracterización del Ethos Legal." In *Evolución de la Cultura Jurídica Chilena*, ed. Agustín Squella. Santiago: Corporación de Promoción Universitaria.

Pepino, Livio, ed. 2001. *L'eresia di Magistratura Democratica: Viaggio Negli Scritti di Giuseppe Borrè*. Milano, Italy: FrancoAngeli.

Pérez-Barros Ramírez, J. E. 1984. *Composición de la Corte Suprema de Justicia: 1824–1984*. Santiago: Universidad de Chile, Facultad de Derecho.

Pereira, Anthony. 2005. *Political Injustice: National Security Legality in Brazil and the Southern Cone*. Pittsburgh: University of Pittsburgh Press.

Peretti, Terri Jennings. 1999. *In Defense of a Political Court*. Princeton, NJ: Princeton University Press.

Phelan, John Leddy. 1976. *The Kingdom of Quito in the Seventeenth Century*. Madison: University of Wisconsin Press.

Popkin, Margaret. 2000. *Peace without Justice: Obstacles to Building the Rule of Law in El Salvador*. University Park: Pennsylvania State University Press.

Pozo, Felipe. 1983. "Momento Judicial: Presidente Habemus." *ANALISIS* (May): 9–10.

Precht Pizarro, Jorge. 1987. "Derecho Material de Control Judicial en la Jurisprudencia de la Corte Suprema de Chile: Derogación Tácita e Inaplicabilidad (1925–1987)." *Revista de Derecho y Jurisprudencia* 84(1): 87–107.

Prillaman, William. 2000. *The Judiciary and Democratic Decay in Latin America*. Westport, CT: Praeger.

Ramseyer, J. Mark. 1994. "The Puzzling Independence of Courts: A Comparative Approach." *Journal of Legal Studies* 23: 721–747.

Ramseyer, J. Mark, and Erik B. Rasmusen. 2003. *Measuring Judicial Independence: The Political Economy of Judging in Japan*. Chicago: University of Chicago Press.

Rawls, John. 1971. *A Theory of Justice*. Cambridge, MA: Harvard University Press.

Raz, Joseph. 1979. *The Authority of Law*. Oxford: Clarendon Press.

Remmer, Karen. 1984. *Party Competition in Argentina and Chile, Political Recruitment and Public Policy, 1890–1930*. Lincoln: University of Nebraska Press.

Report of the Chilean National Commission on Truth and Reconciliation. 1991. Santiago: Ministerio Secretaria General del Gobierno de Chile.

Rial, Juan. 1990. "The Armed Forces and the Question of Democracy in Latin America." In *The Military and Democracy: The Future of Civil-Military Relations in Latin America*, ed. Louis W. Goodman, Johanna S. R. Mendelson, and Juan Rial, Lexington, MA: Lexington Books.

Rigby, Andrew. 2001. *Justice and Reconciliation: After the Violence*. Boulder, CO: L. Rienner Publishers.

Rohde, David W., and Harold J. Spaeth. 1976. *Supreme Court Decision Making*. San Francisco: W. H. Freeman.

Roht-Arriaza, Naomi. 2005. *The Pinochet Effect: Transnational Justice in the Age of Human Rights*. Philadelphia: University of Pennsylvania Press.

Rojas, Juanita. 1990. "Conversando con Nelson Muñoz." *ANALISIS* (September 24–30): 25–27.

Rosenberg, Gerald N. 1991. *The Hollow Hope: Can Courts Bring about Social Change?* Chicago: University of Chicago Press.

Rubin, Edward L. 1991. "Beyond Public Choice: Comprehensive Rationality in the Writing and Reading of Statutes." *New York University Law Review* 66:1 (April): 1–64.

———. 2002. "Independence as a Governance Mechanism." In *Judicial Independence at the Crossroads: An Interdisciplinary Approach*, ed. Stephen B. Burbank and Barry Friedman. Thousand Oaks, CA: SAGE Publications.

Rueschemeyer, Dietrich. 2003. "Can One or a Few Cases Yield Theoretical Gains?" In *Comparative Historical Analysis in the Social Sciences*, ed. James

Mahoney and Dietrich Rueschemeyer. New York: Cambridge University Press.

Rueschemeyer, Dietrich, Evelyne Huber Stephens, and John D. Stephens. 1992. *Capitalist Development & Democracy*. Chicago: University of Chicago Press.

Russell, Peter H. 2001. "Toward a General Theory of Judicial Independence." In *Judicial Independence in the Age of Democracy: Critical Perspectives from Around the World*, ed. Peter H. Russell and David M. O'Brien. Charlottesville: University Press of Virginia.

Russell, Peter H., and David M. O'Brien, eds. 2001. *Judicial Independence in the Age of Democracy: Critical Perspectives from Around the World*. Charlottesville: University Press of Virginia.

Sanchez Noguera, Ana María. 1991. *Reforma Judicial de 1927: Causas y Consecuencias*. Santiago: PUC.

Sartori, Giovanni. 1962. *Democratic Theory*. Detroit: Wayne State University Press.

Schattschneider, E. E. 1960. *The Semisovereign People: A Realist's View of Democracy in America*. New York: Holt, Rinehart and Winston.

Scheppele, Kim Lane. 2000. "Constitutional Interpretation after Regimes of Horror." Paper available at: http://papers.ssrn.com/paper.taf?abstract_id=236219.

2001. "Democracy by Judiciary (Or Why Courts Can Sometimes Be More Democratic than Parliaments)." Paper presented at conference on Constitutional Courts. Washington University, November 1–3. Available at: http://law.wustl.edu/igls/Conconfpapers/Scheppele.pdf

2002. "Declarations of Independence: Judicial Reactions to Political Pressure." In *Judicial Independence at the Crossroads: An Interdisciplinary Approach*, ed. Stephen B. Burbank and Barry Friedman. Thousand Oaks, CA: SAGE Publications.

2003. "Constitutional Negotiations: Political Contexts of Judicial Activism in Post-Soviet Europe." *International Sociology* 18(1): 219–238.

2005. "Dissociation under Emergency: Comparative Judicial Responses to the Anti-Terrorism Campaign." Paper presented at the Annual Meeting of the Law and Society Association, Las Vegas, Nevada, July 2–5.

Schmidhauser, John R., ed. 1987. *Comparative Judicial Systems: Challenging Frontiers in Conceptual and Empirical Analysis*. Boston: Butterworths.

Schor, Miguel. 2003. "The Rule of Law and Democratic Consolidation in Latin America." Available at: http://darkwing.uoregon.edu/~caguirre/schorpr.html

Schubert, Glendon A. 1965. *The Judicial Mind: Attitudes and Ideologies of Supreme Court Justices, 1946–1963*. Evanston, IL: Northwestern University Press.

1974. *The Judicial Mind Revisited: Psychometric Analysis of Supreme Court Ideology*. New York: Oxford University Press.

Schweitzer, Daniel. 1975. "Jurisdicción de la Corte Supreme: Sus Facultades Conservadores y Disciplinarias frente a los Tribunales Militares." *Revista de Derecho Procesal* (June): 3–35.

Scott, James C. 1985. *Weapons of the Weak: Everyday Forms of Peasant Resistance*. New Haven, CT: Yale University Press.

Segal, Jeffrey, and Harold Spaeth. 1993. *The Supreme Court and the Attitudinal Model*. New York: Cambridge University Press.

Selznick, Philip. 1968. "The Sociology of Law." *International Encyclopedia of the Social Sciences* 9: 50–59.

Sen, Amartya. 1999. *Development as Freedom*. New York: Knopf.

Shapiro, Ian. 1996. *Democracy's Place*. Ithaca, NY: Cornell University Press.

Shapiro, Martin. 1981. *Courts: A Comparative and Political Analysis*. Chicago: University of Chicago Press.

Shapiro, Martin, and Alec Stone. 1994. "The New Constitutional Politics of Europe." *Comparative Judicial Studies* 26 (January): 397–420.

Shklar, Judith. 1986. *Legalism: Law, Morals, and Political Trials*. Cambridge, MA: Harvard University Press.

1987. "Political Theory and the Rule of Law." In *The Rule of Law: Ideal or Ideology*, ed. Allan C. Hutchinson and Patrick Monahan. Toronto: Carswell.

1989. "The Liberalism of Fear." In *Liberalism and the Moral Life*, ed. Nancy Rosenblum. Cambridge, MA: Harvard University Press.

Sieder, Rachel, Line Schjolden, and Alan Angell, ed. 2005. *The Judicialization of Politics in Latin America*. New York, Palgrave MacMillan.

Sigmund, Paul. 1977. *The Overthrow of Allende and the Politics of Chile, 1964–1973*. Pittsburgh: University of Pittsburgh Press.

Silva Cimma, Enrique. 1977. *El Tribunal Constitucional de Chile (1971–1973)*. Caracas: Editorial Jurídica Venezolano.

2000. *Memorias Privadas de un Hombre Público*. Santiago: Editorial Andrés Bello.

Simpson, A. W. Brian. 1989. "The Judges and the Vigilant State." *Denning Law Journal*: 145–167.

Smith, Rogers M. 1988. "Political Jurisprudence, the 'New Institutionalism' and the Future of Public Law." *American Political Science Review* 82:1 (March): 89–108.

Smulovitz, Catalina. 1995. "Constitución y Poder Judicial en la Nueva Democracia Argentina." In *La Nueva Matriz Política Argentina*, compiled by Carlos H. Acuña. Buenos Aires: Nueva Visión.

Solomon, Peter H., Jr. 1996. *Soviet Criminal Justice under Stalin*. New York: Cambridge University Press.

Soto Kloss, Eduardo. 1986. "Una Revolución Silenciosa." *Revista de Derecho y Jurisprudencia* 83(1): 157–162.

Soto Kloss, Eduardo, and Iván Aróstica Maldonado. 1993. "La Destrucción del Estado de Derecho: 1970–1973." *Revista de Derecho Público* 53/54: 57–96.

Spaeth, Harold J., and Jeffrey A. Segal. 1999. *Majority Rule or Minority Will: Adherence to Precedence on the U.S. Supreme Court.* New York: Cambridge University Press.

Spence, Jack. 1979. *Search for Justice: Neighborhood Courts in Allende's Chile.* Boulder, CO: Westview Press.

Squella, Agustín, ed. 1988. *La Cultura Jurídica Chilena.* Santiago: Corporación de Promoción Universitaria.

ed. 1994. *Evolución de la Cultura Jurídica Chilena.* Santiago: Corporación de Promoción Universitaria.

Stanton, Kimberly. 1997. "The Transformation of a Political Regime: Chile's 1925 Constitution." Paper presented at the 1997 meeting of the Latin American Studies Association, Guadalajara, Mexico, April 17–19. Available at: http://136.142.158.105/LASA97/stanton.pdf.

Staton, Jeffrey K. 2004. "Judicial Policy Implementation in Mexico City and Mérida." *Comparative Politics* 37(1): 41–60.

Stone, Alec. 1992. *The Birth of Judicial Politics in France.* New York: Oxford University Press.

Stone Sweet, Alec. 2000. *Governing With Judges: Constitutional Politics in Europe.* New York: Oxford University Press.

Summary of the Truth and Reconciliation Commission Report. 1991. Santiago: Chilean Human Rights Commission and Centro IDEAS.

Sunstein, Cass. 1987. "Lochner's Legacy." *Columbia Law Review* 87: 873–919.

Tamanaha, Brian Z. 2002. "The Rule of Law for Everyone?" In *Current Legal Problems*, Vol. 55, ed. M. D. A. Freeman. New York: Oxford University Press.

Tate, C. Neal. 1987. "Judicial Institutions in Cross-National Perspective: Toward Integrating Courts into the Comparative Study of Politics." In *Comparative Judicial Systems: Challenging Frontiers in Conceptual and Empirical Analysis*, ed. John R. Schmidhauser. Boston: Butterworths.

1992. "Comparative Judicial Review and Public Policy: Concepts and Overview." In *Comparative Judicial Review and Public Policy*, ed. Donald W. Jackson and C. Neal Tate. Westport, CT: Greenwood Press.

1993. "Courts and Crisis Regimes: A Theory Sketch with Asian Case Studies." *Political Research Quarterly* 46:2 (June): 311–338.

Tate, C. Neal, and Stacia L. Haynie. 1993. "Authoritarianism and the Functions of Courts: A Time Series Analysis of the Philippine Supreme Court, 1961–1987." *Law & Society Review* 27(4): 707–40.

Tate, C. Neal, and Torbjörn Vallinder, eds. 1995. *The Global Expansion of Judicial Power*. New York: New York University Press.

Tavolari, Raúl. 1995. *Habeas Corpus: Recurso de Amparo*. Santiago: Editorial Jurídica.

Taylor, Matthew. 2006. "Veto and Voice in the Courts: Policy Implications of Institutional Design in the Brazilian Judiciary." *Comparative Politics* 38(3): 337–355.

Teitel, Ruti. 1997. "Transitional Jurisprudence: The Role of Law in Political Transformation." *Yale Law Journal* 106 (May): 2009–2080.

2000. *Transitional Justice*. New York: Oxford University Press.

Thelen, Kathleen. 1999. "Historical Institutionalism in Comparative Politics." *Annual Review of Political Science* 2: 369–404.

Thelen, Kathleen, and Sven Steinmo. 1992. "Historical Institutionalism in Comparative Politics." In *Structuring Politics: Historical Institutionalism in Comparative Analysis*, ed. Sven Steinmo, et al. New York: Cambridge University Press.

Thome, Joseph R. 1971. "Expropriation in Chile under the Frei Agrarian Reform." *American Journal of Comparative Law* 19: 489–513.

Tocqueville, Alexis de. 1969. *Democracy in America*. New York: Harper and Row.

Toharia, José. 1974–1975. "Judicial Independence in an Authoritarian Regime: The Case of Contemporary Spain." *Law and Society Review* 9: 475–496.

1975. *El Juez Español: Un Análisis Sociológico*. Madrid: Editorial Tecnos.

2001. *Opinión Pública y Justicia*. Madrid: Consejo General del Poder Judicial.

Touraine, Alain. 1997. *What Is Democracy?* Boulder, CO: Westview Press.

Tushnet, Mark. 1999. *Taking the Constitution Away from the Courts*. Princeton, NJ: Princeton University.

Unger, Roberto M. 1986. *The Critical Legal Studies Movement*. Cambridge, MA: Harvard University Press.

United States Congress. 1975. Senate. Select Committee to Study Governmental Operations with Respect to Intelligence Activities, *Hearings Volume 7: Covert Action*, 94th Cong., Senate Resolution 21, December 4–5.

Valenzuela, Arturo. 1978. "Chile." In *The Breakdown of Democratic Regimes*, eds. Juan J. Linz, and Alfred Stepan. Baltimore: Johns Hopkins University Press.

1989. "Chile." In *Democracy in Developing Countries: Latin America*, ed. Larry Diamond, Juan J. Linz, and Seymour Martin Lipset. Boulder, CO: Lynne Rienner.

1995. "The Military in Power: The Consolidation of One-Man Rule." In *The Struggle for Democracy in Chile*, ed. Paul W. Drake and Iván Jaksic. Rev. ed. Lincoln: University of Nebraska Press.

Valenzuela, Arturo, and J. Samuel Valenzuela. 1983. "Los Orígenes de la Democracia: Reflexiones Teóricas sobre el Caso de Chile." *Estudios Públicos* 12 (March): 5–39.

Valenzuela Somarriva, Eugenio. 1990. "Labor Jurisdiccional de la Corte Suprema." *Estudios Públicos* 41: 137–169.

1991a. "Informe Final sobre Reformas al Sistema Judicial Chileno." *Estudios Públicos* 41: 171–292.

1991b. "Proposiciones para una Reforma al Poder Judicial." *Mensaje* 400: 242–245.

Vallinder, Torbjörn. "The Judicialization of Politics – A World-Wide Phenomenon: Introduction." *International Political Science Review* 15: 2 (1994): 91–99.

Vargas Viancos, Juan Enrique, and Jorge Correa Sutil. 1995. *Diagnóstico del Sistema Judicial Chileno*. Santiago: Corporación de Promoción Universitaria.

Vaughn, Robert G. 1993. "Proposals for Judicial Reform in Chile." *Fordham International Law Journal* 16: 577–607.

Velasco, Eugenio. 1986. *Expulsión*. Santiago: Copygraph.

Verdugo Marinkovic, Mario, ed. 1989. *La Experiencia Constitucional Norteamericana y Chilena sobre Separación de Poderes*. Santiago: Ediar Conosur.

Verdugo M., Mario, Emilio Pfeffer U., and Humberto Nogueira A. 1994. *Derecho Constitucional*. Santiago: Editorial Jurídica.

Verdugo, Patricia. 1986. *Rodrígo y Carmen Gloria: Quemados Vivos*. Santiago: Aconcagua.

1990. *Tiempos de Días Claros: Los Desaparecidos*. Santiago: Ediciones Chile América.

1991. "Hubo una Acción Planificada del Alto Mando." *Apsi* (February 25): 10–12.

2001. *Chile, Pinochet and the Caravan of Death*. Miami: North-South Center Press at the University of Miami.

Verner, Joel G. 1984. "The Independence of Supreme Courts in Latin America." *Journal of Latin American Studies* 16: 463–506.

Volcansek, Mary L. 2000. *Constitutional Politics in Italy: The Constitutional Court* New York: St. Martin's Press.

Waisman, Carlos H. 1989. "Argentina." In *Democracy in Developing Countries: Latin America*, eds. Larry Diamond, Juan J. Linz, and Seymour Martin Lipset. Boulder, CO: Lynne Rienner.

Waldron, Jeremy. 1999. *Law and Disagreement*. New York: Oxford University Press.

Waltman, Jerold L., and Kenneth M. Holland, eds. 1988. *The Political Role of Law Courts in Modern Democracies*. London: Macmillan.

Weber, Max. 1946. "Politics as a Vocation." In *From Max Weber: Essays in Sociology*, ed. H. H. Gerth and C. Wright Mills. New York: Oxford University Press.

Whittington, Keith. 2003. "Constitutional Theory and the Faces of Power." In *Alexander Bickel and Contemporary Constitutional Theory*, ed. Kenneth Ward. Albany: State University of New York Press.

Wiarda, Howard J., and Harvey F. Kline, eds. 1985. *Latin American Politics and Development*. Boulder, CO: Westview Press.

Widner, Jennifer A. 2001. *Building the Rule of Law*. New York: W. W. Norton.

Woods, Patricia. 2005. "Israel's Court-Driven Constitutional Revolution." Paper presented at the Annual Meeting of the APSA, Washington, DC, September 1–4.

Young Debeuf, Marcel. 1992. "Sobre Jueces, Militares, y Políticos." *Mensaje* 415 (December): 565–567.

Zakaria, Fareed. 2003. *The Future of Freedom: Illiberal Democracy at Home and Abroad*. New York: W.W. Norton.

Zalaquett, José. 2001. *The Pinochet Case: International and Domestic Repercussions*. Toronto: University of Toronto Faculty of Law.

Zuckert, Michael. 1994. "Hobbes, Locke, and the Problem of the Rule of Law." In *Nomos XXXVI: The Rule of Law*, ed. Ian Shapiro. New York: New York University Press.

INDEX

abogados integrantes (substitute judges),
  255–256
Aburto, Marcos, 84, 85
activism, judicial (Chile), 63–70, 73–77,
  83–88, 93, 100
  under Allende, 83–88
  conservatism and, 73–100
  under Frei, 76–77
AD. *See* Democratic Alliance
Africa. *See* South Africa
Agrarian Reform Law, Chile, 79
agricultural reform, in Chile,
  64–65
Alcaino Barros, Alfredo, 81
Alessandri, Jorge, 111
Alessandri Palma, Arturo, 56
Allende Gossens, Salvador, 11, 29, 30,
  38, 76, 103
  audiencias populares under, 97–98
  Chilean Supreme Court under,
  96–100
  judicial activism under, 83–88
  judiciary v. executive branch conflicts
  under, 77, 86–88, 98
  overthrow of, 102
Altamirano, Carlos, 80
Alvarez, Oscar, 96
amnesty law (of 1978), Chile, 113–114,
  196

judicial treatment of, 127, 155–156,
  181, 189, 190–191, 198–199, 200,
  212
  under 1980 Constitution, 212
anti-politics, ideology of, 6, 33, 38, 101,
  103–104, 132, 150, 174, 227, 228,
  235
Anti-Terrorist Law, Chile, 197
apartheid, 2
apoliticism, as concept or ideal, 8, 41, 63,
  244–245, 247–248
  authoritarianism and, 8, 244, 249
  Chilean judges and, 33–40, 41–42, 71,
  72, 93, 99–100, 104, 168–176,
  211–213
  conservatism from, 247–250
  institutionalized, 5–6, 72, 224–229,
  239
  in Italy, 229–230, 233
  in Japan, 233–234
  judges and, 5–6, 225, 227–228
  judicial ideology of, 5–6, 33, 50–51,
  93, 233–234, 248–249
  judicial structure constructed around,
  5–6, 34–36, 229–232, 247–248
  in South Africa, 234–235
  in Spain, 230–231, 233
  in Tanzania, 235
  in United States, 235–236

287